Molly Blooms

Molly Blooms

A Polylogue on "Penelope" and Cultural Studies

Edited by

Richard Pearce

THE UNIVERSITY OF WISCONSIN PRESS

The University of Wisconsin Press
114 North Murray Street
Madison, Wisconsin 53715

3 Henrietta Street
London WC2E 8LU, England

Printed in the United States of America

Library of Congress Cataloging-in-Publication Data
Molly Blooms: a polylogue on "Penelope" and cultural studies / edited by
    Richard Pearce.
        302 p.   cm.
        Includes bibliographical references and index.
        ISBN 0-299-14120-9 (cl)   ISBN 0-299-14124-1 (pb)
        1. Joyce, James, 1882–1941. Ulysses. Episode 18.   2. Women and literature—
    Ireland—History—20th century. 3. Joyce, James, 1882–1941—Characters—Molly
    Bloom. 4. Joyce, James, 1882–1941—Characters—Women. 5. Bloom, Molly
    (Fictitious character) 6. Women—In literature. I. Pearce, Richard, 1932–   .
    PR6019.O9U6843   1994
    823'.912—dc20   93-39641

Contents

Part 4. Molly as Consumer

Part 5. Molly as Body and Embodied

Contributors

Susan Bazargan's odyssey brought her, in 1978, from Tehran, Iran, to the United States. She is now Associate Professor at Eastern Illinois University. She is the co-editor of *Image and Ideology in Modern/Postmodern Discourse* (1991) and is working on *Narrative and History in "Ulysses."*

Kimberly J. Devlin, Associate Professor of English at the University of California, Riverside, is the author of *Wandering and Return in "Finnegans Wake"* (1991). Her articles on Joyce have appeared in *James Joyce Quarterly, PMLA, Novel,* and various essay collections.

Margaret Mills Harper, Associate Professor of English at Georgia State University, is the author of *The Aristocracy of Art: Joyce and Wolfe* (1990) and co-editor of volume 3 of *Yeats's "Vision" Papers* (1992). She is working on a study of Georgie Yeats's collaboration with her husband in the occult experiments that led to Yeats's *A Vision.*

Joseph Heininger teaches at the University of Michigan. He has published essays on Joyce in *James Joyce Quarterly* and in the MLA's *Approaches to Teaching Joyce's "Ulysses."* He is currently writing a book on wartime narratives and transformations of gender in English fiction, 1910–1922.

Cheryl Herr teaches at the University of Iowa. She is the author of *Joyce's Anatomy of Culture* (1986) and editor of *For the Land They Loved: Irish Political Melodrama* (1992). She has recently completed a book tentatively called *How to do Cultural Studies.*

Garry Leonard has published articles on James Joyce in *Novel, James Joyce Quarterly, Modern Fiction Studies, Nineteenth Century Studies,* and *College Literature.* He was the guest editor of the *James Joyce Quarterly Special Issue on Joyce and Advertising* (Fall 1993). His most recent work is *Reading Dubliners Again: A Lacanian Perspective* (1993).

Kathleen McCormick is Associate Professor in the Rhetoric, Language, and Culture Department at the University of Hartford. Her most recent book is *The Culture of Reading and the Teaching of English* (1994). She is also the author of *"Ulysses," Wandering Rocks, and the Reader* (1991), the co-editor of the MLA volume on *Approaches to Teaching Joyce's "Ulysses"* (1993), and the co-author of *Reading-to-Write: Exploring a Cognitive and Social Process* and the textbook *Reading Texts* (1987).

Richard Pearce, Professor of English at Wheaton College in Massachusetts, has published widely on modern literature. He is the author of *Stages of the Clown: Perspectives on Modern Fiction from Dostoyevsky to Beckett* (1971), *The Novel in Motion: An Approach to Modern Fiction* (1983), and *The Politics of Narration: James Joyce, William Faulkner, and Virginia Woolf* (1991). His most recent essays on Joyce have appeared in the MLA's *Approaches to Teaching "Ulysses"* (1993) and *The Return of the Repressed in Joyce* (1993).

Brian W. Shaffer, Assistant Professor of English at Rhodes College, is the author of *The Blinding Torch: Modern British Fiction and the Discourse of Civilization* (1993) and essays in *PMLA, James Joyce Quarterly, Joyce in Context* (1992), *Journal of Modern Literature,* and *Conradiana* (1990/1992).

Carol Shloss, Associate Professor of English at West Chester University, is the author of three books and many essays on James Joyce. She is currently writing *Modernism's Daughters: Families, Law, and the Inheritance of Literature.*

Jennifer Wicke is Associate Professor of Comparative Literature at New York University, where she teaches literature, film, and cultural theory. She has written widely on modernism, gender, and culture, and she explores Joyce at length in *Advertising Fictions: Literature, Advertisement, and Social Reading* (1988). Her forthcoming book is called *Consuming Subjects.*

Ewa Ziarek is an Assistant Professor of English at the University of Notre Dame. Her publications include articles on Melville, Kafka, Joyce, Levinas, Kristeva, and Marianne Hauser. She is currently completing a book manuscript entitled *Rhetoric of Failure: Skepticism, Modernism, Deconstruction.* She was a Lilly Fellow during the 1991–92 academic year.

Molly Blooms

Introduction

Molly Blooms—A Polylogue on "Penelope"

Richard Pearce

Molly Bloom has the last word in *Ulysses,* both literally and figuratively. For—coming after the novel's main line of action, after the quests of father and son, beyond the Homeric superstructure, beyond so complete a picture of male Dublin that (as Joyce told Frank Budgen) it could be reconstructed out of his book—Molly's episode functions as an epilogue. And the purpose of an epilogue, according to the Russian formalist Boris Eikhenbaum, is to "set the perspective by a shift in time scale and orientation."[1] No wonder Molly has assumed such (dis)proportions as reflected in the critical views of her as an earth goddess or shrewish whore. Molly is in a position of great power, and these characterizations limit the broad perspective her epilogue provides not only on the novel's singular hero, but on the male quest story, the Western literary tradition, Irish culture, colonialism, patriarchal power, and, perhaps most important, the very language or set of discourses that have defined our understanding of "perspective."

A fuller view of Molly Bloom has been developing in the last decade,[2] but our book is the first full-length study of Molly Bloom that attempts to restore Molly and her perspective on the world of *Ulysses.* We do so by looking at "Penelope" through the lenses of cultural studies—which include feminism, new historicism, popular culture, postcolonialism, and postmodernism, and which therefore produce a

multiplicity of Molly Blooms and illuminate the multiplicity of positions she occupies within the novel. Indeed, an emerging assumption
of cultural studies is that positions are multiple and changing; therefore, the very notion of an epilogue must be expanded. For the shift
in orientation does not provide an independent perspective. It creates
an intertextual relationship, where relations of first and last, dominant and subordinate, container and contained, inside and outside
are continually shifting. Or, to be more specific, the questions are
not whether Molly is determined by or escapes from the narratives
of gender, class, patriarchy, colonialism, and consumption in order to
provide a perspective on them. Rather, we need to ask how Molly reproduces, negotiates, and resists these narratives—as she looks back
at the men of Dublin, deals with the double disenfranchisement of
Irish women in a period of benevolent paternalism, theatricalizes and
mimics the roles of a woman, recalls her childhood in Gibraltar in
ways that focus her position in colonized Ireland, shifts back and forth
between what Mikhail Bakhtin calls "authoritative" and "internally
persuasive discourse," engages in the "erotics" of shopping and does
the "work" of consumption at a time when British advertising was
moving into its modern phase, and is embodied in images of natural
and mechanical reproduction.

Our book evolved from panels at the 1987 James Joyce Symposium
and the 1989 MLA into a polylogue, where many voices argue and
interweave, maintaining their own integrity, learning from but not
always convincing one another, and opening the way for new voices.
It is designed to maintain the dynamic of interacting voices and evoke
a burgeoning multiplicity of interrelated views—hence the title *Molly
Blooms*. As a result, I am faced with the problem of how to arrange and
introduce a collection of essays without imposing a reductive order
and an authoritative frame on them. And this problem is complicated
for me, as a male editor who does not want to be defined as the father
and framer of a feminist project.

My solution is to construct the introduction as a preview and hope
you will see the arrangement of essays less as an order than as a provisional map: "Molly and the Male Gaze," "Molly in Performance,"
"Negotiating Colonialism," "Molly as Consumer," and "Molly as Body
and Embodiment." This map is designed to give you a general sense
of the geography without limiting the way you can navigate it. But I
want to stress that the essays are also interrelated and overlapping,
that there may be different or better ways to order them, and that in
fact to impose an order is a way of imposing limits on our project. The

following previews are designed to reflect as closely as possible the different positions and voices in our polylogue.

Part 1, "Molly and the Male Gaze," begins with Kathleen McCormick re-visioning the critical reception of Molly Bloom. Indeed, her "Revisionist History of the Reception of 'Penelope,' 1922–1970" is the virtual introduction to this volume, for it not only illuminates the historical stages of Molly's reception, it initiates our new project of self-conscious re-vision by historicizing, and therefore problematizing, all of our own re-visions. McCormick describes how Molly has been not only received but produced by those who introduced, evaluated, and taught *Ulysses*—from 1922 to 1970, when the way we read Molly Bloom began to change. McCormick also makes use of what Tony Bennett calls "reading formations"—the constellation of textual features and social factors that affect the ways we think of ourselves as readers, the ways we think about the text as an object to be read, and the ways we read the texts. Her goal is not simply to label the reading formations but to understand the historical circumstances that produced them as well as the forces that shape our current reading formation and what is at stake in the current critical debates. Two distinct reading formations of Molly held sway from the time *Ulysses* was banned and brought over to this country in brown paper covers to the period when the feminists entered the critical scene. The first developed between 1922 and the 1940s, when critics were trying to establish Joyce's reputation as a literary genius, and Molly was, for the most part, desexualized in her glorified manifestation of earth goddess. The second developed in the 1950s and 1960s, when Molly was a character in a canonized text, and antifeminism was dominant. Now Molly was seen "realistically," as a bitch or a whore, and critics took a prurient interest in the exact number of her lovers. But McCormick also shows, by highlighting the emotional disruptions in both the positive and negative critical discourses, that the two reading formations were not that different. For they both reflected the shock, tensions, and fears Molly engendered in a male-dominated establishment, and, equally important, the way gender-specific assumptions about the nature of women were encoded in society. "By situating readings of the past in larger literary and cultural contexts rather than either accepting them as part of the capaciousness of the text or dismissing them as simply wrong," McCormick's analysis focuses on "the social and the historical, which is where meanings actually get negotiated, and in so doing will attempt to implicate our own reading positions and enable us to interrogate further the terms of our own debates."

If Kathleen McCormick shows how Molly has been the object of a critical male gaze that produced the image seen by most readers until relatively recently and perhaps even today, I focus on the way a male gaze in the text of *Ulysses* operates and is subverted in "Penelope." My question—"How Does Molly Bloom Look Through the Male Gaze?"— is threefold: how does Molly appear within the frame of the male gaze, how does she achieve an active look of her own, and what is the effect of her look? I begin with the model of the male gaze identified and theorized by Laura Mulvey in regard to classical Hollywood film but with implications for traditional narrative in general. And I apply Mulvey's three "looks" to *Ulysses*: the way the characters look at each other, the ways we are made to identify with the male point of view, and the ways in which the male gaze is inscribed in the technology of cinema and the medium of the novel, as well as the means of production and distribution, the education and training of those who produce films and novels, canonization, and the classroom. My main argument, though, is how *Ulysses* in general and Molly in particular subvert the male gaze. But I do not end at this point, for I want to deal with the problem of a male feminist writing about how a strong woman looks *through* the male gaze. I want to question my stake in arguing that a male writer can overcome the historical, social, and psychological limits of his gender—and my stake in showing that the novel ends on a positive note. The second half of the essay, then, building on the feminist film critics who followed Laura Mulvey, interrogates the first—to fashion a dialogic essay that foregrounds the interrelated positions of reader and text, and maintains the instability of "Penelope."

Cheryl Herr extends her argument in *Joyce's Anatomy of Culture*, which was about "Circe," the Victorian and Edwardian stage, and the construction and instability of gender. She introduces part 2, "Molly in Performance," by developing all the puns in " 'Penelope' as Period Piece." Building on the Dublin theatre of the period as well as Penelope's theatrical role in *The Odyssey* and a close reading of the episode, she considers "Penelope" as a theatrical performance. It is specifically a "star turn," or bill topper, in the music hall. Indeed, she argues that Molly is "not a character but rather a role to be enacted by this or that major artiste of the era"—who may indeed have been one of the famous crossdressing males. Herr also develops the other ways "Penelope" is a period piece: the way it "fleshes out, literalizes, the *point* with which Ithaca ends," as well as the way it "theatrically and historically represents Molly's premenstrual and menstrual thoughts." And, finally, she explores the way secretions or excretions in "Penelope" connect the periods of modernism and postmodernism.

Kimberly J. Devlin begins with an important distinction (developed by Carole-Anne Tyler) between female masquerade and female mimicry. In female masquerade a woman passively and unconsciously internalizes cultural images of femininity and flaunts them. In female mimicry she consciously repeats, parodies, appropriates, and flouts them—thereby unmasking the social construction of woman's "nature." Devlin builds on Herr's argument that Molly is not a character but a role, and also on a point Susan Bazargan develops about Molly's "monologue" being dialogic. Devlin shows how the "monologue" is actually a "concatenation of roles, an elaborate series of 'star turns' that undermines the notion of womanliness as it displays it." By analyzing the theatricality of Molly's performance, she reframes Molly's contradictions so that we see them as products of her role playing and as reflections of the cultural contradictions she has internalized—but also "weaves and unweaves." Molly "participates in the female masquerade insofar as she often attempts to conform herself to cultural images of femininity, dramatizing them reflexively. But she also functions as the critic of female masquerade through her repeated gestures of female impersonation that amount to a form of parodic gender mimicry." Devlin not only extends our theoretical understanding of Molly's shifting positions, she uses theory in its original sense of witnessing—reading and re-visioning "Penelope" with acumen and an awareness of the political problems of mimicry as a subversive strategy.

Carol Shloss extends the frame in which we can understand Molly's subversive performance from gender to national politics; hence she takes us into part 3, "Negotiating Colonialism." Though Molly appears apolitical, indeed hostile to politics, Shloss shows that she is in fact both knowledgeable and politically aware. Of course her primary concerns are private rather than public. Nonetheless, "her sensitivity to the issues of authority, privilege, and financial dependence in her relationships with men corresponds with sentiments held by Irish Nationalists in their dealings with England. Both women in marriage and the Irish population in thrall to a colonial government faced a kind of benevolent paternalism that sought to disguise the internal contradictions of union in the language of equity and concern." George Wyndham developed a policy of reform that convinced the Irish of the benefits of English rule. This policy improved the material circumstances of the Irish, while discouraging the desire, or impetus, for home rule, and ensured their powerlessness in achieving what might be in their own self-interest. Within this context, Shloss argues, Molly's "speech acquires a political status simply by being a kind of 'guerilla' tactic that was, in 1904, common to any Irish resistance to unionism." Shloss also gives us an account of Molly's legal position, her status as citizen, wife, and mother in 1904—doubly disenfranchised and silenced as an Irish woman. And she illuminates the strategies by which Molly withholds consent, asserts her complaints, and engages "in acts of subterfuge that undermine the structures of authority that bind her life."

Susan Bazargan moves us from Ireland to the larger context of English colonialism. She shows how, by "placing Molly Bloom's beginnings in Gibraltar," Joyce focuses the issue of British imperialism and elaborates the politics and psychology of colonialism in *Ulysses*. Moreover, he draws an intricate "portrait of the modern female colonial identity in which complications of race and religion are compounded by those of nationality, language, and gender." Bazargan draws on a deep reservoir of languages, history, postcolonialist scholarship, and theory, especially on Bakhtin. She shows how Molly has internalized structures of thought and language that belong to both the colonized and the colonizer, and that connect colonial and sexual domination. She demonstrates that Molly's shifting back and forth in time and space reflects intricate historical interconnections. And she establishes the case for Molly's "monologue" as dialogic. For her speech is addressed to an ideal listener; the pattern of "Yes . . . because" structures her thoughts as an explanation. Moreover, her speech is the site of many conflicting voices. Molly's dialogic reflects the complexities of a colonized psyche, a self caught between inside and outside, the self and the other, master and slave, as well as between competing systems of belief. And it provides her the opportunity to negotiate, mock, and resist the forces of domination. While Molly's contradictions are "signs of a colonized psyche," they also reflect a critical awareness, a sense of perpetual displacement and transition, and an aptitude for survival.

Brian Shaffer brings into focus and clearly explains a theoretical frame, which evolves throughout the polylogue on Penelope, and within which we can more clearly understand Molly's performance and resistance as a doubly colonized Irish woman. He begins with the question of how to assess the degrees of Molly's conformity and subversive power, but goes on to ask broader questions. What cultural processes keep Molly from recognizing the implications of her subjugation as a colonized, lower-class woman? And "by what processes is she able to gain limited enlightenment and subvert those ideologies that would forever keep her in the dark?" Shaffer finds his answers in Freud and Bakhtin. Freud explains the power of ideology to coopt those it suppresses by what he calls the "narcissism of minor differences"—the narcissistic satisfaction gained by suppressed classes by identifying with their masters, or by embracing an ideology where minor differences grant those who are suppressed a sense of superiority. The plebeian is harassed by debt and military service, but as a Roman citizen he shares in ruling over other nations. Molly can ignore or evade her victimization as a lower-class Irish woman by enjoying her sexual prowess—and therefore her superiority over other women. Indeed Shaffer shows how whenever she thinks of politics or the English empire, her thoughts turn back to sexual experiences or fantasies. But he also shows how Molly challenges the social order and its reigning discourses by his explanation and application of Bakhtin. Language, according to Bakhtin, lies "on the borderline between oneself and the other." It becomes one's own when we appropriate it for our own "semantic and expressive intention." "Authoritative discourse"—like the language of religion or science—"binds us" even though it might not "persuade us internally." "Internally persuasive discourse" is language we have adapted to our own intentions. The struggle between authoritative and internally persuasive discourse, sometimes in a single word, is the struggle for "ideological becoming." And Shaffer traces this struggle through the dialogic of Molly's "monologue."

Joseph Heininger initiates the discussion of "Molly as Consumer," part 4, by focusing on advertising as a form of social communication—which not only produces messages about commodities for consumption in the marketplace, but does the cultural work of promoting social and political ideas. The goal of early advertising was to create an image of commercial firms as reputable provisioners of generic products, but in the 1890s large firms, like Pears soap and Lipton's tea, began an "advertising war" to corner mass markets by securing brand loyalty. Advertising in Ireland, then, became doubly imperialistic, since it was designed to colonize mass markets for individual firms. Because these firms were based in England, advertising was a way of extending the power of the Empire in its nearby colony. Building on Edward Said, Heininger also shows how Molly's reception and transformation of advertising messages were forms of colonialized resistance. Examining the role of advertising images, particularly from *The Gentlewoman* magazine, he shows not only how Molly is constructed by but also how she resists the ideology and appropriates its images and symbols. And he argues that Molly finally disengages herself from the world of commodities and mass-produced symbolic images by choosing the "emotionally charged personal image" of the "flower of the mountain." Though acknowledging that the image of woman as flower derives from a poetic tradition connected with the portrayal of women in advertising and indeed had become a reified product in the "cultural marketplace" of Molly's time, he maintains that her appropriation was a way of resisting the spectacle of consumption, subverting the political dominance of British advertising, and asserting her personal history. In doing so he begins an argument that is taken up by other authors of this volume.

Jennifer Wicke, author of *Advertising Fictions: Literature, Advertising, and Social Reading,* develops her 1990 *James Joyce Quarterly* essay and elaborates on the characters' complex mediated positions as consumers in *Ulysses.* Commodities are mediated by Britain's domination over Ireland—since the commodities come from England, when characters buy or even think of a particular commodity, they act and think as colonized subjects. And Molly is mediated by her gender and her youth spent in Gibraltar. Not only does Wicke connect Heininger's essay on advertising as a form of colonization with Bazargan's essay on the role of Gibraltar in *Ulysses,* but she also extends the reach of Molly, "when she's at home," geographically and historically. Molly's private meditation is not trivialized by its obsession with consumption but reflects the international conditions of modernity. Most important, Wicke shows that consumption is not a passive, mindless activity or a form of victimization. It is "a mode of work," an active and intricate "process of culture making and psychic self-fashioning." Molly's housework, her skills in making a home for a family with an unstable income, her efforts in "constructing a petty-bourgeois identity," and her choices of what to wear when she pleads with Mr. Cuffe to save Bloom's job or asserts her sexual independence from her husband— all require knowledge, strategy, and determination, or "work which is as rhetorical and ardent and political as the rest of *Ulysses.*"

Garry Leonard takes us from consumption to "lifestyle," a term that has changed in meaning from a person's basic (organic and precultural) character to a person's or a group's "established patterns of consumption and social exchanges." Following Rachel Bowlby, Leonard shows lifestyle to be the way a consumer transforms commodities to create a theatrical spectacle of him or herself for the consumption of a mass audience. Making use of Lacan and Baudrillard, and working with specific examples not only from the media but also the fashion industry in both Joyce's and modern times, as well as from the nineteenth-century theatre and Joyce himself, Leonard examines the activities of shopping as well as the strategies of display and performance. He also illuminates the erotics of shopping in the new form of market economy, the new style of merchandise display, and the new pattern of "individual" mass consumption—based on the double meaning of "spending" in Victorian times as well as the role of pornography. As a result he expands the arguments of Jennifer Wicke, Cheryl Herr, and Kimberly Devlin and adds new dimensions to, or produces still another, Molly Bloom.

Margaret Mills Harper establishes the bridge from "Molly as Consumer" to part 5, "Molly as Body and Embodied," in an argument that might be called, following Gayatri Spivak, strategic essentialism. Poststructuralism has taught us to be wary of dehistoricized myth and mythic structures. Yet, Harper argues, myth was a vitalizing force in the modernist movement. Therefore to ignore or repudiate the modernists' use of myth is to diminish its power in shaping Molly, as well as to leave out important history. What she advocates is to historicize the mythic approach, to elaborate and enhance it through the insights of poststructuralism. Harper compares the ways the body is dressed and undressed on many levels in *Ulysses* and *The Odyssey*. She focuses on the bodies of Molly and Penelope, the clothes that they wore and wove, the bodies of the male and female texts, and the weave of intertexts. And she shows how "Penelope" strains the gender divisions underlying cyclical myth and temporal narrative, as well as narrative and subject positions, to reflect the "worn repair" of these structures in Joyce's time and in our own.

In the last essay, Ewa Ziarek begins with questions of space and location that lead to questions of the role and meaning of the female body in "Penelope." Two of these locations become especially pertinent: Molly fantasizes her elopement with Boylan "jaunting in a train,"[3] and she recalls Bloom's proposal on the blossoming hill of Howth. Ziarek examines this combination of locations, discourses, embodiments, and meanings within the frame of Walter Benjamin's "Work of Art in the Age of Mechanical Reproduction." On the one hand Molly's body is associated with nature, organic discourse, and a restorative memory that could preserve the "aura" of immediacy and authenticity. On the other hand it is associated with the train (as well as photos, ads, newspapers, magazines, and mass-produced clothes), urban experience, mechanistic discourse, inauthenticity, and infidelity. Infidelity is the key because it implies the breakdown not only of patriarchal marriage, but of unified sexual identity, memory, experience, and language. Moreover, it is the source of the chapter's instability. By locating the female body between natural and mechanical reproduction, Ziarek shows why Molly is both faithful and unfaithful, and how "Penelope" both appeases and frustrates the modernist desire for a more authentic experience rooted in memory, how it is both conventional and subversive.

Let me conclude by reiterating the disclaimer with which I began. This is not an introduction, not a frame, but a way into our polylogue, a set of previews, a provisional map to help you begin your own navigation among the Molly Blooms and add your own argument to ours.

Notes

1.   Quoted in Torgovnick (11).

2.   In parts of books like Suzette Henke and Elaine Unkeless's *Women in Joyce*, Bonnie Kime Scott's *Joyce and Feminism* and *James Joyce*, Christine van Boheeman's *The Novel as Family Romance: Language, Gender, and Authority from Fielding to Joyce*, Cheryl Herr's *Joyce's Anatomy of Culture*, Frances L. Restuccia's *Joyce and the Law of the Father*, Patrick McGee's *Paperspace: Style as Ideology in Joyce's Ulysses*, Vicki Mahaffey's *Reauthorizing Joyce*, Mary Lowe-Evans' *Crimes Against Fertility: Joyce and Population Control*, Suzette Henke's *James Joyce and the Politics of Desire*, Kimberly Devlin's *Wandering and Return in "Finnegans Wake": An Integrative Approach to Joyce's Fictions*, and my *The Politics of Narration: James Joyce, William Faulkner, and Virginia Woolf*, as well as the Autumn 1989 *Modern Fiction* issue on *Feminist Readings of Joyce*.

3.   All citations are from *Ulysses: The Corrected Text*, edited by Hans Gabler (New York: Vintage, 1986).

Works Cited

Devlin, Kimberly J. *Wandering and Return in "Finnegans Wake": An Integrative Approach to Joyce's Fictions*. Princeton: Princeton University Press, 1991.

Henke, Suzette. *James Joyce and the Politics of Desire*. New York: Routledge, 1990.

Henke, Suzette, and Elaine Unkeless. *Women in Joyce*. Urbana: University of Illinois Press, 1982.

Herr, Cheryl. *Joyce's Anatomy of Culture*. Urbana: University of Illinois Press, 1986.

Lowe-Evans, Mary. *Crimes Against Fertility: Joyce and Population Control*. Syracuse, N.Y.: Syracuse University Press, 1989.

McGee, Patrick. *Paperspace: Style as Ideology in Joyce's Ulysses*. Lincoln: University of Nebraska Press, 1988.

Mahaffey, Vicki. *Reauthorizing Joyce*. Cambridge: Cambridge University Press, 1988.

Pearce, Richard. *The Politics of Narration: James Joyce, William Faulkner, and Virginia Woolf.* New Brunswick, N.J.: Rutgers University Press, 1991.

Restuccia, Frances L. *Joyce and the Law of the Father.* New Haven: Yale University Press, 1989.

Scott, Bonnie Kime. *Joyce and Feminism.* Bloomington: Indiana University Press, 1984.

Scott, Bonnie Kime. *James Joyce.* Atlantic Highlands, N.J.: Humanities Press, 1987.

Torgovnick, Marianna. *Closure in the Novel.* Princeton: Princeton University Press, 1981.

van Boheeman, Christine. *The Novel as Family Romance: Language, Gender, and Authority from Fielding to Joyce.* Ithaca, N.Y.: Cornell University Press, 1987.

PART 1

MOLLY AND THE MALE GAZE

1

Reproducing Molly Bloom
A Revisionist History of the Reception of "Penelope," 1922–1970

Kathleen McCormick

I

Seen as obscene by many reviewers in the twenties, an earth goddess in the thirties and forties, a whore in the fifties and sixties, a realistic product of her historical formation in the seventies, and most recently a symbol of "écriture féminine," Molly Bloom has been the subject of intense critical debate throughout the history of the reception of *Ulysses*.[1] But while critics have continually revised their positions on what Molly signifies, their fundamental premises about the author, the text, and the reader have, in large part, remain unchanged. While critics such as Patrick McGee argue that "the . . . effect of Joyce's work is not immanent but institutional," and that "Joyce is the effect of historical process [which] . . . does not come to a halt with the completion of his work" (425), most critics from the twenties to the present do not agree. Rather, they tacitly assume that the text of *Ulysses* contains within it transcendent meanings which can be traced directly to Joyce's "intention" and grasped in a fairly objective fashion by those readers capable of careful and close reading.[2]

Following this model of the text and the reader, critics have tended to explain the differences among interpretations of Molly either as a sign of the capaciousness of the text or the capriciousness of the critics. Mark Shechner, for example, has argued that "it is revelatory of Joyce's greatness as a writer that the terms of his ambivalence are each

17

so powerfully communicated that the two faces of Molly [earth mother and whore] have given rise to two coherent critical responses" (203).[3] This position has been recently rearticulated by Suzette Henke who writes: "By virtue of her capacious monologue, Molly can be envisaged as both goddess and whore, Dublin housewife and archetypal precursor to Anna Livia Plurabelle, the great mother/lover of Finnegans Wake" (*Desire* 7). And even a clearly defined post-structuralist critic such as Christine van Boheeman-Saaf, who argues that Molly's voice is "that of the Other," still attributes her own reading to an understanding of Joyce's intention: "Joyce can generate a deconstructive text like *Ulysses* owing to his identification with the idea of the woman as original other" (98).[4] In celebrating the text of "Penelope" itself or the genius of Joyce as the transcendent and sole source of meaning, this perspective avoids analyzing the historical factors that help to produce and privilege different readings of Molly at different historical moments.[5]

An even more common explanation for the critical divergence provoked by Molly has been that particular interpretations can simply be proved to be "wrong" with reference to "the text." Apparently erroneous readings are explained away as moments of critical "subjectivity" in which critics let their "personal opinions" get in the way of an objective reading of "the text itself."[6] What is perhaps most interesting about this kind of argument is the way it has been repeated, nearly verbatim, by successive generations of critics. Critics in the fifties and sixties, for example, asserted that earlier readings of Molly as earth mother were "obviously wrong" (Richardson 177) because there does not exist "evidence in the text" (Morse 139) to support them.[7] And yet critics of the seventies came to use the same such allegations of misunderstanding and misinterpretation against the critics of the fifties and sixties. Phillip Herring, for example, argues that the negativity of critical responses to Molly of the fifties and sixties resulted from critics' judging Molly on the basis of "personal taste" (49) rather than some more "objective" standard. David Hayman, similarly, contends that such criticism is "partial or subjective," and that it tends to "ignore the text and avoid basic questions" (133). While such arguments are rhetorically powerful for the critic who asserts that he or she has gained objective access to the true meaning of the "text itself," they, like those discussed above, fail to take into account how and why particular interpretations—including their own— are able to take hold at particular moments, and why interpretations change over time.

Underlying both sets of critical statements is a model of reading that regards interpretation as either an objective or a subjective act, controlled either by a text/author or a reader. Here, I will employ a different model of reading with a different set of premises about authors, texts, and readers to reexamine the history of the reception of Molly Bloom. Using contemporary Marxist and cultural theories of textual production and reception, I will argue that reading is an interdiscursive act that occurs within changing determinations that affect both texts and readers. This perspective sees texts not as transcendent, stable entities with universal significances, but as material objects that are both produced and reproduced under changing historical and ideological conditions.[8] Likewise, it assumes that readers (and authors) are not unique individuals who spontaneously create their own texts or meanings, but rather that they are subjects in history who are also traversed by a variety of complex and often conflicting discourses.

Thus, rather than talking about "the text itself," or the text's history as simply the time in which it was written, I seek to replace the concept of the autonomous text by the concept of the "text-in-use" (Bennett and Woollacott 265), that is, "the concrete and varying, historically specific functions and effects which accrue to 'the text' as a result of the different determinations to which it is subjected during the history of its appropriation" (Bennett, *FM* 148). Such an approach will not allow us simply to dismiss readings of the past that, from the current perspective, may look obviously "wrong;" nor will it allow us to defend our own positions merely on the basis of their "faithfulness" to the text. Rather, it will require us to explore in detail the larger literary and general ideological determinations that have helped to produce different texts and different readers of "Penelope." I should add that this position does not imply that one cannot take a stand for or against certain interpretations. Quite the contrary. The stand one must take, however, is not in relation to the supposed objective rightness of a particular interpretation with reference to the "Penelope" episode "itself," but in relation to the material antecedents and consequences of a position within a given historical moment.

I focus my analysis on the period between 1922 and 1970 when Molly was either extolled as an earth goddess or decried as a whore and the symbol of world destruction. Feminist critics in the eighties were the first to suggest that these earlier readings of Molly could be traced to broader cultural assumptions, that they were laid down, not merely by individual (predominantly male) critics, but by a more general encoding of deep-seated western patriarchal assumptions about the nature and roles of women.[9] The obviousness of this analysis (once it was made), however, precluded a more detailed study of the diverse and complex literary and social factors that enabled these interpretations of Molly to be produced. What has not yet been addressed is how other literary and social determinations interacted with those patriarchal forces to enable certain interpretations of Molly to develop *when* they did, why certain perspectives on Molly which were voiced in the twenties were very strikingly rearticulated thirty years later, and how the *effectivities*, that is, the diverse and often contradictory consequences, of those positions changed from one period to another. It is my hope that this analysis will not only inform us about the past, but that it will also enable us to interrogate more fully the historical and ideological antecedents and implications of our own contemporary debates and interpretations.

As Bennett and Woollacott state, texts can be said to serve "as a basis for one set of meanings when hooked into a particular set of ideological and cultural co-ordinates and for another set of readings when uncoupled from those co-ordinates and connected to new ones" (240–41). I argue that while the earth mother and satanic mistress interpretations of Molly have perhaps even more in common than contemporary feminists have contended, their differences can be best understood as the product of divergent, though at times overlapping, sets of literary and more general ideological determinations.

In the twenties through the forties, the primary set of ideological coordinates into which the "Penelope" episode was hooked were functioning to canonize *Ulysses*. Critics extolled Molly as an earth mother not to preserve her reputation, but to establish Joyce's—as (in whatever sense) a major author or a literary genius. Much of the shock engendered by *Ulysses* and Molly in the early reviewers of the twenties had to be outwardly suppressed during the thirties and forties if the novel was to be seen as a work of high art, and representing Molly as a symbolic earth mother figure worked to aestheticize much of what might have been regarded as immoral in "Penelope." This interpretation of Molly, however, was a response not only to certain literary determinations, but to broader patriarchal ones as well. Although Molly's beliefs and actions may seem "conventional" to most readers today (Unkeless), when read from a more traditional patriarchal perspective, much of her sexual behavior threatens dominant notions of masculinity. The earth mother interpretation not only offers praise of Molly—which was necessary to aid in the canonizing process of *Ulysses*—it also, more subtly and indirectly, provided a means of neutralizing the threat of Molly's sexuality—which was necessary if she was to be accepted by dominant patriarchal discourses.

By the fifties and sixties, "Penelope" was hooked into a different set of ideological coordinates. The shock Molly initially caused which had been repressed to some extent in the thirties and forties was able to resurface safely in the fifties at least in part because Joyce's reputation had been secured, and a lashing out at Molly was no longer to be confused with a lashing out at Joyce. Further, since the postwar period was a time of strong antifeminist sentiment, expressions of rage and horror at Molly's overtly sexual nature were fueled and encouraged by the general ideology. Thus, the critical responses to Molly of the fifties and sixties were not a kind of aberration, as so many have contended, but instead constituted a culmination of tensions and fears surrounding Molly that had been being expressed in one form or another since the publication of *Ulysses*. What is most surprising is not that such negative responses to Molly emerged, but rather how long it took.

While texts are constituted differently in different reading contexts, there are also tensions and contradictions within any specific context, and while particular interpretations of a text may be dominant at a particular time, interpretations are never unified or without conflict. In the thirties and forties, the dominant critical position on Molly was to extol her as an earth mother, but she was also criticized for her "obscenities of thought" (Budgen 263), her "animal placidity" (Levin 125),[10] and her apparent lack of respect for men.[11] In the fifties and sixties, dominant interpretations of Molly decried her as a whore and an embodiment of evil and destruction, but her sexuality was also depicted as alluring.[12] Thus, when I speak of dominant interpretations, I am not implying that these positions were completely agreed upon, unified, or unopposed. Nor is there ever—it needs to be emphasized within this theoretical framework—a one-to-one correspondence between a particular social or literary determination and a certain representation of Molly. While it is clear that such factors as dominant attitudes toward women, the increasingly canonical status of *Ulysses*, and the history of past readings of the text, may all work to determine ways in which Molly will be reproduced in different contexts, the reading situation is always overdetermined. It is the interaction of all these factors within a particular historical conjunction, not one of them alone—let alone a text being read outside a historical context—that enables the development of a particular interpretation.

II

If texts can be said to change from one reading context to another, it is nonetheless still possible to construct what Dave Morley calls a "preferred reading" of a text, that is, the reading privileged by the dominant discourse at the particular time in which the text is being read (167). This reading is not to be confused with the author's intention; neither is it the only reading that different readers can develop at any given time. It is, simply, the reading that is most likely to be constructed by readers at a particular historical moment. In 1922, Sisley Huddleston articulated what, for a significant period of time, was the "preferred reading" of *Ulysses* when, in a fairly sympathetic review, he asked: "What . . . is the good of a book which . . . only a handful of people will read, and which will be found unspeakably shocking even by that little handful?" (Deming 214). Many early reviewers of *Ulysses* were shocked by it on both moral and literary grounds, asserting that it was an "Odyssey of the sewer" (Deming, *Quarterly Review* 207) written by "a perverted lunatic" (Deming, *Pink'Un* 192) who "goes down to that level where seething instinct is not yet illuminated by intellect" (Deming, *Dublin Review* 204). While Molly was not discussed extensively in the early reviews, what one observes is that indictments of her are generally linked with indictments of Joyce or the novel in general. So, for example, Shane Leslie's comment in the *Dublin Review* that the "Penelope" episode is "a very horrible dissection of a very horrible woman's thought," was part of a more general condemnation of the book as a whole as "a fearful travesty on persons, happenings and intimate life of the most morbid and sickening description" (Deming 200–201).

While comments such as these are still often quoted today, critics have not sufficiently analyzed their relation to early laudatory readings of Molly. In this initial period, when Joyce's reputation had yet to be established, critics and reviewers who wanted to argue that *Ulysses* was a major work of art had to develop interpretations of it—and particularly of the "Penelope" episode which Joyce himself said was "probably more obscene than any preceding episode" (*Letters* 1.170)—which would defend Joyce and the novel against such attacks of immorality.[13]

In the twenties, when the shock elicited by the novel was the strongest, even the most positive critics addressed the issue of the book's alleged pornography. Valery Larbaud, for example, felt obliged to argue that Joyce's "intention" in *Ulysses* "is neither salacious nor lewd," and he defended the alleged "obscenity" of "Penelope": "the English language has a very great store of obscene words and expressions, and the author of *Ulysses* has enriched his book generously and boldly from this vocabulary" (Deming 262). Holbrook Jackson acknowledged that *Ulysses* is an "affront" as well as an "achievement," and then, like Larbaud, defended it by arguing that "there is not a salacious line in it" (Deming 198). Huddleston, somewhat more ambivalently, wrote that Molly's reverie is "the vilest, according to ordinary standards, in all literature," but then goes on to argue: "And yet its very obscenity is somehow beautiful and wrings the soul to pity. Is that not high art?" (Deming 216). It became impossible to discuss the novel without addressing the preferred reading of moral shock, even if the critical goal was to refute that reading. The terms of the debate had thus been set out: if *Ulysses* was to be established as a work of high art, it had to be proven either that it was not obscene or that its obscenity served a higher purpose.[14]

Within this movement to demonstrate that *Ulysses* was a work of high art, Molly was assigned a preferred reading as a symbolic earth mother figure. The early critics of the thirties and forties spoke of her as "the voice of nature herself" (Gilbert 400), "the eternal feminine" (Levin 125), and the "center of natural life" (Tindall, *JJ* 233). Although the adulation expressed in these early interpretations has on occasion been attributed to the fact that these critics were writing in a time when women had recently received the vote in Britain and the United States and when they had greater freedom and greater protection under the law (Scott, *Joyce* 159), the dominant ideology still saw women's sexuality as "passive," expected women to put marriage before a career, and regarded "emancipated" women as a danger to the family.[15] And since the criticism of the thirties and forties attacked Molly as much as it apparently praised her, the motivation for idealizing her should not necessarily be attributed to an incipient feminist ideology.

The earth mother interpretation is most commonly thought to have attained dominance because it was the one authorized by Joyce himself. Three sources for this interpretation are generally cited: the mythic invocation of "Gea Tellus" in the "Ithaca" episode, and two of Joyce's letters, one to Frank Budgen and one to Harriet Weaver. At the end of "Ithaca," Molly is described in the following manner:

In what posture?
Listener: reclined semilaterally, left, left hand under head, right leg extended in a straight line and resting on left leg, flexed, in the attitude of Gea-Tellus, fulfilled, recumbent, big with seed. (17.2311–14)

To Budgen, Joyce wrote:

Penelope is the clou of the book. The first sentence contains 2500 words. There are eight sentences in the episode. It begins and ends with the female word *yes*. It turns like the huge earth ball slowly surely and evenly round and round spinning, its four cardinal points being the female breasts, arse, womb and cunt expressed by the word because, bottom (in all senses bottom button, bottom of the class, bottom of the sea, bottom of his heart), *woman, yes*. Though probably more obscene than any preceding episode it seems to me to be perfectly sane full amoral fertilisable untrustworthy engaging shrewd limited prudent indifferent *Weib. Ich bin der [sic] Fleisch der stets bejaht*. (*Letters* 1.170)

And in a significantly abbreviated description of Molly, Joyce wrote to Harriet Weaver: "In conception and technique I tried to depict the earth which is prehuman and presumably posthuman" (*Letters* 1.180).

When we looks at Joyce's words today, however, we can see that they could have authorized many readings, and that they, no less than the "Penelope" episode, are texts-in-use. Because of the particular social and ideological relations of reading *Ulysses* at the time—the need to defend Joyce and *Ulysses* against attacks of immorality—particular, historically specific effects "accrued" (Bennett, *FM* 148) to Joyce's comments, effects which they clearly may not have had in a different reading context. Critics of the time virtually ignored those aspects of Joyce's letters that emphasized the "obscenity" of the episode or the sense of Molly's active female sexuality and used Joyce's remarks to authorize a sanitized and aestheticized reading of Molly in which she could comfortably be reduced to a symbol of "the teeming earth with her countless brood of created things" (Budgen 262).

Bonnie Kime Scott points out that for all their symbolic interpretations of Molly, the early critics seem to have ignored much of what is symbolized in the mythic allusion of the episode. Scott argues that to see Molly primarily as a symbol of fertility is a "reduction and oversimplification" of both Molly and the various mythic figures to whom she is compared (*Joyce* 158)—such as Penelope, Gea Tellus, and the goddesses of the *Tain Bo Cuailgne*—all of whom are strongly sexual and many of whom play powerful social roles. In various versions of the *Odyssey*, for example, Penelope is portrayed as an unfaithful wife; the goddesses of prehistory are depicted not only as sources of fertility, but as prophets, warriors, healors, and lawmakers (Scott, *Joyce* 9); and the menstruating Medb in the *Tain* is wanton and domineering as well as fertile (O'Corrain, 10).

None of these sexually and socially aggressive characteristics are foregrounded in discussions of Molly during the thirties and forties because to have done so, given the literary and more general ideological climate of the time, would have intensified the episode's provocativeness and lessened the possibility of canonizing *Ulysses* and establishing Joyce's greatness. By connecting "Penelope" with classical sources, rather than focussing on the potentially threatening detail of those sources, critics could demonstrate that the episode served a higher aesthetic function than might be immediately apparent. Gilbert, for example, in linking Molly with Homer's faithful Penelope, argues that Molly is "faithful too—in her fashion" (395), thereby deemphasizing the apparent immorality of Molly's affair with Boylan. He attempts further to reduce the impact of Molly's affair by suggesting that Joyce's portrayal of *her unfaithfulness* may simply be the result of *his faithfulness*, faithfulness, that is, to the variant versions of the *Odyssey*: "Homer's account of the absolute fidelity of Penelope was not endorsed by later classical writers" (395). Molly's adultery, therefore, loses much of its threatening potential because, rather than symbolizing the lusty sexual drive of a woman, it comes to symbolize Joyce's knowledge of and connection to such writers as Herodotus and Butler.

As I noted above, however, there is never a one-to-one correspondence between a social or literary determination and a particular representation of Molly. Thus, the impulse to aestheticize Molly's sexuality was determined by more than simply the literary goal of canonizing *Ulysses*. This impulse can also be linked to the deep-seated need in Western patriarchy to reduce the apparent threat to masculinity engendered by the female body. Eva Feder Kittay, for example, suggests that "in idealizing the maternal aspects of women, men reduce the full scope of woman's human capabilities to her reproductive functions," and thereby attempt to render women less threatening (107). This seems to be one of the effects of turning Molly into a fertility symbol, and although critics of the time do not seem to want to say this explicitly, it is, in the words of Pierre Macherey what their texts appear to be "*compelled* to say" in order to say what they "*wanted*" to say (94).

Critics repeatedly express a sense of relief after developing a symbolic interpretation of Molly as an earth mother. Budgen, for example, writes: "It is clearly in her symbolical character as fruitful mother earth that Molly speaks, . . . for what individual, socially limited woman, if she were capable of entertaining such thoughts, would not be secretive enought to suppress them?" (263). The answer, of course, is Molly Bloom. The need for secrecy and suppression arises from a culture which seeks to censor women's sexuality, and perhaps particularly the sexuality of "socially limited" women.[16] And in exalting Molly as an earth mother, that is exactly what this and other like interpretations do. Budgen goes on to comment that if Molly "lived in our world we should criticize her morals, and good mothers would warn their sons to have nothing to do with her, but she is out of reach of our yardstick and scales. She dwells in a region where there are no incertitudes to torture the mind . . . where there are no regrets, no reproaches, no conscience and consequently no sin" (265). Note the relief this interpretation brings, and note that Budgen is speaking of the (male) reader's reality, not Molly's, for hers is certainly a world of regrets and reproaches. It is as if Budgen were saying that if Molly were real, men would need their mothers who are "good" to protect them from her, but so long as men can reduce her to a principle, "devivify" (Theweleit 107) her by idealization, they are safe, safe from "sin," that is, safe from the threat of female sexuality. Klaus Theweleit, in a study of the male fantasies of the German Freikorpsmen, writes of the tendency to abstract and depersonalize women in all of Western literature: "exaltation is coupled with a negation of women's carnal reality" (285). This tradition of abstracting women's bodies to negate their carnal reality is clearly one of the determinations of such readings of Molly, whether or not it is a conscious goal of the criticism.

Tindall's comment that Molly is the "essential being of everywoman . . . [a]s fundamental and symbolic as her cat" (*JJ* 36) similarly functions both to praise her (in order to aid in the canonization process of *Ulysses*) and to desexualize—indeed, dehumanize—her in order to discharge some of the threat she poses. While he contends that "it is as a person in a story, and not as a many-leveled symbol, that she must appeal to the common reader" (*JJ* 38), it is her symbolic nature on which he dwells. In fact, writing a decade later and still extolling Molly's symbolic function as the "flowering fruitful earth" (*Guide* 233), he makes it clear that "as a person" Molly could not appeal to the (decent) common reader. In a statement that, in a remarkably explicit way, establishes himself as a common (male) reader, he confesses: "born on Depot Street, reared on Main Street, onetime scholar of two Sunday schools (one Episcopalian, the other Congregationalist), member of a poor but decent profession, I am glad not to be married to this particular embodiment of everything" (*Guide* 232). Considered as a woman, Molly is too much for any typical man, but as an archetype, as a "creative principle" (*Guide* 234), she is more easily negotiated. Main Street male readers can safely assume a position of dominance over Molly the archetype, and are able, with relieved benevolence, to enact the lessons of their Sunday school training and can, in an obvious act of identification with Bloom, "forgive" Molly the woman (*Guide* 232).

Tindall's stance of dominance through abstraction leads us to another unspoken aspect of the "earth mother" symbology: it opens

Molly's body to be used or mined by men in whatever way they see fit, and in so doing, it once again secures their fundamental superiority to women. Theweleit argues that because women have never been the "direct agents" of "dominant historical processes," they "have always remained objects and raw materials, pieces of nature awaiting social- ization. This has enabled men to see and use them collectively as part of the earth's inorganic body—the terrain of men's own productions" (294). By calling Molly an earth mother, the critics are in effect saying that Molly—and by implication women generally—are uncultivated raw materials that need to be controlled by men. As an earth mother she is attributed with such traits as "animal placidity" (Levin 125) and "absence of mind" (Tindall, *Guide* 234). She is described as "teeming" (Budgen 262), and "compliant," and "ripe" (Levin 125). Blackmur is perhaps most explicit about the uses to which Molly should be put when he says: "Molly is necessary to any culture but not as its foun- dation; she is rather the basic building material: the problem that first and last must be controlled" (114). And how will she be controlled? By being kept in her place, in which she is to be "ploughed, penetrated, seeded like the earth" (Blackmur 115).

I contended above that interpretations are produced by multiple de- terminations within any reading context. While I have certainly not specified all of the social and ideological conditions that helped to produce the earth mother interpretation of Molly, I have attempted to locate it in a larger historical and cultural context. Rather than seeing it simply as an interpretation "objectively" authorized by Joyce or by the text, or as a product of the critics' personal or "subjective" read- ings of Molly, I have suggested that the particular social and literary climate at the time produced particular kinds of readers for *Ulysses* and produced *Ulysses* as a particular kind of text. To argue that these critics read as subjects in history with particular biases is not to in- dict them for a lack of objectivity, but rather to make the point that in any reading context, critical texts are constructed and constrained by a variety of determinations as they work to organize and delimit the particular ways in which a primary text is to be consumed. The earth mother interpretation of Molly gained dominance because of a convergence of particular ideological coordinates including the need to canonize *Ulysses* and the need to neutralize the threat of Molly's sexuality. When that interpretation began to seem "wrong," it was not that critics became more objective (or more subjective) readers who saw more (or less) clearly the meaning of the text itself, but that the ideological coordinates had shifted and that different functions and effects were being assigned to the text-in-use.

III

Critics of the fifties and sixties openly villified Molly as a "bitch" (Richardson 183), a "whore" (O'Brien, *CJJ* 211; Morse 140), and a "slut" (Adams, *Common* 166) and suggested that she was an embodiment of evil and destruction (Kenner, *DJ* 262; Morse 141). In making such accusations, they are generally seen as directly opposing the "paeans of praise" (Shechner 203) of the earth mother critics, and they have been attacked from many sources for their supposedly "personal" and "subjective" responses to Molly. I want to argue that while there are important differences between these readings of Molly and earlier ones, they are not as divergent as most critics have assumed, and that, far from being "subjective," the interpretations of this period are closely linked historically with earlier readings of the text.[17] Further, I will contend that their differences are not so much a result of a change in critical views of Molly, as is generally thought, but a change in critical views of Joyce which caused a different set of effects to accrue to "Penelope" as a text-in-use.

Few have noted that the accusations of the critics of the fifties and sixties against Molly are similar both in tone and content to those made by many early reviewers against Joyce or *Ulysses*. While Joyce was accused by early reviewers of having "a diseased mind that sees and feels life only in its deformed relationship to sex" (*Carnegie Magazine*, Deming 244), and *Ulysses* was said to be "morbid and sickening" (Leslie, Deming 201), "a corrupt mass of indescribable degradation" (Noyes, Deming 274), which contained all the "foulness conceivable to the mind of madman or ape" (Noyes, Deming 274), in the fifties and sixties Molly was accused of being "the product of enflamed, not healthy nerve ends" (Richardson 184), "a frightening venture into the unconsciousness of evil" (Adams, *Common* 166), and "the center of paralysis" (Morse 141) who had the power to "darken the intellect and blunt the moral sense of all Dublin" (Kenner 262). The same sense of shock and moral outrage of which Huddleston spoke in 1922 underlies all these comments: in the fifties, however, it is displaced from Joyce and the novel and transferred completely onto Molly.

In exploring the relationship of the criticism of the fifties and sixties to that of the thirties and forties, Suzette Henke and Elaine Unkeless suggest that both the earth mother and satanic mistress interpretations are similar in their desire to reduce women to stereotypes (xii).[18] While this analysis may seem obvious today, we still need to address the differences as well as the similarities in how those stereotypes functioned. We need to examine the historical determinations that could have enabled critics of the fifties and sixties both to transfer the outrage of the twenties against Joyce and *Ulysses* onto Molly, and to articulate explicitly the shock against Molly that was spoken of only indirectly in the thirties and forties.

As I have argued, the primary set of ideological coordinates into which the "Penelope" episode was hooked during the thirties and forties was the canonization of *Ulysses*. These coordinates forced critics to suppress the shock that Molly evoked in them for fear that in impugning Molly's reputation, they would tarnish Joyce's: to call Molly a whore was to indict the author who created her. By the time critics were publishing attacks against Molly in the fifties and sixties, however, Joyce's reputation as a canonical Modernist was well established. The number of critical studies of his work was increasing dramatically, and the years between 1958 and 1966 saw the publication of such important texts as Stanislaus Joyce's *My Brother's Keeper*, Richard Ellmann's biography, and the three volumes of Joyce's letters, as well as the establishment of a journal devoted solely to the study of Joyce's work. Further, the question of whether *Ulysses* was pornographic was long since closed.

Once *Ulysses* had been canonized, the "Penelope" episode became connected to a different set of coordinates and different functions and effects began to accrue to Molly. Perhaps the most significant change was that critics had a freedom to respond to the patriarchal irritants of the episode without fear of impugning the text or Joyce's reputation, or without themselves looking reactionary. In fact, since the critics of the previous generation had avoided addressing Molly's sexuality directly, the critics of the fifties and sixties could, paradoxically, appear innovative or "advanced" simply for rearticulating earlier expressions of outrage against the novel, and for bringing to the fore attacks against Molly that had been significantly muted in the earth mother interpretation.

Although the canonization of *Ulysses* was probably the most important factor contributing to the apparent shift in readings of Molly, the convergence of determinations that enabled these readings involved more than the literary. The intensity of the attacks on Molly was in part fueled by an extreme antifeminist backlash in America in the fifties and sixties. Schechner (197) and Scott (*Joyce* 159–60), among others, have noted this in passing, but a somewhat more detailed examination of the language of the critics and the language of some antifeminist statements outside the literary can help to suggest the multiplicity and complexity of discursive determinants that mediated the relations between the "Penelope" episode and its readers in this particular conjuncture.

The cultural formation after the war endorsed an attitude of explicit hostility toward "promiscuous" women, and as John D'Emilio and Estelle Freedman comment, "sex appeared as an uncontrollable force that spawned social chaos when its power was let lose" (284). Elaine May observes that the fear of women's increased sexual activity "extended beyond the traditional fear of prostitutes and 'loose women' to include 'good girls' whose morals might [have] unravel[led] during wartime" (69). A federal commission warned returning soldiers to avoid the good girl gone bad: "She is more dangerous to the community than a mad dog" (quoted in May 69). Molly, in fact, is nearly likened to a mad dog in one essay in which she is characterized as "howling like a bitch in heat" (Richardson 184).

Such exaggerated attacks on the evils of adultery typified criticism of Molly during this period. O'Brien, for example, argues that "For all Molly's attractive vitality, for all of her fleshly charms and engaging bravado, she is at heart a thirty-shilling whore" (*CJJ* 211). The reasoning behind this remark is that: "it seems silly to quibble, as critics have done, over lists and numbers with Boylan's visit a fact" (*DMB* 144). In other words, the "fact" of one affair automatically "proves" Molly to be a whore. Adams and Morse, among others, concur with this assessment of female promiscuity. In discussing whether Molly "made herself available" to any of his list of possible lovers, Adams comments parenthetically "and if to one, why not to all?" (*SS* 38), and Morse suggests that Molly's guilt is proven simply by what people think of her: "She is a dirty joke. No one [in the book] regards her as anything but a whore" (140).

D'Emilio and Freedman point out that in the early 1950s, sexual frankness was increasingly resisted for fear that it would, in the words of a congressional report, "weaken the moral fiber of the future leaders of our country" (quoted, 282). Sexuality, therefore, needed to be contained for national as well as domestic security. Thus, discovering and naming Molly as a "whore" in the fifties and sixties took on a different ideological significance from what it would have had earlier. No longer was such a reading associated with an attack on Joyce or pornographic writing; rather it became connected to discovering and purging all that is evil within society. The ideological coordinates through which the episode was being read had thus shifted significantly since the thirties and forties; however, in linking evil with the female body, the critics are not only employing the discourse of antifeminism dominant in the postwar period, but are also participating in the Western tradition of gynophobia which has blamed women since Eve for evil in the world, a tradition, as we saw above, that in part also served as an underpinning of the earth mother interpretation.

For many of the critics of this period, Molly not only comes to symbolize evil, but she is also directly linked with death and world destruction. Hugh Kenner, for example, asserts, without discussion, that Molly's "Yes" is "the 'Yes' of consent that kills the soul" and has "authority" over the "animal kingdom of the dead" (262). Richardson similarly argues that Molly's "universe contains the seed of its own destruction," and contends that "that destruction will inevitably include Bloom and Stephen" (184). That neither critic feels the need to elaborate on such extreme attacks, far from suggesting the "personal" or "subjective" nature of these interpretations, points to the degree to which connecting female sexuality to world destruction was culturally sanctioned and seemed "normal" at this particular conjuncture. May, for example, notes that an open expression of sexuality was literally equated with the possibility of world destruction during this period. The slang term, "bombshell," developed in the thirties to describe the "devastating power" of the sexual woman, was literalized in World War II when thousands of fighter planes were decorated with iconography of sexy women (May 69).[19] A civil defense pamphlet (see fig. 1.1) depicted the alpha, beta, and gamma rays of radiation as three sexy women with open mouths and large breasts ready to burst out of their strapless bathing suits. The pamphlet explains that "these rays are potentially both harmful and helpful," and, as May notes, is presumably saying the same things about the sexy women (110). The message was clear: unless their sexuality was controlled, women could kill you. "This is not life, this is death; this is the center of paralysis," Morse writes of Molly (141).

The accusations of the postwar critics are, then, on the surface, significantly more virulent than those of the earlier critics at least in part because, with the canonization of *Ulysses,* it became possible to separate attacks on Molly from attacks on Joyce. The sense of shock and hostility that these critics manifest in reaction to female sexuality, however, although fueled by the strong antifeminism of the period, is part of the same gynophobic tradition underlying the earth mother interpretation. While the early critics sought to diminish the threat Molly posed by apparently denying the existence of her sexual attributes and turning her into a devivified abstraction, the postwar critics attacked more directly. Each group was able to develop the particular readings of Molly that it did, however, not simply because the "Penelope" episode is complex and ambiguous, but because of the historical convergence of particular literary and more general ideological determinations.

Linking Molly with death, for example, is perhaps the most over-

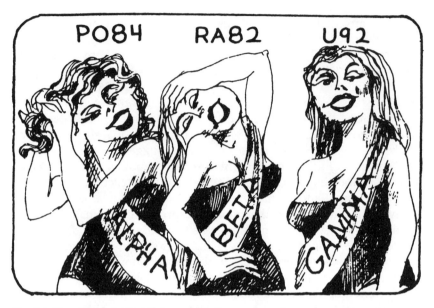

Fig. 1.1. *Your Chance to Live*, Defense Civil Preparedness Agency pamphlet. Courtesy of Far West Laboratory, San Francisco, California, 1972.

determined interpretive act of the critics of the fifties and sixties. Molly came to symbolize death because death literally became associated with female sexuality during and after World War II. This symbolization occurred, in part, as an act of patriarchal wish-fulfillment— for only in death will women's bodies cease to threaten—and in part because the later critics were acting out the legacy of unspeakable shock of the earlier group of critics. Turning Molly into a death force may, finally, not be all that different from turning her into an earth mother. For earth mothers, as devivified by the critics of the thirties and forties, are, if I may develop a train of associations: unthinking. Compliant. Like the earth. No longer threatening. Able to be extolled. Of the earth. The earth. Dirt? In their place. In the earth. Dead?

IV

I have attempted to develop a revisionist history of Molly Bloom by locating past readings of "Penelope" in more complex historical contexts. I have contended that it is not productive to talk about the "text itself" as a transcendent metaphysical entity, because such a position does not allow us to analyze how "Penelope" has functioned in "the historically varying forms of . . . [its] social use and inscription" (Bennett and Woollacott 264)—including its use in our own contemporary reading contexts. In reexamining the varying uses to which "Penelope" was put between 1922 and 1970, I have studied past interpretations in relation to larger literary and social determinations, in particular, to the institutionalization of *Ulysses* and to traditional patriarchal beliefs about female sexuality. I have also examined readings of Molly, not only in terms of their content, but in terms of their *effectivities*. While the earth mother interpretation may seem reductive to us today and clearly a product of the encoding of traditional gender-specific assumptions about women, its effect was quite radical in helping to enabling *Ulysses* to circulate. The overt expression of the satanic mistress interpretation participated in perpetuating the traditional patriarchal recoiling at female sexuality, but also—in part because of its extreme nature—eventually forced the literary establishment to look critically at such expressions.

If we can recognize some of the ways in which literary and more general ideological determinations helped to produce past readings of "Penelope," we might begin to interrogate further the terms of our own contemporary debates about Molly. Over the last two decades, dominant interpretations of Molly have changed significantly. In particular, there have been far more readings of Molly that are sympathetic to feminist concerns. While feminist criticism is highly varied, and includes Marxist, deconstructive, and psychoanalytic approaches, there seem to be two primary orbits of contemporary concern into which discussions of Molly and the "Penelope" episode have predominantly been drawn.

The first, which began over a decade ago and which Henke and Unkeless initially termed "contextual" (xi), situates Joyce's women characters, including Molly, within the complex cultural, historical, political, and economic forces that were part of turn-of-the-century Dublin.[20] While work in this area varies in the degree to which it embraces post-structuralist notions of textuality and subjectivity,[21] it shares a focus on how Molly's language, desire, and even her very subjectivity have been produced by her historical formation. The most contentious issue among these critics is whether Molly's subjectivity is completely contained within the dominant patriarchal discourses of her social formation, or whether her thoughts, actions, and desires are to some extent resistant to them.[22]

The second orbit of concerns into which Molly has been drawn involves not whether, as a character, she is capable of resisting the forces of patriarchy, but whether Joyce's use of language somehow frees it

from patriarchal authority. French feminists such as Hélène Cixous
and Julia Kristeva have argued that Joyce's prose works to dissolve
sexual difference, and that Molly's language of flow and overflow is an
example of "écriture féminine" (Cixoux 255). Over the last decade, a
number of critics have argued forcefully for this position with specific
reference to Molly,[23] although the argument recently has been modu-
lated by Suzette Henke who contends that: "Molly Bloom's discourse
is fluid and feminine, deracinated and polymorphic, uncontained by
the limits of logocentric authority. But the contours of her monologue
are fearfully phallomorphic, determined by the pervasive presence of
a male register of desire" (*Desire* 130).

Others, however, have argued against the "inherently" feminine
nature of Molly's language. Gayatri Spivak remarks that she finds
"something comical about Joyce rising above sexual identities" (144).
Sandra Gilbert and Susan Gubar have articulated perhaps the most
violent opposition to the argument, contending that far from being a
language of flow and *jouissance,* Joyce's language is in fact a language
of "densest condensation" and "*puissance*" (261). Diana Henderson
develops a similar position, focussing specifically on Molly, arguing
that the structure that organizes "Penelope" is "the male authorial
fist" (521).

It is tempting to see these debates—because they are part of our
own historical moment and we have naturalized them—as those that
the "text itself" raises. And clearly as a feminist, I would certainly
acknowledge that I find analyses of Molly's degree of agency significantly more compelling than analyses of her morality. But while
contemporary readers may find the particular questions that they put
to the episode more interesting than those put to it in the past, we
should not lose sight of the fact that our questions are no less interested than those of the past: they have been produced by particular
literary and social determinations, and they, like the readings of the
past, have particular ideological antecedents and implications. It is
on the basis of those antecedents and implications, not on the basis
of having "objectively" apprehended Joyce's "true intention," that we
need to argue for the value of one reading over another.

Thus, as we analyze contemporary readings of Molly and attempt to
take up a position within them, we need to look back at the complex literary and social determinations that produced the readings of the past
and ask what larger literary and ideological determinations underlie
current perspectives? Contemporary feminist readings are opposed in
a number of powerful and important ways to many of those of the
past. Yet one might ask what continuities could usefully be explored

in order to help analyze the implications of current positions? To what extent are contemporary readings that seek to demonstrate that Joyce was "really" a feminist or that the language of "Penelope" is "actually" an expression of *écriture féminine* mediated by determinations such as the canonical status of *Ulysses* or the institutional authorization of feminist discourse? What is at stake in the debates about the construction of Molly's subjectivity and about her degree of agency? Why can we have these particular debates about Molly now, and what are the consequences—for the status of Joyce, *Ulysses*, and the critic making the argument—of taking up one position over another? What are some of the implications of applying to Molly and the "Penelope" episode, in the name of feminism, a variety of theoretical perspectives such as Marxism and deconstruction that have been used in other contexts for more traditional masculinist ends? While the answers that we can develop from such questions will necessarily always be partial—we cannot step outside our own reading context and see it objectively— asking such questions can continually remind us that larger literary, social, and institutional determinations inform all our acts of reading, and that, as we attempt to make "Penelope" repeatedly readdress our own historical condition, those determinations have consequences.

Notes

1.   For early comments on Molly, see Colum, Deming 233, and Leslie, Deming 202. For earth goddess interpretations, see Budgen, Gilbert, Levin, and Tindall (*Guide* and *JJ*). For readings of Molly as a whore, see Richardson, O'Brien (*CJJ* and *MB*), Morse, Adams (*Common* and *SS*). For readings that attempt to contextualize Molly as a realistic character, see Hayman, Unkeless, and Scott (*Joyce* and "Character"). For readings of the "Molly" episode as *écriture féminine*, see MacCabe, Henke and Unkeless, Henke (*Desire* and *JMS*), and Levitt.

2.   For an argument similar to McGee's, see Attridge 548–53 and 561–62.

3.   Although Shechner notes that the criticism of the fifties and sixties was probably influenced by "the hardening of sensibility in postwar America" (197), he does not develop the analysis.

4.   See Hayman 103–4, and Card 17 for similar arguments that credit Joyce and the text itself as the sources of divergent critical readings.

5.   For an analysis of the effects of locating the author and the text as the immanent source of meaning, see Foucault's discussion of the "author function" (148–53).

6.   See, for example, Richardson 177; Morse 139; Steinberg 55; Herring 49; Hayman 133.

7.   Steinberg suggests that these critics "misunderstood" Molly perhaps

because they were "led astray" by the excesses of Gilbert and of Budgen (55), while Morse hypothesizes that they simply may have been too "inexperienced" and too "gallant" to understand that "any sexually indiscriminate woman" is not "a fertility symbol" (139).

8. See, for example, Macherey 66–101; Jauss 3–45; Eagleton 44–63; Bennett, *FM* 127–66.

9. Henke and Unkeless xii; Scott, *Joyce* 157–61.

10. See also Tindall, *Reader's Guide* 232–35, and Blackmur 114–15.

11. Tindall, *Reader's Guide* 233; Gilbert 389–95; and Budgen 264–65.

12. See Adams, *Common* 166; O'Brien, "Determinant," 143–49; Shechner 217.

13. In 1982, Leslie Fiedler recalled that as an adolescent in 1932, he had found the novel quite like an aphrodisiac, and he suggests that "to read *Ulysses* . . . without being titillated represents as inadequate a response as reading it without laughing or weeping" (29). While Fiedler can in the early eighties, easily praise the pornographic elements of *Ulysses,* to contend in 1932 that Molly or the book in general was salacious or "titillating" was to take a stand against the novel and against Joyce.

14. This, of course, is exactly what Judge Woolsey argued when he declared that while in many places the book appeared to be "disgusting," he did not consider any of it to be "dirt for dirt's sake," nor anywhere did it tend to be an "aphrodisiac" (x, xii).

15. Lewis 112–141; D'Emilio and Freedman 222–35; May 47–57.

16. Theweleit, for example, notes that accusations against women's sexuality in Western patriarchy are particularly directed toward women of the lower classes (70–84).

17. See, for example, Herring 60; Schechner 197; Scott, *Joyce* 158–62; Henke, *Desire* 6.

18. While the criticism of the fifties and sixties is certainly more extreme, the nature of its attacks on Molly are quite consistent with earlier critiques of Molly's sexuality and lack of respect for men. See, for example, Budgen's criticism of Molly's "obscenities of thought" (263). See also Tindall, *Reader's Guide,* 233; Gilbert 389, 395; and Budgen 264–65.

19. A picture of Rita Hayworth, the Hollyword sex symbol, was in fact attached to the hydrogen bomb that was tested on the Bikini Islands (May 110).

20. Henke and Unkeless xii–xv; Unkeless 150–68; Scott, *Joyce* 162–79.

21. See, for example, Scott, "Character" 158–62 and van Boheemen-Saaf 93–98.

22. Pearce 66–70; Scott, *Joyce* 162–63; van Boheemen-Saaf 93–98; Unkeless 150–68; and Shloss in this volume, p. 00.

23. See, for example, MacCabe, 131–32; Henke and Unkeless xiv; Levitt 507–16.

Works Cited

Adams, Robert. *James Joyce: Common Sense and Beyond.* New York: Random House, 1966.

Adams, Robert. *Surface and Symbol: The Consistency of James Joyce's "Ulysses."* New York: Oxford University Press, 1967.

Attridge, Derek. "Molly's Flow: The Writing of 'Penelope' and the Question of Women's Language." *Modern Fiction Studies* 35 (1989): 543–65.

Bennett, Tony. *Formalism and Marxism.* London: Methuen, 1979.

Bennett, Tony, and Janet Woollacott. *Bond and Beyond: The Political Career of a Popular Hero.* London: Macmillan, 1988.

Benstock, Bernard, ed. *James Joyce: The Augmented Ninth.* Syracuse, N.Y.: Syracuse University Press, 1988.

Blackmur, R. P. "The Jew in Search of a Son." *The Virginia Quarterly Review* 24 (1948): 96–116.

Budgen, Frank. *James Joyce and the Making of "Ulysses."* 1934. Bloomington: Indiana University Press, 1960.

Card, James Van Dyck. " 'Contradicting': The Word for Joyce's 'Penelope.' " *James Joyce Quarterly* 11 (1974): 17–26.

Cixoux, Hélène. "The Laugh of the Medusa." Marks and de Courtivron 245–64.

D'Emilio, John, and Estelle B. Freedman. *Intimate Matters: A History of Sexuality in America.* New York: Harper and Row, 1988.

Deming, Robert. *James Joyce: The Critical Heritage.* Vol. 1. New York: Barnes & Noble, 1970.

Eagleton, Terry. *Criticism and Ideology.* London: New Left Books, 1976.

Ellmann, Richard. *James Joyce.* 1959. Rev. ed. New York: Oxford University Press, 1982.

Fiedler, Leslie. "To Whom Does Joyce Belong? Ulysses as Parody, Pop, and Porn." *Light Rays: James Joyce and Modernism.* Ed. Heyward Ehrlich. New York: New Horizon Press, 1984. 26–37.

Foucault, Michel Paul. "What Is an Author?" *Textual Strategies: Perspectives in Post-Structuralist Criticism.* Ed. Josue V. Harari. Ithaca: Cornell University Press, 1979. 141–60.

Gilbert, Sandra M., and Susan Gubar. *The War of the Words.* New Haven: Yale University Press, 1988. Vol. 1 of *No Man's Land: The Place of the Woman Writer in the Twentieth Century.* 2 vols. to date. 1988–.

Gilbert, Stuart. *James Joyce's "Ulysses": A Study.* New York: Knopf, 1952.

Hayman, David. "The Empirical Molly." *Approaches to "Ulysses": Ten Essays.* Ed. Thomas F. Staley and Bernard Benstock. Pittsburgh: University of Pittsburgh Press, 1970. 103–35.

Henderson, Diana E. "Joyce's Modernist Woman: Whose Last Word?" *Modern Fiction Studies* 35 (1989): 517–28.

Henke, Suzette. *Joyce's Moraculous Sindbook: A Study of "Ulysses."* Columbus: Ohio State University Press, 1978.

Henke, Suzette. *James Joyce and the Politics of Desire.* New York: Routledge, 1990.

Henke, Suzette, and Elaine Unkeless, eds. *Women in Joyce.* Urbana: University of Illinois Press, 1982.

Herring, Phillip. "The Bedsteadfastness of Molly Bloom." *Modern Fiction Studies* 15 (1969): 49–61.

Jauss, Hans Robert. "Literary History as a Challenge to Literary Theory." *Toward an Aesthetic of Reception.* Trans. Timothy Bahti. Minneapolis: University of Minnesota Press, 1982. 3–45.

Joyce, James. *The Letters of James Joyce.* Vol. I. Ed. Stuart Gilbert, 1957; rev. Richard Ellmann, 1966. New York: Viking Press, 1966. Vols. 2 and 3. Ed. Richard Ellmann. New York: Viking Press, 1966.

Joyce, Stanislaus. *My Brother's Keeper.* London: Faber, 1958.

Kenner, Hugh. *Dublin's Joyce.* Bloomington: Indiana University Press, 1956.

Kittay, Eva Feder. "Womb Envy: An Explanatory Concept." *Mothering: Essays in Feminist Theory.* Ed. Joyce Trebilcot. Totowa, N.J.: Rowman and Allanheld, 1983. 94–128.

Kristeva, Julia. "Woman Can Never Be Defined." Marks and de Courtivron 137–41.

Levin, Harry. *James Joyce.* Norfolk, Conn.: New Directions, 1941.

Levitt, Annette Shandler. "The Pattern Out of the Wallpaper: Luce Irigaray and Molly Bloom." *Modern Fiction Studies* 35 (1989): 507–16.

Lewis, Jane. *Women in England 1887–1950: Sexual Division and Social Change.* Bloomington: Indiana University Press, 1984.

MacCabe, Colin. *James Joyce and the Revolution of the Word.* London: Macmillan, 1979.

McGee, Patrick. "Reading Authority: Feminism and Joyce." *Modern Fiction Studies* 35 (1989): 421–36.

Macherey, Pierre. *A Theory of Literary Production.* Trans. Geoffrey Wall. Boston: Routledge and Kegan Paul, 1978.

Marks, Elaine, and Isabelle de Courtivron, eds. *New French Feminisms.* New York: Schocken Books, 1981.

May, Elaine. *Homeward Bound: American Families in the Cold War.* New York: Basic Books, 1988.

Morley, Dave. "Texts, Readers, Subjects." *Culture, Media, Language.* Ed. Stuart Hall. London: Verso, 1980. 163–73.

Morse, J. Mitchell. "Molly Bloom Revisited." In *A James Joyce Miscellany.* Ed. Marvin Magalaner. Carbondale: Southern Illinois University Press, 1959. 139–49.

O'Brien, Darcey. *The Conscience of James Joyce.* Princeton: Princeton University Press, 1968.

O'Brien, Darcey. "Some Determinants of Molly Bloom." *Approaches to "Ulysses": Ten Essays.* Ed. Thomas F. Staley and Bernard Benstock. Pittsburgh: University of Pittsburgh Press, 1970. 137–55.

O'Corrain, Donncha. "Women in Early Irish Society." *Women in Irish Society: The Historical Dimension.* Ed. Margaret Maccurtain and Donncha O'Corrain. Westport, Conn.: Greenwood Press, 1979. 1–13.

Pearce, Richard. *The Politics of Narration*. New Brunswick: Rutgers University Press, 1991.

Richardson, Robert. "Molly's Last Words." *Twentieth Century Literature* 12 (1967): 177–85.

Scott, Bonnie Kime. *Joyce and Feminism*. Bloomington: Indiana University Press, 1984.

Scott, Bonnie Kime. "Character, Joyce, and Feminist Critical Approaches." Benstock 158–64.

Shechner, Mark. *Joyce in Nighttown: A Psychoanalytic Inquiry into "Ulysses."* Berkeley: University of California Press, 1974.

Spivak, Gayatri Chakravorty. *In Other Worlds: Essays in Cultural Politics*. New York: Methuen, 1987.

Steinberg, Erwin. "A Book with a Molly in It." *James Joyce Review* 2 (1958): 55–62.

Theweleit, Klaus. *Male Fantasies*. Vol 1. Trans. Stephen Conway. Minneapolis: University of Minnesota Press, 1987.

Tindall, William. *James Joyce: His Way of Interpreting the Modern World*. New York: Scribner, 1950.

Tindall, William Y. *A Reader's Guide to James Joyce*. New York: Noonday Press, 1959.

Unkeless, Elaine. "The Conventional Molly Bloom." Henke and Unkeless 150–68.

van Boheemen-Saaf, Christine. "Joyce, Derrida, and the Discourse of 'the Other'." Benstock 88–102.

Woolsey, Judge John M. "Decision." In James Joyce, *Ulysses*. New York: Random House, 1961. vii–xii.

2

How Does Molly Bloom
Look Through the Male Gaze?

Richard Pearce

Line-of-sight weapons—those in which one can see the opposition while firing . . . are prohibited to women as *offensive*
weapons in most western militaries . . .

Susan Jeffords

Leopold Bloom has a good eye for an ad. He imagines one for Wisdom
Hely's stationery: "a transparent showcart with two smart girls sitting
inside writing letters. . . . catch the eye at once" (8.132). Bloom's ideal
ad would still catch *the* eye. But it is designed for the male, not the
female eye. And it focuses the dilemma of women as spectators and
authors, or authors (the smart girls are writing letters) of their own
imaginative desires, when they are trapped in the male gaze.

In *Ulysses* Joyce creates Molly Bloom as an apparently independent
woman, who, given her interior monologue, would seem to be the
author of her own thoughts and fantasies, her own gaze and desire.
Indeed, Brenda Maddox concludes in her biography of Nora, "when
Joyce made Leopold Bloom recall Molly's pleading, 'Give us a touch
Poldy. God I'm dying for it,' he gave his country, and his century, the
voice of female desire" (381). But by the time we reach the last episode, Molly has been framed by the quest stories of Stephen Dedalus
and Leopold Bloom, and her image has been shaped by the aggregate
male view. So we might ask the deliberately ambiguous question: how
does Molly look through the male gaze—or the transparent showcart
of the male gaze? I am not asking this question rhetorically, for I do
not intend to come to a conclusion, or a closure. Indeed, I want to
write a dialogic essay, where the second part interrogates the first.

And I want to do so not only because this book is designed to be dialogic, but because the contradictory positions reflect my dilemma, as a male feminist,[1] writing about a strong female character—*looking* through or looking *through* the male gaze.

I

Let me begin by describing and developing Laura Mulvey's concept of "the male gaze" ("Visual Pleasure"), which, though designed to illuminate the dynamics of Hollywood film, also exposes an element of traditional realistic narrative, especially male narrative, that retains a residual power in *Ulysses*. For, despite the undermining of conventions, the play of language, the shift in perspectives, and the intervention of styles, it is important to remember that we are drawn to Joyce's realistic characters and follow their actions along a realistic storyline.

The power of the gaze, according to Mulvey, derives from the pleasure we take in looking when we are not seen. The movie theatre is an ideal place in which to indulge our scopophilia or voyeurism, for it is dark, and we are safely distanced from the objects of our desire that are magnified on the lighted screen. Indeed movies resemble the dream world. So our desires and fantasies can be both reflected and shaped by the films we watch—as long as the seamless editing and realistic conventions keep us from realizing that film is materially and socially constructed. And let me suggest that we take similar pleasure in reading a traditional realistic novel, where, sitting alone, we picture the objects of our desire. And these fantasies are shaped by a trustworthy narrator who limits our view while leading us to feel that we are seeing from a universal vantage, who leads us from one scene to the next in a way that seems natural and logical, who makes us forget that we are looking at print and turning the pages of a book, who obscures the fact that our expectations are governed by a publishing industry—and that he is authorized by a sense of culture defined by the dominant (male) class of our society.

Since our pleasure in looking depends on our distance from the spectacle, we establish a relationship limited to two positions: subject and object. Which means that we deny the object of our desire its subjectivity—and a desire of its own. (Bloom is wrong when he thinks that everyone is "dying to know" what the girls in the show-cart are writing—though he may be reflecting his own singular curiosity.) Moreover, desire is aroused by what we do not possess, or what is Other and therefore threatening to us. And we control this threat by repressing, sublimating, or transforming it into a fetish—

that is, an object which, in symbolically resembling ourselves, makes the Other safe.

I have been using the plural "we," at the risk of alienating my women readers, to demonstrate my point about the Hollywood camera eye and the traditional realistic narrator. Without acknowledging it as a choice, I have positioned the male as subject and the female as object—and limited the woman reader to my subject position. That is, I have constructed the reader as male, or the kind of male that makes men like me uncomfortable.

According to Mulvey, there are three "looks" in the Hollywood film, which can be translated into looks in traditional realistic fiction. The first is reflected in the way the characters look at each other within the diegesis, or storyline. And we focus on far more men looking at women than women looking at men. Moreover, when a woman looks at men, she usually looks from the vantage of the object rather than the subject, seeing men as active agents, or being concerned about how men will see her. I want to emphasize the term "vantage" here, for women also look as subjects. Indeed Robyn Warhol shows how the women in Jane Austen's works, particularly in *Persuasion*, look at men from a subject position, deriving from their sensibility a look that is both empowering and authoritative. Moreover, as Beth Newman argues in her discussion of *The Turn of the Screw*, being the object of a gaze can be sustaining, indeed necessary for one's self, or subjectivity, especially when one's position is destablized by gender and class. Nonetheless, in both cases, women are *also* framed by the male gaze. The strong women in classic Hollywood films begin by being framed as subjects with their own desires, but end by looking the way their husbands wanted them to look. In *Blonde Venus,* when Marlene Dietrich returns to her husband, wearing an elegant black gown that sets off his dour shabbiness, she kneels behind her child's crib, her bare shoulders censored by its bars, so that she literally looks up to him. In *Dark Victory,* Bette Davis ends up happily married to the doctor who discovered her illness, but pays the ultimate price by going blind and dying for her early assertions of independence and presumptions of power.

The second "look" is realized by our identification with the male point of view. The narrative voice-over in Hollywood *film noir* accentuates the power of the first-person film narrator, who is traditionally male. For we are compelled to identify with the storyteller as we see what has happened to him from his limited point of view. But, the source of his voice is absent, at least for the most part. Indeed, Kaja Silverman argues that the male voice-over gains its power by issuing from a source beyond the gaze of not only the viewer but also the camera, thereby identifying it with the godlike origin of the text. The dying investigator of *Double Indemnity* begins by talking into his dictaphone, but this device was soon seen as too contrived; now the scene of narration is rarely shown. Either way, what we see seems to be objective, and the first-person narrator takes on the authority of third-person omniscience. The narrative voice-over, then, helps us understand that the omniscient, third-person narrator also limits our view, for unless coded female, he is implicitly male due to our associations with male authority in a patriarchal tradition. But he nonetheless makes us feel that what we see is natural, objective, and universal. At least as insidious is the way women are framed as passive or alluring objects—and the way we see them from the perspective of the hero.

Identifying with the hero—who provides coherence to most Hollywood films and traditional novels—leads to another form of pleasure, according to Mulvey. While her notions of scopophilia and voyeurism come from Freud, here she makes use of Lacan—who goes back to the moment when a baby catches the first glimpse of itself in a mirror. For, while it is not completely coordinated at that time and has no sense of itself as coherent or separate from the world around it, the mirror reflects an image that appears both whole and independent. This false image becomes an ego ideal, which requires continual confirmation—offered most commonly by women, who, as Virginia Woolf observed, "have served . . . as looking-glasses possessing the magic and delicious power of reflecting the figure of man at twice its natural size" (35). The false image of the ego-ideal is also reinforced when we identify with a hero who provides continuity, coherence, explanations, salvation, and reward.

The third "look" of the male gaze is inscribed in the technology. In film it is shaped by the way the camera selects and focuses on events, but also by the way directors and cameramen are trained, the way the film is edited, and the way the studio is run. Moreover, it is realized in the way the camera developed from the box Alberti invented to establish an ideal vantage and impose the system of perspective, which we have come to accept as realistic. As Joel Snyder points out, Alberti recognized that perspective was a construction, or a "rational structure of perceptual judgments" (515). Further, this third "look" of the male gaze is shaped by agencies of advertising and distribution, and by the expectations of the audience. In traditional realistic fiction (which, as Alan Spiegel shows, has been affected by the development of the camera) the male gaze is inscribed in the controlling and unifying point of view, in the education of writers, in the publishing industry, in advertising and the modes of distribution, and in the way people are taught to read.

Successful representation of the male gaze depends on its seeming natural, or on suppressing the medium. It depends, that is, on suppressing the fact that we are watching a film or reading a book, that the actors and actresses are made up or that the characters are conventionalized, that spontaneity is calculated, that the camera or narrator focuses from this rather than that angle, that a shot or a scene is composed to direct our view and understanding, that the cutting from one shot or scene to another only seems seamless, that the production of a film or book requires labor, and that its distribution (the way it gets to us) is part of the capitalist system. Successful representation also depends on imposing unity through coherent narration, causal structures, unified characters, central characters, recurrent motifs, satisfying endings. And this unity denies Otherness by ignoring it, repressing it, sublimating it into a unifying ideal, fetishizing it into a safe form, punishing it for its threatening desires, or recuperating it into the accepted system.

According to Mulvey, then, unless women become resisting viewers, they are presented with the undesirable options of identifying either with the male point of view, which results in false consciousness or self-destruction,[2] or with the female object, who has no look of her own, who has neither agency nor subjectivity, who can neither choose nor desire for herself. And women readers are in a similar bind, though critics like Beth Newman and Robyn Warhol are opening up new possibilities.

Molly Bloom contends with all three looks of the male gaze. She contends with the fact that she is seen for seventeen out of eighteen episodes from her husband's point of view. And Leopold is a voyeur—who continually gazes at women from a safe distance not only at the Mutoscope in Capel street, but as he follows "the moving hams" of his next door neighbor, as he watches a stylish woman climb into the carriage, as he pictures "those pretty little seaside girls," as he imagines the caretaker courting his wife in the graveyard, as he masturbates while watching Gerty lean back to see the fireworks. And in the nighttown of his guilty thought, as he pictures Gerty accuse him of seeing "all the secrets of my bottom drawer" (15.384), and being punished for his voyeurism by Mrs. Bellingham and Mrs. Barry, and peeking through the keyhole to watch Molly and Blazes make love.

We not only watch the main character gazing at women throughout the novel, we are continually led to identify with a more general male point of view. We are asked to identify with the quests of the father and son. We see most of what happens through Stephen's and

Bloom's eyes. We listen to men's stories in the funeral coach, in the newspaper office, in the library, in the woman's lying-in hospital, and in the Blooms' kitchen. Moreover, until the final episode, our image of Molly is derived solely from the male point of view. Bloom continually thinks of Molly as he leaves home and wanders through Dublin. The men he meets continually ask about his wife and her singing tour, and continually wonder about who's getting it up. Lenehan tells the story about being lost in Molly's Milky Way. Simon Dedalus puns that "Mrs Marion Bloom has left off clothes of all descriptions" (11.496). The nameless narrator of "Cyclops" tells us she has "a back like a ballalley" (12.503–4). The men in the cabman's shelter gaze at the photo with "her fleshy charms on evidence" (16.1428). Bloom speculates about her eighteen lovers. And it took scholars half a century of careful reading to discover that Molly was not promiscuous, for Boylan was her first adulterous lover.

That we accepted the male point of view for so long without taking Molly's monologue seriously reflects the power of the third look of the male gaze—which is inscribed in the technology of traditional narrative that Joyce developed to new limits even as he undermined it. It is inscribed in the very concept of the point of view, to which Joyce and other male modernists gave such scrupulous attention. (I argue in my *Politics of Narration* that Woolf helped initiate an alternative line of modernism in part by developing a point of view that is not scrupulously limited to individual characters but is relational and intersubjective.) It is reinforced by the mythic framework of male heroes and system of male allusions, especially to Homer and Virgil. (We see Bloom wandering in the path of Odysseus. We judge Bloom and Stephen not as peeping Toms, as they pee beneath Molly's window, but as the modern Virgil and Dante trying to outdo each other while looking up at the beatific vision.) Finally, the male gaze is inscribed in the canon in which Joyce is taught, and in the traditional way students have been taught to read him.

But the male gaze is continually broken in *Ulysses*. It is broken by the parodies of classical myths—the kind of parodies where, according to Mikhail Bakhtin, what was sacrosanct and beyond question is brought in close, drawn into "a zone of crude contact" (23), fingered familiarly on all sides, turned upside down, inside out, peered at from above and below, taken apart, dismembered, laid bare, and exposed. It is broken by the continually shifting perspectives—which destroy the coherence upon which the power of the male gaze depends. And it is broken by the multiplicity of perspectives, which engender heterogeneity and the multiplicity of self.

The male gaze is also broken by our being situated in the woman's position in "Nausicaa." Gerty MacDowell may have internalized the male construction of an ideal woman of magazine advertisements and popular novels. And she may have idealized Bloom as a dashing foreign gentleman. But, as Kimberly Devlin points out, Gerty sees him as a physical man whose masturbating gives her pleasure (136–40).

Most importantly, the male gaze is broken by Molly's monologue. For it is contained in a gratuitous chapter that was not part of *The Odyssey*, nor required by the novel's plot. Moreover, it is a break from the concerns and perspectives of the father and son. And, since we never hear Bloom's request for breakfast in bed, it is initiated by a physical break in the text. Fritz Senn and Hugh Kenner ingeniously argue that Molly misunderstood Bloom's rambling about the "roc's auk's egg" (17.2328–29), but in doing so they naturalize Joyce's daring omission.[3]

Further, as Susan Bazargan points out in this volume, Molly's chapter is not a monologue. It is a dialogue—"Yes . . . because" being an explanation to an ideal listener.[4] And I would add that Molly's ideal listener is a woman, with whom she can share her restlessness, her physical desires, her fantasies, her cynical views of men, as well as her realistic views of motherhood and menstruation that don't come from the dominant discourses of her society.

I have been considering Molly in relation to the dominant, realistic storyline, which is structured to seem natural and coherent, to reinforce the male gaze, and to appropriate Molly. The storyline is continually undermined by parodies, shifts in perspective, and the foregrounding of style and textuality. But it is undermined in a new way in "Penelope." As Derek Attridge demonstrates, the long unpunctuated sentences do not convey a realistic sense of natural flow. Indeed we need a new orientation to deal with their materiality. Moreover, the pauses we make in reading are arbitrary and ambiguous. The monologue or dialogue is filled with puns and what Frances Restuccia calls a "playful leapfrogging." And, in the midst of her most female-centered thoughts, Molly breaks through with "O Jamesey let me up out of this pooh" (18.1128–29).

Moreover, while many of her recollections and fantasies are passive, even masochistic, Molly is an active agent. She asserts her own views, turns Bloom, Blazes, and other Irishmen into objects of her gaze, directs the course of her thoughts, and even argues with her creator—or demands that he stop prying into her private life or making her pose as a natural woman in the transparent showcart of his novel. And she breaks through the realistic illusion that supports the reader's imaginative gaze.

Her final assertion of independence appears at the climax of her affirmation, when she blends together Leopold Bloom and Lt. Mulvey. While she began her chapter by defining Bloom as an assertive husband who demands his breakfast in bed after cavorting in nighttown, or by constructing him as a manly man, she ends by denying him his agency—in a gaze that is independent, indifferent, all-embracing. And I want to focus on these three qualities.

To elaborate on her independence, I can do no better than quote Kimberly Devlin: As Molly "thinks back to the day she spent on Howth with Bloom . . . she recalls, 'I gave him all the pleasure I could leading him on till he asked me to say yes and I wouldn't answer first only looked out over the sea and the sky *I was thinking of so many things he didn't know* of Mulvey and Mr Stanhope and Hester and father and old captain Groves' [18.1580–83, emphasis added]—what follows is the elaborate recollection of Gibraltar in which Bloom starts to merge with Mulvey. Molly's closing reveries interweave two distinct but not mutually exclusive memories: a moment of union and tacit understanding balanced by a concurrent sense that her private female past is uniquely and irrevocably her own" (Devlin 153).

To say that Molly's gaze is indifferent may be to deny her the kind of love that makes the ending so satisfying—though this may say more about "our" needs, or the needs of the reader constructed as male. To see her gaze as indifferent may be to see her as cold and selfish as some male critics have seen her—though this may say more about the dilemma of women in fiction. Our identity, as Devlin points out following Lacan, depends upon the way we imagine ourselves being seen by the Other. And Bloom worries, "See ourselves as others see us. So long as women don't mock what matter" (Devlin 114). But for the Other's gaze to be indifferent is to deny the subject his existence. Or his position and power.

Molly's gaze is not only indifferent but all-embracing. Therefore it redefines the subject in relation to another subject, as well as an object to be distanced and appropriated. And now let me suggest that Molly's monologue or dialogue or polylogue embodies an alternative to the male gaze—and the male narrative—which allows not only an alternative way of looking but a multiplicity of desires and an intersubjectivity. The multiplicity of desires may, as Luce Irigaray argues, arise from multiple erogenous sites on the woman's body (205–18). But there is more. Jessica Benjamin gives us the model of a mother holding a child, or watching and "being with" rather than dominating her child at play. In both instances the mother creates a transitional space, where inner meets outer, where the child is both dependent and independent, where play and creativity are encouraged. I realize that my use of Irigaray and Benjamin may lead toward essentializing and a dualistic argument of women's vs. men's ways of seeing. But the male gaze is hegemonic, which can only be broken by first imagining an alternative way of looking.

So how does Molly look through the transparent showcart of the male gaze? Yes, she looks the way the men want her to look: admiringly (as she thinks about Bloom looking "very handsome . . . trying to look like Lord Byron"), narcissistic (as she thinks of herself "so plump and tempting in my short petticoat"), defensive (when she worries about her belly being "a bit too big"), motherly (bandaging Bloom's corns), forgiving ("Ill give him one more chance Ill get up early in the morning"), catty (as she recalls the cleaning woman "padding out her false bottom to excite him"), dependent (needing "to be embraced 20 times a day . . . to look young" and hoping that Blazes "was satisfied with me"), seductive ("Ill put on my best shift and drawers and let him have a good eyeful"). Moreover, she also satisfies Jamesey Joyce's voyeuristic and, as Frances Restuccia argues, masochistic needs.

But she also looks back at the men who author-ize her: critically ("because theyre so weak and puling when theyre sick and want a woman to get well"), indignantly (when she recalls how Blazes slapped her behind and went away "so familiarly"), haughtily (when she complains about his "pulling off his shoes and trousers there on the chair before me so barefaced without even asking permission and standing out in that vulgar way in the half of a shirt they wear to be admired like a priest or a butcher"), realistically (when she thinks that "anyway its done now once and for all with all the talk in the world about it people make its only the first time after that its just ordinary"), cynically (when she realizes "thats all they want out of you"), unflatteringly (when she recalls "that determined vicious look in [Blazes'] eye" and "the lord Mayor looking at me with his dirty eyes").

And she looks out as a subject with a variety of her own desires: for "some nice looking boy" ("Id let him see my garters the new ones and make him turn red looking at him seduce him"), with unladylike joy ("I was coming for about 5 minutes with my legs round him . . . O Lord I wanted to shout all sorts of things fuck or shit or anything"), taking lesbian pleasure in recalling "the storm I slept in her bed she had her arms round me," playful (pulling Mulvey off in her handkerchief, tormenting the life out of him, "rousing that dog in the hotel rrrssstt awokwokawok"), transsexual ("I wouldn't mind being a man and get up on a lovely woman"), voyeuristic (watching "the fine young men . . . down in Margate strand from the side of the rock standing up in the sun naked like a God or something and then plunging into the sea"), and deeply moved by "that long kiss" Bloom gave her sixteen years ago, "yes he said I was the flower of the mountain."

But she also looks out, as well as within, in a way that is all-embracing and positions herself as a subject in relation to other subjects as well as to objects. When Jessica Benjamin's model of a mother watching her child is applied to "Penelope," we can see that Molly not only contends with and asserts her independence from Bloom, Blazes, Mulvey, and the other men in her thoughts, but also accepts them, especially Bloom, as they are. It is important to remember that mothers need to assert their independence too, and express their feelings of resentment; indeed this is one of the important points Marianne Hirsch makes in *The Mother/Daughter Plot*. So I am not claiming that Molly always accepts the men in her thoughts as they are. Moreover, to be independent requires a degree of indifference. Not indifferent in the sense of attaching no importance, but in the first meaning of the word: being impartial or neutral. Thinking of Mulvey while she is thinking of Bloom is not making either less significant than the other, although Bloom would certainly think so. It is a way for Molly to reflect her multiplicity of desires, without asserting a hierarchy, and to maintain her independence while allowing the subjects of her thoughts their independence as well as their interdependence. Her thoughts become a space for creative play in that they are not totalizing, and in the ways they can engage the reader to see that interrelationships continually change. But let me end this point about Molly's gaze being like the mother's embrace by saying that neither exists in the isolated way I have focused them. They always exist in relation to other social and historical frames, and the relationships are always vying for dominance and always changing—as Kathleen McCormick's history of Molly's reception and production reflects.

At the end of his travels, Bloom accepts Molly's desire with equanimity, and then lies in the fetal position. Molly is not completely liberated from the male gaze, which has established such a base of power in the traditional realistic narrative, and which she has to some extent internalized. But her chapter is structured to undermine the male gaze, to establish an independent gaze, and to represent or enact or *embody* the space of holding, of "being with," of mutuality, intersubjectivity, creativity, where a variety of female desires can play themselves out. I use the word "play" to suggest both free play and performance. For another way of describing the ways Molly looks out of the male gaze is to consider them a series of performances that undermine the forces of gender construction and regulation, and that constitute her agency as a subject. Judith Butler argues that gender identity is neither a substance nor a construction. It is a performance, or series of performances. The subject is produced by a *"regulated process of repetition"* (145). And agency results from the possibility of varying the repetition, subverting it.[5] Cheryl Herr and Kimberly Devlin elaborate on the ways in which Molly's performances establish her agency.

II

At least I would like to think so. But, as I pause to consider my desire for a happy ending, I have to consider Judith Butler's warning that parody is not necessarily subversive, that it "depends on a context and reception in which subversive confusions can be fostered" (139). I also have to wonder about my position as a male feminist Joycean. What is my stake in wanting to think that Joyce has created an alternative to the male gaze, and that *Ulysses* ends on a positive note? Don't I as a Joycean have a stake in maintaining Joyce's reputation as an extraordinary writer? Don't I as a male feminist have a stake in proving that a male writer can overcome the historical, social, and psychological limits of his gender? So while it would be nice for the novel to end on such a positive note, several questions linger in my mind, doubts provoked by the work of Ann Kaplan, Annette Kuhn, Mary Ann Doane, and Kaja Silverman, feminist film theorists who build on and depart from Laura Mulvey.

In classical Hollywood film (and, I would add, in classical narrative) woman is identified with her body. Kaja Silverman describes the voice as "privileged to the degree that it *transcends the body*." (49) At one extreme is the disembodied voice-over, which issues from beyond the diegesis, is empowered by its distance in space and time, and belongs to the *film noir* male. At the other extreme is the embodied voice-over, which "loses its power and authority with every corporeal encroachment, from a regional accent or idiosyncratic 'grain' to definitive localization, the point of full and complete embodiment" (49). Her voice may be the voice of a letter as in Max Ophul's *Letter from an Unknown Woman* or seem like an interview as in John Schlesinger's *Darling*, or, more significantly, it may be a "talking cure" with a female patient addressing a male doctor, as in many "women's films" or family melodramas of the 1940s.

Applying Silverman's model to *Ulysses*, we can distinguish Molly's interior monologue from Stephen's and Bloom's. First, the men are located very generally as they meander along the strand in "Proteus" and "Nestor," while Molly is, specifically located, lying in bed or sitting on the pot. Second, though Stephen closes and opens his eyes, urinates or masturbates, and picks his nose, and though Bloom unsticks himself, these are exceptional moments. Stephen's monologue is almost entirely abstract, and Bloom's hardly ever calls attention to his body—especially when we compare it to Molly's. And, third, though we can distinguish Bloom's from Stephen's monologues by their rhythms and subject matter, the language is literate, whereas Molly's is marked by its "idiosyncratic 'grain' "—bad grammar, spelling, and malapropisms—and is embodied in its run-on sentences that call attention to their materiality.

One way the woman is identified with her body in classic Hollywood film and traditional narrative is when the camera or narrator brakes the momentum of the storyline, impedes the narrative to catch the woman in its look, to hold her in its gaze; she is immobilized, transfixed, turned into a spectacle. In *Ulysses* women's bodies are often specularized, most often when the story is being told from Bloom's perspective, though also when Lenehan tells of being lost in the Milky Way and when Molly's picture is passed around from man to man in the cabman's shelter. But, given the continual stylistic intrusions and shifts in perspective, which brake the momentum and break the continuity of the storyline, the specularization is achieved by convention rather than by narrative strategy. That is, readers have been conditioned to look at women's bodies in a different way than they look at men's and at other objects. The real break and brake in the storyline comes at the end of the seventeenth episode—as Molly begins a monologue that is not required by the (male) storyline and seems mostly independent of the male gaze. But is Molly's monologue really independent? Isn't it caught, transfixed, immobilized by being situated, framed for us, outside the male storyline?

Ann Kaplan convincingly argues that the language of the woman's body in *film noir* constitutes a subversive counter to the forward pull of the narrative voice-over. I have been developing a similar argument in relation to the male plotline of *Ulysses*. But how powerful is the subversion? Why has it taken so long for the subversion to be identified? Wasn't Molly easily recuperated or vilified in what Kathleen McCormick describes as the first two reading formations of *Ulysses*. Wasn't her recuperation or vilification made easy because her voice was embodied in the "idiosyncratic grain" of her unpunctuated sentences? Isn't the reader carried along by the momentum of the male storyline, despite the brake or break and shift to Molly's new narrative? Isn't Molly turned into a spectacle of an independent woman, talking endlessly to herself while lying in bed, in the penumbra of the masterplot? Indeed, isn't she eroticized for the implied (male) reader by the display of her desires?

This leads to the important distinction that Annette Kuhn draws, and on which Mary Ann Doane elaborates, between "the gaze" and "the address." "The gaze" relates to the way the spectator is positioned by the camera or the narrative voice and eye; it is discussed in psychoanalytic and semiotic terms. "The address" refers to more or less conscious narrative strategies, which are socially and historically explicit. In *Ulysses* (and perhaps in all verbal narrative) the gaze and the address come together (perhaps because the gaze must be achieved through a narrative voice rather than a narrative eye). From the very beginning of the novel, the reader is addressed as one who has had a classical education, which in Joyce's time was limited to men; hence the reader is historically male. He is also addressed as a psychologically male reader, driven to show off his classical education through an understanding of the erudite allusions, but also driven to achieve independence—to transcend the limitations of this education and become independent of its authority. And he is addressed as a historical and psychological male, who can take on Joyce in the ceremonial combat of reading the novel—just as students of Clongowes Wood, Belvedere, and University College had to take on their masters.[6] He has to hold as much as Joyce could hold in his mind, rebuild Dublin from the factual details scattered through the novel, handle the radical shifts in perspective, keep from flinching at the stylistic intrusions.

"Penelope" does not require the same intellectual muscle flexing, but we are nonetheless addressed as having developed our intellectual muscles through the combative education accessible only to men and the tough exercises of male modernism that Joyce put us through in the earlier part of the novel. (Frank Lentricchia shows how modernism developed in reaction to what Eliot called the "Feminine principle in literature" and what Pound called the "aunt Hepsy" [176].) That is, we are addressed as readers who can hold the first seventeen episodes in our heads in order to grasp Molly's fleeting allusions and at least narrow the possible antecedents of her "hes." Moreover, we are encouraged, as we were throughout the novel, to be accomplices in framing—and recuperating—Molly by recuperating the epic title Joyce deliberately left out. For by calling her independent episode "Penelope," we situate her in the male story of Odysseus and Telemachus, and by extension, of Bloom and Stephen. And our desire for a happy ending, for at least the possibility of a reconciliation between Bloom and Molly, is a form of recuperation. For a happy ending would restore Molly to the norm of wife. It would define her as an essentialized, idealized figure of feminine vitality. It would complete the story of the husband's return. It would restore order and bring an ideal closure to the male plot.

Another way of understanding how we are addressed as male readers and made into accomplices in the framing of Molly's performance, is by seeing her monologue in the tradition of the female complaint. And it is helpful to come to this tradition by following Lauren Berlant, who describes a 1985 hit rap song called "Roxanne, Roxanne" by the UTFO (which stands for "Untouchable Force"). In the song, each (male) rapper tries to provoke a response from the "autonomous and unyielding" Roxanne. As one rapper puts it, "She's all stuck up (why do you say that) because she wouldn't give a guy like me no rap even though I'm in UTFO" (241). And each rapper ends with "Roxanne, Roxanne, don't you understand," implying that she was too dumb to understand the skill of their rapping and, therefore, to succumb to the power of their seduction. One day a "real" Roxanne, named Roxanne Shantee, was infuriated by the rappers and, between loads of her mother's wash, cut a song called "Roxanne's Revenge." She complained about the UTFO making a record "bout me, the R-O-X-A-N-N-E" and refused to be defined, let alone silenced, by their narrative. Sixteen response songs followed, two by other "real" Roxannes. And some of them were reproduced on the UTFO's *Complete Roxanne*. The result is a contextualizing, or framing, of the women's assertions by the male rappers, especially the one by a rapper who claims to be Roxanne's psychiatrist. This framing reduces their songs—like all forms of the traditional female complaint—to nagging, whining, or hysteria.

We might ask, then, what happens when we consider Molly's monologue as a form of hysteria? Some feminists argue that hysteria is a positive form of assertion against being trapped in male plots–by the male gaze. Molly (as Juliet Mitchell, Charles Bernheimer, and Claire Kahane say of Freud's Dora) embodies, exposes, and breaks through patriarchal repression. For seventeen episodes she has been denied her desires as a woman and as a female subject, as well as the language that could express her desires. Her monologue, or dialogue, like the narrative of the hysteric, follows the laws of its own desire and constitutes itself out of their free play.[7]

But if hysteria can be a liberating force, it can easily be reframed and recontextualized by those—from Freud to the UTFO—who are in control of language, the assumptions of psychology, and the conventions of literary tradition and pop culture. Indeed, the traditional way of reading "Penelope" is as what Breuer and Freud called a "talking cure," or "chimney sweep": once Molly lets it all out, she'll be recuperated, come back to being a good wife. And indeed we are complicit as readers in this recuperation since we have been put in the position of the unauthorized auditor of her private monologue or dialogue, who can reframe her complaint.

I don't want to draw this essay to a conclusion, for that would be to impose closure on *Ulysses*; rather I want to recognize the instability of its ending and maintain the dialogic of my unstable position as a male feminist. From one perspective we can see Molly telling a story of her own, looking back at the men of Dublin, and exposing them. But it doesn't take much of a turn to see that her independent episode is contextualized, if not literally framed, by the first seventeen episodes. Kimberly Devlin argues convincingly in this volume that Molly's performance is mimicry (in contrast to masquerade), that she is a female female impersonator, who exposes and sometimes transcends traditional female roles at the same time that she confirms them. But isn't her mimicry contained, contextualized, coopted by the overpowering male masterplot? Doesn't the apparent independence of her chapter from the rest of the novel set it apart as a spectacle, and invite us to recall Leopold Bloom's ideal ad. Doesn't it lead us to see the last chapter of *Ulysses* as a transparent showcart in which Molly is mimicking the female stereotype of her time—and acting out the role of an independent woman with a subjectivity of her own for the pleasure of the implied (male) reader? As scholars and teachers we can shift the balance by illuminating the positive potential of Molly's performance and the role of mimicry. But we must recognize the formal and historical context, and the power of "Penelope's" frame.

Afterword: Fionnula Flanagan's Re-vision of Molly

In a new dramatic reading of "Penelope," presented (as this volume was at the press) in New York on Bloomsday 1993 and later that month at California Joyce in Irvine, Fionnula Flanagan illuminated a new dimension of Molly—and set her in a different frame from those I have been considering. Flanagan played Molly as a performer, but not as a performer mimicking the role imposed on her. And while she may affirm Bloom, she does so not as a happy or even possibly happy ending of the marriage plot, but by situating him in the material reality, and frame, of her own story—or the desolation of her life at the end of *her* long day.

Flanagan's re-vision was achieved, it seems to me, as a result of two daring theatrical decisions. The first was to slow the pace of reading; it took three hours and fifteen minutes. The second, related to the first, was *not* to build to a crescendo of flower images and yeses, as Siobhán McKenna had done. These choices enabled Flanagan's Molly to register the differences among the wide range of responses, or what I have described as Molly's looks: surprise, defensiveness, cattiness, admiration, narcissism, motherliness, seductiveness, joy in being able to express her own desire, anger at being used as a sex object, dependency, cynicism, resentment, affection, affirmation—and, now we understand, desolation, though not despair.

Flanagan's Molly displays a depth of resources as well as intelligence in the way she registers an open-eyed confrontation with her past and present. While her innocence and her solecisms give rise to much laughter, to me this laughter was not condescending; rather it reflected our recognition of a kind of independence and resistance. Dale Bauer, developing a feminist model of Bakhtin's carnival, focuses on the disruptive excesses of female characters who extend the role of the traditionally male fool. Freedom for the fool in Bakhtin is not wisdom and wit, as it was for Shakespeare, but incomprehension. Following Mary Russo, Bauer argues that "stupidity (a form of resistance) forces the unspoken repressions into the open, thus making them vulnerable to interpretation, contradiction, and dialogue" (678). Molly as fool exposes the repressions fostered by priests, doctors, British colonizers, popular culture, and a generally patriarchal society—represented, despite his ambivalence, in Leopold Bloom.

At the end of Flanagan's monologue, the flower imagery and the yeses did not tumble one after another toward a final crescendo of joyous affirmation. Indeed, flower imagery barely registers as an accumulating pattern. And the yeses change in tone—so that the joyous yeses affirm only those (probably romanticized) moments in distant Gibraltar, and we become aware of their distance in both space and time. The memory of Mulvey's kiss by the Moorish wall leads us to realize the distance between a romanticized event (she can't even remember his first name, "Jack Joe Harry Mulvey was it yes I think a lieutenant" [18.818]), Bloom's kiss on the Howth four years later, and Bloom's recent kiss on "the wrong end of me" sixteen years after that (18.1401)—a meager trajectory in a nearly barren life. Moreover, in this performance we come to realize that Lt. Stanley G. Gardner, whose name is fully remembered, was Molly's measure of love. But he went off to the Boer War with the 8th Battalion of the 2nd East Lancers Regiment to die of enteric fever. (In Flanagan's reading of this passage— "I hate the mention of their politics after the war that Pretoria . . ."

[18.387–88]—we can hear echoes of Gretta Conroy's nostalgia over-
laid with a conscious resentment toward the patriarchal society that
fosters just those shows of manliness both women admire.) Boylan
was exciting, even though she resents being treated without respect,
but what she registers just as strongly is simple relief and open-eyed
awareness of her situation: "O thanks be to the great God I got somebody to give me what I badly wanted to put some heart up into me
youve no chances at all in this place like you used long ago" (18.732–34, my
emphasis as a result of Flanagan's reading).

And we become more fully aware in this reading that it is not just
men who have been missing from Molly's empty life. She didn't know
her mother ("whoever she was" [18.846–47]), only a surrogate aunt, or
friend of her father's, Mrs. Stanhope, who sent her a dress from Bon
Marche. She has very warm, even erotic, memories of Hester, who
slept with her arms around her. But she left and wrote only one letter—"Lord how long ago it seems centuries of course they never came
back and she didnt put her address right on it either" (18.666–67). The
only friend she had in Dublin was Josie, but she is remembered only
as a rival. And of course there was Milly, but in this reading we become more aware not only that she has left home, but of the quarrels
when she was still there, of the time Molly cracked her across the ear,
of Molly's remorse but also of her continuing jealousy, and of the way
she identifies with Milly when she recalls "her lips so red a pity they
wont stay that way I was too" clearly pitying herself as well (18.1066).

At one point, as I was watching Fionnula Flanagan early in the
performance, relatively immobile in an overstuffed chair, I was reminded of *Happy Days,* and wondered if Beckett had been inspired by
"Penelope." Here was Molly with the same spirit as Winnie, finding
endless possibilities and endless hope not from the mundane objects
she pulls from her purse but from the mundane events she pulls from
her past and present. And she finds a great deal to affirm in her life in
Gibraltar as well as in her life with Bloom. But the affirmations vary
as she is less or more aware of her need to find something colorful,
romantic, or just positive. By the end of the monologue, when the affirmations become literal yeses, spaced apart from one another due to
Flanagan's pacing, they develop two different meanings with minor
variations. The joyous yeses register Molly's romanticized memories
of a distant past in Gibraltar. But the other yeses register almost as
if she were checking off a list of recollected facts—beginning with:
"them saying theres no God . . . *ah yes* I know them well" (from here
on, quotes are from 18.1564 through to the final page, my emphases).
And this note is maintained, at least as a strong note in the complex

chords of recognition as she recalls their love-making on Howth. "I got him to propose to me *yes* first I gave him the bit of seedcake"— this is much closer to a factual recognition, like "*yes* that was 16 years ago," than it is to an affirmation. Even the yeses in "*yes* he said I was a flower of the mountain *yes* so we are flowers all" are read as more facts being ticked off than breathless recollections. And as she approaches what has been traditionally a climax—"*yes* that was why I liked him because I saw he understood or felt what a woman is"—the yes is certainly positive, but Flanagan reads it as insufficient; moreover it leads to her recognition that Bloom's power is vulnerable—"and I knew I could always get round him and I gave him all the pleasure I could leading him on till he asked me to say yes and I wouldnt answer first." Flanagan leads us to go beyond Kimberly Devlin in recognizing the way Molly preserved the independence of a "private female past," as she recalls her ideal moment of union with Bloom while "thinking of so many things he didnt know of" (Devlin 153). For their moment of union has a tragic dimension. Bloom is a good man, he was even handsome, but he would provide insufficient physical and emotional satisfaction. Moreover, Molly, who is so romantic, full of life, and intelligent in this reading, has been confronting the reality of her position as a married woman in colonized, patriarchal Ireland. In the end she checks off as matters of fact—"yes . . . yes . . . yes"—the points that led her to draw "him down to me so he could feel my breasts all perfume *yes* and his heart was going like mad and *yes* I said *yes* I will Yes." Flanagan's Molly, full of intelligence as well as vitality, ends in tears as she faces the fact, yes, that she locked herself in 7 Eccles Street when she got Bloom to say yes. Like Winnie, she has the capacity to find much in her narrowing world to make this a truly happy day. But also like Winnie, her eyes are fully open.

Notes

1.   Stephen Heath opens the hotly contested issue of men's relation to feminism by saying that it is impossible. See Alice Jardine and Paul Smith's *Men in Feminism.* Also see Joseph A. Boone and Michael Cadden's *Engendering Men* for Boone's argument with Heath, and Jardine and Smith, and for applications as well as theories, including those of gay men.

My own position on male feminism has been developing, especially since Wheaton College went coed five years ago. I had taught at a woman's college for twenty-three years, the last ten of which had involved a successful collaborative effort on the part of most faculty to "mainstream" feminist studies. When we started teaching men, I became self-conscious of contradictions in my position. Indeed, I have been working with Linda Alcoff's notion of positionality. Alcoff argues that positionality is the logical step for feminists to take after cultural feminism and post-structuralism. Cultural feminism celebrates, appropriates, and transvalues the devalued values of women's culture, so that passivity becomes a form of peacefulness, subjectivism and narcissism become ways of being in touch with oneself, and sentimentality becomes caring and nurturing. But cultural feminism tends toward essentialism, identifies women with their bodies, and perpetuates biological determinism. Post-structuralism, on the other hand, exposes "essence" and "femininity" as social and linguistic constructs. But in showing these constructs to be overdetermined by a wide range of social institutions and forces, it denies women agency, choice, and the possibility of change—and it renders gender invisible.

Teresa de Lauretis shows us a way out of the bind between cultural feminism and post-structural determinism by arguing that we are constructed through a continuous and ongoing interaction with the practices, discourses, and institutions that shape value, meaning, and feeling. Alcoff extends this to the notion of positionality. The self, rather than having an essence or being overdetermined, is a constellation of positions, formed by changing historical and personal relations. And agency is a matter of choosing to take this or that position or negotiating among them.

This doesn't mean that, as a male feminist, I take a woman's position. Only that I am a constellation of positions, the most powerful of which are constructed by social and historical frames that have positioned me as male, some of which I can resist or negotiate. This essay is an attempt at just such a negotiation.

2.   See Laura Mulvey's discussion of *Duel in the Sun* in "Afterthoughts."

3.   Senn proposed the notion in a symposium; Kenner developed it in *Joyce's Voices* (87).

4.   This point is more fully developed in her "Monologue as Dialogue."

5.   Butler goes further. She argues convincingly that there is no basis for distinguishing between gender as culturally constructed and sex as a biologically fixed basis of identity. Therefore agency results from the subversion and destabilization of sex, and therefore from sexuality—subjects that none of us in this volume have considered.

6.   See Walter Ong for a historical account of traditional Western education as ceremonial combat.

7.   I am paraphrasing Minrose Gwin here in her important argument about Rosa Coldfield in *Absalom, Absalom.*

Works Cited

Alcoff, Linda. "Cultural Feminism Versus Post-Structuralism: The Identity Crisis in Feminist Theory." *Signs: Journal of Women in Culture and Society* 13.3 (1988): 405–36.

Attridge, Derek. "Molly's Flow: The Writing of 'Penelope' and the Question of Women's Language. *Modern Fiction Studies* 35 (1989): 543–68.

Bakhtin, Mikhail M. *The Dialogic Imagination: Four Essays by M. M. Bakhtin.*

Ed. Michael Holquist. Trans. Caryl Emerson and Michael Holquist. Austin: University of Texas Press, 1981.

Bauer, Dale. "Gender in Bakhtin's Carnival." *Feminisms: An Anthology of Literary Theory and Criticism.* Ed. Robyn R. Warhol and Diane Price Herndl. New Brunswick, N.J.: Rutgers University Press, 1991. 671–84. First published in Bauer's *Feminist Dialogics: A Theory of Failed Community.* Albany: State University of New York Press, 1988.

Bazargan, Susan. "Monologue as Dialogue: Molly Bloom's 'History' as Myriorama." *Works and Days 10: Essays in the Socio-Historical Dimensions of Literature and the Arts* 5 (1987): 63–77.

Benjamin, Jessica. "A Desire of One's Own: Psychoanalytic Feminism and Intersubjective Space." *Feminist Studies/Critical Studies.* Ed. Teresa de Lauretis. Bloomington: Indiana University Press, 1986. 78–101. Developed in Benjamin's *The Bonds of Love: Psychoanalysis, Feminism, and the Problem of Domination.* New York: Pantheon, 1988.

Berlant, Lauren. "The Female Complaint." *Social Text* 19/20 (1988): 237–59.

Bernheimer, Charles. *In Dora's Case: Freud—Hysteria—Feminism.* Ed. Charles Bernheimer and Claire Kahane. New York: Columbia University Press, 1985.

Boone, Joseph A., and Michael Cadden. *Engendering Men: The Question of Male Feminist Criticism.* New York and London: Routledge, 1990.

Butler, Judith. *Gender Trouble: Feminism and the Subversion of Identity.* New York and London: Routledge, 1990.

de Lauretis, Teresa. *Alice Doesn't.* Bloomington: Indiana University Press, 1984.

Devlin, Kimberly. *Wandering and Return in "Finnegans Wake": An Integrative Approach to Joyce's Fiction.* Princeton: Princeton University Press, 1991.

Doane, Mary Ann. *The Desire to Desire: The Woman's Film of the 1940's.* Bloomington: Indiana University Press, 1987.

Gwin, Minrose C. *The Feminine Faulkner: Reading (Beyond) Sexual Difference.* Knoxville: University of Tennessee Press, 1990.

Heath, Stephen. "Male Feminism." *Men in Feminism.* Ed. Alice Jardine and Paul Smith. New York and London: Methuen, 1987. 1–32.

Hirsch, Marianne. *The Mother/Daughter Plot: Narrative, Psychoanalysis, Feminism.* Bloomington: University of Indiana Press. 1989.

Irigaray, Luce. *The Sex Which is Not One.* Ithaca, New York: Cornell University Press, 1985.

Jardine, Alice, and Paul Smith, eds. *Men in Feminism.* New York and London: Methuen, 1987.

Jeffords, Susan. "Point Blank: Shooting Vietnamese Women." *Vietnam Generation* 1.3–4 (1989): 152–68.

Kahane, Claire. "Introduction: Part Two." *Dora's Case: Freud—Hysteria—Feminism.* Ed. Charles Bernheimer and Claire Kahane. New York: Columbia University Press, 1985. 19–32.

Kaplan, E. Ann. *Women and Film: Both Sides of the Camera.* New York: Methuen, 1983.

Kenner, Hugh. *Joyce's Voices.* Berkeley: University of California Press, 1978.

Kuhn, Annette. *Women's Pictures: Feminism and Cinema.* London: Routledge and Kegan Paul, 1982.

Lentricchia, Frank. "The Resentments of Robert Frost." *American Literature* 62 (1990): 175–200.

Maddox, Brenda. *Nora: The Real Life of Molly Bloom.* Boston: Houghton Mifflin, 1988.

Mitchell, Juliet. *Women: The Longest Revolution.* New York: Pantheon, 1966.

Mulvey, Laura. "Afterthoughts on Visual Pleasure and Narrative Cinema Inspired by King Vidor's *Duel in the Sun* (1946)." In *Visual and Other Pleasures.* 29–38.

Mulvey, Laura. "Visual Pleasure and Narrative Cinema." In *Visual and Other Pleasures.* 14–28.

Mulvey, Laura. *Visual and Other Pleasures.* Bloomington: Indiana University Press, 1989.

Newman, Beth. "Getting Fixed: Feminine Identity and Scopic Crisis in *The Turn of the Screw.*" *Novel* 26 (1992): 43–63.

Ong, Walter. "Agonistic Structures in Academia: Past to Present." *Daedalus* 103 (1974): 229–38.

Pearce, Richard. *The Politics of Narration: James Joyce, William Faulkner, and Virginia Woolf.* New Brunswick: Rutgers University Press, 1991.

Restuccia, Frances L. "Molly in Furs: Deleuzean/Masochian Masochism in the Writing of James Joyce." *Novel* 18 (1985): 101–16. Revised in Restuccia's *Joyce and the Law of the Father.* New Haven: Yale University Press, 1989. 124–76.

Silverman, Kaja. *The Acoustic Mirror: The Female Voice in Psychoanalysis and Cinema.* Bloomington: Indiana University Press, 1988.

Snyder, Joel. "Picturing Vision." *Critical Inquiry* 6 (1980): 499–526.

Spiegel, Alan. *Fiction and the Camera Eye: Visual Consciousness in Film and the Modern Novel.* Charlottesville: University of Virginia Press, 1976.

Warhol, Robyn R. "The Look, the Body, and the Heroine of *Persuasion*: A Feminist-Narratological Reading of Jane Austen." *Novel* 26.1 (1992): 5–19.

Woolf, Virginia. *A Room of One's Own.* New York: Harcourt Brace Jovanovich, 1957.

PART 2

MOLLY IN PERFORMANCE

3

"Penelope" as Period Piece

Cheryl Herr

When Richard Pearce asked me to participate in the initial "Historical Molly Bloom" panel in Milwaukee in 1987, I was happy for the opportunity to float a companion piece to work that I had done in *Joyce's Anatomy of Culture* (1986). In that book, I had explored some forms of communication typical of Joyce's era, media that he had exploited in his various fictions not only thematically but also formally. It was my contention that the sermon, the newspaper, the pantomime, and the music hall turn—all of which Joyce parodied in form and content in his narratives—not only signified the endless dialogue among cultural institutions (press, stage, and pulpit) but also performed specific ideological work in and through Joyce's Ireland. Repeated semiotic messages inhered in these media forms, and Joyce's fiction entered into dialogue—often startling, comic, or revisionary—with the major institutional communicative modes of his time. Although I had not been able to devote space in *Joyce's Anatomy of Culture* to theatrical monologues, I knew that in "Penelope," Joyce turned to the theatrical mono-showpiece as a form not only highly typical of Victorian drama but also bursting with clichéd ideas that were grist to Joyce's mill.

Turning the Milwaukee conference presentation into an essay published in 1988, I added to my original argument a consideration of Molly's monologue as an unstable link, a disappointed bridge, if you

will, between nineteenth-century theatre and the postmodern aesthetic of novelist Don DeLillo: in *White Noise*, DeLillo obliquely appropriates Molly's voice for his own narrative uses. Along the way, I also
pursued a supporting "slant"-argument that our usual concepts of
literary-historical periodization are inflected by Joyce's play with various kinds of periods, including Molly's menstrual cycle and Bloom's
own narrative assimilation to the female anatomy. "Penelope" adds
to the abundant evidence for the body's necessary unspeakableness
in any form of institutional communication, even though the body's
representative formulae shift from period to period, from gender to
gender, and from genre to genre. This essay, written in 1987, attends
to that specific moment in Joycean studies; in a sense, it is offered here
as itself a period piece.

Book twenty-three of *The Odyssey* deals with the rapturous re-
encounter of the newly unmasked Odysseus and that valorized home-
body, Penelope. Big finish. End of story. Period.

But not quite—the following and final book narrates a drama, literally identified as such in the work, of Penelope's playing a role when
she meets the suitors; she is, in her initiation of the bow-stringing
contest that facilitates her husband's vengeance, quintessentially an
actress; she actualizes her name, which translates to "countenance
of webs" or mask. Penelope's final action in her twenty-year stalling
scene is to pretend that things are other than they are and to make the
suitors believe in that pretense, too. This specific Odyssean backdrop
to *Ulysses* seems to me especially worth noting when we recall that
among all of his famous, adjective-heavy, epistolary descriptors for
"Penelope," Joyce calls the episode the *clou* of the book, a word that
the editor of Joyce's letters translates in its theatrical sense of "star
turn" or topper on a music hall bill.[1] Like a music hall star, Molly is
the headliner, the turn last on, the act anticipated from the beginning
of the narrative.

I propose that we take seriously this symmetry between Penelope's
acting a part and Molly's finale framing of *Ulysses*, that we examine the
theatrical elements of Molly's soliloquy, and that we read them against
the historical ground of Joyce's dramatic experience, especially taking
into consideration (1) the popularity in turn-of-the-century Dublin of
stock scenes played by major performers, (2) the kind of play with
which Molly is familiar and tends to identify, and (3) the fact that
Molly recalls getting her period at the Gaiety when she and Bloom
went there to see the Kendals in *The Wife of Scarli* (18. 1110–21). My
aims are to position Molly's monologue in its social setting (emphasis

on social) and to understand why Joyce ends *Ulysses* with so many theatrical flourishes and gestures. Certainly, it is important that the "Penelope" episode is a script (the handiest one in *Ulysses*, if we are to judge by its almost too frequent stagings) and that the projected actor of Molly's role may be, as in all theatrical performances, either a woman or a man.

One of the things that strikes a contemporary browser in the newspaper theatre columns and daybills from Joyce's era is the penchant for performing a fairly static repertoire. A regular theatregoer like Joseph Holloway eventually saw just about everything possible for the stage at the time—and he saw these works repeatedly. An outgrowth of this repetitive repertoire was the performance, usually by well-known actors, of selected big scenes from classics like *MacBeth* and *Hamlet;* if the performer happened to be an opera star, the pieces would be beloved arias. Imposing the structure of variety revues on the legitimate stage indicates that audiences were sufficiently familiar with various major stage pieces so that transmission of the story could be eliminated; knowledge of the overall action was assumed. More important, speeches and arias were valued quite apart from their function in the works from which they were drawn; they were prized as tours de force that provided opportunities for an actor's talents to be measured and savored. Molly's soliloquy, a star turn in a variety performance, has this quality. There is a sense in which the notes she hits have less to do with the narrative's issues than we might expect or even wish. Molly's operatic thrusts seem to me emotive gestures that are not intrinsically motivated by the larger work. This is to say that for most purposes "Penelope" shows us a singer doing her most famous aria, a performer delivering the somewhat scandalous speech that made her notorious. Comically reinforcing this theatrical frame is the fact that Molly and Boylan get together on June 16th to rehearse for their concert.

Along these lines, it is important not to downplay the "writtenness" of the episode. It *is* like the famous letters that Joyce received from his female correspondents, letters big on flow and short on punctuation. But it is just as similar to the typically unpunctuated speeches of many working playscripts which assumed that the actor would disambiguate the piece in the act of speaking it. This clarification, of course, actually happens when someone like Siobhan McKenna or Colleen Dewhurst has performed Molly's monologue. They have spoken in a way that necessarily removes the syntactic ambiguities that we enjoy so much in the reading experience. They accomplish this feat of clarification mostly by adding periods, and it is the status of the punctuating full stop that the narrative brings into question by way of pursuing a crucial submerged pun in *Ulysses*. By removing most of the punctuation from the "Penelope" episode, Joyce emphasizes the function—grammatical, aesthetic, and social—of periodicity. Molly's weight and balance are achieved by removing some of the signs that ordinarily mark those features in quotidian discourse.

On the one hand, Joyce eliminated many periods, which, even while syntactically indicating full stops, quite obviously call forth varying degrees of pausing and silence, varying tones of finality. This function of modulating coherence and silence was passed on to Molly's famous affirmations; instead of punctuation, we often encounter the word "yes," which, as Derrida and others have argued, takes on multiple shades of meaning in Joyce's text.[2] On another structural level, the breaking of "Penelope" into two handfuls of massive "sentences" creates a comprehensive rhythm generally taken to allude to the beat of the menstrual cycle, the monthly changes of the moon, the flow of the tide, and other natural patterns. So the full stop is both a grammatical and a natural-biological category that Joyce exploits in staging Molly's star turn.

Ambiguities that resonate on the psychosocial level crop up when we turn, say, to the many definitions of "period" catalogued in the *Oxford English Dictionary:* "regular recurrence," "orbit of a heavenly body," a rounded and complete sentence of some magnitude and complexity, the "cycle of the four Grecian games," an indefinite historical unit "characterized by the same prevalent features or conditions," the moment of ending or consummation, the peroration, death, the acme, any "particular point in the course of anything," a spatial limit, a goal, a pause, a "complete musical sentence." These definitions, all operative or recuperable when "Penelope" was composed, are richly suggestive: death, they assert, is both an end and an acme or consummation. History is composed of sentences of varying length and complexity but recurrent features. Spatial limits are somehow similar to perorations and musical compositions; Molly's stasis moves her both to monologue and to sing. All of the episode's events are as choreographed as the Grecian games over which Odysseus' wife presides. And the monologic form of the episode, which takes place in two-dimensional space, is also fleshed out into rounded, cyclic recurrences in a history that we can predict because we have the script. Among other things, both theatre and menses take on historical weight and participate in social meaning systems that, like orbiting bodies, can be charted.

In more than one way, then, the "Penelope" episode is a period piece. It fleshes out, literalizes, the *point* with which Ithaca ends. It responds to historical constraints on meaning, representation, and desire in its portrayal of Molly's premenstrual and menstrual actions and thoughts. This focus on menses as constraint and possibility conditions my reading of Molly's monologue. However, before I turn to Molly's projected period, I need to linger for a moment on the theatrical context within which her menstruation takes place.

If we entertain the notion that "Penelope" works on some level as an unmotivated, showcased theatrical monologue, we might wonder what work Molly's monologue is rightly a part of. An answer to this question can be derived from two contexts: the operatic repertoire and that of late nineteenth-century popular "problem" drama—the plays that raised more or less of an uproar during the days of Molly's theatregoing.

On the operatic scene, viewing Molly's phrasing as operatic provides some useful interpretive clues to her role as *clou*. Even without Bloom's repeated thoughts of Zerlina's "should I or shouldn't I" song from *Don Giovanni*, we could easily place her in Mozart's world, where precisely because adultery has such grave and permanently hellish consequences the Donna Annas and Donna Elviras of the world appear to be overdoing their outrage more than a little. Although Zerlina's role as "innocence preserved" does not fit Molly's personal style, Zerlina's comically knowing song of mock-decision does resonate with Molly's role-playing vis-à-vis her equally knowing husband and her prolific lover. It seems to me that the whole of Molly's monologue might be viewed as an extended operatic meditation, one that poses challenges to the singer who must sustain breath from one immense "sentence" to another. And the whole point is to rehearse a comical ambivalence that is already irrelevant. The fact that Molly is miscast in singing Zerlina's role becomes more significant when we notice the "donjuanesque" quality of her conviction that she can seduce *anyone* if she puts her mind to it. (Of course, there's a sense, too, in which Molly's song is a Wagnerian piece—in that it is a continuous work of musical prose which moves forward rather than going back obsessively to rehearse gestures established in the initial section. Isolde's long, ecstatic death has obvious symmetries, despite the tonal differences from Molly's speech.)

On the scene of the Ibsen-inspired serious drama, the most likely candidate for the play that Molly's speech is part of would *not* be the play that she seems most attracted to—*The Only Way*. Molly would like to think that her lover would follow Sydney Carton to the gallows for her benefit, but she also knows that such a fellow would likely be a bit soft in the head. Her ambivalence does not find a place in the Dickensian world of *The Only Way*. A more likely play of origin is *The Wife of Scarli* in that it summarizes a fixation of late Victorian drama with marital issues. Molly recalls seeing the play and identifies with the adulterous heroine—to the point of remaining with her husband, as Scarli's wife decides to do. The value of noting Molly's position in this drama rests not in the specifics of Greene's play but rather in its exemplification of a type of play that included, by association, most of Shaw's domestic dramas, much of Pinero's work, and Dumas' *La Dame aux Camelias*. *Camelias* and Pinero's *The Second Mrs. Tanqueray* share the limelight in this genre partly because they initially raised censorship issues for the Lord Chamberlain and the general public and partly because the female leads in these plays were appropriated by the big female stars of the era, actors like Sarah Bernhardt, whose acclaim resounded in Dublin as well as in other world capitals, and Eleonora Duse, who was a personal favorite of Joyce's.[3]

The popularity of La Duse is underscored by William Archer in his 1893 reviews of her part in the London season. Including Dumas's play in her repertoire, she shone in *Mrs. Tanqueray* and occasioned Archer's addressing an issue very much in the minds of theatre critics of his day—that of the line between the novel and the drama:

Some critics objected to Mr Pinero's *Lady Bountiful* that it was rather a novel than a play; whereupon I argued that this was, in itself, no valid objection, the real trouble being that the novel was a poor and commonplace one. It is the highest praise, then, that I can find for *Mrs Tanqueray* to say that its four scenes are like the crucial, the culminating, chapters of a singularly powerful and original novel. In the fact that we would fain see the intermediate chapters written and the characters of Tanqueray and Paula worked out in greater detail, we touch one of the aforesaid limitations of the dramatic form. (Archer 132).

Archer goes on to say that Paula's characterization lacks enough information about "her parentage, her girlhood, her education, antecedents" to explain her contradictory behavior, and that he wishes for some "retrospective analysis" to illuminate "the underlying harmony of certain superficial discords" (Archer 133). I emphasize the parallels between Paula Tanqueray and Molly Bloom because both women combine a respect for "ordinary decencies" with sexual behavior considered daring in their era. Also, the terms in which Archer positions Pinero's play—novel vs. drama, character development via retrospective arrangement—outline the dilemmas of Victorian theatre that eventually forced Joyce off the stage and exclusively into a narrative mode that is relentlessly dramatic in its orientation, its issues, and its call for disambiguating performance. The fact that Paula Tanqueray spends the day of the first act in the ultimately seductive maneuver of writing a long retrospective confession seems compelling, also, in positioning Molly's monologue—the self-revelatory speech that Paula might have made had the dramatic form been able to overcome the decorum of the Victorian stage.

Contextually, Molly's monologue is thus the narrative version of material that viewers like Archer and Joyce felt the need of on the contemporary stage; to put it in the clichéd terms of our own era, her monologue is the "absent other" of the existing drama of the day. To say this is, for me at least, to argue that Molly need not occupy solely the level of narrative reality that we have normally granted her. Although in some sense I am willing to accept the fictive actuality of the arm that in "Wandering Rocks" flings from a window a coin for the one-legged sailor, I can no longer find it in myself to grant the Molly of "Penelope" any reality-value whatsoever—not as Earth Mother, not as Celtic goddess, not as ordinary Dublin Hausfrau.[4] None of the terms that describe Molly in the Joyce criticism with which I am familiar, from Tindall to, say, Unkeless, discovers the Molly that I detect.[5] For me, "Penelope" projects simply an actor reading a script, a star singing an aria. If I had to guess what play the speech is in, I would say that it is a composite opera-problem play, a formal sign of Joyce's times. If I had to guess what actor is "doing Molly," I would have to say *not* the "sparrowfart" (18.879) singers that she detests, *not* the truly histrionic Bernhardt, but rather La Duse, whom Archer usefully compares to Bernhardt to the former's advantage, mostly because of La Duse's controlled southern European style and "simplicity" (Archer 146–47).

Molly's monologue is thus a sign for the theatrical issues of Joyce's era—the limitations of dramatic form, the topical and linguistic limitations imposed by overt and implicit censorship, and the question of Northern versus Southern "temperament" that continued to challenge Lawrence, Fitzgerald, and other modernist writers as well as Joyce. Molly's monologue-ing, her sartoriocentrism, her stylized gestures, her great sentences sustained as an operatic tour de force—these contribute to my assessment of her as not a character but rather a role to be enacted by this or that major artiste of the era. Along these lines, it is surely significant that Molly's life is recalled on what appear to be stage sets—Molly by the Moorish wall, Molly on promenade with an officer in Gibraltar, Molly on Howth. And it is not entirely off the mark to suggest that the performer who gives us this star turn is not necessarily a woman at all. Why not, in that era of relentless comic cross-dressing, a male performer? Why not a male performer doing a good imitation of La Duse doing a good imitation of a Dublin Hausfrau with trendily late Victorian "excess libido"? This is not a frivolous suggestion but rather one motivated by the fact that Joyce's one absolute advance over the theatre of his era is less his sexual explicitness than it is his enactment "on stage" of menstruation. The question of why Molly menstruates has been variously answered, but one explanation is simply that menstruation signifies femaleness in a way that is incontestable. Characteristically, Joyce uses this signal of the feminine to mask, playfully, the conventions and implications of the theatrical machinery which make up "Penelope."

One of Joyce's masterstrokes is having Molly recall getting her period during a performance of *The Wife of Scarli*. Adultery and periodicity are part and parcel of one another for Molly—maybe it is, as she says, all of that rooting around that makes the connection for her. Although Molly thinks of her period as the "usual monthly auction" (18.1109), her only recollection of the event is cued to a theatrically charged context—the evening at the Gaiety and the narratively suppressed scene of Boylan's afternoon visit. Menstruation is, in a sense, only a theatrical event for Molly. She remains remarkably free from cramps or discomfort; she is incommoded only by having to sit on the broken commode. This fact, and the significance of menstruation as a dramatic event, were brought home to me recently when a graduate student in my *Ulysses* seminar, talking about "Nausikaa," spoke of Gerty's "PMS nastiness." Until that moment I had never given much *interpretive* emphasis to the coincidence of Gerty's and Molly's—and even Martha's—premenstrual status. But surely no one today can miss the fact that PMS—a rampant 1980s "syndrome" with its own aggressively reductive, totalizing, and ultimately antiwoman ideology[6]—is precisely what Molly does not experience. In the terms of her era, she is not much of a woman because unlike Gerty and Martha as Bloom sees them, she is *not* "a devil before her period."

The most obvious candidate in *Ulysses* for PMS nastiness is rather Bloom himself.[7] Surely we cannot avoid recognizing the periodicity of Bloom's body rhythms, something that takes on extra meaning in two frames of reference—Molly's insistence that women suffer quietly while "if his nose bleeds youd think it was O tragic" (18.24) and the recurrent medical and psychoanalytic fascination with the phenomenon of what was called "male menstruation." Sander Gilman's 1987 article in *Critical Inquiry* addresses this issue, specifically through studying the Freud-Fliess correspondence over the psychopathology of perceived periodic nosebleeds in Jewish males. Medical texts such as Ashwell's *Practical Treatise on the Diseases Peculiar to Women* (1848) make similar observations and consider the dangers attendant on the menopausal "extinction" or necessary evacuation of *excess* blood from the body. For instance, Ashwell becomes exercised over the "Case of Frederick P——."

A young man subject to plethora and to large discharges of blood from the nose every spring, having for some time laboured under mental vexation and anxiety, missed, during last spring (1840) his usual epistaxis. He became somnolent, morose, and dejected, and at length, after some bodily exertion, fell into a sort of fainting fit. Under the direction of Mr. Symes of Tavistock Square, he was largely bled, with apparent relief. Having been placed in bed, he lingered for some hours, with a sense of weight and oppression about the heart, which gradually terminated in death. (Ashwell 149n)

Ashwell uses this example in a discussion of menopause. Kindly and well-disposed, the doctor nonetheless views women as another species ("Nother dying" [3.199]); hence the text projects some distress over this unseemly end for an unfortunate man who somehow came to share the female hazard.

What was going on, psychosocially speaking, in such medical texts? What is going on in *Ulysses* when Joyce makes Bloom subject to periodicity to the extent of an "O tragic" response to nosebleeds as well as to the displacement of his PMS distress onto provoking the Citizen into throwing biscuit tins? The kindest interpretation, and the one that comes most readily to mind in the current critical climate, would find Joyce asserting the essential symmetry of male and female biology, the attractiveness as well as the experiential reality of androgynous cyclicality. But I find myself stopping short of this unifying gesture to focus again on the staginess of Molly's theatrically positioned and symptomless menstruation. Surely the bill "topper" who is reading the "Penelope" script is not a woman but a male or gender-indeterminate actor, and we have all along been manipulated into discovering female truths in Molly's peroration when in fact the narrative in some sense ended at the big period that closes "Ithaca." As a primer of reification, "Ithaca" undoes the cyclic wholeness and regenerative power of the fluids that it deals in—cocoa, water, urine. "Penelope" plays out that hegemonic control of fluidity when it presents a reified body masqueing as real. And Molly's coda, a suppressed or discarded scene from late Victorian dramatic performance, formally and literally evokes itself as period piece in order to mask the relentlessly male ideology of the era. Molly's need not be a believable female voice, although women of her day certainly spoke in her rhythms, willy-nilly, as men ventriloquized through female bodies the patterns and ideas (essentialism, necessity, "the feminine," eternal return) that they wanted to find. Joyce's seemingly liberating assimilation of Bloom to female periodicity signifies the same phenomenon—the erasure of unambiguously female (and real) voices and female body space in the novel, on the stage, and in history as our culture suggests we experience it.

Perhaps asking for something unambiguously female is to miss the contextual point, but certainly viewing Molly's monologue as a liberated or liberating voicing of female desire is to see something that was highly unlikely at the time that Joyce wrote it and Molly supposedly lived it. Hence, Bloom's periodicity strikes me as not theatrical but rather appropriating of female power, and even Molly's instances of menstruation strike me as merely playacting. As we all point out to one another these days, we look for a sign of essentialism, of the recovered feminine voice, of return and resurrection, and of origin because our culture has taught us to do that, but Joyce's final move remains that of a historically constructed masculinity that desperately wants to recover the body in all of its hormonal and behavioral ambiguities but discovers in its place only the frightening category of the "flesh" (as in "the world, the flesh, and the devil"), Molly as temptation ("Devils they are when that's coming on them" [13.822]), and the feminine as a dramatic trope that still moves us even though we know that in 1904 its major characteristic was its absence. Even today, when women listen to themselves, they discover endless ambiguities, resistances, and inexplicable bits that stimulate further self-exploration amidst dominant and alien discourses (a linguistic situation which should find echoes in the colonial position of Ireland in 1904). But Molly's dramatic monologue, although contradictory and in need of punctuating performance for utmost clarity, has little in it of an interiorized ambiguity or a truly somatized registering of the dialogue between hormones and history. It is a performance of roles and tropes and motions that were, even in 1922, so naturalized by stage and narrative that their very seamlessness and consistency signal their inauthenticity.

Inauthenticity, however, merely signals the constructedness of gender and gesture—by now old news. Newer news involves periodicity of a slightly different kind from Molly's and even from that of her historical era. The question that occurs next is how, in our own time with its own constraints on semantic systems, we are to assign a periodic marker to Molly's performance. Is this a text of modernism, for instance, or is it more properly received as a postmodern piece? For

Ulysses as a whole, that determination has been made in favor of both sides, with Joyce's status as postmodern precursor mostly agreed upon. But Molly's flowing discourse appears to lead backward, toward a modernist naturalism that favors if not the seamier, at least the more graphic, aspects of narrative description, in a mode that links those details to some larger concept of natural law. I find the choice of modernism versus postmodernism far less interesting, however, than the simple fact that some of the more lively postmodernist theory helps to illuminate aspects of Joycean enactment. Consider the following: "The political code . . . is about power operating today in the language of the aesthetics of seduction (where seduction is parodic of excrementia); its emotional mood oscillates between boredom and terror; it is populated by parasites . . . and its psychological signs are those of detritus, decomposition, and disaccumulation" (Kroker and Cook 10).

This is Arthur Kroker and David Cook discussing Eric Fischl's extraordinary painting "The Old Man's Boat and the Old Man's Dog" as part of their inquiry in *The Postmodern Scene* into what they, following Baudrillard, call "excremental culture." The phrase emphasizes the cultural scenario of the present, one in which all art is not just excess but positively oozing with contradictions, the excretions of the contemporary "bodiless" era. In their version of the postmodern world, Kroker and Cook assert the body's inability any longer to excrete; it is a world in which "writing the body"—a modernist, not to say feminist, preoccupation, has given way to denaturalizing the body. It is an art of the periphery and extraneous, of a debased nude that Sir Kenneth Clark would have been hard-pressed to recognize. Not that Fischl's bodies are unrecognizable as bodies; on the contrary, their fleshiness is all too apparent. But they communicate a pointless animalism that hovers on the verge of the sexual without ever quite getting there. Curiously static, a bit like Henry James's characters whose clothes did not come off, these characters are clearly unable to dress themselves; the few attempts at sartorial skill depicted in his paintings illustrate clearly that these people, bred on velcro, just have not gotten the subtleties of shoe tying or dress buttoning. Kroker and Cook introduce their discussion of this lugubrious loss of cultural control by saying "that postmodernism comes directly out of the bleeding tissues of the body—out of the body's fateful oscillation between the finality of 'time's it was' (the body as death trap) and the possibility of experiencing the body (*au-dela* of Nietzsche) as a 'solar system'—a dancing star yes, but also a black hole—which is the source of the hyper-nihilism of the flesh of the postmodern kind" (Kroker and Cook 10).

"Hyper-nihilism of the flesh" is the kind of phrase one loves to produce in talking to a class, off the tip of the tongue and somewhere near the edge of the irrational. But I suspect that there are some contradictions in Kroker and Cook's vision of excremental culture that bear discussion if we turn to Joyce's great exemplar of fleshiness, Molly Bloom. Clearly, even given the flowing quality of the prose, Molly's fleshiness—her inertness—is a great part of her charm. Although I would not care to label her a postmodern woman nor the episode a postmodern event, I would suggest that the notion of excremental culture (even of culture-as-excrement) obviously has a lot to do with the episode. And although I would not willingly speak of the hypernihilism of her flesh, I might be persuaded to discover a sufficiency of annihilation there to grant that there's a touch of the postmodern about Molly Bloom.

And Molly's body *is* aggressively denaturalized; it undergoes and initiates seduction, but it also positions seduction as a kind of bodiless exercise or excretionless exchange (excretionless because Bloom verifies the earlier presence of Boylan in his jingling bed not by semen stains on the sheets but rather by the remains of potted meat and by an indentation in the mattress—a primitive simulacrum, if you like— left by the collision of the "jaunty" and the "jingle"). In fact, *persona*-Molly's theatrical body does not suffer the sea-changes even of the postmodern body; rather than succumb to what Kroker and Cook call the "poststructuralist diseases" of AIDS and herpes, which are intent on "privileging the ruin of the surface of the body," *persona*-Molly thrives on her sexual experience. If anything, it firms her up ("yes I think he made them a bit firmer sucking them like that" [18.535]) instead of eroding her flesh in the fashion of AIDS, a disease which has led, socially speaking, to our current cultural idea of "sex without secretions" (Kroker and Cook 13).

The question of secretions, intersecting as it does the sliding signifier of excrement, brings us full circle to the implied reality-status of Molly and of her monologic role in *Ulysses*. In this inquiry, the question that seems most pertinent to me is not "Why does Molly menstruate?" but rather "Is her menstruation real?" The answer, I think, is that Molly does not menstruate but only enacts menstruation because she is "actually" a man, or rather, an undecidable act(or)/ (ress). The *fact* of enactment also helps to clear up the question of why so many putatively postmodern characteristics can be found in a socalled high modernist work, the dramatic emphasizing as it does the elements of a contemporary culture in ways that predict the future extensions or transformations of those elements. Hence it is no surprise that, when we think of Molly Bloom, we immediately interrogate and refuse the formulation of Kroker and Cook on gender instability: "The absorption and then playing back to its audience of the reversible and mutable language of sexual difference is the language of postmodern capitalism" (Kroker and Cook 20). As I have argued in *Joyce's Anatomy of Culture,* much of the point of the "Circe" episode is to play out this mutable language and to highlight for the reader the messages of gender construction and gender instability that were currency on the Victorian and Edwardian stage. Molly has seemed to most readers the very embodiment of the static, inert, untransformable feminine, and for that reason the reintroduction of the theatrical metaphor in her monologue works to Joyce's ends, which are naturalist ends that enact postmodern possibilities—or rather, the postmodern-as-possible.

As a sidenote, it is useful to recall the argument of Fredric Jameson and others that postmodernism does not consist of a set of characteristics that constitute its difference from and continuity with high modernist productions; rather we must recognize that modernism and postmodernism are discontinuous precisely because "the two phenomena . . . remain utterly distinct in their meaning and social function, owing to the very different positioning of postmodernism in the economic system of late capital, and beyond that, to the transformation of the very sphere of culture in contemporary society" (Jameson 59). The question of what might constitute signs of the postmodern in Irish literature, even today, remains open: the interplay between technologies that stimulate postmodernity and a traditional culture marks contemporary Irish life in ways that have yet to be theorized. Speaking simply to the persistent terminological difficulty in literary study, we might find it useful to think of Joyce not as a modernist, high modernist, or postmodernist but as an ultra- or supermodernist.

Molly's body space, her flesh as an abstract category and a "real" fictive presence, is the stage on and around which Joyce enacts a drama that problematizes the supermodernist motives of *Ulysses* precisely at the points of excremental and secretionist openness. The modernist nostalgia for the body, for the body of the mother and for all of the secure, lush fullness that it promises, is nowhere more urgently attested to than in our usual readings of the script that *persona*-Molly playacts. And yet the primary vehicle of that atavistic desire, not the body itself but body-oozes, provides an undeniable link between Joyce's cultural moment and our own world in which the literally self-purgative drama of "industrial culture" artists like Throbbing Gristle and Mark Pauline moves beyond possible pornographic titillation (depending on one's tastes, of course) to the "emetic" properties detected in *Ulysses* long ago by the decorous but enlightened Judge John M.

Woolsey. Perhaps the messages of the flesh remain consistent, whatever mask we decide to put on them; we just do not always hear those messages in the same key. Like the language that ends the "Oxen of the Sun episode," culture in the making is a kind of excrement, an excess that the social body produces and casts off in endless moments of self-birthing. Like the entrails that ancient priests pored over for predictions, Joyce's contributions to his own excremental culture slip, slide, shift their signifying force depending on the angle of vision, our position in relation to the footlights.

For this reason, an undeniably with-it writer like Don DeLillo can play out the messages of Molly's theatrical nonessence, calibrating his fiction to cues that exist in the most famous line in *Ulysses*. DeLillo's *White Noise* thus presents a trendy, pop psych marital conversation about sex in which neither partner wants to dominate and so no love is ever made. Instead, they discuss whether they will read "sexy stuff" first, who will read, what the person will read, and who enjoys the reading more. Finally, Babette tells Jack that she will read, "But I don't want you to choose anything that has men inside women, quote-quote, or men entering women. 'I entered her.' 'He entered me.' We're not lobbies or elevators. 'I wanted him inside me,' as if he could crawl completely in, sign the register, sleep, eat, so forth. Can we agree on that? I don't care what these people do as long as they don't enter or get entered."

"Agreed."
" 'I entered her and began to thrust.' "
"I'm in total agreement," I said.
" 'Enter me, enter me, yes, yes.' "
"Silly usage, absolutely."
"Insert yourself, Rex. I want you inside me, entering hard, entering deep, yes, now, oh." (DeLillo 29)

It is not until the end of the following chapter that Babette's "yes" is less ironic, and then she is merely semi-attending to her children's comments, "Yes yes yes" (DeLillo 34). Later still, to encourage an infant's eating, Babette again says, "Yes yes yes yes yes yes yes" (DeLillo 209) in a way that oddly disengages itself from the page and finds echoes only a few paragraphs later when she tries to convince her husband not to investigate her use of a suspicious drug. As Jack notes, "Babette is not a neurotic person. She is strong, healthy, outgoing, affirmative. She says yes to things. That is the point of Babette" (DeLillo 221). But the reader knows, as does Jack, that her affirmations have become merely acontextualized quotations. *White Noise*, a novel relentless in its disavowals, permits the trace of Molly's playacting to surface in oblique parody—parody which does not seek to undo the imagined Joycean transfigurative moment so much as to highlight its inadequacy to the postmodern scene—and to say, if short of the mark now, also then. After all, the narrator tells us with Joycean relevance, "The world is full of abandoned meanings. In the commonplace I find unexpected themes and intensities" (DeLillo 184).

In one sense, following the idea of excremental culture from Joyce to DeLillo maps out the obvious—that Joyce's supermodernism, founded as it was on a critique of forms and genres as much as on a critique of language, necessarily foreshadowed much of what we know as the calmer forms of postmodernism. Simultaneously, we might note that it requires only a momentary reversal of terms, from art-as-excrement to excrement-as-art to arrive at the kind of performance art that uses excretions and secretions as its medium and the body as its field. This exchange of terms Joyce adumbrated in concatenations like Stephen's protean urination and poetry composition, in Bloom's *Tit-Bits* reading and defecation, in Molly's Poulaphouca voiding, in the choreography of Stephen and Bloom's nocturnal micturition, in the seductive soft-porn plopping of stays and the softer plops of equine refuse, and, even before *Ulysses*, in Stephen's question, "Can excrement or a child or a louse be a work of art?" (*Portrait* 214).

One might make the point here that all such productions are process-based and rhythmic, ultimately organic and affirming, but I doubt that this is an adequate response to Stephen's query. In contrast, *Ulysses* embraces the excremental notion of culture, pausing, as always, over those female productions that question the excremental aesthetic at its heart, in its taxonomy. Is a child different from *merde*? Is menstrual fluid properly seen as excremental or secretional? The productions of the female body, in excess of the male's mostly less colorful manifestations, can be neither refused by Joyce's texts nor incorporated as lived experience. Childbirth, afterbirth, menstruation—these enter the fictions in highly stylized forms and remain unrealized matter that the language struggles to recuperate fully into art. Unable to contain the feminine, Joyce turned to theatrical form in a characteristic motion of discomfort; he provides a stage for what remains unknown, a period piece drama in place of a primal scene. And *persona*-Molly has seemed refreshingly real to many readers precisely because it is in her monologue that the struggle to bring all into words finds a predictable end. We free ourselves to the self-indulgence of the comfortable, the melodramatic, while Molly, ignoring our gaze, exudes the aplomb of actors used to exteriorizing feelings even while their subjectivity takes place on another stage. As a woman, both Irish and generic, Molly has her script forced on her, and *persona*-Molly responds out of an elsewhere-subjectivity that knows itself most profoundly in its unspeakable secrets and secretions.

Notes

1.   Letter to Frank Budgen, 16 August 1921, in Ellmann, *Selected Letters* 285. In his *Ulysses on the Liffey*, Ellmann returns to this point about "Penelope" as the "star turn" (162).

2.   I am indebted to Christina O'Shea for demonstrating the punctuating function of Molly's use of "yes" and to my colleague Herman Rapaport for discussions about the "failed ending" of *Ulysses* in which Molly's "yes" becomes "no." For Derrida on *oui*, see *Ulysse gramophone*.

3.   Stanislaus Joyce tells us about his brother's fascination with Eleonora Duse. Joyce went to London to see La Duse act in a D'Annunzio piece and had occasion to hear William Archer speak of La Duse as a better actress than Sarah Bernhardt. Joyce kept her picture, for a time, on his desk, and wrote her some poetry (*My Brother's Keeper* 188–89).

4.   Elaine Unkeless has been the most prominent spokesperson for Molly's role as ordinary homemaker. Bonnie Kime Scott also addresses this dimension of Molly's character in her fine discussion of critical approaches to Molly (Scott 156–83).

5.   I remind the reader that this essay was written in 1987 and first published in 1988.

6.   The issue of PMS as emergent from the nineteenth-century ideology of female pathology finds useful treatment in Laws, Hey, and Eagan, and in Rome.

7.   I am indebted to Jean Zida for directing my attention to Bloom's nosebleeds as a possible surrogate form of menstruation and to the discussion of male menstruation in Gilman. The concept of male menstruation is especially interesting when considered along with Ellmann's important chapter in *Ulysses on the Liffey*, "Why Molly Bloom Menstruates." Specifically, Ellmann asserts that "Menstruation is Promethean" (p. 171), a statement that appropriates a female function for masculine uses, replicating the medical gesture of appropriation.

Works Cited

Archer, William. *The Theatrical 'World' for 1893*. London: Scott, n.d.

Ashwell, Samuel. *Practical Treatise on the Diseases Peculiar to Women: Illustrated by Cases, Derived from Hospital and Private Practice*. Philadelphia: Lea and Blanchard, 1848.

DeLillo, Don. *White Noise*. New York: Viking Press, 1985.

Derrida, Jacques. *Ulysse gramophone: Deux mots pour Joyce*. Paris: Editions Galilee, 1987.

Ellmann, Richard. *Ulysses on the Liffey*. New York: Oxford University Press, 1972.

Ellmann, Richard, ed. *Selected Letters of James Joyce*. New York: Viking Press, 1975.

Gilman, Sander L. "The Struggle of Psychiatry with Psychoanalysis: Who Won?" *Critical Inquiry* 13 (Winter 1987): 293–313.

Herr, Cheryl. *Joyce's Anatomy of Culture*. Urbana: University of Illinois, 1986.

Jameson, Fredric. "Postmodernism, or the Cultural Logic of Late Capitalism." *New Left Review* 146 (1984): 59–92.

Joyce, James. *A Portrait of the Artist as a Young Man*. New York: Penguin, 1956.

Joyce, Stanislaus. *My Brother's Keeper*. Ed. Richard Ellmann. London: Faber, 1958.

Kroker, Arthur, and David Cook. *The Postmodern Scene: Excremental Culture and Hyper-Aesthetics*. New York: St. Martin's, 1986.

Laws, Sophie, Valerie Hey, and Andrea Eagan. *Seeing Red: The Politics of Pre-Menstrual Tension*. London: Hutchinson, 1985.

Rome, Esther. "Premenstrual Syndrome (PMS) Examined Through a Feminist Lens." Pp. 145–57 in Virginia L. Olesen and Nancy Fugate Woods. *Culture, Society, and Menstruation*. New York: Hemisphere, 1986.

Scott, Bonnie Kime. *Joyce and Feminism*. Bloomington: Indiana University Press, 1984.

Unkeless, Elaine. "The Conventional Molly Bloom." Pp. 150–68 in Suzette Henke and Elaine Unkeless, eds. *Women in Joyce*. Urbana: University of Illinois Press, 1982.

4

Pretending in "Penelope"
Masquerade, Mimicry, and Molly Bloom

Kimberly J. Devlin

Feminist theorists have recently reexplored the concept of the female masquerade, formulated initially by Joan Riviere.[1] Mary Ann Doane characterizes the masquerade as "a hyperbolisation of the accoutrements of femininity," as a flaunting of the cultural signifiers of womanliness (Doane, 82). Carole-Anne Tyler, however, draws a distinction between flaunting those signifiers and flouting those signifiers: if the former constitutes female masquerade, the latter becomes a sort of female mimicry. The female masquerade, after all, is a potentially oppressive gender identity, but female mimicry is a potentially playful one: consider the slight but critical difference between a Marilyn Monroe and a Madonna. As Tyler points out,

miming the feminine, playfully "repeating" it, produces knowledge about it: notably that it is a role and not a nature, and an exploitative role at that. . . . The mimic as performance artist denaturalizes ideology by questioning the terms in which she is produced and circulated as commodity, calling attention to the conventions that encode her as woman, representing representation and so unmasking through a conscious masking (mimicry) the masquerade of (woman's) nature as nature, as what precedes cultural construction. She "does" ideology in order to undo it. (21–22)[2]

The distinction between female masquerade and female mimicry allows women's interactions with representations of the feminine to

80

take contrasting forms: on the one hand, women may assume and internalize those culturally determined images passively and unconsciously; but on the other hand, they can appropriate them ironically, manipulate them from an internal critical distance.

The concept of women doing and undoing ideological gender acts is relevant to the last episode of *Ulysses*, where Molly recurrently foregrounds theatricality (both female *and* male) in her so-called "monologue"—a critical term misleading in its implications, as I will suggest later. Molly often conceptualizes human behavior as dramaturgical performance, dictated by putative gender "traits." Thinking about an explicitly male hypochondria, she recalls her husband at the City Arms hotel "pretending to be laid up with a sick voice doing his highness" (18.3). Figuring out how to recapture Bloom's gaze, she casts herself as the imperturbable, elusive, and hence exquisitely desirable femme—"Ill do the indifferent" (18.1529). Imagining bringing Stephen breakfast in bed if he had agreed to stay the night, she tells herself, "I could do the criada" (18.1482–83), assuming the position of stereotypical female servitude. Theatricality mediates Molly's visions of self and other, sometimes explicitly, for instance when she recollects Stephen as a child: "he was an innocent boy then and a darling little fellow in his lord Fauntleroy suit and curly hair like a prince on the stage" (18.1311–12).

In Molly's thoughts, identity is inextricably linked to signifiers in a variety of forms: appellative (names, or rather "parts" in the dramatis personae), verbal (statements, or rather "lines"), sartorial (clothing, or rather "costumes"), proprietorial (possessions, or rather "props"), and gestural (actions, or rather "poses," stage-directed "stances"). In the course of the episode, she tries on new self-figurations ("suppose I divorced him Mrs Boylan" [18.846]); recalls those that eluded her ("I could have been a prima donna only I married him" [18.896]—a phrase whose ambiguous syntax casts Bloom in a new "part," nominatively female); and explores a repertoire of roles, conventional and yet varied. A weaver and unweaver of identity itself, Molly dons multiple recognizable masks of womanliness, appropriating femininity in many familiar figurations. She stages herself as Venus in Furs, the indignant and protective spouse, the jealous domestic detective, the professional singer, the professional seductress or femme fatale, the teenage flirt, the teenage naif, the unrepentant adulteress, the guilt-ridden adulteress, the narcissistic child, the exasperated mother, the pining romantic, the cynical scold, the female seer/fortuneteller (hence her "natural" attraction to "one of those wildlooking gipsies" [18.1413]?), the frustrated housewife, the female confidante and adviser, the female misogynist, et cetera, et cetera. Molly

Bloom is all of these femininities, and hence none.[3] Commenting on the theatrical elements in the "Penelope" episode, Cheryl Herr points out in this volume that Molly's Homeric counterpart is "quintessentially an actress; [Penelope] actualizes her name, which translates to 'countenance of webs' or mask." She argues that Molly's episode is an analogous mask/masque: "[her] monologue-ing, her sartoriocentrism, her stylized gestures, her great sentences sustained as an operatic tour de force—these contribute to my assessment of her as not a character but rather as *a role* to be enacted by this or that major artiste of the era [who Herr points out could be either male or female] (emphasis added)." I would qualify this point by suggesting that Molly's monologue (for temporary lack of a better term) is a concatenation of roles, an elaborate series of "star turns" that undermines the notion of womanliness as it displays it. If gender is one of several ideologically dominant tropic differences, with masculinity and femininity divisible into many subtropes, then Molly is surely a polytropic "woman."

Molly Bloom, as a narrative/dramatic representation of "woman," has provoked an ongoing debate among Joyce scholars: can she be defended as an archetype or should she be stigmatized as a stereotype? Is her womanliness wonderfully quintessential or shamefully derivative? I would argue that the difference between archetype and stereotype is contrived, ultimately nonexistent: sexual archetypes, in particular, are often stereotypes decked out as literary concepts or masquerading as inherent psychological categories; they are sometimes merely "positive" stereotypes, embraced by the gender they are assigned to only when they are flattering or self-serving. The nondifference between the two terms is reflected in their various definitions. According to *Webster's Third New International Dictionary*, a stereotype is "something repeated or reproduced without variation," "a standardized mental picture held in common by members of a group." Organized around a Platonic conception of reality, an archetype is "the original model, form, or pattern from which something is made or from which something develops"; but, in Jungian terms, it is also *"an inherited idea or mode of thought* [emphasis added] derived from the experiences of the race and present in the unconscious of the individual"—which, if one disregards the mystical explanation for its perdurance, sounds suspiciously like a stereotype. *Webster's* further defines an archetype as at once "a perfectly typical example" (i.e., a norm) and "the most extreme example" (i.e., hyperbole, an exaggeration of the norm—a stereotype, perhaps?). The distinction between stereotype and archetype relies on, first of all, the contradictory concept of original copies, on a belief that some representations (the "model, form, or pattern") are more authentic than others, and, second, a contradictory definition of archetype itself—a definition that posits absolute norms and essences from which deviations and excesses can then be measured, and a definition that revealingly claims, moreover, the norm and the exaggeration of it are one and the same.[4]

If archetypes are always already stereotypes, then Molly's "archetypal" status is in fact bogus, a fraudulently transcendent way of describing her stereotypical nature. But to claim Molly is a stereotype in a straightforward, unqualified way is to miss the subtleties of Joyce's representation of "woman" in *Ulysses'* last episode. In an attempt to define Molly as a realistic character, Elaine Unkeless implies that there is a quintessential "she" who is the quintessence of conventional notions of femininity—naive, passive, dependent, illogical; the paradox of convention (which is always re-presentation) being quintessential remains unexamined. Unkeless elides the fact that for every conventional guise of femininity in "Penelope," there is a counterguise that contradicts it, undermining any female essence. Molly's well-known contradictions, which often lead to the critical assessments of her as "illogical," are very much a result of her role as roleplayer, of her ability to strike varying poses of womanliness and to parrot varying attitudes toward social myths and institutions. Molly's contradictions are internalized cultural contradictions: she weaves and unweaves ideological clichés. Molly is interesting to examine as an engendered character, insofar as Joyce represents her not as the feminine but as cultural femininities—constructed, labile, assumable, rejectable. Returning to Herr's dramaturgical framework for the episode, I suspect that Molly would be a challenging character to enact: the actor/actress playing her would have to foreground gender acts, to highlight staginess rather than to naturalize or conceal it in the ways "realistic" theater often mandates. One of Molly's dramatic pretexts is Nora Helmer of *A Doll's House*—a role (or rather, a series of roles) that requires the actor/actress to perform a woman who is constantly performing. The representation of Molly as a gender performance artist raises an inevitable question about the nature of the performances themselves—unquestioning masquerade or subversive mimicry?

Like Stephen and Bloom, Molly is represented as a character situated within representation, as a reader of popular culture, as a consumer of textual artifacts. Joyce makes it clear that her assumed roles are often by-products of identifications with specific texts of femininity available to her at her particular historical moment and locus. Molly, I will argue, participates in the female masquerade insofar as she often attempts to conform herself to cultural images of femininity, dramatizing them reflexively. But Molly also functions as the critic of the female masquerade through her repeated gestures of female female impersonation that amount to a form of parodic gender mimicry. Alternately flaunting and flouting her feminine signifiers, she functions as both the dupe and the deconstructer of media representations of received ideas about what constitutes womanliness. Her vacillation between the two positions supports the theoretical claim that there is no permanent critical vantage outside ideology.

Molly's belief in the importance of large breasts, an elaborate wardrobe, extremely smooth and soft skin, and youthful beauty in general strongly suggests that she has bought into the female masquerade, that she places credence in a hyperbolic brand of femininity. This construct of womanliness is often reinforced and elaborated through her appropriations of conventional representations of femininity available from the textual warehouse of popular song, advertisement, theater, and historical hearsay. When Molly fantasizes about running off with Boylan, for instance—"suppose I never came back what would they say eloped with him that gets you on on the stage" (18.373–74)— she forms a rough unconscious identification with a historical figure she explicitly recalls shortly afterward: Lillie Langtry, the reputedly second-rate actress who was nonetheless enormously popular due to her beauty and the patronage of her lover, Edward, Prince of Wales. Molly acknowledges here the illogical though by no means unusual causal connection between sexual scandal and commercial success, and envisions herself conventionally as the female artist who needs male sexual admiration and endorsement in order to succeed. It is worth noting, however, how frequently Molly's textual identifications do not really work, how often the received female costume does not fit, as it were. As Herr notes, Molly's role as Zerlina, the sexually tempted woman whose innocence is ultimately preserved, is surely a case of ironic miscasting: alone with their respective Don Giovannis, Zerlina screams while Molly willingly succumbs. When Molly remembers Mrs. Maybrick, the woman who surrendered to erotic temptation, she must radically dis-identify with the figure, because the figure was punished, ostensibly for murder but surely also for the illicit passion that supposedly motivated it. Positive images of female sexual desire are apparently a shortage in the textual warehouse of Anglo-Irish popular culture at the turn of the century.

One of Molly's most explicit textual identifications and subsequent self-dramatizations is provided by the song "In Old Madrid." Fantasizing about a liaison with Stephen, she recalls the ballad and then enters it, turning herself into the female figure in the musical narrative: "two

glancing eyes a lattice hid Ill sing for him theyre my eyes . . . two eyes
as darkly bright as loves own star" (18.1338–40). The textual imago of
the self here is a cultural cliché: Molly envisions herself as the female
with the seductive look, the female alluded to earlier in the banal
query from "Nausicaa"—"Why have women such eyes of witchery?"
(13.107). But to explore the imago further, it is necessary to look at the
song in its entirety, for the second verse of the musical narrative tells
us that "a convent veil those sweet eyes hid": the woman in "In Old
Madrid" has renounced desire and become a nun when her lover dies
in war, although she is still haunted by his romantic serenade.[5] What
sounds in the context of *Ulysses* like a potentially positive narrative of
female passion is in fact a negative one insofar as the fulfillment of
that passion remains perpetually deferred, eternally frustrated. The
textual identification is hence ironic—Molly is no pining nun, as she
herself well knows ("a nun maybe like the smutty photo he has shes
as much a nun as Im not" [18.21–22])—and yet it also records some revealing psychic truths: the identification reiterates unconsciously her
feelings of sexual abandonment and physical confinement as well as
her nostalgic desire for romance. Significantly, however, Molly revises
the song, turning the woman's "sparkling eyes" in the actual lyrics
into "glancing eyes" in her faulty recollection of them. The revision restores sight—however oblique—to the song's female persona, doubly
occluded behind lattice and veil, by transforming the feminine I/eye
from an aesthetic object (i.e., "sparkling eyes") into a seeing subject
(i.e, "glancing eyes"). Molly's association of herself with the song's
heroine further revises the heroine in the very process of association
itself: Molly takes the seemingly positive image of female passion that
is in fact negative and makes it positive by recuperating through a
distinctly lustful identification the desires the heroine has ostensibly
abandoned. The identification, in other words, is thoroughly conventional, and yet works revisions into the convention itself. Molly inter-
acts dialectically with received ideas about femininity, altering the
masquerade to make it fit.

Another seemingly conventional gender identification in "Penelope"
reveals unwitting insight into the process whereby women are produced as textual images. Recalling Bloom's suggestion that she seek
employment as an artist's model, Molly first visualizes herself in idealized form as the aestheticized female nude that hangs over the marriage bed (although conceding a slight difference between visual text
and self) and then pictures herself in a more debased guise as a specific pornographic tableau. The envisioned self-theatricalization in the
artist's studio leads directly to comparable images of staged female

flesh: "he said I could pose for a picture naked to some rich fellow in Holles street when he lost the job in Helys . . . would I be like that bath of the nymph with my hair down yes only shes younger or Im a little like that dirty bitch in that Spanish photo he has" (18.560–64). Bloom's suggestion that she permit herself to be reified out of financial necessity leads to an immediate and doubled self-reification in her own imagination, Molly imitating mentally the patriarchal practice of female objectification. But Molly's doubled identification also contains residues of trenchant understanding. Associating *The Bath of the Nymph* with pornography, Molly intuits, first of all, the sexual impetus behind seemingly "refined" artistic representations of the female. In her passing note of the model's age, she also sees the real women behind the representation, the female subject the painted object elides (it is clearly the person, the "she"—and not the image, the "bath of the nymph"—that is "younger," static images, in a sense, being ageless). And finally, Molly recognizes unconsciously, in the reflexive association her thoughts create here, that both of those women may have resorted to the occupation of the artist's or photographer's model out of sheer economic need (a condition she herself is all too familiar with). Molly explicitly likens herself to the women in the pictures, but also implicitly likens those women to herself, recuperating their humanness in the identification process.

Molly's textual identifications with the pristine nymph and the dirty bitch border on narcissism: she perceives herself *through* these clichéd tropes of femininity (if not quite *as* them) and views neither term of the polarity (i.e., virgin or whore) critically. Such a mode of female self-conception might support the contention that Molly is represented as a female stereotype, the by-product of Joyce's limited imagination, that she is "woman" unknowingly confined to the traditional female masquerade by a knowing male author. But a countercurrent in the final episode suggests that Molly's monologue can be read as a savvy critique of gender performance, as Joyce's self-conscious anatomy of feminine as well as masculine roles—roles in the sense of theatrical personae. Joyce creates in Molly a woman who is frequently conscious of her own theatricality, shrewdly aware of the assumed nature of her own gender acts. Recalling Bloom's courtship of her, for instance, Molly remembers when "he wrote me that letter with all those words in it . . . after when we met asking me have I offended you . . . and if I knew what it meant of course I had to say no for form sake dont understand you I said" (18.318–25). Molly remembers herself not, strictly speaking, behaving properly, but rather, more accurately, acting properly (in the dramaturgical sense of the phrase). Joyce makes it clear

that Molly's disingenuous gender performance is a function of a patriarchal ideology that mandates sexual ignorance as the norm for nubile
young women—an ideology that is at once successfully repressive
and pathetically self-delusional.

The key term in distinguishing female impersonation or mimicry
from female masquerade is distance—a critical distance (in both
senses of the phrase) that Joyce critics sometimes elide. James H.
Maddox, Jr., for example, acknowledges the divisions in Molly, the
potential distances between one "self" and another, but only in order
to meld her disparate personae ultimately into one seamless and atemporal whole: "[Molly] has . . . a complete, unmediated identification
with her own past. . . . She wanders back and forth between her different selves with delight and with no feeling that one of her serial
personalities is really separate from another. . . . Carrying her own
past inside her with virtually no barriers between her and it, Molly has
the extraordinary power actually to reduplicate and relive it" (213–15).
Discussing the passage where Molly remembers Lieutenant Mulvey,
David Hayman makes similar claims, suggesting that it creates "the
sense that time is one continuous erotic present" and that in it "Molly
has genuinely experienced and now re-experiences a romantic-erotic
moment" (127–28). This supposed temporal seamlessness of Molly's
thoughts is, I suspect, a textual illusion, created by a purely formal
device, the lack of punctuation. The content of Molly's recollections
often renders explicit the distance and difference between former
selves, as when she views, for instance, an earlier persona critically:
"O wasnt I the born fool to believe all his blather about home rule
and the land league" (18.1187–88). Molly's memories, moreover, are
often predicated on a double gap, a double distance: a critical distance between past and present and between actress and projected
persona within the recollected experiences themselves. This double
gap—temporally and ontologically dramatic—is most readily seen in
that passage centered on Mulvey, which Hayman selectively cites to
support his claims.

When Molly thinks about her first suitor, the dramaturgical dimension of the courtship is recurrently foregrounded. She recalls playfully
creating a dramatic persona for herself, telling her young admirer that
she is engaged to "the son of a Spanish nobleman named Don Miguel
de la Flora" (18.773–74), and she works other fictive elements into her
projected self-image as well: she claims "a few things I told him true
about myself" (18.776), implying that there were many other things
she told him that were false. Mentally recreating her early sexual experience with Mulvey, she recalls not so much a prior self as a prior

self-dramatization—and hence is at a distance from "Molly" in both
the past and the present. Like an actress remembering a particular costume, she inventories in detail the apparel she wore on the occasion;
she also paraphrases her lines ("I told him [OHaras tower] was struck
by lightning" [18.783–84]; "I said I was tired" [18.789]—whether she
really was or not remains unclear); and she remembers leaning over
her suitor at a theatrically advantageous angle, knowing "the left side
of my face the best" (18.798). The erotic scenario takes place "in broad
daylight . . . in the sight of the whole world you might say they could
have put an article about it in the Chronicle" (18.828–30): Molly conceptualizes the experience as a dramatic performance for a posited
general audience, a performance that might be followed by a write-
up in the newspaper. The indeterminacy of her partner's identity—
"what was his name Jack Joe Harry Mulvey was it" (18.818)—is thus
not surprising: from Molly's point of view, he has merely played a
part in response to her own so that his specificity as an individual is
entirely forgettable. Recalling the culmination of the sexual scenario,
Molly thinks to herself, "how did we finish it off . . . I pulled him off
into my handkerchief pretending not to be excited" (18.809–10). She
intentionally impersonates in this scene the unseducible young girl:
there is a clear and conscious gap between the projected female persona and the person behind it, the self that really is aroused but knows
better than to betray it. This dissembled sexual imperturbability might
be mistaken for a conventional gesture of coyness, but it is in fact a
cagey act of self-protection. Molly remembers what the old servant
Ines has told her about being left "with a child embarazada" (18.802)
and knows she is safest not to reveal the keenly felt sexual pleasure
that may leave her vulnerable to full seduction. What looks like female
masquerade here is really female mimicry, an intentional manipulation of a particular gender act, and female mimicry, moreover, that
functions ultimately as contraception.

Theatricality is also heavily embedded in Molly's sexual fantasies
focussed on Stephen. Her envisioned seduction of him is a private
melodramatic tableau, with Stephen suggestively cast in the stereotypical female role ("Ill make him feel all over him till he half faints
under me"), that ends in public notoriety ("then hell write about me
lover and mistress publicly too with our 2 photographs in all the
papers when he becomes famous" [18.1363–66]). The material specificity of the last part of the fantasy suggests that it may be inspired by
the media: lapsing back into masquerade, Molly may be unconsciously
identifying with an unspecified adulteress, celebrated in verse and
in the news. An unconscious intertext likewise lies behind the comic

theatrical trick Molly thinks of playing on her fantasy guest: "pretend we were in Spain with him half awake without a Gods notion where he is dos huevos estrellados senor Lord the cracked things come into my head sometimes" (18.1485–88). Although Molly passes off this thought as an original whim that has randomly entered her mind, it bears an uncanny resemblance to the second part of the Induction of *The Taming of the Shrew*. Christopher Sly's experiences in the Induction as a whole nicely parallel Stephen's on the night of 16 June. An inebriated Sly has broken glasses in an alehouse, whereupon the Hostess threatens to fetch a constable; he falls into a drunken sleep and is discovered by a Lord who decides to play a trick on him: he will be taken to the Lord's house, put to bed, and when he awakens, he will be treated like a lord, waited upon by servants (including the real Lord himself), and then shown the play proper of *The Taming of the Shrew*. The similarity of Molly's fantasized trick may be mere coincidence, as there is no direct evidence she is familiar with the play, although she may have dipped into Bloom's copy of Shakespeare's *Works* (17.1365). But Joyce, of course, is familiar with the play and stages Molly staging an analogous drama—but with an interesting reversal. If Sly watches *The Taming of the Shrew*, Stephen—in Molly's imagination, at least— will see its inverse: *The Taming of the Errant Husband*.

Stephen, however, will be not only a witness to this transformative drama, but also a participant, as the ensuing trajectory of Molly's thoughts suggests: "Id love to have a long talk with an intelligent welleducated person Id have to get a nice pair of red slippers like those Turks with the fez used to sell or yellow and a nice semitransparent morning gown that I badly want or a peachblossom dressing jacket like the one long ago in Walpoles only 8/6 or 18/6 Ill just give him one more chance" (18.1493–98). The envisioned arrival of Stephen leads Molly to thoughts of a new costume for herself, a costume scripted by contemporary advertising (an ongoing dominant textbook for the female masquerade), as the prices and unmistakable ad lingo ("semitransparent," "peachblossom") make clear; it remains deliberately equivocal, however, as to whom this garb is meant to appeal. The fantasy of an erotico-intellectual liaison with Stephen segues into a fantasy of marital reconciliation and the tactics (including seductive apparel) that will effect it. Molly imaginatively stages, in other words, the oedipal "drama" with a twist: in her version of it, the son-figure's desire for the mother must not be repressed, but rather actively encouraged. The son's desire is the agency that will solidify the family unit by provoking the father's jealousy and renewed desire for the mother—hence the sequence of Molly's fantasies, culminating in the vision of the errant husband "tamed," back within her sphere of control, manipulated—paradoxically—into a position of active sexual longing ("then Ill go out Ill have him eying up at the ceiling where is she gone now make him want me thats the only way" [18.1538–40]). Molly's earlier theatrically mediated imago of Stephen ("a darling little fellow in his lord Fauntleroy suit and curly hair like a prince on the stage" [18.1311–12]) not only announces a variant of the Freudian family romance—a wish for highborn offspring (as opposed to parents) through the appropriation of another's child; it also reveals her conception of him as a "character." Molly psychically casts the vocationless Stephen into a specific and functional role: the oedipal son, the heir apparent, suitably figured in Lord Fauntleroy himself.[6]

Staginess permeates the interpersonal throughout the "Penelope" section, where dramaturgical sexuality lays bare a hidden agenda of theater itself: to "grig" the other, to incite mimetic desire ("I wish some man or other would take me sometime when hes there and kiss me in his arms" [18.104–5]). The persistently dramatic contours of Molly's fantasies, her recurrent sense of an implied audience, records the psychological imprint on her consciousness of the Other and the sociohistorical imprint of a theatrical culture. Envisioned romantic triangles have a decidedly melodramatic cast to them, with each participant playing a scripted part:

> I know they were spooning a bit when I came on the scene he was dancing and sitting out with her the night of Georgina Simpsons housewarming and then he wanted to ram it down my neck it was on account of not liking to see her a wallflower . . . after that I pretended I had a coolness on with her over him . . . supposing he got in with her again and was going out to see her somewhere . . . alright well see then let him go to her she of course would only be too delighted to pretend shes mad in love with him that I wouldnt so much mind Id just go to her and ask her do you love him and look her square in the eyes she couldnt fool me but he might imagine he was and make a declaration to her with his plabbery kind of a manner (18.171–95)

Molly claims that she was never genuinely jealous of Josie (Powell) Breen in the past, but that she merely performed the expected response, given "the scene," by acting the part of the sexually competitive woman. She then imagines Mrs. Breen in the present pretending to be in love with Bloom, herself pretending to care in a dramatic confrontation, and Bloom pretending, in sheer delusion, that his passions for Josie are equally intense. When I first speculated about the motives behind this fantasy, I was certain that they were defensive, that Molly imagines romantic pretense to deny the possibility of genuine feeling between Bloom and another woman. But the larger pattern of Molly's Weltanschauung, oddly enough, suggests otherwise: she does not blindly block out possible realities with theatrical scenarios of fraudulent emotion; rather she perceptively recognizes in the seemingly real the paradox of the genuinely fraudulent.

Molly is consistently accorded a sort of X-ray vision that enables her to recognize artifice, various simulacra of the real immediately. Perhaps as a result of her own participation in melodrama, she identifies the behavioral genre in others easily ("if his nose bleeds youd think it was O tragic and that dyinglooking one off the south circular . . . Miss Stack . . . trying to imagine he was dying on account of her to never see thy face again" [18.24–29]). Molly is adept at recognizing the inauthentic in all guises: "a bottle of hogwash [Larry ORourke] tried to palm off as claret" (18.453–54); "that Mary we had in Ontario terrace padding out her false bottom to excite him" (18.56–57); Mrs. Rubio "with her switch of false hair on her" (18.752). These remarks could be taken as mere cranky and aggressive skepticism, aimed at denigrating others, if Bloom's earlier thoughts did not confirm the fact that Molly does indeed have unusual powers of penetration: "Sharp as needles they are. When I said to Molly the man at the corner of Cuffe street was goodlooking, thought she might like, twigged at once he had a false arm. Had, too" (13.913–16). The pattern behind many of these insights emerges as a refusal to see the cultural as natural, as an ability to recognize the constructedness of various perceptual illusions. The everyday counterparts to stage props and staged gestures fail to fool her. Molly can distinguish cultural deviance, in the form of veiled exhibitionism, from a genuine "call of nature" ("that other wretch with the red head . . . when I was passing pretending he was pissing standing out for me to see it" [18.545–47]) and even sees the subtleties of inauthenticity embedded in the patently inauthentic itself: "those statues in the museum one of them pretending to hide it with her hand" (18.540–41). Molly perceptively recognizes the art object here as doubled mimesis: as a representation of representation; as a simulacrum of a pose of feminine modesty, sexual coyness; as a marmoreal staging of a specific socially sanctioned gender act.

Molly's position as critic of cultural fraudulence might seem to align her with nature, in the traditional ways she has been in many earlier readings of her. But such an alignment is problematic, not only because the barrier between nature and culture is extremely porous in "Penelope," as Derek Attridge has suggested (560), but also because Molly understands the cultural so thoroughly. Her ability to critique its artifices and representations stem from her own involvement in (and sometimes complicity with) those signifying systems themselves. Her ironic disclaimer—"I hate that pretending of all things" (18.491)— is hence a lie and a truth simultaneously: a lie insofar as her alternate gestures of masquerade and mimicry make her a pretender *par excellence,* and a truth insofar as she sets herself up as a deconstructer of pretense, as a woman who challenges cultural pretense—not through the "alternative" of nature—but through parodies of cultural pretense, through hyperbolic elaborations of it.

Molly's critical, penetrative vision is repeatedly leveled at her spouse, whom she represents as a fraud, a relentless impersonator. Odyssean masquerade becomes most transparent under the Penelopean gaze, where we see Bloom as the klutz posing as the athlete ("if anyone asked could he ride the steeplechase for the gold cup hed say yes" [18.955–56]); as the partial plagiarist posing as the original romantic ("his mad crazy letters My Precious one everything connected with your glorious Body everything underlined that comes from it is a thing of beauty and of joy for ever something he got out of some nonsensical book" [18.1176–78]); as the ecletically educated man posing as the certified scholar ("of course he pretended to understand it all probably he told him he was out of Trinity college" [18.1330–32]); and as the philanderer posing as the earnest breadwinner, creating one fictional persona in his letter to Martha (Henry Flower) while masking it with yet another, in a complicated tableau of figurative and literal cover-ups ("he covered it up with the blottingpaper pretending to be thinking about business" [18.48–49]). From Molly's perspective, Bloom's mode of being is shamelessly imitative, derivative—even his quirky and seemingly individualistic sleeping habits bear traces of mimetic representation: "breathing with his hand on his nose like that Indian god he took me to show one wet Sunday . . . imitating him as hes always imitating everybody" (18.1200–5). Bloom anticipates the dreamer of *Finnegans Wake,* who is known only through encyclopedic self-mediating figurations, a panoply of mimetic masks—and who is hence likewise accused of "immutating aperybally" (460).

As it is recorded in Molly's monologue, the Blooms' relationship emerges as an ongoing drama (in the literal sense of the word), a protean theater of multiple genres. Some moments from their courtship are marked as sentimental romance, with Bloom using mimesis to back his mimetic fantasies and Molly impersonating the compliant and impressed fiancée, concealing her X-ray vision in her perfect replication of the appropriate gender act: "all the things he told father he was going to do and me but I saw through him telling me all the lovely places we could go for the honeymoon Venice by moonlight with the gondolas and the lake of Como he had a picture cut out of some paper of and mandolines and lanterns O how nice I said" (18.983–87). Other episodes border on fetishistic comedy, with Bloom contriving elaborate and transparent ruses to get a look at the bed that harbors her body and to use the soap that he hopes (deludedly) has touched her hands: "the very 1st opportunity he got a chance in Brighton square running into my bedroom pretending the ink got on his hands to wash it off with the Albion milk and sulphur soap I used to use and the gelatine still round it O I laughed myself sick at him that day" (18.1192–95). Scenes from their marriage vacillate between the theater of farce and the theater of cruelty:

Id never again in this life get into a boat with him after him at Bray telling the boatman he knew how to row . . . then it came on to get rough the old thing crookeding about and the weight all down my side telling me pull the right reins now pull the left and the tide all swamping in floods in through the bottom and his oar slipping out of the stirrup . . . theres no danger whatsoever keep yourself calm in his flannel trousers Id like to have tattered them down off him before all the people and give him what that one calls flagellate till he was black and blue (18.954–63)

Bloom's fondness for role-playing becomes most explicit in his contrived sex game, where he performs his own personal rendition of *The Wife of Scarli*, the popular drama about adultery, ingeniously casting himself simultaneously as both the cuckold and the cuckolder: "who is in your mind now tell me who are you thinking of who is it tell me his name who tell me who the german Emperor is it yes imagine Im him think of him can you feel him" (18.94–96). In addition to playing both male leads, Bloom assumes in this scenario the position of the stage director, telling Molly how he wants the cuckolder to be cast, but in other scenes Molly herself assumes the directorial position. When she thinks he is on the verge of proposing to her against the backdrop of an inappropriate stage set ("he was on the pop of asking me too the night in the kitchen I was rolling the potato cake theres something I want to say to you" [18.198–99]), she makes it clear to him that his timing is off, that such gestures demand a better mise-en-scène. The power struggles in the Blooms' relationship can be conceptualized as a battle for the director's chair, for the position which determines the genre of the drama and hence its outcome.

When Molly recollects the mini-dramas of their relationship, she recurrently "does" the voice of her spouse:

the hotel story he made up a pack of lies to hide it planning it Hynes kept me who did I meet ah yes I met do you remember Menton and who else let me see (18.37–39)

who is in your mind now tell me who are you thinking of who is it tell me his name who tell me who the german Emperor is it yes imagine Im him think of him can you feel him trying to make a whore out of me what he never will (18.94–97)

the night in the kitchen I was rolling the potato cake theres something I want to say to you (18.198–99)

after when we met asking me have I offended you (18.320–21)

measuring and mincing if I buy a pair of old brogues itself do you like those new shoes yes how much were they (18.469–70)

plottering about the house so you cant stir with him any side whats your programme today (18.507–8)

every blessed hat I put on does that suit me yes take that thats alright (18.521–22)

that place in Grafton street I had the misfortune to bring him into . . . saying Im afraid were giving you too much trouble (18.524–26)

the weight all down my side telling me pull the right reins now pull the left (18.957–58)

its a mercy we werent all drowned he can swim of course me no theres no danger whatsoever keep yourself calm (18.959–61)

Joyce represents Molly not just as a figurative mimic, in her conscious recreations of her own performed gender acts, but also as a literal mimic, in her conscious parrotings of the voice of the Other. As her imitation of Bloom's studiously nonchalant response to her "catechetical interrogation" (17.2249) makes clear (the first example cited above), mimicry is often a means of exposing the inauthentic, of re-presenting self-representations in ways that highlight their fraudulence. Frequently Molly simply gives paraphrases of others' speech—paraphrases marked by the past tense and appended with a "he said" or a "she said" (e.g., "he said wasnt it terrible to do that there in a place like that" [18.278–79])—but at other points she clearly reproduces in her thoughts others' idiosyncratic linguistic inflections and tonalities:

her father was an awfully nice man he [Mat Dillon] was near seventy always goodhumoured well now Miss Tweedy or Miss Gillespie theres the piannyer (18.721–23)

those romps of Murray girls calling for her can Milly come out please (18.1024–25) her tongue is a bit too long for my taste your blouse is open too low she says to me the pan calling the kettle blackbottom (18.1033–34)

Molly's repertoire includes the "speech" of animals ("he used to break his heart at me taking off the dog barking in bell lane" [18.634–35]; "I loved rousing that dog in the hotel rrrsssstt awokwokawok" [18.812–13]) as well as the voice of a priest, which comes through quite distinctly, only to break down in a moment of nonrecollection: "where . . . but whereabouts on your person my child on the leg behind high up was it . . . was it where you sit down . . . and did you whatever way he put it I forget" (18.108–12). Joyce endows Molly with a memory that is virtually photographic—she remembers not only the wording of texts but also typography (e.g., "Gardner lieut Stanley G 8th Bn 2nd East Lancs Rgt of enteric fever" [18.389])—and virtually "taperecordic": she reduplicates the utterances of others nearly verbatim (occasionally her mimicry is flawed by pronominal confusion, e.g., "asking me questions is it permitted to enquire the shape of my bedroom" [18.286–87]). The documented inaccuracies and contradictions in her recall of general facts—we will never know for certain how many times Molly and Boylan had intercourse—stand in sharp contrast to the textual specificity of recalled inscriptions *and* voices. Susan Bazargan in this volume has thus noted that "although critics have usually referred to the 'Penelope' episode as Molly's monologue or stream-of-consciousness, in fact her discourse is anything but univocal. It is dialogic not only because it seems directed toward an interlocutor, but also because it is informed by a variety of rhetorical stances." I agree that Molly's discourse posits a listener, but a listener, I would add, who is expected to hear her speaking internally her own listenings. The ongoing parodic caricatures of others' voices rupture the ostensible flow of her thoughts, further rendering inaccurate the concept of a "monologue" or "soliloquy": her playful and various mimic vocalities are better described as a "polylogue" or "polyloquy."

Of all Molly's acts of mimicry, my personal favorite is the mental skit she performs that I call the priest and the penitent. Bazargan claims that, in the course of recollecting that well-known confession scene, Molly reproduces a comic dialogue "by alternating between roles, by mimicking voices, her own and that of Father Corrigan." The recollection is actually a trialogue insofar as three distinct intonations can be heard in the passage: the pseudo-penitent plaints of the female confessee (e.g., "he touched me father"), the solemn tones of the male priest (e.g., "whereabouts on your person my child"), and the critical voice of the actress herself (e.g., "O Lord couldnt he say bottom right out and have done with it" [18.107–11]), who recognizes the other two voices as mere acts, easily reenacted in memory. I would argue that Molly does not, strictly speaking, imitate her own voice, as Bazargan suggests, but rather an assumed voice, the voice of a female cultural caricature. In recollection, she mimics her own mimicry, reperforms her own performance. The element of travesty in Molly's rendition of the priest and the penitent makes her, in a sense, both a female male impersonator and a female female impersonator. If a female female impersonator is at all difficult to conceptualize, one needs only to think of the contemporary entertainer Dolly Parton, who, according to Carole-Anne Tyler, opened her 1987 variety show by "announcing that if she had been born a man, she would have been a female impersonator" (45). Feminist critics have argued that mimicry is often a subversive practice, "a time-honored tactic among oppressed groups, who often appear to acquiesce in the oppressor's ideas about it, thus producing a double meaning: the same language or act simultaneously confirms the oppressor's stereotypes of the oppressed and offers a dissenting and empowering view for those in the know" (129).[7] Molly's past mimicry in the confessional is precisely such a double gesture: it validates the priest's belief in female devotion to the patriarchal church, but as a mere act, as a simulacrum of piety, it affords Molly the distance to view that institution critically, to recognize the incongruous combination of fastidious verbal evasion and displaced auditory voyeurism (auditeurism?) inherent in the priest's inquiries. Molly's female female impersonation in the narrative present is likewise a critical act, predicated on an awareness of the constructed nature of "the devout woman," on a sentient penetration of this particular female masquerade.

I find several other instances of these anatomizing gender performances in Molly's thoughts, particularly in her recollected interactions with men in symbolic positions of authority. In her recalled encounter with Mr. Cuffe, she attempts to manipulate a hyperbolic femininity against capitalist economic power and mimics in her musings the conventional voice of the male employer who speaks to the beleaguered wife in tones of genuine condescension and spurious sympathy ("he gave me a great mirada once or twice first he was stiff as the mischief really and truly Mrs Bloom . . . but he changed the second time he looked . . . I could see him looking very hard at my chest . . . Im extremely sorry Mrs Bloom believe me" [18.512–31]). Genuinely dissatisfied with her flawed costume in this scenario, Molly seems very much *into* her performance, but it becomes clear in her final self-conceptualization that she knows it is just that—a performance: "and me being supposed to be his wife" (18.532). Remembering her visit

to "that dry old stick Dr Collins" (18.1153), Molly's parodic repetition of male speech mocks the voice of clinical authority, a conventionally venerated discourse. As Paula A. Treichler notes, "medical
diagnosis stands as a prime example of an authorized linguistic process (distilled, respected, high-paying) whose representational claims
are strongly supported by social, cultural, and economic practices.
Even more than most forms of male discourse, the diagnostic practice is multiply-sanctioned" (70–71). Molly's mimicry of Dr. Collins
questions those representational claims by highlighting their circum-
locutory nature and the consequent slippage between signifier and
supposed signified: "could you pass it easily pass what I thought he
was talking about the rock of Gibraltar the way he put it" (18.1163–
64). If Molly recognizes the auditeur in the confession box and the
voyeur in the cattle dealer's office, she also perceives the sadist in
the doctor's chair, associating Collins with a specific male tyrant from
popular fiction: "I wouldnt trust him too far to give me chloroform
or God knows what else . . . frowning so severe his nose intelligent
like that you be damned you lying strap" (18.1171–74). Molly's penetrative vision exposes the veiled taboo pleasures available to men in
culturally sanctioned positions of power.

And yet for all her derision of these masculine figures, Molly still
maintains a modicum of admiration for them, recalling Mr. Cuffe's
politeness ("it was nice of him to show me out in any case" [18.530]) or
Dr. Collins's diagnostic reliability ("still I liked him when he sat down
to write the thing out" [18.1172–73]). Her ambivalence toward cultural tropes of masculinity comes through most clearly in her thoughts
about Boylan. On the one hand, she is highly attracted to his particular version of maleness, a specifically dramatic convention of maleness—the character of the rake: the amoral, insensitive, and sexually
predatory figure, often also financially extravagant, that finds its most
familiar incarnation in Don Giovanni. Molly's pragmatic, exploitative
response to this embodied dramatic convention is dramatically uncon-
ventional ("he has plenty of money and hes not a marrying man so
somebody better get it out of him" [18.411–12]). But on the other hand,
Molly criticizes Boylan for his crude familiarity and macho "acts" (e.g.,
slapping her on the rear) and, in her last assessment of him on 17 June,
she dismisses him as a joke: "standing out that vulgar way in the half
of a shirt they wear to be admired like a priest or a butcher or those
old hypocrites in the time of Julius Caesar of course hes right enough
in his way to pass the time as a joke" (18.1373–76). Molly seems at
points to buy into a phallocentric order quite literally, in her well-
known moments of penis worship, and yet there is also a decided

contrast between her representation of the conventional *male* estimate of the phallus as the impressive monumental signifier ("some fellow or other trying to catch my eye as if it was 1 of the 7 wonders of the world" [18.551–552]) and *her own* idiosyncratic and deflationary assessments, assessments that figuratively domesticate the phallus through comparisons to household items ("sticking up at you like a hatrack" [18.543–44]; "like a sausage or something" [18.558]; "some kind of a thick crowbar" [18.147–48]). Molly's critique of phallocentrism is also felt in her refusal to buy into the phallus in the symbolic (Lacanian) sense: that is, the phallus as cultural signifier of significance (an elevating title, a prestigious position, an impressive reputation, etc.). Her gaze highlights the ironic gap between the signifiers (title, reputation) and the men behind them ("mouth almighty and his boiled eyes of all the big stupoes I ever met and thats called a solicitor" [18.42–44]; "he says that little man he showed me without the neck is very intelligent the coming man Griffiths is he well he doesnt look it thats all I can say" [18.385–86]). Refusing to be impressed by arbitrarily determined cultural differences, Molly reduces a president/general to a nobody ("general Ulysses Grant whoever he was or did supposed to be some great fellow landed off the ship" [18.682–83]) and sees Edward VII as an ordinary man ("I suppose hes like the first man going the roads only for the name of a king theyre all made the one way" [18.482–83]). From her point of view, the names of venerated authors and philosophers are not worth remembering ("some old Aristocrat or whatever his name is" [18.1241]), their cultural positions are exposed as pious fraud, and their works are esteemed as mere pretensions of cultured entertainment ("the works of Master Francois Somebody supposed to be a priest about a child born out of her ear because her bumgut fell out a nice word for any priest to write and her a—e as if any fool wouldnt know what that meant" [18.488–91]). Molly's relationship to the phallocentric order is best represented in the image of her drawing the penis and then tearing it up (18.557–58): although it can be read as a denigrating tableau of a woman with a childish genital obsession, it also can emblematize a woman who represents images of masculinity—describing and impersonating simulacra of "manliness"—only to dismantle and de-signify them through parody and critique. Molly is the poseur who nonetheless sees through all poses—actress, stage director, *and* critic of the gender theater itself.

In the polylogue of "Penelope," Bloom is criticized for his lack of two signifiers of manliness, the beard (18.30) and the pipe (18.508–9), but also praised for his former feminine beauty (18.208–10) and his transsexual knowledge of the Other: "I saw he understood or felt what a woman is" (18.1578–79). "Circe" has revealed, of course, that Bloom's experience of femininity is theatrical ("It was Gerald converted me to be a true corsetlover when I was a female impersonator in the High School play *Vice Versa*" [15.3009–11]) in the same way that Molly's experience of masculinity is. Although critics sometimes assume that Molly wants to *be* a man, her language makes it clear that she simply wants to try on the part, and only temporarily: "I wished I was one myself for a change *just to try* with that thing they have swelling up on you so hard and at the same time so soft" (18.1381–83, emphasis added). She views the penis here as a sexual prop, a detachable object, a part of the costume of maleness. Given this theatrical conception of gender difference, her later paean to Bloom's essential transsexuality is ironic and vexed by paradox. At the moment when Molly seems to affirm feminine essence ("he understood or felt what a woman *is*" [emphasis added]), she also undermines it by refusing to link femininity to the female body or female subjectivity. "Penelope" suggests, moreover, that what a woman (or a man, for that matter) "is" is what she/he is not—a construct, an assumable gender mask worn for the other. As Cheryl Herr has noted in her important rereading of "Circe," "*Ulysses* argues that sexuality is sheer theater, at least on the social stage on which we dramatically construct the selves we play" (154). Bloom does indeed know that what a woman "is" is what she is not, for he is the one and only male character in "Penelope" who is accorded the power of recognizing a gender act as an act: "he wrote me that letter with all those words in it . . . after when we met asking me have I offended you with my eyelids down of course he saw I wasnt he had a few brains" (18.318–22). He is briefly dramatized as knowing that what Molly "is" is a function of the exigencies of ideological gender conventions.

Although I have mentioned "Joyce" in passing and have acknowledged that Molly is "Joyce's representation of 'woman,'" I have thus far deliberately avoided the obvious: that "Molly" is really a male female impersonation, a "man" doing a "woman" who in turn does both genders. What is the possible purpose of this regress of mimicry? Who is intended to benefit from it? As I have argued above, Molly as a "character" clearly does, insofar as mimicry affords her a tentative albeit unstable critical vantage on various cultural institutions. But with the brief exception of Bloom in his days of courtship, no other characters in this dramatic fiction seem to recognize Molly's gender acts as such, to notice that she often consciously dons various masks; on the contrary, most of the men who discuss her emphasize her female essence, her excessive presence, her substantiality. Menton describes her as "a good armful" (6.697), Lenehan opines that "she has a fine pair, God bless her" (10.559–60), and the nameless narrator of "Cyclops" calls her "the fat heap he married . . . with a back on her like a ballalley" (12.503–4). Carole-Anne Tyler has discussed the problems inherent in the reception of gender impersonations, the difficulties inherent in their legibility:

> The best intentions guarantee nothing. A woman's intending to repeat the feminine with a difference may enable her to have a different relationship to femininity but may have no such effect on men—or other women, for that matter. In short, the mimic could find herself in the same old story. . . . Mimicry is not a strategy that will always and everywhere be subversive because the perception of irony does not depend on the author's intentions or on the text itself. . . . Rather irony—and mimicry—are produced by reading a difference into what could be mere repetition, mere masquerade. Seeing a difference depends on a difference of point of view, which is enabled by a different history. . . . (31–32)

Given the necessity of a different—and critical—point of view, I suspect that the potential audience of Molly's (and Joyce's) gender impersonations is constituted by readers of *Ulysses* itself: the show is aimed at us. We are invited to see ourselves in Joyce-doing-Molly-doing-whoever, to recognize our own en-gendered in-scriptings—for in order to read gender players as players, perhaps "it takes one to know one," perhaps this is one requisite of that different point of view. Writing Molly, Joyce forges a female voice that exposes, in gestures of travestic imitation, the en-gendered linguistic performances of her culture. It is significant, though not surprising, that only in the act of male female impersonation, that only in the act of trying on the female masquerade himself, was Joyce enabled to feel the discomforts of the construct (hence the recurrent images of claustrophobia in "Penelope"?) and to find a way out of its confines in subversive gender play. Putting on "womanliness" that repeatedly puts on "manliness" allowed Joyce to articulate one of his canniest critiques of the ideology that produces the oppressive categories themselves.

Notes

1. Joan Riviere's seminal essay, "Womanliness as Masquerade," was first published in 1929 in the International Journal of Psychoanalysis.
2. My essay is indebted to this dissertation, and I thank Tyler for granting me permission to quote from it.
3. I am deliberately echoing here Judith Williamson's contention about the photography of Cindy Sherman: "The fact that it *is* Cindy Sherman per-

forming each time is precisely what undermines the idea that any one image is 'her'. It reminds me of the Cachet ad: 'It won't be the same on any two women . . . the perfume as individual as *you* are.' This promise is followed by a bunch of images of different 'femininities,' each of which is meant to be a different *woman* (using Cachet); whereas what Sherman shows is that anyone can 'be' all of them, and none" (105).

4.   The most recent analysis of Molly as an archetypal character is John H. Lammers's "The Archetypal Molly Bloom, Joyce's Frail Wife of Bath." Lammers's argument, which starts by documenting the critical tradition of archetypal approaches to Molly, is plagued by the spurious distinction between terms I discuss above. After mapping Molly's "archetypal" resemblance to the Wife of Bath, he concedes that the female archetype may be a function of specific psychosocial conditions, describing it in terms that resonate of a stereotype: "As the imaginative creation of men . . . , the archetype of the Wife and Molly suggests other types of realities—the opinions, beliefs, and emotions regarding women of Chaucer, Joyce, and possibly, as [Darcy] O'Brien concludes, the majority of men in her (the archetype's) society" (497).

5.   The lyrics for "In Old Madrid" are printed in the pamphlet *The Joyce of Music,* with notes by James Hurt, p. 23. This pamphlet accompanies the tape of the same name, performed by the New Hutchinson Family Singers.

6.   Don Gifford with Robert J. Seidman note that in the novel *Little Lord Fauntleroy,* "the naive but winning American-born boy becomes heir to an English title and estate" (629).

7.   Tania Modleski is discussing a point initially made by Luce Irigaray in *The Sex Which is Not One,* trans. Catherine Porter (Ithaca: Cornell University Press, 1985), 76.

Works Cited

Attridge, Derek. "Molly's Flow: The Writing of 'Penelope' and the Question of Women's Language." *Modern Fiction Studies* 35 (1989): 543–65.

Doane, Mary Ann. "Film and the Masquerade: Theorising the Female Spectator." *Screen* 23.3–4 (1982): 74–87.

Gifford, Don, with Robert J. Seidman. *Ulysses Annotated: Notes for James Joyce's "Ulysses."* Berkeley: University of California Press, 1988.

Hayman, David. "The Empirical Molly." *Approaches to "Ulysses."* Ed. Thomas F. Staley and Bernard Benstock. Pittsburgh: University of Pittsburgh Press, 1970. 103–35.

Herr, Cheryl. *Joyce's Anatomy of Culture.* Urbana: University of Illinois Press, 1986.

Joyce, James. *Finnegans Wake.* New York: Penguin, 1978.

Lammers, John H. "The Archetypal Molly Bloom, Joyce's Frail Wife of Bath." *James Joyce Quarterly* 25 (1988): 487–502.

Maddox, Jr., James H. *Joyce's "Ulysses" and the Assault upon Character.* New Brunswick: Rutgers University Press, 1978.

Modleski, Tania. "Feminism and the Power of Interpretation: Some Critical Readings." *Feminist Studies/Critical Studies.* Ed. Teresa de Lauretis. Bloomington: Indiana University Press, 1986. 121–38.

New Hutchinson Family Singers. *The Joyce of Music.* Urbana: University of Illinois Press, 1983.

Riviere, Joan. "Womanliness as Masquerade." *Formations of Fantasy.* Ed. Victor Burgin, James Donald, and Cora Kaplan. London: Methuen, 1986. 35–44.

Treichler, Paula A. "Escaping the Sentence: Diagnosis and Discourse in 'The Yellow Wallpaper.' " *Feminist Issues in Literary Scholarship.* Ed. Shari Benstock. Bloomington: Indiana University Press, 1987. 62–78.

Tyler, Carole-Anne. "Female Impersonation." Diss. Brown University, 1989.

Unkeless, Elaine. "The Conventional Molly Bloom." *Women in Joyce.* Ed. Elaine Unkeless and Suzette Henke. Urbana: University of Illinois Press, 1982. 150–68.

Williamson, Judith. "Images of 'Woman.' " *Screen* 24:6 (1983): 102–16.

PART 3
NEGOTIATING COLONIALISM

5

Molly's Resistance to the Union
Marriage and Colonialism in Dublin, 1904

Carol Shloss

What can James Joyce's character, Molly Bloom, tell us about Anglo-Irish politics at the turn of the century? If we agree with M. M. Bakhtin that the "internal politics of [a novel's] style (how the elements are put together) is determined by its external politics (its relation to alien discourse)" (284), then it is interesting to ask what elements of Molly's soliloquy at the end of *Ulysses* can act as indexes of the external political situation of women in Dublin in 1904. A soliloquy is not a dialogue, but it can be a form of responsive speech that reflects upon other relationships. Seen dialogically, Molly's knowledge, her silence, her biases, and her dissatisfactions can all signal much more than they might if we considered them in isolation. Even her relationships with men can reveal something about the conjugal suppression of Irish women in 1904 as well as the more general civil suppression of the Irish under George Wyndham's Unionist government during this part of her lifetime.

Not surprisingly, Ireland's status as a colonial nation, with England playing "the predominant partner" in the Empire, affected the institution of marriage within Ireland where questions of autonomy within partnership could also be at issue. We might say that the Irish nationalist drive toward Home Rule in the early 1900s left its mark on the ideas of individual men and women who were faced in the private sphere with home rule issues of their own: to what extent did one cooperate in the success of one's marriage, actively sorting out the differences between reciprocal obligations, legitimate grievances, and oppression? At what point and in what ways did one withdraw from or protest the inequitable demands of union? Ultimately Molly's rambling thoughts and reflections raise a question that is central to all people to whom effective political self-definition is denied: what strategies of resistance can be used when the means of redressing perceived inequities are not immediately at hand?

At first this seems to be a particularly elusive question to answer, for Molly Bloom gives the impression of being apolitical and even hostile to the problems of collective life. She disparages Mrs. Riordan for having "too much old chat in her about politics" (18.608), and although we could read this as a mark of her unhappiness about Mrs. Riordan's former intimacy with Bloom, Molly insists on separating herself from women who speak their minds in public: "Miss This Miss That Miss Theother lot of sparrowfarts skitting around talking about politics they know as much about as my backside" (18.627).[1] Priding herself on knowing "more about men and life when I was 15 than theyll all know at 50" (18.627), she turns her attention to the lover who had just left her, to the idiosyncrasies of her husband, and to memories of girlhood, courtship, and the early years of her marriage.

Despite these disclaimers, Molly Bloom is not without knowledge of political life, and, in fact, it is often dislike of what she knows that leads her to turn back to the private sphere and toward its implicit possibilities for change and renewal. "I hate the mention of politics" (18.616), she repeats as she goes into the details of war in the Transvaal: "Pretoria and Ladysmith and Bloemfontein where Gardener Lieut Stanley G 8th Bn 2d East Lancs Rgt . . . they could have made their peace in the beginning . . . the old Krugers go and fight it out between them instead of dragging on for years killing" (18.616–17). It is only later that we learn that Gardner was someone she had once known who was killed in South Africa.

Other aspects of her political awareness seem to have come either from reading newspapers (she mentions *The Irish Times, Lloyd's Weekly News, Freeman's, Photo Bits,* and *The Gentlewoman's Chronicle*) or from conversations with her husband about everything from Christ's status as the first socialist (18.612) to British field marshal Sir Garnet Wolseley's maneuvers at Khartoum in the Sudan (18.623). Her most recurrent thoughts are those that deal with problems closer to home. Molly thinks about problems with Bloom, and she disagrees with his assessment of certain issues. At one point she remembers that "all the

Doyles said he was going to stand for a member of Parliament O wasnt I the born fool to believe all this blather about home rule and the land league . . . [and] rigmaroling about religion and persecution" (18.634).

At another time, she speaks about Arthur Griffith, whose news-paper articles about "The Resurrection of Hungary" were appearing in *The United Irishman* in 1904. Griffith had written these essays to suggest a parallel between the Hungarians, who had used a unified passive resistance to secure their independence from the Austrian Empire, and the Irish, who might use a similar pacifism as an alternative to the physical force policy of the Irish Republican Army or the co-operative incremental policy of the Irish Parliamentary Party (O'Neal 49). Bloom, as we know from his musings during the day, concurs with Griffith, and rumor has it that "Bloom gave the idea for Sinn Fein to Griffith" (12.275). It is through her husband's eyes that Molly sees Griffith: "he says that little man he showed me without the neck is very intelligent the coming man Griffiths is he" (18.616).

But these instances of specific political knowledge do not negate the generally private nature of Molly's thought during the night. She remains primarily concerned with men, with issues of relationship, and with a sense of being that is firmly rooted in the body. Never unaware of the husband who is sleeping "upside down" beside her, her thoughts return to him, to the sexual experience she has just had with Blazes Boylan, and to the significance of her own behavior. Her memories bring pleasure as well as dissatisfaction, and, indeed, it is the interplay between these poles of feeling that lends Molly's rev-eries special interest. For in her rambling assessment of her situation, we can see a pattern of response, which far from being irrelevant to the Irish political situation, acts as a gauge for it. Although pri-vate and public remain separate domains in Molly's consciousness, it is nonetheless true that her sensitivity to the issues of authority, privilege, and financial dependence in her relationships with men cor-responds with sentiments held by Irish nationalists in their dealings with England. Both women in marriage and the Irish population in thrall to a colonial government faced a kind of benevolent paternal-ism that sought to disguise the internal contradictions of union in the language of equity and concern. For both groups, responses to domi-nation had to be forged without any general agreement about what constituted an effective strategy of resistance or even a consensus about how to articulate grievances clearly. In 1904 both groups were disorganized and emerging out of silence, poised before the "speech act" of 1916 when the Easter Rising made clear the limits of nation-alist patience and long before the road to female suffrage had been paved, a movement which was not effectively organized until the Irish Women's Franchise League (I. W. F. L.) was formed in 1908.

The social and legal parameters of Molly's life would have been shaped by George Wyndham who, in 1904, had been Chief Secretary in Ireland for four years. The friend and successor of Gerald Balfour, he believed that the policy that he had inherited could be "progressively developed" (O'Halpin 24). He focused his attention on the land issue, on the demand for university education for Catholics, and somewhat later, on bureaucratic reorganization and the "devolution" of political power to local boards. Like the Balfours, he believed that the reason for Irish restlessness within the Empire lay in a series of widespread social and economic grievances; and, like them, he believed that disposing of or "ameliorating" these grievances would guarantee acquiescence in the union.

Balfour's most famous (notorious) statement of purpose had been produced in 1895 for a *National Review* symposium on "Unionist Policy for Ireland" and was reported in the 17 October 1895 *Times*. Here he generated the phrase "kill[ing] home rule with kindness" to describe the intentions of his party:

I do not for a moment suggest that that implies that the majority of the Irish people have lost their desire for home rule. On the contrary, I have not the slightest doubt that, if they had to vote again on the subject tomorrow, they would again vote for home rule as they voted for it at the last election. . . . We should be glad enough, no doubt, to kill home rule with kindness if we could, but whatever may be the result of our efforts, our intention is to do our utmost to introduce and pass such measures as will really promote the interests of the material prosperity of Ireland. (cited in Gailey 35)

Although his statement clearly distinguished between the innate rightness of his remedial measures (they will "promote the interests of the material prosperity of Ireland") and the intent to "kill" Home Rule, it was the phrase itself that was decontextualized and remembered by nationalists and unionists alike. Wyndham knew that the heart of Balfour's strategy had been "coercion and conciliation," that is, that he had tackled the root economic causes of unrest in Ireland while dealing severely with disorder. Although he modified the balance of Balfour's plan, leaning more on concession than on force for the containment of disorder, he essentially carried forward the practical commitments and political philosophy of his predecessor. Both men were imperialists who believed fervently in the moral rightness of the British Empire.

Judging the greatest agitation in Ireland to be provoked by the issues of land ownership, Wyndham first turned his attention in 1901 to major land reform. In doing this, he was opposing party feeling in Britain, where issues of law and order were more popular than the " 'invisible' economic measures of official policy" (Gailey 176). He was in turn opposed by the Irish Parliamentary Party which, "spurred on by the United Land League [U.L.L.] on its flank, indulged in obstructive tactics not seen since Parnell's heyday" (177). Writing to the editor of *The Spectator*, a Professor Dicey of Magee College expressed British sentiments when he observed that "it is the merest delusion that we can keep on friendly terms with nationalists. There must be fighting and incessant fighting, though the fight must be carried on fairly" (178). Wyndham was fully aware of these English attitudes, but he felt that relentless coercion would throw Redmond's Parliamentary party fully to the U.L.L. and in the end strengthen his Irish opposition. Consequently, he stalled on implementing coercive measures, but by 1902 the British cabinet had compelled him to put the Crimes Act into effect, "proclaiming" fully half the country including Dublin (182). What he feared happened, for the alienated Irish withheld their support of his first land bill which had to be withdrawn from Parliament.

This stalemate was partially resolved by changes in government personnel: Arthur Balfour became prime minister; C. T. Ritchie took over the Irish Office of the Treasury, and Anthony MacDonnell became Wyndham's new undersecretary. MacDonnell, a forty-year veteran of the Indian civil service, not only shared Wyndham's imperialist perspective but was also an expert on land reform and famine prevention. He seemed a superb ally to have at this moment, for he had already dealt successfully with the problems that faced Wyndham in Ireland, a "cycle of famine, popular agitation and political terrorism" (Gailey 184). Together they reapproached the British cabinet to urge its support for land reform, tax relief, and a Catholic university as the basis for future Irish loyalty to the Empire.

When John Shawe-Taylor called for a conference of landlord and tenant representatives in 1902, Wyndham saw this as an opportunity to win back his initiative in Irish politics. When John Redmond (I.P.P.) and William O'Brien (U.L.L.) also came out in support of such a conference, Wyndham felt, once again, that the "land war" in Ireland could be settled definitely. By 1903 negotiations over the legal and financial terms of the bill were accomplished: essentially the imperial Treasury would make up the difference between what the tenant could pay and what the landlord could afford. With this, the land structure of rural Ireland was transformed.

This abbreviated account of land reform in 1903 leaves out the intricacies of persuading the cabinet, the Treasury, and the party to act together, but it does let us see a structure of decision-making and a concomitant set of social attitudes. For this plan to work, the chief secretary had to usurp some of the Treasury's authority for financing Irish programs, but he remained antagonistic to any Irish attempts to wrest authority for self-governance from him.

Although there was undoubted good will and British consensus involved in this piece of legislation, Wyndham never forgot that the ultimate goal of such reform measures was the acquiescence of the Irish to beneficent British rule. He did not really want the cooperation of the two countries as partners with full parity, but he saw the measure, instead, as a sign that the Irish would henceforth consider the Castle a "remedial and beneficent instrument" (Gailey 187) responsible to Irish needs and would cease to press for independent decision-making powers. "Ireland is in a plastic state," he wrote to Balfour on 4 November 1903. "We can mould her almost at will provided that we go on doing something over here. We must give the Irish something sensible to think about and work for. Otherwise they relapse into a position of being mere pawns in a game between rival politicians" (quoted in Gailey 198).

Wyndham's predictions about future consensus proved to be wrong—both because he had not fully quieted the Irish opposition (Michael Davitt, for example, remained against the bill) and because his future dealings with his own undersecretary on the "devolution issue" (which came to a head in 1904) made clear his essential opposition to Home Rule and his continued belief in an all-powerful paternalistic state that would rule in the "best interests" of the ruled (Gailey 187).

Without delving more deeply into the conflict of internal loyalties and prejudices that characterized the Unionist government in these years, it is still possible to see the strategic position that was left to Irish nationalists as a consequence of these kinds of policy-making procedures. Because they were designed to coopt opposition by material benefit, one could acquiesce in gratitude for gain, or one could resist. One could accept a consultative role, or one could agitate. But in no circumstance could the Irish initiate national policy with the expectation of success. The effect of Wyndham's mode of governance was to leave people in better material circumstances but powerless to ensure their own continued self-interest.

It is this situation of corporate powerlessness within a supposedly benign partnership that provides, for me, the most interesting context for Molly Bloom's grumblings on the evening of 16 June. For, seen in this light, her speech acquires a political status simply by being the kind of "guerilla" tactic that was, in 1904, common to any Irish resistance to unionism.

Joyce could not have been unaware of the rhetorical implications of such heckling, of "speech acts" like Molly's that are inherently political but that lack the power to make effective change. Indeed, one way to read Joyce's earlier work, *A Portrait of the Artist as a Young Man,* is to follow Stephen Dedalus's assault upon different kinds of corporate authority as he attempts to reconstitute his own power, or, as Vicki Mahaffey has argued so persuasively, to "reauthorize" himself by noncompliance.

This relationship between authority and verbal noncompliance is one of the issues that underlies Stephen's reflections on the English priest's insistence that a "tundish" is really a "funnel." He is confronted with one language that, in seeming to represent two cultures—the English and the Irish—succeeds only in expressing the voice of oppression:

—The language in which we are speaking is his before it is mine. How different are the words *home, Christ, ale, master,* on his lips and mine! I cannot speak or write these words without unrest of spirit. His language, so familiar and so foreign, will always be for me an acquired speech. I have not made or accepted its words. My voice holds them at bay. My soul frets in the shadow of his language. (189)

In this passage, Joyce articulates the linguistic dilemma of a colonial nation whose own cultural identity has been eclipsed by an invading authority. Stephen knows that English precludes Gaelic and that its ascendancy places him in history at a point when he, as a writer, can only borrow the words of one language and seek darkly for the older tongue whose use has been denied him. Caught between the foreign and the unknown, he locates authenticity in an "unborn" future that his writing will help to create.

What Stephen and the priest do in the face of their unvoiced antagonism is important to notice, for their behavior is emblematic of a strategy that many people, both men and women, use to negotiate unequal power relationships: knowing nothing of Stephen's bitterness, the priest urges him to persevere and to anticipate a successful end to his studies. A Belvedere professor then comes into the room to begin a lecture on applied science, while Stephen fades into the company of his fellow schoolmates who listen with increasing restlessness and ill-concealed rudeness: "Moynihan leaned down towards Stephen's ear and murmured:—What a price ellipsoidal balls! Chase me, ladies, I'm in the cavalry! . . . Moynihan . . . began to call with the voice of a slobbering urchin:—Please, teacher! Please, teacher! This boy is after saying a bad word, teacher" (192–93). Amid this heckling, "[t]he droning voice of the professor continued to wind itself slowly round and round the coils it spoke of, doubling, trebling, quadrupling its somnolent energy as the coil multiplied its ohms of resistance" (194).

Like the electrical demonstration that he conducts in front of the students, the professor's voice coils and is met by recoil. Although he has control of the discourse, his speech engenders its own resistance. The young men in the gallery show their unwillingness through "guerilla" tactics similar to the ones Molly Bloom uses at the end of the day: knowing that their conflicts with this particular representative of English authority cannot be resolved through argument and rebuttal, they snipe, they heckle, they mock. They refuse to acquiesce, but they stop short of open rebellion. Stephen dislikes his classmates. "Can you say with certitude," he asks, "by whom the soul of your race was bartered and its elect betrayed—by the questioner or by the mocker?" (193–94); but we should remember that it is his denigration of Others, it is his decision to give up on them and to leave, that has led us to ignore the unexpressed, or barely expressed, or badly expressed, desperation of those who are left behind in Ireland and who remain below the level of political discourse. Like rude and ineffectual children, Stephen's Irish compatriots whisper "two and two behind their hands" (192).

Molly's disorganized speech can be read, then, in the terms established by the classroom in *Portrait*, where science and nonscience, authority and a discredited Other confront one another in unequal battle. The distinction lies, of course, in the issue of gender, for the terms of domination and suppression, of expression and silence, have been transformed from "England" and "Ireland" in their struggle with the union to "male" and "female" without changing the issues of marginality and the inadequacy of cultural representation that remain at the heart of Joyce's concern in both books. In fact, what remains in *Ulysses* is evidence of the double alienation that history has generally bestowed upon women under colonial rule, where gender has established yet another mode of dispossession from the political and cultural arena. "How different are the words . . . on his lips and on mine! I cannot speak or write these words without unrest of spirit" (*Portrait* 189) might serve to express Molly's sentiments as well as those of Stephen Dedalus. "His language," he or she might say, "so familiar and so foreign, will always be for me an acquired speech. I have not made or accepted its words" (189).

Certainly these are the thoughts of anyone who has been dispossessed by the world he or she is forced to inhabit or who understands, however obliquely, that the script of the dominant culture precludes authentic self-expression. Like Stephen who uses language as a weapon, Molly drones on at the end of *Ulysses.* "My voice holds them at bay" (*Portrait* 189). For each of them, the act of speaking, however inchoately, is itself a political act, an act of assertion, a search for definition in the face of a domineering Other.

What else could Molly Bloom have done in 1904 had she wanted to assert herself more effectively in the world? Neither her legal position nor her status as a citizen, wife, and mother would have empowered her. If we look at 1904 not only as a year in the struggle for Irish independence from England but also as a year in the movement of women for citizenship in the British Isles, we would find an equally compelling (and discouraging) set of circumstances that would have confronted Molly. All of them would have affected the way that she experienced her marriage and, indeed, her very sense of the reaches of her own authority in life.

She would have had some rights and protections.[2] The "Poor Law Guardian, Ireland (Women) Act" of 1896 would have made her eligible to be a Poor Law Guardian, and the "Irish Local Government Act" of 1898 had reorganized local government so that women who had been previously excluded from the municipal franchise were made eligible for Rural and District Councils (Blackburn 270). But, even barring the great issue that faced British and Irish women alike—the right to vote in national elections—Ireland lagged far behind England in other matters of legal concern for women. Molly would not have been allowed, even in cases of aggravated assault, to get a separation order; she would not have been given custody of Milly, had divorce been possible; she had no right to the money she earned by singing in concert, nor could she have invested money or held property in her own name. The home at 7 Eccles Street did not belong to her. Had Bloom died, the court would not have appointed her guardian of her own child unless he had specified it as his wish, nor would she have had claim to even a minimum share in his estate had he died intestate.[3] In short, quite apart from the fact of her political disenfranchisement on the national level, Molly would have known herself to be the lesser member of a marital union with a male "predominant partner." This would have been so no matter how much kindness or private affection may have tempered Bloom's responses to her. In 1904 Irish marriage was from the legal perspective very much like Wyndham's unionist rule of Ireland. Both were institutions predicated on an unequal distribution of power over property, finance, inheritance, and "voice," and both sought to finesse, accommodate, and neutralize resistance by means of conciliatory gestures.

Given her unequal status in so intimate an institution as marriage, it is little wonder that Molly's thoughts remain so consistently rooted in the intricacies of personal relationships, for they were the very forms through which the political world made its power known to her. She had no direct access to authority nor even an organization for voicing opposition. The movement to make Irish women citizens lay several years in the future, and even its later vicissitudes showed how fully issues of parity between the two genders informed the nationalist drive for Home Rule.

Far from being "acutely sensitive to the relativity of language . . . to political power," as Joseph Valente (59) has argued,[4] the Irish Nationalists would prove to be as determined to keep women voiceless as the English had been with regard to them. When the general election of February 1910 shifted the balance of power between the Liberal government and the Unionists in England, the Irish Party found itself able to press the Liberals for another Home Rule Bill as a condition for their continued support (Ward 22). Clearly British "kindness" had not succeeded in mitigating their desire for independence.

But as Anna Haslam, Hanna Sheehy-Skeffington, and Gretta Cousins, all active Dublin feminists, were to discover, this did not prevent the Party's being unkind to them. Not only did the Irish Party reject the idea of a "predominant partner," but they also rejected the idea of partnership altogether. John Redmond, the leader of the Irish Nationalists, was vehemently opposed to women's enfranchisement, and although the I.W.F.L. was intent on ensuring that votes for women be incorporated within the proposed Home Rule Bill (Ward 24), he persisted in believing that including women in the bill would divide the nationalist ranks and also lead to the resignation of British Prime Minister Asquith. Should the Liberal government fail, Redmond reasoned, the Home Rule Bill would be jeopardized just as completely as it had been in the time of Parnell. Kitty O'Shea, in one generation, and the women suffragists in the next, played the role of demon lovers whose acknowledgment had broken/would break the solidarity and effectiveness of the Irish Party. Despite a variety of tactics on the part of women—some of them rhetorical and some of them violent[5]—the Home Rule Bill of 1913 left the women of Ireland without a vote.

C. P. Scott, editor of *The Manchester Guardian*, "tried to urge [Redmond] to reconsider his attitude by pointing out the inconsistency of a Home Rule party betraying the very principle of Home Rule—'that emancipation for Irish men [would be] purchased at the cost of its refusal for women' " (David Morgan, quoted in Ward 26), and the Irish-women's Suffrage Federation reiterated his view, saying "that nationalist opposition to the principle of woman suffrage contained in the Conciliation Bill would be 'an act of hostility to Irish women' " (Ward 26), but to no avail. Under Home Rule, women were to suffer from circumstances analogous to the repression that men and women had both endured under the English Unionist Party. Only when Padraic Pearse read the Republican Proclamation in front of the General Post Office at the Easter Rising of 1916 was the principle of equal citizenship for Irish men and Irish women reaffirmed. In 1922 the franchise was finally extended to women.

All of these struggles for women's independence lay ahead of Molly in 1904. Anna Haslam, a Quaker woman whose interest in higher education and employment for women had resulted in the foundation of the Queen's Institute (Molesworth Street), was active in her support of women's suffrage in Dublin (Blackburn 129), but no organized, vocal group existed for Molly to join, even had she possessed a more militant temperament.

Instead, Molly's resistance to the union—whether we understand "union" to mean the tie between England and Ireland or that between Bloom and herself—has been reduced to insurgency: she can withhold consent, she can complain, and she can engage in acts of subterfuge that undermine the structures of authority that bind her life. She does all three.

If she has not understood how to use knowledge or power or even how to imagine the full ramifications of her own cultural position, she has mastered a more fragmentary critical art. Like the students in Stephen Dedalus's physics lecture, she has learned how to heckle, to snipe, and to mock the script that continues to write limited cultural roles for her: "we have to be thankful for our mangy cup of tea itself as a great compliment to be noticed the way the world is divided" (18.617). Her dissatisfactions can be considered the beginning signs of insurrection, just as, on another level, her decision to take a lover is a second refusal of paternalistic tradition. Seen in this light, the political importance of Molly's affair with Blazes Boylan lies precisely in its symbolic "uncoupling" of that which has coupled her unjustly. It is a "speech act" against marriage, a refusal of its bonds.

To say this is not to make any claims about Leopold Bloom's strengths or deficiencies as a husband. But it is to notice the complexity of Irish marriage at the turn of the century, to insist on its analogy to colonial rule, and to see the structural inequities of both institutions with regard to women. If Molly's soliloquy is a catalogue of vigorous complaints and a litany of vague hopes for more autonomy ("they darent order me about the place its his fault" [18.632]), and if it only contains the rudiments of a narrative construct that might serve as a counterpart to Bloom's view of their marriage ("I declare some-body ought to put him in the budget if I only could remember the one half of the things and write a book out of it" [18.621]), it nonetheless shows the possibility of female resistance to male domination in 1904. The French historicist Michel Foucault would call Molly's coming-into-speech, in whatever halting way, "an insurrection of subjugated knowledge." Similarly, the American feminist Adrienne Rich would call it a "re-vision" or a seeing-again of cultural institutions that have seemed immutable but that are, in fact, the consequences of patriar-chal modes of organizating structures of knowledge, structures of art, and structures of social engagement. When Foucault was asked to explain the meaning of his terminology, he said:

I believe that by subjugated knowledges one should understand . . . a whole set of knowledges that have been disqualified as inadequate to their task or insufficiently elaborated: naive knowledges, located low down on the hier-archy, beneath the required level of cognition or scientificity. I also believe that it is through the reemergence of these low-ranking knowledges, these unqualified, even directly disqualified knowledges . . . that criticism performs its work. . . . To emancipate [them] from that subjection [is] to render them . . . capable of opposition and of struggle. (82–85)

Rich, whose interest in subjugated knowledge is more directly fo-cused on the suppression of women's knowledge of themselves, is, perhaps, a more appropriate critic to call on here, for she took the inspiration for one of her most influential essays from Henrik Ibsen, the dramatist who so deeply influenced Joyce. Amplifying the themes that she saw in Ibsen's *When We Dead Awaken*, she contended that "the sleepwalkers are coming awake": "Until we can understand the assumptions in which we are drenched we cannot know ourselves. [We should ask] how we have been led to imagine ourselves, how our language has trapped as well as liberated us; and how we can begin to see . . . afresh" (35). Rich's project was not, and is not, one that has been completed; and it was certainly not achieved by the Molly Bloom whom Joyce gives to us in the midst of tired, nighttime musings.

But both Foucault and Rich help us to understand how Molly's soliloquy is a kind of speech that is beginning to emerge and to be "capable of opposition and struggle." Given the limited political choices that she faced in 1904, we can see that "struggle"—the ability to say "no"—was as important to Molly as the ability to say "yes." And to be able to say "yes" need not have been an overwhelming endorsement of "love," even though Richard Ellmann would have liked us to think that.

Marriage demands loyalty that is inevitably divided between self-interest and the desires of the Other; it requires mediation between corporate and individual welfare; it is supported by the ability to negotiate differences. Domination rarely serves these goals, nor does unquestioned yielding. That Molly withholds consent from the terms of her marriage on Bloomsday is as significant as remembering that she said "yes I will" to Bloom years earlier on the hill of Howth.

Foucault, Rich, and Bakhtin would all have endorsed her contrariness. Bakhtin called these tendencies toward disunification "heteroglossia" or "dialogue" (272). He recognized that such verbal strategies, however disruptive, were at the same time dynamic, the sign that language "is alive and developing" as it must be in any union that strives to obliterate the need for a "predominant partner" and to maintain the social life of gendered languages.

Notes

1. In "Women, the Vote and Revolution," M. MacCurtain reports the comment of a parish priest in Ventry, County Kerry, who said "it was a sure sign of the breakup of the planet when women took to leaving their homes and talking in public" (49). This remark tells us not only that the priesthood opposed women's voices in political life at this time but also that Molly's view is a male-identified one, one acquired from the clergy. Her comment is also interesting in light of John Redmond's (the leader of the Irish Parliamentary Party) fear, articulated in 1911, that votes for women would increase the power of the Church.

2. As Countess Markievicz asserted in *The Irish Citizen*, "three great movements were going on in Ireland in those years, the national movement, the women's movement and the industrial one." To the students of the National Literary Society, Markievicz said in 1909, "Fix your minds on the ideal of Ireland free, with her women enjoying the full rights of citizenship in their own nation" (quoted in MacCurtain 52, 53).

3. Compare the 1830 and 1873 Custody of Infants Acts, 1878 Matrimonial Causes Act, 1870 Married Women's Property Act, 1886 Guardianship of Infants Act, and 1890 Intestates Act (Blackburn 271–72).

4. The full quotation is: "A national culture rediscovering itself amid another dominant one, awakening to its long-alienated language and customs, and feeling its everyday lifestyle correspondingly alien, will be even more acutely sensitive to the relativity of language, especially its relativity to political power" (Valente 59).

5. For an excellent discussion of the various suffrage movements in Ireland and the varieties of political strategies they chose, see Margaret Ward.

Works Cited

Bakhtin, M. M. *The Dialogic Imagination.* Austin: University of Texas Press, 1981.

Blackburn, Helen. *Women's Suffrage: A Record of the Women's Suffrage Movement in the British Isles.* Oxford: Williams and Norgate, 1902.

Ellmann, Richard. "Preface." *James Joyce Ulysses: The Corrected Text.* Edited by Hans Walter Gabler. New York: Vintage, 1986. xi–xiv.

Foucault, Michel. "Two Lectures." *Power/Knowledge.* New York: Pantheon, 1980.

Gailey, Andrew. *Ireland and the Death of Kindness: The Experience of Constructive Unionism, 1890–1905.* Cork: Cork University Press, 1987.

Ignota. "The Present Legal Position of Women in the United Kingdom." *Westminster Review* 163 (1905): 513–29.

Joyce, James. *A Portrait of the Artist as a Young Man.* New York: Viking, 1965.

MacCurtain, M. "Women, the Vote and Revolution." Pp. 46–64 in Margaret MacCurtain and Donccha O'Corrain, eds., *Women in Irish Society: The Historical Dimension.* Westport, Conn.: Greenwood Press, 1979.

Mahaffey, Vicki. *Reauthorizing Joyce.* Cambridge: Cambridge University Press, 1988.

O'Halpin, Eunan. *The Decline of the Union: British Government in Ireland, 1892–1920.* Syracuse: Syracuse University Press, 1987.

O'Neal, Daniel. *Three Perennial Themes of Anticolonialism: The Irish Case.* Denver: University of Denver Monograph Series in World Affairs, 1976.

Rich, Adrienne. "When We Dead Awaken: Writing as Revision." *On Lies, Secrets and Silence.* New York: Norton, 1979.

Valente, Joseph. "The Politics of Joyce's Polyphony." Pp. 56–72 in Bonnie Kime Scott, ed. *New Alliances in Joyce Studies.* Newark: University of Delaware Press, 1988.

Ward, Margaret. "'Suffrage First—Above All Else!' An Account of the Irish Suffrage Movement." *Feminist Review* 10 (1982): 21–36.

6

Mapping Gibraltar
Colonialism, Time, and Narrative in "Penelope"

Susan Bazargan

We start transparent, and then the cloud thickens. All history
backs our pane of glass.

Virginia Woolf, *Jacob's Room*

I begin with a simple question: Why Gibraltar as Joyce's choice of
origins for his Penelope? In "Toward an Historical Molly Bloom," an
important essay that supplies much needed information concerning
the realistic background of Molly's life in Gibraltar, Phillip Herring
explains Joyce's interest in the colony in terms of epic geography and
biographical significance: Dante's Ulysses had to navigate the Pillars
of Hercules, part of the "end of the world" as Gibraltar was known to
ancient sailors; Nora's Willie Mulvey was stationed in Gibraltar, and
Nora hailed from Galway, a city with Spanish connections (518). I suggest—without trying to establish Joyce's intentions—that the significance of Gibraltar can be mapped in yet another territory. By extending
the topography of his text to Gibraltar, Joyce was able to (1) synec-
dochically represent British imperialism, (2) project colonialism in its
contemporary, international guise in his study of the displaced and the
dispossessed, and (3) associate the theme of colonialism and its implications with his female persona. Placing Molly Bloom's beginnings
in Gibraltar enabled Joyce to offer us an intricately drawn portrait of
the modern female colonial identity in which complications of race
and religion are compounded by those of nationality, language, and
gender.

Gibraltar's position as a synecdochic representation of British imperial power is well described in one of the sources Joyce used to gather information on the peninsula, Henry M. Field's *Gibraltar:*

> Gibraltar . . . may be considered the centre of the military life of England. True, the movements of the Army are directed by orders from the Horse Guards in London. But here the military feature is the predominant, if not the exclusive, one; . . . [I]f you are interested in the history of modern wars, . . . you may not only read about them in the Garrison Library, but see the very men that have fought in them. . . . A regiment recalled from Halifax is quartered near another just returned from Natal or the Cape of Good Hope; while troops from Hong Kong, or that have been up the Irrawaddi to take part in the late war in Upper Burmah, can exchange experiences with their brother soldiers from the other side of the globe. Almost all the regiments collected here have figured in distant campaigns, and the officers that ride at their head are the very ones that led them to victory. (48–49)[1]

But besides being an imperial crossroad, Gibraltar, occupied by the British, in population African, Spanish, Jewish, Moroccan, Maltese, and Genoese, presents the modern-day colonial situation in which the categories of the colonizer and the colonized are splintered to reveal multiple layers of subcolonization, conflictual interests among oppositional groups of various nationalities, which are separated not only by class and economic distinctions but also by race and religion. In Gibraltar, colonialism, as in its many contemporary forms, infected not only the main players and counterplayers (the British vs. the Spanish) but also exiles and refugees—often fleeing war and persecution—such as the Arabs and the persecuted Sephardim, the Spanish Jews. The latter people's history of exile includes settlements in Morocco (beginning in the fourteenth century) and resettlements in Gibraltar (beginning in the fifteenth century and extending to the nineteenth).[2] As Herring reminds us, "Eleven years before Molly Bloom's birth, in 1858, over 3,000 Moroccan Jews fleeing the impending Spanish-Moroccan War arrived in Gibraltar, where they camped in tents on the North Front, and were supported in large part by local Jews, whom the refugees outnumbered" (510). Molly's mother, Lunita Laredo, was a local Jew, with Moroccan associations. Thus Gibraltar also made it possible for Joyce to introduce Jewish and Arab elements in his heroine's genealogy, opening the way for him to explore a theme that appears in as early a work as "The Sisters" and reverberates in *Ulysses:* Orientalism.

The complications in Molly's genealogy instigate the series of ambivalences characteristic of modern-day émigrés and exiles with divided allegiances to dual (sometimes multiple) nationalities and languages. The divisions can best be scrutinized by projecting Gibraltar not tangentially, as an "exotic" landscape, but as a space of colonization with significant political and psychological dimensions. These contours often find dyadic or dialogical shape, a chiasmatic chain binding issues of language, power, and temporality.[3] Thus, unlike Herring, who is ultimately dissatisfied with Joyce's portrayal of Molly, I find her a most convincing representation of a modern-day colonized identity. Despite his careful delineation of Molly's "real" history, Herring dismisses Gibraltar as "a dash of local color in the drab landscape of Dublin that was never meant to be examined closely, one of the many qualities in a composition that is Molly Bloom. . . . In the final chapter of *Ulysses* Joyce was faced with an artistic problem which, given his publishing deadlines, he hadn't the time or space to resolve very effectively" (516, 518). Among the reasons Herring cites for Molly's lack of credibility are her ignorance of such facts as the existence of appalling poverty and disease in Gibraltar (505). More important, according to Herring, is the "problem" of Molly's language; given her fifteen years of life in Gibraltar, she must be "surprisingly forgetful" to lose her Spanish and keep her "undiluted Irish brogue" (516). But both of these elements, a repression of the horror of life in the colony (often transformed into the idealized lost Eden for the likes of Kipling), alongside the desire for belonging to (or quickly assimilating into, in the case of immigration) the parent culture, often at the expense of eliding the native one, are at the crux of an identity formed in a colonial setting.

At the core of the colonial psyche lie ambivalence and contradiction since colonialism, in essence, operates on opposing principles. The colonizer's position as " 'the Father and the oppressor . . . just and unjust' . . . reinscribes both colonizer and colonized" (Bhabha, "Sly Civility" 74). Colonialism is built on institutions which incarcerate human beings while "civilizing" them. To use Homi Bhabha's succinct formulation: "The barracks stand by the church which stands by the schoolroom; the cantonment stands hard by the 'civil lines' " ("The other question" 172). The identity of the colonized, then, in its barest outlines, is shaped by dualistic forces engendering a divided existence. Molly's case is made even more complicated by the fact that she has lived both in Gibraltar (as the daughter of a "Major") and in Ireland, and has thus internalized structures of thought and discourse associated with both the colonizer and the colonized. Reflecting such spatial dislocations and discrepancies is Molly's splintered, internally dialogic language.

The ambivalence at the heart of the colonial identity is evident in Molly's contradictory constructions of beginnings and endings in respect to her birthplace. The first mention of Gibraltar in her internal

dialogue occurs at a rare moment of contemplation on fear, punish-
ment, and sin, when she recalls awakening to the sound of thunder.
The occasion echoes Vico's notion on beginnings—it was the fear of
thunder that first drove human beings into caves, where human civilization began. But it also bears apocalyptic messages of doom: "till that
thunder woke me up God be merciful to us I thought the heavens were
coming down about us to punish us when I blessed myself and said
a Hail Mary like those awful thunderbolts in Gibraltar as if the world
was coming to an end" (18.134–37). Yet, in contrast to this mapping of
the territory, associated with wrathful, punitive beginnings and endings, is the euphoric, exotic image of Gibraltar as it appears in the
climactic scene of her narrative. And in between these two diverging
images unfolds Molly's history as lived and recollected by her.

Divergences and hierarchical divisions are of course built into the
rituals of daily life in a colony. Molly remembers the gunshots that
began the day at dawn and at sunset announced the closing of gates
which barred all natives from entering the garrison after dark (18.685–
89). This division of life into two territories occupied by the rulers
and the ruled has its clear boundaries, marking inside and outside.
But Joyce, as if to point out the sheer artifice of the master/slave di-
chotomy, endows Molly with a social status that places her in that
ambiguous third zone, the "median category" (Said 58), the category
most difficult to analyze in discussions of colonialism. The ambiguity
of Lunita Laredo's origin, a Jewess and perhaps a prostitute, in turn
makes Molly's position one that vacillates between the inside and the
outside, even if she would like to remain within the safe boundaries
of the gates. Having no place in the garrison, Lunita was replaced by
Spanish servants like Mrs. Rubio. Although clearly resentful toward
the conquerors (18.754–56), Mrs. Rubio seems to have integrated African and Spanish elements of life on the Rock—she worships "her
black blessed virgin with the silver dress" (18.759)—and to have cared
enough for Molly to introduce her to the work of the Renaissance poet
Juan Valera Y Alcalá Galiano (18.1475). Molly, of course, prefers to
read English novels such as *The Shadow of Ashlydyat* rather than a book
given to her by a representative of the outside, a "rock scorpion," a
racial epithet used by the British garrison to describe native residents
of Gibraltar.

Besides the issue of parental race and social origin, Molly's nationality also contributes to her ambivalence. She is keenly aware of Irish
subservience, as it is registered in linguistic deflections. She worries
that Gardner "mightnt like my accent first he so English" (18.889–90).
Her father, Tweedy, is at best a second-order citizen in the British

army. Based on his military experiences, he deserves, perhaps, to be a true "Major" but is only a drill sergeant.[4] Tweedy falls into that category Paulo Freire calls the "sub-oppressors" (30). As "hosts" of the oppressors, the colonized, the oppressed—whose only models of existence have been supplied by those in power—find that *"to be is to be like,* and *to be like* is *to be like the oppressor"* (33). At home, with Molly "lighting their pipes for them" (18.691), Tweedy and "captain" Grove occupy themselves by getting drunk and swapping tales of military exploits.

Having been schooled, as servant to a servant, in military colonialism, Molly, even after twenty years in Dublin, cannot extricate herself from British colonial aspirations. That she has retained some of her British sympathies despite her apparent Irishness ("I had a map of it all" 18.378) is shown in her support for the Boer War, which has cost her dearly. A year before, having angered the nationalists (who vehemently opposed the British conduct during the Boer War), she was replaced by "little chits of missies they have now singing" at St Teresas Hall (18.375–76). She recalls wearing a brooch for Lord Roberts, the Indian-born, Anglo-Irish commander-in-chief of the Boer War, and singing Kipling's propaganda song "The Absentminded Beggar" (Gifford and Seidman 614).

In less obvious ways, Molly is interpellated by colonial ideology, whose chiasmatic links of power and language bind together political authority and sexual dominance. Ashis Nandy, in his penetrating study of colonialism, focuses on this dyadic interrelation:

The homology between sexual and political dominance which Western colonialism invariably used . . . was not an accidental by-product of colonial history. . . . The homology, drawing support from the denial of psychological bisexuality in men in large areas of Western culture, beautifully legitimized Europe's post-medieval models of dominance, exploitation and cruelty as natural and valid. Colonialism, too, was congruent with the existing Western sexual stereotypes and the philosophy of life which they represented. It produced a cultural consensus in which political and socio-economic dominance symbolized the dominance of men and masculinity over women and femininity. (4)

British rule in India, as Nandy mentions, was to a great degree established when both the British rulers and the Indians had internalized "the language of the homology between sexual and political stratarchies" (6). In British analyses of Irish culture, too, we find the same homology operating. Matthew Arnold—whose face appears in the context of Stephen's broodings on British "palefaces" or conquerors (1.166)—produced some of the most influential arguments promoting

British rule in Ireland based on the superiority of the "masculine" Teutons against the Irish, who were "an essentially feminine race" (Cairns and Richards 46, 48).

The homology between colonial and sexual dominance is beautifully captured in a central icon in Joyce's text: the Blooms' bed, a piece of one colony transported into another, the space in which we locate Molly both at the beginning and the ending of the day/book. Unlike Bloom, Molly knows the real origins of the bed: a pawnshop, as a colony often is. Besides commenting ironically on its Homeric counterpart, Bloom's misconceptions about the bed—that it belonged to the governor of Gibraltar—serve to underline his illusions about correlations between political power and sexuality. A persecuted Jew in Irish society—because he is "not Irish enough" as Molly puts it (18.379)—Bloom in bed has to urge Molly to "think of him [the german Emperor]" "yes imagine Im him" "can you feel him" (18.95–96). Molly, of course, finds the idea revolting: "trying to make a whore of me"; and yet both her and Bloom's sexual identities cannot extricate themselves from colonial teachings on power, biological stratification, and sexual stereotypes. The most blatant of these is Bloom's preoccupation with Molly as the "Oriental" woman, a construct of male Western imagination, an object of both desire and terror. She is thus fetishized by him, as colonial subjects often are. Bhabha's analysis of the fetish may illuminate the sexual dynamics unfolding at 7 Eccles Street:

> The fetish or stereotype gives access to an 'identity' which is predicated as much on mastery and pleasure as it is on anxiety and defence, for it is a form of multiple and contradictory belief in its recognition of difference and disavowal of it. This conflict of pleasure/unpleasure, mastery/defence, knowledge/disavowal, absence/presence, has a fundamental significance for colonial discourse. For the scene of fetishism is also the scene of the reactivation and repetition of primal fantasy—the subject's desire for a pure origin that is always threatened by its division, for the subject must be gendered to be engendered. ("The other question" 161–62)

Bloom's fascination with his Semitic origins, evident all through the text, is fraught with deep ambivalence, as revealed by his contrasting reveries on the Orient during his early morning stroll (4.191–230). The same process of identification/disavowal, absence/presence, pleasure/unpleasure is replicated in his relationship with Molly. As fetish and stereotype, Molly may give access to Bloom's desire for (and simultaneous fear of) his Oriental origins; and yet ironically such an "origin" has to be divided, adulterated for Bloom to be "gendered." Hence his unconscious fantasies, dramatized in the "Circe" episode, in which he watches Boylan and Molly having intercourse, or his more obvious acts of pimping for her.

Molly's sexual fantasies, her preoccupation with men, in turn also reflect a divided subject whose struggle to acquire agency can best be understood in light of critiques of colonialism. Franz Fanon, commenting on the formation of a black man's ego, writes:

> For him [the black man] there is only one way out, and it leads into the white world. Whence his constant preoccupation with attracting the attention of the white man, his concern with being powerful like the white man, his determined effort to acquire protective qualities—that is, the proportion of being or having that enters into the composition of an ego. . . . [I]t is from within that the Negro will seek admittance to the white sanctuary. . . . Ego-withdrawal as a successful defense mechanism is impossible for the Negro. He requires a white approval. (51)

Fanon's remarks to a great extent explain Molly's aspirations toward men and her attempts to protect and compose an ego by making entries into the male world. But it seems to me that she is granted what Fanon does not observe in the black man: ego-withdrawal as a defensive measure. While colonialism is imbricated in Molly's writing of the self, she also makes it—and its gender-based ramifications—to a great extent a subject of scrutiny, even mockery. Her resistance is shown in ways that Carol Shloss describes in this volume, but what empowers Molly as agent is also the hybridity, the dialogism, in her language. Bhabha has discussed the power of hybridity which allows the colonized to appropriate the language, the texts, the knowledge of the colonizer in such a way as to "estrange the basis of its authority—its rules of recognition" ("Signs" 175). It is the power of hybridity that enables the colonized to challenge "the boundaries of discourse," and which "breaks down the symmetry and duality of self/Other, inside/outside" (177) and establishes another space of power/knowledge.

If language is born in time/space, then the dialogism in Molly's narration can be examined more closely in the context of not only the rhetorical but also the temporal dimensions of her inner geographical space, the space in which Gibraltar and Dublin coalesce. This mental arena I will call, echoing Molly, a myriorama, a panoramic, shifting display of her past and present. A myriorama, the *OED* tells us, is a kind of "landscape kaleidescope" or a large picture composed of separate sections, which can be combined to form numerous scenes. "Pooles Myriorama" (18.40), which Molly visits, was a "travelogue with running commentary" (Gifford and Seidman 610), a progenitor of silent movies, in which often an obliging live narrator (sometimes accompanied by music) projected his voice on the screen. Molly's myriorama fuses these elements—spectacle and drama, commentary and song—in her complex, revolving mental kaleidescope. Thus my choice of the trope serves to describe her many-faceted mental odyssey, but more importantly, it coalesces time and space in describing Molly's writing or narration of the self—elements which have often been torn asunder in readings of this episode, at the expense of time (qualifiers such as "timeless" or "eternal" are often used to describe the narrative).

The temporal dimension of Molly's myriorama can be described as "chronotopic," a term that accentuates the modulatory qualities of time/space and links them to dialogical features of Molly's language and identity. Chronotope, as defined by M. M. Bakhtin, is "time space," the "intrinsic connectedness of temporal and spatial relationships that are artistically expressed in literature" (84). Unlike Kant, who used time and space as transcendental categories, Bakhtin insists on binding them to "immediate reality" (85). Furthermore, in its derivation from Einstein, chronotope maintains its grounds in variation and relativity. Meaning is made in time space or chronotope; as Gary Morson and Caryl Emerson have remarked, chronotopes "as senses of the world . . . may implicitly dispute (or agree with) each other. That is, the relation of chronotopes to each other may be *dialogic*" (369). Such dialogics are featured not only in the chronotopes of Molly's myriorama but also, as we shall see, in the rhetorical features of her discourse. Bakhtin relates the variation of chronotopes to genres, each with its own particular bindings of time and space. The chronotopes of Molly's narrative are characterized by an organic, concrete relation between time and space. Time, in her case, is phenomenological and cyclical, wedded intrinsically to geographical space, the space of colonization.

But let us momentarily depart from this general characterization of the chronotope informing Molly's narrative and consider the term in a more specific and heuristic manner, as a reference to the multiple variations and differentiations—the dialogics—in time space that cause the shifts in her myriorama. The variety of chronotopes in Molly's discourse indicate the liberating power of memory to fracture the past to make the present. The relativity in time/space resists authoritarian versions of history and chronology, linear models of history, which in Western cosmology have often supported domination and imperialism.[5] The shifting chronotopes in Molly's narrative are not, as her critics have alleged, a sign of her lack of a sense of time. Rather they affirm a sense of history and meaning in which time need not be uniformly defined but is invested with a sense of design by the knower/narrator who can mold, accentuate, and differentiate alternate experiences. Consider, for example, the following passage:

how long ago it seems centuries of course they never came back and she didnt put her address right on it either she may have noticed her wogger people were always going away and we never I remember that day with the waves and the boats with their high heads rocking and the smell of ship those Officers uniforms on shore leave made me seasick he didnt say anything he was very serious I had the high buttoned boots on and my skirt was blowing she kissed me six or seven times didnt I cry yes I believe I did or near it my lips taittering when I said goodbye she had a Gorgeous wrap of some special kind of blue colour on her for the voyage made very peculiarly to one side like and it was extremely pretty it got as dull as the devil after they went I was almost planning to run away mad out of it somewhere were never easy where we are father or aunt or marriage waiting always waiting to guiiiide him toooo me waiting nor speeeed his flying feet their damn guns bursting and booming all over the shop especially the Queens birthday and throwing everything down in all directions if you didn't open the windows when general Ulysses Grant whoever he was or did supposed to be some great fellow landed off the ship and old Sprague the consul that was there from before the flood dressed up poor man and he in mourning for the son (18.666–84)

Here Gibraltar comes to life in a variety of time spaces charged with a range of cognitive and emotional significance. Inside the larger temporal framework ("it seems centuries") are multiple time spaces, recording precise differentiations among experiences, their immediate impact, and their greater consequence. The sense of abandonment and insularity, characteristic of life in a colony where the desire is always to "go home," is conveyed through such precise moments as when Molly notes the absence of an address, signifying the loss of connection with life beyond Gibraltar; while her less specific references capture a more overwhelming feeling of desertion: "they never came back" and "people were always going away." Conveying a deeper understanding of loss are time spaces of two different parting scenes. The significance of Hester Stanhope's departure is revealed in the length and graphic details of the description, but intruding on the time space of this transitional scene is the silence of another—"he [Mulvey] didn't say anything"—brief in comparison, but perhaps keener in affect. Colonial insularity and the desire for escape are then seen in a broader context: the life of women, "never easy" and "always waiting." The words from the romantic song "Waiting," usually sung by the woman patiently waiting for the hero's return, here reinscribed—juxtaposed to "their damn guns bursting"—highlight the discrepancy between idealized versions of epic deeds and the actual violence and brutality of adventures abroad. Molly defuses the myth of the epic romance energizing many male concepts of heroism, adventure, and conquest. Heroes, even the real Ulysses in her story, are hardly glamorized. Greeting general Ulysses Grant, "whoever he was," is Sprague, the broken-down American consul, overcome by age and grief. Thus, in the amalgamation of various chronotopes, Molly not only displays the "thickness" of history as lived by her and others, but also reveals her resistance to authorized, male-empowered forms of time and recognition.

The chronotopic richness of Molly's myriorama is embedded in its rhetorical grounds, in the hybridity, the dialogism of her language. Readers of the "Penelope" episode usually refer to it as Molly's monologue or stream-of-consciousness, but in fact her discourse is anything but univocal. Molly's narrative is dialogic not only because it seems directed toward an interlocutor and informed by a variety of rhetorical stances, but also because it is characterized by those features essential to dialogism: her narrative is the site of interaction of a multiplicity of competing voices ("heteroglossia") and is imbricated by hybrid constructions that contain "two utterances, two speech manners, two styles, two 'languages,' two semantic and axiological belief systems" (Bakhtin 304).

Such hybridity characterizes a "dialogic self," one that reinscribes the duality of inside/outside, self/other, master/slave. Thus it seems to me that Bakhtin's theories on dialogism have direct applications to discussions of the interrelation of language and colonialism. Besides highlighting the hybrid element in colonial discourse, Bakhtin's writings on the "other" are particularly useful in analyzing the complexities of a colonized psyche, a self caught in that median category between the inside/outside, between competing belief systems. To realize a self, according to Bakhtin, one has to imagine oneself from the outside, address oneself to an other. This does not mean, however, that the self is actualized *only* from the outside. Bakhtin's theory of the self is in fact a triadic model, the three categories being "I-for-myself (how my self looks and feels to my own consciousness) . . . I-for-others (how my self appears to those outside it) and . . . the-other-for-me (how outsiders appear to my self)" (Morson and Emerson 180). The interaction among these categories generates the dialogic self; existence as "the condition of being addressed" (Holquist 27) and as responses to that condition, as "answerability." Thanks to the other (or others), the self is always incomplete and multiple. Without an other, one lives as if one had "an alibi for living" and aesthetic activity

degenerates into fantasy, which does not allow for or need otherness. And yet the relation between the self and other is always based
on nonfusion (Morson and Emerson 180–84). In fact, in authoring
the self, one needs to assimilate and reaccentuate language as given
("already made" belonging to others, i.e., authorial voices) to create
"innerly persuasive discourse" (one's own language). But the linchpin
in this process is the interlocutor who understands. Iris Zavala has put
it succinctly: "The 'listener' of the utterance (the 'third,' the one who
understands), establishes the relationship between the 'said' and what
is implied and what is unspoken: the 'given' and the 'created'" (46).

In a colonial context, the dynamics of addressivity and answerability are saturated with issues of power and domination. The
"already made," the authorial voices, daily reminders of the masters'
supremacy, constantly threaten to overwhelm one's innerly persuasive speech.[6] Hence the crucial significance of the listener, the "third"
in this case. Indeed, the existence of a third, the other who understands, is signaled by Molly's opening words, "yes" and "because,"
and implicit throughout her discourse:

> Yes because he never did a thing like that before as ask to get his breakfast
> in bed with a couple of eggs since the City Arms hotel when he used to be
> pretending to be laid up with a sick voice doing his highness to make himself
> interesting for that old faggot Mrs Riordan that he thought he had a great
> leg of and she never left us a farthing all for masses for herself and her soul
> greatest miser ever was actually afraid to lay out 4d for her methylated spirit
> telling me all her ailments she had too much old chat in her about politics and
> earthquakes and the end of the world let us have a bit of fun first God help the
> world if all the women were her sort down on bathingsuits and lownecks of
> course nobody wanted her to wear them I suppose she was pious because no
> man would look at her twice . . . her dog smelling my fur and always edging
> to get up under my petticoats especially then still I like that in him (18.1–16)

The *medias res* feature of these statements insinuates the tacit understanding of an ideal listener or confidante who presumably is familiar
with the implied, unspoken main clause of Molly's protest (which
begins with an adverbial clause, "because . . .") and now demands
the rest of the story. Thus the inaugural "yes" functions as a media-
tor, the bridge between the speaker and a nonthreatening listener,
between the given and the created, the understood and the articulated. Similarly "because" indicates a communicative gesture, an act
of answerability; it is an effort to explain, to justify her surprise at
Bloom's unusual request. Rhetorical embellishments in her language
such as "of course" and "I suppose" also mark its addressivity, evident in the variety of rhetorical positions she assumes. She *argues* her

case by presenting evidence from the past. The argumentative stance, however, is followed by a judgmental and critical one, in turn pursued by exhortative statements ("let us have a bit of fun first"), then by sarcasm and disdain ("of course nobody wanted her to wear them . . . I hope I'll never be like her") before it turns to an appreciative one ("still I like that in him").

The obvious question that must be raised at this point concerns the interlocutor in Molly's self-actualization. One might say that the "third" for Molly is a woman, her "superaddressee," the one who *really* understands, who "embodies a principle of hope" (Morson and Emerson 135) embedded in virtually every human utterance. Thus her listener is not unlike that of her progenitor, the distressed Penelope, lying awake in bed, speaking to a "dark dream image" in the likeness of her sister, a figure sent by Athene.[7] But one might also argue that the "other(s)" that Molly imagines are also male spectators. In authoring or writing a self, Molly has to consider what, in this volume, Richard Pearce discusses as the "male gaze." And inevitably, she has to assimilate male language in the dialogic self, even if her superaddressee is a woman. Molly's dialogic narration, then, emanates from the interaction of various competing internal and external forces, inscribed in the multiple turns of her narrative. As Bakhtin reminds us, "The internal politics of style . . . is determined by its external politics. . . . Discourse lives, as it were, on the boundary between its own context and another, alien, context" (284). Thus in investigating Molly's narrative, her innerly persuasive discourse (her "own" language), we need to consider both political realms: the external politics, which refer to the general context of colonialism and its dyadic components of sexual and political domination; the internal dynamics, which depend to some extent, on "I-for-myself."

The latter is shaped by but also resists the "alien context" of her language. Thus Molly's discourse emanates not exclusively from a colonial subtext but also from an interior bodily space (a space *not* defined by the male gaze), unverbalized, but manifested largely as a fluidity.[8] We might say that the highly individualized rhythm of her language is *analogous* to what Julia Kristeva calls the "semiotic rhythm," that "vocal and kinetic rhythm," the "air or song beneath the text," traces of the maternal body and that enigmatic space, the *chora,* which has no *law* (unlike the symbolic) but gestural and rhythmic organization (21–30). The semiotic in Molly's language can be associated with the deluge of her uninterrupted discourse that guards and determines the unique poetics of her expressions. Although the semiotic obviously does not dissolve the symbolic ordering of her language, it does infiltrate it to yield its unique shape, music, undulations, song, gestures—its poetry. In other words, it is the transgressive force of the semiotic that irrupts and remodels the symbolic drive of her narration.

In examining the mutations of Molly's text, Kristeva's distinction between the semiotic and the symbolic might offer us a heuristic device to approach Joyce's cryptic statement on this episode: "*Penelope* is the *clou* of the book. . . . Its four cardinal points being the female breasts, arse, womb and cunt expressed by the words because, bottom . . . woman, yes" (*Letters* 170). The association drawn here between erogenous zones and words such as because (signifying a causal, "logical" relationship) and "yes," denoting a *response* (an act of communication) may remind us of the two linguistic trends Kristeva associates with the two modalities of the semiotic and the symbolic. The first trend connects linguistic relations to the psychosomatic realm, linked to erogenous "zones of the fragmented body" (28). The second trend relegates itself to semantics and pragmatics, to language with "deep structures." Such a division is of course highly theoretical in nature: as Kristeva explains, "The subject is always *both* semiotic *and* symbolic" (24). Thus the signifying process of language is indebted to both these inseparable trends, locked in dialectical opposition, with the semiotic referring to instinctual drives within the body and the symbolic to the highly social realm of logical and intercommunicational skills.

The dialectical conflict between the semiotic and symbolic, the two modalities operating in language, can serve as a homology to explain the politics of Molly's narration. The semiotic mutations of her speech, registered in its rhythmic flow, are checked, "colonized" by symbolic orderings of language, and, furthermore, by her own desires toward addressivity in a territory—geographical and mental—of male discourse and domination. Molly's ambitions to know and express the self, including her own body, have to be realized in a sociopolitical realm controlled by symbolic logic and forms of communication, eventually enforced by male institutions. Thus in actual situations of addressivity and response involving men, Molly's verbal exchanges produce comic scenarios of frustrated communication. Witness, for example, her re-creation of a confession scene, the comic, futile dialogue with Father Corrigan. Alternating between roles, mimicking voices, her own and that of the priest, she produces a little drama replete with hybrid utterances. The "alien context" intruding on Molly's word is Father Corrigan's reproduction of the master discourse on sexuality. Offered by the Catholic church since the Middle Ages, this language, as Foucault has pointed out, has exploded into "distinct discursivities which took form in demography, biology, medicine, psychiatry, psychology, ethics, pedagogy, and political criticism" (33). Empowering this master discourse was, first, its positioning of sex as that which, "above all else, ha[d] to be confessed." Sex was presented as a "disquieting enigma" always hiding, "the insidious presence that speaks in a voice so muted and often disguised that one risks remaining deaf to it" (35). Second, while the Church took charge of sex and promised to "allow it no obscurity," it did so ironically "[u]nder the authority of a language that had been carefully expurgated so that it was no longer directly named" (20). The contradiction between the instigation to examine meticulously all movements of the body and soul but in a language that does not name itself generates much of the comedy in Molly's dialogic performance. Her resistance to the language of sexuality, as prescribed by the Church, is shown not only in the apostrophic asides—"what harm if he did"—but also in her overall refusal to yield to sexual mystification and indirect naming:

then I hate that confession when I used to go to Father Corrigan he touched me father and what harm if he did where and I said on the canal bank like a fool but whereabouts on your person my child on the leg behind high up was it yes rather high up was it where you sit down yes O Lord couldnt he say bottom right out and have done with it what has that got to do with it and did you whatever way he put it I forget no father and I always think of the real father what did he want to know for when I already confessed it to God (18.106–13)

The basic contradiction of confession vs. concealment operating in the above dialogue compels Molly's interpretive note marking the redundancy of the act: "what did he want to know for when I already confessed it to God." This instance is one among many other contradictory situations Molly finds herself in, thus earning the word "contradiction" as a logo for her verbal tapestry.[9] Yet contradiction is the *modus operandi* of a colonized psyche in which the duality of inside/outside has to be constantly challenged and shifted to establish one's own time/space and language.

Perhaps the most striking indications of Molly's efforts to resist the boundaries of discourse are found in her references to the texts most familiar to her, songs and lyrics. (Close to thirty of these are alluded to in "Penelope.") By recontextualizing a line from a ballad or lyric, in which sexual stereotypes are often reenforced, Molly produces alternate knowledge/power. As one example, we may refer to the following passage in which a phrase from "After the Ball" appears. This sentimental ballad, as Gifford and Seidman tell us, was "the story of an old man who has remained celibate because long ago his 'true love' apparently, but not really, deceived him: 'I believ'd her faithless, after the ball' " (616). The ballad insinuates the woman's guilt in causing the man's suffering. In Molly's appropriation of the line, this age-old scenario is corrected; the scene has changed dramatically but not radically. Male suffering here occurs in the form of masochistic sex games—"the ball"—in which the woman has become an involuntary participant: "that Ruby and Fair Tyrants he brought me that twice I remember when I came to page 50 the part about where she hangs him up out of a hook with a cord flagellate sure theres nothing for a woman in that all invention made up about he drinking the champagne out of her slipper after the ball was over" (18.492–96).

But Molly's ability to disperse authorial systems of power can best be witnessed in the context of the "primal" scene of her colonization, the space of Gibraltar. Witness, for example, her encountering what one might call, after Lacan and Althusser, a scene of misrecognition, that is, the moment when one class accepts and adopts its subordinate status by realizing the subservient image preferred to it by the ruling class (Cairns and Richards 13). Joyce's version, of course, is replete with comedy. Molly's literal exposure to British colonial "power" occurs at the focal point of Gibraltar's public life, in the Alameda Gardens. At the center of the Gardens—"where the statue of the fish used to be"—a Cameron Highlander, "the Queens own," exposes himself to Molly by pretending that "he was pissing standing out for me to see it" (18.547). But Molly has her way of deflecting the image, by thrusting it back on the aggressor, thus subverting him. Recollecting the night when, walking home with Bloom she had to use the men's facilities, she observes: "a pity a couple of the Camerons werent there to see me squatting in the mens place" (18.556–57).

The contradictions in Molly's narrative, while signs of a colonized psyche and its chiasmatic involutions, are also channels of critical awareness (contra-dict: to speak against). To echo Stephen, Molly's "errors" may be those of a "[wo]man of genius," leading to "portals of discovery" (9.229)—but at the cost of a split ego, temporarily healed through those final ambivalent, doubly resonant "yes"'s that attempt a fusion of presence and absence, of Gibraltar and Dublin, of the Moorish Wall and Howth Hill. Her history is that of the survival of the modern ego in exile, suffering from colonial angst, in perpetual displacement and transition, tracing, writing/seeing itself (and being seen) in and through the pane/pain of history.[10]

Notes

1.   As Field explains, Gibraltar was a key colonial post for the British. In a passage with rich symbolic resonances in *Ulysses* he says: "The object of this Rock fortress is to command the passage into the Mediterranean. The arms of Gibraltar are a Castle and a Key, to signify that it holds the key of the Straits" (120–21). Field's text is itself a fascinating example of colonial discourse in the sense that it is torn by a series of contradictions and ambivalences. On the one hand, Field exclaims his veneration for soldiers (48) and devotes the longest chapter in the book to "The Great Siege" of Gibraltar, but on the other, he confesses his hatred for guns: "As you climb the Rock, it fairly bristles with guns. You cannot turn to the right or the left without seeing these open-mouthed monsters, and looking into their murderous throats. Everywhere it is nothing but guns, guns, guns!" (22–23). (Field also describes the gun shots heard at dawn and sunset, and especially at the Queen's birthday, which Molly recalls.) Full of admiration for the British "masters" and "glad to see that they bring their English ideas and English customs with them" (32), Field, nonetheless, goes on to say "There is one thing in Gibraltar which strikes me unpleasantly, and yet . . . it is the very thing which has made it so attractive, viz., the English occupation" (110). While most of Field's text concerns itself with military life on the Rock, he seems most moved by its natural beauty and landscape. At sunset, once the sounds of guns have silenced and the gates of the garrison closed, "Then the sky is aflame where the sun has gone down in the Atlantic; and . . . the Straits . . . shine as if they were the very gates of gold that open into a fairer world than ours" (17). Field also mentions the flowers of Gibraltar, an emblem attached to Molly Bloom: "[W]ild flowers spring up almost as in Palestine" (12). He mentions "the almond-tree and the myrtle . . . the fragrance of locust and the orange blossoms . . . the clematis . . . and the red geranium" (13). But Field's depiction of the people of Gibraltar reveals his own racist prejudices: besides the Spaniards and the Moors, "Here are long-bearded Jews in their gabardines; and Turks with their baggy trousers, taking up more space than is allowed to Christian legs; with a mongrel race from the Eastern part of the Mediterranean, known as Levantines; and another like unto them, the Maltese; and a choice variety of natives of Gibraltar, called 'Rock scorpions,' with Africans blacker than Moors, who have perhaps crossed the desert, and hail from Timbuctoo. All these make a Babel of races and languages, as they jostle each other in these narrow and crowded streets, and bargain with each other, and I am afraid, sometimes swear at each other, in all the languages of the East" (33–34).

Ironically, in future decades, British colonialism in Gibraltar would impact the Irish directly. See, for example, Ian Jack's fascinating essay "Gibraltar," in which he unravels the killings of three IRA volunteers, gunned to death on their arrival on the Rock on 6 March 1988. Since no bomb was found on the three bodies, the British government had to go to great lengths to justify the murders. Jack's depiction of Gibraltar tragically highlights the problems of Northern Ireland, "mocked" in another colonial setting:

Regiments come here [Gibraltar] after tours of duty in Northern Ireland, in part for rest and relaxation but also to keep in shape for further tours: according to reports, one of the Rock's large caverns contains a mock Ulster village made of wood—a main street, four side-streets, two shops, a Roman Catholic church called St Malachy's, a school and a women's lavatory. What goes on here under artificial light? Raids, seiges and patrols, one assumes, stun bombs thrown into the ladies' loo, the school stormed, sanctuary denied at St Malachy's. (26–27)

(For a relatively recent study of Gibraltar, see Stewart.)

 2. The Spanish, of course, had fought with the Arabs for centuries over the possession of the Rock. As Field notes, "For nearly eight hundred years it was the prize of war between the Spaniard and the Moor, and its legends are all of battle and of blood. Ten times it was besieged and passed back and forth from conqueror to conqueror, the Cross replacing the Crescent, and the Crescent the Cross. . . . When, at last, in 1598 the Spaniards drove the Moors out of Spain, they remained masters of Gibraltar, and held it . . . for a little more than a hundred years" (63).

 3. I am using the term "chiasmatic" to indicate the dialogical interactions of language, power, and temporality. The chiasmus (Greek, "crossing") is central to Joyce's *Ulysses* not only as a rhetorical figure but also a spatial one, appearing in the form of multiple crossings and crosses in the text. In his provocative essay, "DissemiNation," Homi Bhabha writes about "the ambivalent and chiasmatic intersections of time and place that constitute the problematic 'modern' experience of the western nation" (293).

 4. On Tweedy's dubious rank and his various military expeditions, see Raleigh (78–79, 33–34).

 5. To resist colonialism in India, Gandhi emphasized myth rather than history, and argued for a noncausal relation between public consciousness and history through "memories and anti-memories" (Nandy 57). He drew upon Indian notions of time, which conceptualized the past not as an incontestable authority but as "a special case of present," the latter being capable of fracturing and generating alternate, even competing pasts, leading to a remaking of the present (57). We might say that Joyce, too, whose ambition was to "forge" the consciousness of his race, offers us a model of temporality as "memories and anti-memories" in which the past is amenable to change and revision. But this does not mean denying objective time; in "Penelope," the so-called "timeless" episode, Molly gives us the most precise clock times recorded in *Ulysses*.

 6. On innerly persuasive speech, see also Brian Shaffer in this volume.

 7. The dialogue runs thus:

The dream figure
went into the bedchamber passing beside the thong of the door bar,
and came and stood above her head and spoke a word to her:
"Penelope, are you sleeping sorrowful in the inward
heart? But the gods who live at their ease do not suffer you
to weep and to be troubled, since your son will have his homecoming
even yet, since he has done no wrong in the gods' sight."

Circumspect Penelope said to her in answer,
sleeping very sweetly now in the dreams' gateway:
"Why have you come here, sister, now, when you were not used to
come before, since the home where you live is far away from us,
and now you tell me to give over from the grieving and sorrows
that are many upon me and trouble me in my heart and spirit,
since first I lost a husband with the heart of a lion,
and who among the Danaans surpassed in all virtues,
a great man, whose fame goes wide through Hellas and midmost Argos;
and now again a beloved son is gone on a hollow
ship . . . (Homer 86)

   In general Homer, Joyce's most natural ancestor, also treats internalized
mental processes in dialogic frameworks. In such cases, the Homeric hero
may address a god, an external agent (a horse or a river, for example), or
one of his "organs," such as his *kradie* (loosely translated, heart or courage).
As Joseph Russo and Bennett Simon explain, in *The Odyssey*, "no one really
carries on mental activity in isolation. Even when the hero is clearly alone,
his thoughts and feelings are likely to be externalized in the form of a dialogue between 'Himself' and a part of himself." For example, when Odysseus
finally sights Phaecia after being tossed in the sea for two days, his joy turns
to despair when he notices the reefs and rocky coast. His description of the
grave consequences of an effort to approach the coast is an internal speech,
which, nonetheless is introduced as such: "The knees of Odysseus gave way
for fear, and the heart inside him,/ and deeply troubled he spoke to his own
great-hearted spirit" (98). Russo and Simon relate the dialogic form of the
internal monologue in Homer to the concept of the Homeric self as "not en-
capsulated but an open force field." In Homer, there is no coherent concept of
self; instead "character" is often represented by collection of parts. The use of
individual "organs" in *Ulysses* might be seen as a comic endorsement of this
vision of the self, fragmented in modern times in more senses than one.
   8.   While Molly clearly enjoys male spectatorship and is partly constituted
by it, the "I-for myself" component in her resists the gaze through language.
As Emmanuel Levinas reminds us, "Speech cuts across vision. In . . . vision
the object seen can indeed determine an act . . . an act that in some way
appropriates the 'seen' to itself. . . . In discourse the divergence that inevitably opens between the Other as my theme and the Other as my interlocutor,
emancipated from the theme that seemed a moment to hold him, forthwith
contests the meaning I ascribe to my interlocutor" (195).
   9.   For a list of contradictions in Molly's narrative, see Card.
   10.   A portion of this essay, entitled "Monologue as Dialogue: Molly
Bloom's 'History' as Myriorama" appeared in *Works and Days: Essays in the
Socio-Historical Dimensions of Literature and the Arts* 5.2 (1987): 63–77.

Works Cited

Bakhtin, M. M. *The Dialogic Imagination.* Ed. Michael Holquist. Trans. Caryl Emerson and Michael Holquist. Austin: University of Texas Press, 1981.

Bhabha, Homi K. "DissemiNation: time, narrative, and the margins of the nation." *Nation and Narration.* Ed. Homi K. Bhabha. London and New York: Routledge, 1990. 291–322.

Bhabha, Homi K. "The other question: difference, discrimination and the discourse of colonialism." *Literature, Politics, and Theory.* Ed. Peter Hulme, et al. London: Methuen, 1986.

Bhabha, Homi K. "Signs Taken for Wonders: Questions of Ambivalence and Authority under a Tree Outside Delhi, May 1817." *"Race," Writing, and Difference.* Ed. Henry Louis Gates, Jr. Chicago: University of Chicago Press, 1985. 163–184.

Bhabha, Homi K. "Sly Civility." *October* 34 (1985): 71–80.

Cairns, David, and Shaun Richards. *Writing Ireland: Colonialism, Nationalism and Culture.* Manchester: Manchester University Press, 1988.

Card, James Van Dyck. "'Contradictory': The Word for Joyce's 'Penelope'." *James Joyce Quarterly* 11 (1973): 17–26.

Fanon, Franz. *Black Skin, White Masks.* Trans. Charles L. Markmann. New York: Grove, 1967.

Field, Henry M. *Gibraltar.* New York: Charles Scribner's Sons, 1888.

Foucault, Michel. *The History of Sexuality.* Trans. Robert Hurley. Vol. 1. New York: Pantheon, 1978. 2 vols. 1978–1985.

Freire, Paulo. *Pedagogy of the Oppressed.* Trans. Myra B. Ramos. New York: Continuum, 1990.

Gifford, Don, and Robert J. Seidman. *Ulysses Annotated.* Berkeley: University of California Press, 1988.

Herring, Phillip. "Toward an Historical Molly Bloom." *English Literary History* 45 (1978): 501–52.

Holquist, Michael. *Dialogism. Bakhtin and His World.* New York: Routledge, 1990.

Homer, *The Odyssey.* Trans. Richmond Lattimore. New York: Harper and Row, 1965.

Jack, Ian. "Gibraltar" *Granta* 25 (1988): 14–86.

Joyce, James. *Letters.* Vol. 1. Ed. Stuart Gilbert. New York: Viking, 1957. 3 vols. 1957–1966.

Kristeva, Julia. *Revolution in Poetic Language.* Trans. Margaret Waller. New York: Columbia University Press, 1984.

Levinas, Emmanuel. *Totality and Infinity. An Essay on Exteriority.* Trans. Alphonso Lingis. Pittsburgh: Duquesne University Press, 1969.

Morson, Gary Saul, and Caryl Emerson. *Mikhail Bakhtin: Creation of a Prosaics.* Stanford: Stanford University Press, 1990.

Nandy, Ashis. *The Intimate Enemy. Loss and Recovery of Self Under Colonialism.* Delhi: Oxford University Press, 1983.

Raleigh, John Henry. *The Chronicle of Leopold and Molly Bloom.* Berkeley: University of California Press, 1977.

Russo, Joseph, and Bennett Simon. "Homeric Psychology and the Oral Epic Tradition." *Journal of the History of Ideas* 29 (1968): 483–98.

Said, Edward W. *Orientalism.* New York: Random House, 1979.

Stewart, John D. *Gibraltar. The Keystone.* Boston: Houghton Mifflin, 1967.

Zavala, Iris M. "Bakhtin and the Third: Communication as Response." *Critical Studies* 1.2 (1989): 43–63.

7

Negotiating Self and Culture
Narcissism, Competing Discourses, and Ideological Becoming in "Penelope"

Brian W. Shaffer

Whatever else one might say about the closing episode of *Ulysses*, that "eight-sentence" celebration of the provocative and evocative power of Joycean language, none can deny its obsession with the question of subjectivity, the question of how various linguistic, material, and ideological realities conspire to construct Molly Bloom. Indeed, the centrality of the problem of subjectivity in "Penelope" is suggested clearly by the fact that the word "I" appears more than six hundred times in this comparatively short episode (Steppe 127).

I am interested in exploring two interrelated questions concerning Molly's subjectivity, particularly concerning its degree of conformism or subversive power, that have vexed many readers for years: what cultural processes make it difficult for her to recognize the full implications of her unenviable place in the social order—as a lower-middle-class female in turn-of-the-century colonial Ireland—and yet by what processes is she able to gain limited enlightenment and subvert those ideologies that would forever keep her in the dark? Another way of phrasing all of this is to ask how is Molly "mollycoddled" into accepting a situation that many would find objectionable in the extreme, and yet how does she manage to extricate herself, at least partially, from the tangle of discourses that victimize her? However related these questions are when it comes to "Penelope," they first deserve discrete treatments and articulations. To this end, I use late Freudian theory to demonstrate the means by which Molly is blinded to her reality, and Mikhail Bakhtin's conception of the internally dialogic nature of language to reveal the means by which Molly evades the "paralysis" said to unite so many Joycean characters from *Dubliners* to *Finnegans Wake*. In the process, I hope to clarify how conformist or subversive we should take Molly Bloom to be with respect to the culture which defines and is defined by her.

"no man would look at her twice I hope Ill never be like her": Molly's Narcissism of Minor Differences

I begin with a simple question: how is Molly "mollycoddled" into accepting her fate as lower-middle-class Irish woman—and British subject? How are so many significant issues of Molly's material victimization kept from her conscious scrutiny? Another way of posing this question is to ask, as Catherine Belsey does, "Why, since all women experience the effects of patriarchal practices, are not all women feminists?" (45). And I would add, why, since she is a victim, however indirectly, of English colonization, is she suspicious of rather than sympathetic toward the efforts of Parnell and Davitt for political and land reform in Ireland? One understanding of the function of ideology may provide an answer. As Catherine Belsey, following Marx and Althusser, puts it, ideology "is both a real and an imaginary relation to the world—real in that it is the way in which people really live their relationships to the social relations which govern their conditions of existence, but imaginary in that it *discourages a full understanding of these conditions of existence and the ways in which people are socially constituted within them*" (46, my emphasis). "Ideology," Belsey continues, "obscures the real conditions of existence by presenting partial truths. It is a set of omissions, gaps rather than lies, smoothing over contradictions, appearing to provide answers to questions which in reality it evades, and masquerading as coherence in the interests of the social relations generated by and necessary to the reproduction of the existing mode of production" (46). It is this mystifying power of ideology—its ability to *discourage* an understanding of the conditions of Molly's existence as a female in a colonial culture—that interests me here. Yet it is Freud rather than Marx who for me best explains the mechanism by which an oppressive reality is inadequately perceived and articulated by Molly, however much she feels its sting.

In "Joyce and Freud: Discontent and Its Civilizations," I have argued that Gerty MacDowell suffers from what Freud would call the "narcissism of minor differences"; this condition strikes me as relevant to Molly's case as well. In this sense, to invert the old adage, Molly shares with Gerty those mental blinders necessary to keep certain truths about her existence out of mind—and therefore out of sight. In *The Future of an Illusion* Freud puts his argument most clearly:

The narcissistic satisfaction provided by the cultural ideal is . . . among the forces which are successful in combating the hostility to culture within the cultural unit. This satisfaction can be shared in not only by the favoured classes, which enjoy the benefits of the culture, but also by the supressed ones, since the right to despise the people outside it compensates them for the wrongs they suffer within their own unit. No doubt one is a wretched plebian, harassed by debts and military service; but, to make up for it, one is a Roman citizen, one has one's share in the task of ruling other nations and dictating their laws. This identification of the suppressed classes with the class who rules and exploits them is, however, only part of a larger whole. For, on the other hand, the suppressed classes can be emotionally attached to their masters; in spite of their hostility to them they may see in them their ideals; unless such relations of a fundamentally satisfying kind subsisted, it would be impossible to understand how a number of civilizations have survived so long in spite of the justifiable hostility of large human masses. (13)[1]

Molly's culturally encouraged "narcissism of minor differences" limits her focus, helping her to evade, or at least to ignore, the dimensions of her victimization as a lower-class, female, colonial subject. Molly will keep her mind off of such things as long as other distracting tensions, however insubstantial they finally may be, exist to claim her attention.

Countless examples of Molly's narcissism of minor differences, particularly pertaining to her sexual superiority to other women, can be found in "Penelope." While it is not novel to point out that Molly is harder on women than she is on men—Harry Blamires, for example, long ago noted that as "critical as she can be of her husband, it is soon clear that she is even more critical of other *women*" (247)—little attention has been paid to *why* this is the case. Molly takes comfort in the thought that she is far more attractive than most other women, yet this concentration upon "sexual competition" detracts from her ability adequately to size up her situation. Remembering Gibraltar, she imagines that other women would "die down dead off their feet if ever they got a chance of walking down the Alameda on an officers arm like me on the bandnight my eyes flash my bust that they havent passion God help their poor head I knew more about men and life when I was 15 than theyll all know at 50" (18.883–87). Ironically, it is precisely this fixation on her triumph over "men and life" that blinds her to a greater understanding of her victimization by "men and life."

Obsessed with her "mass of hair" (18.213), far "thicker" than her friend Hester's (18.638), with her alluring thighs ("I bet he never saw a better pair of thighs than that" [18.1144–45]), her "plump and tempting" breasts (18.1378–79), her neck (18.301) and feet (18.257), and with her attractive underdrawers ("I promised to give him the pair off my doll to carry about in his waistcoat pocket" [18.305–6]), Molly outdoes her female competitors at every turn. Although she is certainly not as "young" as she used to be, she takes comfort in being the most attractive "wife" around, as Jack Power's wife was "always getting sick or going to be sick or just getting better" (18.1273), while her friend Josie possesses a "face beginning to look drawn and run down" ever since "living with that dotty husband of hers" (18.217–19). Even Molly's last name is more attractive than those of other wives she has encountered, like Mrs. "Breen or Briggs . . . or those awful names with bottom in them Mrs Ramsbottom or some other kind of a bottom" (18.844–45). However badly off Molly is, there are always women even more badly off than she. In this way the "narcissism of minor differences" rationalizes marginal defeat into palpable victory; in this way a Molly who, like Stephen Dedalus, is in fact the "servant" of many "masters," imagines that one day she might possess the "proper servant" she deserves (18.1080). Molly also imagines herself to be a muse to young Stephen's artistic genius, but then worries about the difficulty of negotiating among the numerous men with whom she would be compelled to spend time (18.1359–67).

Indeed, Molly's fantasies of negotiating among various men and of vanquishing various women help keep her mind off of the colonial situation in which she finds herself. Whenever her thoughts turn to politics or to the English empire, they quickly turn back again to sexual matters. On the subject of the Sinn Fein, for example, she thinks, "I hate the mention of their politics" (18.387–88), and soon afterward thinks of "finelooking men" in a military context: "I love to see a regiment pass in review" (18.397–98). Similarly, thoughts of Lieutenant Gardner, who travels to India and South Africa (where he dies in the Boer War), soon turn to thoughts of her first sexual encounter with him, just as the political sentiments she expresses—"wasnt I the born fool to believe all his blather about home rule and the land league" (18.1187–88)—soon give way to sexual ones. Even Molly's "charitable" act of throwing "a penny to that lame sailor for England" (18.346–47) has obvious sexual connotations, as does her often repeated misnomer for the Irish ultranationalist movement, "Sinner Fein," which suggests an illicit sexual side to this organization's political activities.

In these ways, then, Freud's concept of a narcissism of minor differences helps explain how certain reigning ideologies—about male-female, English-Irish, and class relations—lull Molly into accepting her place in the social order. What has not yet been explained, however, is the question of how Molly, despite her narcissism of minor differences, is nevertheless *capable* at many points of challenging these reigning discourses by rendering them profane rather than sacred, interested rather than authoritative. For a conception of how this works I turn to Bakhtin's understanding of the internal dialogue of competing discourses which determine and are determined by the subject in a state of ideological development.

"I suppose he wont find many like me": Competing Discourses and Ideological Becoming in "Penelope"

It is no surprise that the linguistic makeup of Molly's "monologue" has been so fascinating to readers, particularly its quintessentially dialogic nature. In this volume Susan Bazargan, for example, wonders whether Molly's "monologue or stream-of-consciousness" is "univocal" after all; Carol Shloss argues that taken "dialogically, Molly's knowledge, her silence, her biases, and her dissatisfactions can all signal much more than they might if we considered them in isolation"; and Richard Pearce stresses the "instability" of *Ulysses'* ending, suggesting that to view "Penelope" as anything but open and richly dialogic would be to impose closure on Joyce's text.

To be sure, such an interest in the discourse of "Penelope" is nothing new; readers, as Kathleen McCormick shows in this volume, have been variously perplexed and delighted, outraged and amused over the language and figure of Molly ever since the publication of *Ulysses*. But while more traditional readings of this episode have treated its discourse as monologic (as "interior monologue"), and Molly as a unified, autonomous character, more recent readings have treated this discourse as a characterless linguistic trope, and Molly as an expression of "the culture speaking."[2] As Jennifer Wicke correctly notes, "The debates which have swirled around Molly Bloom as character, voice, or *écriture* in the text have tended to collocate around the 'Penelope' chapter, and then to argue the case for Molly as a real woman, or a bad woman, or as not-woman, or as woman under erasure, with varying degrees of theoretical sophistication" (3). I propose to negotiate a path between these positions by suggesting that Molly's discourse is "internally dialogic," one which mediates between the competing discourses of a culturally constructed subjectivity and a subjectively apperceived culture. In other words, I read Molly's selfhood as a particular means of combining and sorting through the many voices within her, rather than as a "single voice" or a site of the random convergence of the culture's many voices. More importantly, I believe that an understanding of the precise contours of this dialogue will determine the degree of subversive power or of conformism we grant to Molly's peroration—an issue central to Molly's ability to see around her narcissism of minor differences and to negotiate the constraining colonial, class, and gender conventions she faces.[3] If, as Carol Shloss maintains in this volume, the act of speaking for Molly and others in Joyce's works "is itself a political act, an act of assertion, a search for definition in the face of a domineering Other," then it is essential to grasp the nature and workings of this speech if we are to understand its ability to confront that "Other." In other words, how does Molly negotiate among the dominant colonial and patriarchal discourses which on some level construct her and determine her conception of self? How does she evade the worst paralyzing effects of a narcissism of minor differences that she exhibits on nearly every page—effects that Gerty MacDowell could never overcome?

On the subject of the dialogic nature of language and the relationship of discourse to subjectivity, few theorists are more illuminating than M. M. Bakhtin. Indeed, he is so compelling a thinker on these issues that an entire recent volume, R. B. Kershner's provocative *Joyce, Bakhtin, and Popular Literature: Chronicles of Disorder*, explores Joyce's early works through a Bakhtinian lens.[4] For me, however, Bakhtin is most enlightening for his conception of the dynamic between "authoritative" and "internally persuasive" discourse in the development of a subject's "ideological consciousness." Moreover, this dynamic allows us to steer a course between conceptions of Molly as a "character speaking her monologue" and a "linguistic trope speaking the culture," as well as to sort through the issue of Molly's ability to subvert those colonizing discourses that oppress her as an Irish female of the lower class.

Bakhtin's conception of the internally dialogic nature of language is laid out most clearly in his "Discourse in the Novel," one of his richest, most complex, and at the same time most neglected essays. Here, Bakhtin explores the means by which words, in addition to being occasioned by other words (born in dialogue with other words), are "internally dialogic" (exist in tension with themselves). This is because "language, for the individual consciousness," lies "on the borderline between oneself and the other. The word in language is half someone else's. It becomes 'one's own' only when the speaker populates it with his own intention, his own accent, when he appropriates the word, adapting it to his own semantic and expressive intention. Prior to this moment of appropriation, the word does not exist in a neutral and impersonal language . . . but rather it exists in other people's mouths, in other people's contexts, serving other people's intentions . . ." (293–94).

In the section of his essay entitled "The Speaking Person in the Novel," Bakhtin addresses the mechanics of this appropriation. He maintains: "Within the arena of almost every utterance an intense interaction and struggle between one's own and another's word is being waged . . ." (354), a struggle between language, as he puts it in his grammar school analogy, retold "in one's own words" and language recited "by heart" (341). Specifically, Bakhtin distinguishes between *authoritative discourse*—language that demands "we acknowledge it" and "make [it] our own," language that "binds us" independent "of any power it might have to persuade us internally," language that we encounter "with its authority already fused to it," the language of "the fathers," the "authority of religious dogma . . . of scientific truth or of a currently fashionable book," for example (342–43)—and *internally persuasive discourse*, language we appropriate from others by adapting it to our own intentions. While these two kinds of discourse may be "united in a single word" in an individual's ideological becoming (342), more often than not this "becoming" is "characterized precisely by a sharp gap between these two categories: in one, the authoritative word (religious, political, moral . . .) that does not know internal persuasiveness, in the other [the] internally persuasive word that is denied all privilege, backed up by no authority at all, and is frequently not even acknowledged in society. . . . The struggle and dialogic interrelationship of these categories of ideological discourse are what usually determine the history of an individual ideological consciousness" (342).

Indeed, it is because "the ideological becoming of a human being" is "the process of selectively assimilating the words of others" (341), and because "selfhood is not a particular voice within, but a particular way of combining many voices within" (Morson and Emerson 221), that Bakhtin's conception of the struggle between "authoritative" and "internally persuasive" discourse is so germane when we consider Molly's case. Such a concept of subjectivity explains how Molly can overcome her narcissism of minor differences at many points. For example, Bakhtin's observation that a "particular language in a novel is always a particular way of viewing the world," and hence that "novels are never in danger of becoming a mere aimless verbal play" (333), speaks directly to the discourse of "Penelope." To be sure, however "rambling" (as Shloss describes them in this volume) and "contradictory" (Card 38–55) Molly's thoughts initially appear, one can discern an order to them in the struggle—or "gap"—between authoritative and internally persuasive discourse. Take Molly's repeated use of clichés, those perfect instances of authoritative discourse, the words "of a father, of adults and of teachers" (Bahktin 342). Whether she thinks, "no fool like an old fool" (18.52), "1 woman is not enough for them [men]" (18.60), Bloom is "too beautiful for a man" (18.210), men "cant get on without us [women]" (18.239–40), "its all very well a husband but you cant fool a lover" (18.354–55), "theres many a true word spoken in jest" (18.775), "it must be real love if a man gives up his life for her" (18.1056), or "God of heaven theres nothing like nature" (18.1558–59), Molly invokes "incontestable truths" in an attempt to validate her place in the social order. And it should come as no surprise that most of these clichés, these subjective expressions hardened into objective truths, center on men and women, beauty, love, and lust—on sexual politics.

Indeed, Molly clearly has absorbed the dogmas of authority, of "the authoritativeness of tradition, of generally acknowledged truths, of the official line" (344)—perpetuated by the colonial situation, by the church, and by the popular culture industry—when it comes to gender relations.[5] While it would be an overstatement to suggest that the novel depicts Irish men colonizing Irish women in the same ways that England colonizes Ireland, it is nevertheless clear, both for men in the first scenario and for England in the second, that the status quo authority and power relations are preferable to any critical reevaluation of them. At one point, for example, Molly cites an ultimate authority, God, to rationalize the state of affairs between men and women generally, and between Bloom and her specifically: "its all his own fault if I am an adulteress . . . God knows its not much doesnt everybody only they hide it I suppose thats what a woman is supposed to be there for or He wouldnt have made us the way He did so attractive to men" (18.1516–20). If God himself has so ordered things, who is Molly to challenge this eternal state of affairs? If heaven itself has ordained the role of temptress and tool for woman, it stands to reason that Molly's mania over her beauty, sensuality, and desirability is as appropriate as it is inevitable.[6] Moreover, there can be little doubt that Molly's obsession with her own sexual prowess, only intensified by her narcissism of minor differences, saps energies that could otherwise be used to question the extra-sexual order of things—Ireland's colonial situation, for example.

Once again reminiscent of Gerty MacDowell (and for that matter

Martha Clifford), Molly invokes the authoritative discourse of "a currently fashionable book" (in this case the pseudo-pornographic tales of formulaic pulp romances like *Sweets of Sin*) to explain her place in the world: "still of course a woman wants to be embraced 20 times a day almost to make her look young no matter by who so long as to be in love or loved by somebody if the fellow you want isnt there sometimes by the Lord God I was thinking would I go around by the quays there some dark evening where nobodyd know me and pick up a sailor off the sea thatd be hot for it and not care a pin whose I was" (18.1407–12). Fluctuating between fantasies of being a love and a lust object of men, and of being a virgin and a whore (a "sweetheart" and a "sweet tart"), Molly's words clearly reflect the authoritative discourses of the colonial patriarchy in which she lives. At one point she betrays a desire to be a prostitute, thinking, "then Ill wipe him off me just like a business" (18.1538), and at another point betrays a rape fantasy, imagining how a man might "attack me in the dark and ride me up against the wall without a word" (18.1418). Molly even imagines herself as what we would consider a porn star ("I could pose for a picture naked . . . Im a little like that dirty bitch in that Spanish photo" [18.560–64]), and at other points succumbs to the "official line" that women should keep entirely out of politics ("Miss This Miss That Miss Theother lot of sparrowfarts skitting around talking about politics they know as much about as my backside" [18.878–80]). She also buys into the popular notion that women are closer to nature than men ("I was a flower of the mountain yes so we are flowers all a womans body" [18.1576–77]), and, as Jung put it five years after the publication of *Ulysses*, that for women "Logos is a deadly boring kind of sophistry" if they are not already "repelled and frightened by it" (124). This final point is evident in Molly's complaint about Bloom's earlier definition of "metempsychosis": "he never can explain a thing simply the way a *body* can understand" (18.566–67, my emphasis).

Nevertheless, to the extent that the "conformist" Molly simply invokes authoritative discourse because distracted by her narcissism of minor differences, the "subversive" Molly attempts to appropriate this discourse to serve her own purposes by making it internally persuasive, thereby beginning the process of freeing herself from the strictures of the "official line." Joseph Heininger, in this volume, is correct but does not go far enough when he states that Gerty and Molly occupy "a physically and socially marginal position in Dublin," yet that "Molly explicitly rejects the inculturated attitudes of female timidity and shame that Gerty has internalized." Indeed, of all Joyce's female subjects, I believe that Gerty and Molly *in this respect* stand at opposite poles, with the former being among the author's greatest conformists (what thoughts of Gerty's escape the "official line"?) and the latter being among his most thoroughgoing subversives.[7]

Indeed, "Penelope," with its unique fluidity of language, and with its teeming contradictions, is perhaps best understood as that represented discourse—that linguistic process—by which Molly begins to liberate herself from "the word of the fathers" and come to "ideological consciousness." "The importance of struggling with another's discourse, its influence in the history of an individual's coming to ideological consciousness, is enormous," Bakhtin argues. "One's own discourse and one's own voice . . . will sooner or later begin to liberate themselves from the authority of the other's discourse" (348). Despite the prevalence of authoritative discourse in "Penelope," then, Molly's "consciousness" might be said to be working, from at least one perspective, "in an independent, experimenting and discriminating way" (345). This accounts for the efflorescence of and struggle among various internally persuasive discourses in the episode. "Our ideological development is just such an intense struggle within us for hegemony among various available verbal and ideological points of view, approaches, directions and values," Bakhtin writes, and hence "the semantic structure of an internally persuasive discourse is *not finite*, it is *open* . . ." (346). This openness is precisely what we see at work in Molly's heteroglot, overdetermined discourse, in which the words of others—whether or not she specifically wills it—are turned to serve her own intentions.

Such an understanding of internal dialogue and ideological struggle sheds light on Molly's much discussed ability to contradict herself— her ability to insist, in the space of less than a page, both that "itd be much better for the world to be governed by the women in it you wouldnt see women going and killing one another" (18.1434–46), and that "I hate that in women no wonder they treat us the way they do we are a dreadful lot of bitches" (18.1458–59). Similarly, the following lines of Molly's betray the gap (and struggle) between authoritative and internally persuasive discourses at the heart of her ideological becoming: "the greatest earthly happiness answer to a gentlemans proposal affirmatively my goodness theres nothing else *its all very fine for them but as for being a woman as soon as youre old they might as well throw you out in the bottom of the ashpit*" (18.744–47, my emphasis). Notice the abrupt shift from approval to disapproval toward the authoritative understanding of gender relations: the prestige conferred upon the woman in accepting the hand of a suitor immediately dissolves (even if it is later reconstituted) in Molly's mind after she recognizes that women are commodities to men, and that when the "goods" no longer carry exchange value they are simply to be discarded. Rather than attributing Molly's contradictoriness to her personality, psychological makeup, or gender, then, as many readers have done, this contradictoriness is more persuasively viewed as part and parcel of Molly's "two steps forward, one step back" progress toward emancipation from the "official line."[8]

Molly renders authoritative discourse internally persuasive in dozens of other places, but two brief examples will suffice here. First, Molly at points plays "manly woman" to Bloom's "womanly man." Imagining what it would be like to be a male "conquering" a female—"God I wouldnt mind being a man and get up on a lovely woman O Lord" (18.1146–47); "all the pleasure those men get out of a woman I can feel" (18.583); "the amount of pleasure they get off a womans body were so round and white for them always I wished I was one myself sometimes" (18.1380–81)—Molly subverts the traditional hierarchy of sexual politics (and of the sex act itself).[9] Second, Molly subverts the discourse of the church confessional by confessing her own curiosity and suspicions about her priest: "what did he want to know for when I already confessed it to God he had a nice fat hand the palm moist always I wouldnt mind feeling it neither would he Id say . . . Id like to be embraced by one in his vestments and the smell of incense off him like the pope besides theres no danger with a priest if youre married hes too careful about himself" (18.113–21). Nevertheless, however subversive Molly's thinking is here, it does not stop her from invoking the authoritative discourse of the church at a later point: "I hope theyll have something better for us in the other world" (18.1210–11). In both of these instances Molly paradoxically subverts, resurrects, and then subverts again the authoritative discourse in question with a rapidity and frequency unparalleled anywhere in *Ulysses*. Nowhere in this text is "ideological becoming" more clearly represented as a function of language, as the negotiation of competing discourses, colonial, sexual, and otherwise. Nowhere in the text is a subject's narcissism of minor differences more clearly challenged by the salutary processes of internal dialogue.

Thus, if Bakhtin is correct in his assertion that each fictional character's "speech possesses its own belief system" (315), then Molly's belief system may be said to be in a state of ideological becoming, at that point where the "official line" begins to resemble something synthetic and alterable rather than untouchable because "in the nature of things." More than any other episode of *Ulysses*, then, "Penelope" represents the internal struggle of discourses that make up subjectivity

and reveals the great extent to which the subject's "interior monologue" is always already dialogic—an open-ended, now subversive,
now conformist dialogue of self and self, self and other. Unlike Gerty,
Molly exhibits the potential to trade in a mystifying self-love for self-
knowledge, to exchange her paralyzing narcissism for the ability to
negotiate between self and culture to her own advantage.

Notes

1.   In *Group Psychology and the Analysis of the Ego* Freud writes, "In the
undisguised antipathies and aversions which people feel towards strangers
with whom they have to do we may recognize the expression of self-love—
of narcissism" (34); and in *Civilization and Its Discontents* Freud puts this even
more plainly: "It is always possible to bind together a considerable number of
people in love, so long as there are people left over to receive the manifestation
of their aggressiveness" (61).

2.   In her ingenious and convincing essay in this volume, for example,
Cheryl Herr argues that "Molly does not occupy the level of narrative reality
that we have normally granted to her. . . . I can no longer find it in myself
to grant the Molly of 'Penelope' any reality-value whatsoever—not as Earth
Mother, not as Celtic goddess, not as ordinary Dublin Hausfrau." Herr goes
on to argue that Molly is less a "character" than "a role to be enacted by this
or that major artiste of the era."

3.   Carol Shloss in this volume concerns herself with the "strategies of
resistance" to be found in Molly's "rambling thoughts and reflections"; and
Cheryl Herr wonders whether it is legitimate to speak of "Molly's monologue
as a liberated or liberating voicing of female desire."

4.   For more on this see my review of Kershner's book in *JJLS*.

5.   Carol Shloss, for example, convincingly argues that Molly's "sensitivity
to the issues of authority, privilege, and financial dependence in her relationships with men corresponds with sentiments held by Irish nationalists in their
dealings with England. Both women in marriage and the Irish population in
thrall to a colonial government faced a kind of benevolent paternalism that
sought to disguise the internal contradictions of union in the language of
equity and concern."

6.   At too many points to count, Molly betrays this obsession. A few such
instances include: "make him want me thats the only way" (18.1539–40); "I
gave him all the pleasure I could" (18.1580); "anything at all only not to look
ugly" (18.589); and "I wish somebody would write me a loveletter" (18.734–
35).

7.   For more on Gerty's inability to counter the discourse of her victimization see my "Joyce and Freud: Discontent and Its Civilizations."

8.   See Schwab for a provocative psychological explanation of Molly's
contradictoriness.

9.   As Kimberly Devlin convincingly argues in this volume, in Molly Joyce

articulates "one of his canniest critiques of the ideology that produces" oppressive gender categories by "putting on 'womanliness' that repeatedly puts on 'manliness'."

Works Cited

Bakhtin, M. M. "Discourse in the Novel." *The Dialogic Imagination : Four Essays.* Austin: University of Texas Press, 1981.

Belsey, Catherine. "Constructing the Subject: Deconstructing the Text." *Feminist Criticism and Social Change: Sex, Class and Race in Literature and Culture.* Ed. Judith Newton and Deborah Rosenfelt. New York: Methuen, 1985. 45–64.

Blamires, Harry. *The Bloomsday Book: A Guide Through Joyce's "Ulysses."* London: Methuen, 1966.

Card, James Van Dyck. *An Anatomy of "Penelope".* Cranbury, N.J.: Associated University Presses, 1984.

Freud, Sigmund. *Civilization and Its Discontents.* New York: Norton, 1961.

Freud, Sigmund. *The Future of an Illusion.* New York: Norton, 1961.

Freud, Sigmund. *Group Psychology and the Analysis of the Ego.* New York: Norton, 1959.

Jung, C. G. *Civilization in Transition.* New York: Pantheon, 1964.

Kershner, R. B. *Joyce, Bakhtin, and Popular Literature: Chronicles of Disorder.* Chapel Hill: University of North Carolina Press, 1989.

Morson, Gary Saul, and Caryl Emerson. *Mikhail Bakhtin: Creation of a Prosaics.* Stanford: Stanford University Press, 1990.

Schwab, Gabriele. "Mollyloquy." *The Seventh of Joyce.* Ed. Bernard Benstock. Bloomington: Indiana University Press, 1982. 81–85.

Shaffer, Brian W. "Joyce and Freud: Discontent and Its Civilizations." *Joyce in Context.* Ed. Vincent Cheng and Timothy Martin. Cambridge: Cambridge University Press, 1992. 73–88.

Shaffer, Brian W. Review of Kershner. *James Joyce Literary Supplement* 4.1 (1990): 25–26.

Steppe, Wolfhard, and Hans Walter Gabler. *A Handlist to James Joyce's "Ulysses."* New York: Garland, 1986.

PART 4

MOLLY AS CONSUMER

8

Molly Bloom's Ad Language and Goods Behavior
Advertising as Social Communication in *Ulysses*

Joseph Heininger

Advertising texts and publicity messages appear everywhere in *Ulysses*. Their language, symbolic content, and place in everyday life are important parts of the novel's representations of modern culture. By representing these forms of communication and their effects on the consciousness and behavior of the characters, Joyce dramatizes the psychological, experiential, and textual dimensions of modernity in *Ulysses*. Max Horkheimer and Theodor Adorno see the professional practitioners of advertising in *Ulysses*, Leopold Bloom and Blazes Boylan, as members of a newly formed "culture industry," and examine advertising's powerful communication technologies and their destructive effects on traditional relationships in European society. I think a more accurate view of the place of advertising and other publicized forms of discourse in Joyce's novel can be achieved by using methods of textual and cultural analysis derived from communication studies, especially studies of social communication. Advertising as social communication connects two processes: producing messages about commodities for consumption in the marketplace, and doing the cultural work of promoting social and political ideas. In other words, advertising symbolizes social goods through the medium of material goods; advertising always produces a political discourse in and through the commodities it sells. In *Ulysses*, Joyce employs advertising and related discourses to represent the cultural politics of social communication and the consumption of goods in 1904 Dublin.

In retelling the story of Odysseus, Joyce exploits the narrative possibilities of advertising and other forms of what Roland Barthes has called "theatricalized" discourse. By appropriating advertising's discourse in and through objects, Joyce establishes a historical and economic context for Ireland in 1904 while enriching the narrative with contemporary forms of language. The episodes, as they trace the complex movements of mind of the individual characters, show that their dealings with such discourse constitute much of what is distinctively modern about them. And Joyce employed discourses such as advertising and journalism to dramatize public life in Dublin in 1904, to portray the cultural work of contemporary ideologies of art, sexuality, colonialism, and nationalism. As an Irishman who kept his skeptical distance from the British presence in Ireland and from the Irish Revival, Joyce knew that an ideology's power to persuade is built on the appeal of carefully chosen symbols. Joyce's pointed critique of British political ideology and of the Irish Revival's romantic cultural ideology in *Ulysses* begins with a critique of their symbols, and of the relations between commodities, needs, and values in consumerism and politics. Thus some famous commodities and familiar images become symbolic through the narrative's characteristic patterns of repetition and accretion in *Ulysses*. For example, the jingle for "Plumtree's Potted Meat," the popular icon of the nubile seaside girl, and the image of the "flower of the mountain" on Gibraltar become identified with Leopold Bloom, Gerty MacDowell, and Molly Bloom, respectively. Through repetition and narrative arrangement, these texts become symbols associated with the characters. Here I want to examine these associations with regard to Molly Bloom's body and imagination, in the realistic, material world of Dublin's corsets, dresses, "anti-fat" patent medicines, flowered wallpapers, and Guinness stout, and in the symbolic, polysemous world the novel constructs from ads and images in the *Gentlewoman* magazine, from the cult of the colonized consumer, and from Molly's image of herself as a "flower of the mountain."

My argument about Molly's ad language and goods behavior has two complementary parts. First, I want to show that the advertising texts Joyce chose to incorporate in *Ulysses* inscribe and interpret the political and social relations of the British and Irish in 1904 Ireland. Although one cannot fit *Ulysses* into neat categories without being reductive, it is true that Joyce's methods redefine the concept of the political novel. In my view, the most interesting dimension of its political character is how the ideologies of mass-culture consumerism and imperial control of colonial peoples become reproduced in much of the discourse about commodities in *Ulysses*. Molly Bloom is centrally important in this regard, as she is in any reading of the novel. For example, the most important discourses in and through commodities in "Penelope" concern a British-made corset advertised in a London fashion magazine, an "anti-fat" patent medicine, and the bedroom's flowered wallpaper. These discourses and Molly's responses to them are integral parts of Joyce's realism and his representation of Irish cultural politics. But if a Defoesque realism is served by the presence of so many material goods and texts about them in *Ulysses,* so too is Joyce's admiration for Blake's creation of a visual and verbal symbolic system to express larger correspondences. The second part of my argument, therefore, deals with the symbolic construction of advertised goods and the images our minds associate with them. By frequent repetition, advertising texts and other texts about commodities in *Ulysses* become icons, symbols and totems—rich sources for the narrative's exploration of states of consciousness.

Joyce's incorporation of advertising's theatricalized discourses in his portrait of life in 1904 Dublin prompts questions about how to approach the artistic modernity of *Ulysses*. Theorists of advertising and communications such as Raymond Williams, John Berger, William Leiss, Stephen Kline, and Sut Jhally, Gillian Dyer, and John Fiske maintain that advertisements are the social texts of consumer society. Both advertisements and novels are understood as fictions and social communications; both have the power to redescribe social and individual reality and make new worlds in place of old. Such texts, they argue, encode political, economic, and gender messages in which multiple, often contradictory, and sometimes subversive meanings can be discerned. The advertising texts incorporated in the last episode of *Ulysses* place Molly's "discourse in and through objects" in the context of her acceptance of and resistance to the dominant British culture's systems of needs and values.

Before looking at Molly's discourse in some detail, I want to sketch the place of advertising in Irish history and culture from 1870 to 1904; that is, from the dates of Molly's birth in Gibraltar to her monologue in Eccles Street. According to Raymond Williams, a significant shift in British advertising's social role began in the 1880s and continued through the first two decades of the twentieth century. In the eighteenth century, British advertisers typically contented themselves with notifying the newspaper reading public that they were reputable provisioners of material goods. But in the 1890s, large British firms such as Pears' soap and Lipton's tea intensified brand competition in an

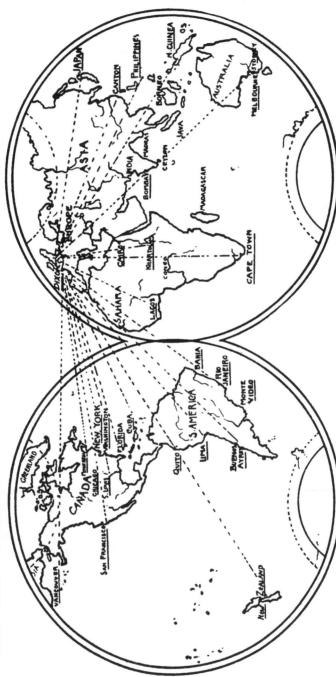

THE SUN NEVER SETS ON THE GOOD ADVERTISER'S CUSTOMERS.

At midnight in London it is early afternoon in the Western States and in the Far West of Canada, there and in Australia and New Zealand, our fellow citizens are benefitting by the Advertising which emanates from these offices.—T. DIXON, 193 & 195, Oxford Street, London.

Fig. 8.1. From the *Advertisers' Guardian*. (London: Thomas Dixon, 1902.)

effort to corner mass markets, and newspaper and magazine "advertising wars" worked to secure the consumers' brand loyalty. By the turn of the century, there was a widespread sense of imperial mission among advertisers, linked inexorably to the political reach and power of the British Empire (see fig. 8.1).[1] Irish men and women who read British journals and papers, such as Leopold and Molly Bloom, witnessed intense competition among large British firms for markets in Ireland. It is not surprising that they witnessed as well the growth of Irish nationalist and revivalist groups such as the Gaelic League, the Land League, and Sinn Fein, which arose in response to calls for Irish, not English, cultural materials and political discourse.

Beginning in the 1910s, and entrenched as standard industry practice by the 1920s, modern advertising in Britain and America no longer sold commodities only, but social goods and cultural models as well. In the fifty years between 1870 and 1920, advertising had become, in Raymond Williams's term, the "magic system," as its messages consistently promised wonderful transformations in the lives of those who consumed the products it promoted. During the period before 1914, most of the commodity advertising published in Ireland was produced in England, and it was, not surprisingly, thoroughly Anglocentric. In 1904, Ireland was entering its second century of British political rule under the Act of Union (1800), but Ireland was also geographically close to Britain, and was considered an important part of the domestic market for British manufactured goods. As Robert Opie's collection of tradecards, packaging, and advertising posters in *Rule Britannia: Trading on the British Image* reveals, contemporary British advertising heavily promoted England's exports of its defining national symbols— John Bull, Queen Victoria, the Britannic lion, the rose and crown—as well as its material commodities. These imperial and national images of England saturated the colonial markets together with the goods they sold.

However, as Edward Said has noticed with regard to Yeats's post-1916 nationalistic poems, there are always "cultures of resistance" at work in the life and art of a colonial people. Accordingly, it is clear that the reception and transformation of advertising messages, especially Bloom's and Molly's, is a form of political resistance that assumes a prominent part in *Ulysses.*[2] Moreover, both Raymond Williams and Seamus Deane have convincingly shown that Ireland's economic domination by British capitalism reinforced its dependent political status as a colony of the Crown. During the heyday of British economic activity in Ireland, from 1890 to the Irish Revolution of 1916, the forces of consumerism and colonialism allied to convert Ireland into a ready source of exports and materials for English domestic use:

especially cattle, dairy products, male soldiers, and female domestic servants. Working in the other direction, consumerism and colonialism also made Ireland a nearby market for importation of British manufactured goods, especially packaged and branded products such as tea, soap, cigarettes, mineral water, ale, patent medicines and other curatives, cosmetics, bicycles, and many kinds of useful and fashionable clothing. (All of these products are in use, on display, or otherwise advertised in *Ulysses*.) In British economic and imperial policy, Ireland, and Dublin in particular, was being urged toward greater dependence on British manufacturers and commodities, always identified by British images. Such commodities are realistic and symbolic texts which consistently convey Anglocentric political and cultural messages.[3]

The consumption of goods in which Molly Bloom and Gerty MacDowell participate clearly functions as an integral part of Irish colonialism's hierarchically organized social system. For both female characters, the political reality of Irish dependence and British rule continually produces the social meanings of those goods they desire and consume. This is so because the mass production of goods, and the system of consumption—modern economic processes which always designate women as the prime consumers—are analogous in their power structures and their symbolic codes to the British political system operating in Ireland through Dublin Castle. In this analogy, the system of consumption has its imperial capitals, London and, of course, Paris, for the most sophisticated devotees. Through advertising, the capital then disseminates its messages to its colonial subjects, Ireland's lower-middle and middle-class women who, cast in the role of inferior provincials, strive to imitate their English models in fashion and taste.

The English-Irish system of commodity consumption in 1904 typically features the image of the Queen, which is used as an advertising icon to display the product's implied quality and the status its ownership confers on the buyer. Queen Victoria, whose Jubilees in 1887 and 1897 saw her image marked on almost every British branded commodity, is first in importance as the advertisers' favorite patriotic icon. Then, during the reign of Edward VII, Victoria is succeeded by Queen Alexandra, whose youthful visage appears on the wrapper of the "queen of ointments" Gerty MacDowell uses for her hands. (Throughout the Victorian and Edwardian eras, many products also displayed Britannia's female heraldic image.) Not to be overlooked are the producers and arbiters of fashionable consumption: "Madame Vera Verity" and other writers in English women's magazines, including Gerty's favorite, the *Lady's Pictorial,* and Molly's *Gentlewoman.* Although both of these "illustrated journals" were published in London to appear every Thursday, each journal targeted a different mass audience: the *Lady's Pictorial* sought the lower-middle and middle-class reader, with advertisements suitable in style and tone; and the *Gentlewoman,* which billed itself, "First in Fashions," aimed for upper-middle-class and upper-class readers. Or, in the words of an advertisement for the magazine, "The *Gentlewoman* is undoubtedly the Leading Illustrated Journal "de Luxe" of refined Society to be found almost universally in the homes of English Gentlewomen." (It also claimed 250,000 readers per issue, according to a trade publication, *The Advertisers' Guardian,* published by Thomas Dixon in London in 1902. See fig. 8.2.) There are many loyal subjects of commodity colonialism, "votaries of dame fashion" such as Gerty, who consume what they can acquire of the desired objects, and who define themselves by such acquired images. However, there are also those who resist, rebellious colonials such as Molly Bloom, who first accept and later reject the imperial culture's images, products, and social goods, in order to create cultures of resistance.

Molly plays a paradoxical role in defining herself vis-à-vis the world of goods and the symbols of well-being in 1904 Dublin. Before "Penelope," Molly is often figured in Dublin's male public discourse as a sexual commodity, as well as a colonized site for male activity and fantasy. Dramatized as a woman speaking in "Penelope," however, Molly first participates in, then resists defining her self-image in terms of the system of commodities that mass consumer culture offers her. Of course, in her thoughts of fashionable dresses, corsets, and "anti-fat" pills, Molly partakes in this culture's symbolic imaging of the middle-class woman's body as visible public property. But in the last section of "Penelope," she chooses to associate herself and her body with an image which invites interpretation as both completely "natural" and highly "artificial": the image of a flower, specifically a "flower of the mountain" on Howth Head.

The image is "artificial" because the floral figuration of a woman's body is a social construct. It was originally a rhetorical figure appropriated from the Italian poets by the English Renaissance poets and became thoroughly popularized as a visual image in late Victorian and Edwardian culture. The floral image is a social construct, whether it appears as a poetic trope or as a mass-produced decorative motif. But Molly's consciousness moves away from the desire to consume toward repetition of scenes from her past, reappropriates the floral image from the public realm of the commodity, and transforms it into

Fig. 8.2. From the *Advertisers' Guardian*. (London: Thomas Dixon, 1902.)

a symbol of personal feeling. In this respect, Molly's rhetorical turn to the flower represents her desire to return to nature and the "natural," that is, to an Edenic, unmediated relation to her body and its public presentation.

Before "Penelope," however, Molly is most often mentioned as a singer, as Bloom's wife and as Boylan's rumored lover. Most men in Dublin speak of her as if she were a piece of goods, a tradeable commodity on the Dublin male sexual exchange. John Henry Menton, who danced with her at Mat Dillon's, speaks of her as "a good armful" when reminiscing with Ned Lambert in "Hades" (6.697). The Nameless One in "Cyclops" says of Boylan, "That's the bucko that'll organise her, take my tip" (12.1002). But Molly also undergoes the process Georg Lukacs terms reification, which in her case is the magical transformation from female character with a personality into a commodity, that publicized object of desire. Her image is featured on a photograph which Bloom shows Stephen in the cabman's shelter in "Eumaeus." This photograph of Molly as a concert singer is displayed much as a commercial tradecard might be: Molly is the pictured object of desire, and Bloom half-invites Stephen to think about bidding for her. In the primarily male discursive space of the first seventeen episodes of *Ulysses*, Bloom, Boylan, and the other male characters represent Molly as a sexual and musical commodity.

But what Molly herself says in "Penelope" about various advertised objects of desire is crucial, because in this discourse she reveals not only her personality, but also attitudes toward her body and toward the clothes she wears. As a middle-class "*Gentlewoman*" of her time, Molly is economically defined by her culture as a consumer, rather than as a producer. Overwhelmingly male-sponsored and produced in this era, advertising advocates a consumer mentality and always knows "a woman's place," as the copy from the *Gentlewoman*'s 1902 promotion to advertisers states matter-of-factly: "Astute advertisers will observe: The *Gentlewoman* is bought by women, read by women, and, as women spend nine-tenths of what men earn, the moral is obvious" (see fig. 8.2). Insofar as Molly Bloom conforms to the consumer mentality she has been assigned by virtue of her gender, "Penelope" contains many references to commodities and consumption, especially clothes and lingerie of high quality and higher-than-average price.

For example, a prized possession she remembers having received from Mrs. Stanhope on Gibraltar is a dress "from the B Marche paris" (18.612–13). She mentions it twice, emphasizing the distinctive label, as someone today might emphasize "Donna Karan" or "Ralph

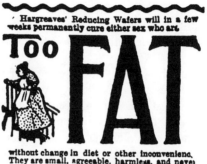

Fig. 8.3. Advertisements for English patent medicines like
the one Molly vows to try again. (Reprinted courtesy of the
Robert Opie Collection.)

Lauren." Molly has reason to be well satisfied. Au Bon Marche, constructed with arcades of glass and steel, was the first department store;
it opened on the Left Bank in 1852, the year after the Crystal Palace
exposition in London. By the 1880s, it was one of the premier fashion
centers of Paris. As Rachel Bowlby has observed, the store was built
as a temple of fashion with sumptuous interior balconies, so that the
spectator could include herself in the consuming vistas and activities
displayed there. But this Parisian dress, a treasure from Molly's past,
is no doubt somewhat out of fashion by 1904. Molly most frequently
speaks of wearing clothes and being seen in the private space of the
Blooms' bedroom, and of clothes as fetish objects and instruments for
seduction. Thus she recognizes that the middle-class woman's clothed

body is the fetishized pleasure-site of the consumer culture. She participates in advertising's promise of magical personal transformations by naming objects she desires—silkette stockings, drawers, a corset—and by making her body an adorned object of desire. Drawers are especially potent fetishes, as she knows: she has worn drawers with Boylan; she plans to wear new drawers to display her body for Bloom. She even comments in a moment of etymological inspiration that the still-daring fashion in women's dress, bloomers, is doubtless named for Bloom, who is always "skeezing" at the girls on the bicycles.

By fetishizing her body to excite male desire, Molly participates in consumerism's perverse dialectic. She assimilates the images of women offered by the commodity system and tries to transform herself by its magic, rather than maintaining her body's singularity and autonomy. For example, she reminds herself to try again "that anti-fat" (18.455–56), one of many patent medicines which promised "to quickly remove all superfluous flesh, improving the health and figure" (see fig. 8.3). These products were heavily advertised in newspapers and magazines at the end of the nineteenth century, and were very popular with consumers. Yet in Molly's misplaced desire to transform her body she is also unwittingly enacting what Frantz Fanon states is the master desire of imperialism: to efface and make illegitimate the colonized person's distinctive culture and history. In this regard, the most illusory advertising language in "Penelope" is a text Molly quotes from a corset ad in the *Gentlewoman:*

yes and the second pair of silkette stockings is laddered after one days wear I could have brought them back to Lewers this morning and kicked up a row and made that one change them only not to upset myself and run the risk of walking into him and ruining the whole thing and one of those kidfitting corsets Id want advertised cheap in the *Gentlewoman* with elastic gores on the hips he saved the one I have but thats no good what did they say they give a delightful figure line 11/6 obviating that unsightly broad appearance across the lower back to reduce flesh my belly is a bit too big Ill have to knock off the stout at dinner or am I getting too fond of it the last they sent from ORourkes was as flat as a pancake (18.442–52)

Here Molly's distinctive discourse style merges approvingly with the style of the advertising copywriter. She fantasizes about wearing this corset, ready to accept the discomforts this fashionable garment will impose on her body. She seems to be persuaded by this advertising's promise of "a delightful figure line" into choosing a cultural politics which would literally and figuratively dis-figure her body's history (see figs. 8.4 and 8.5).

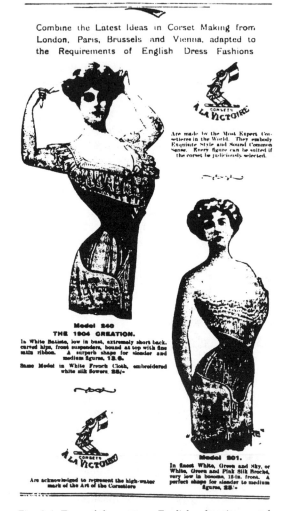

Fig. 8.4. Turn-of-the-century English advertisement for corsets. (Reprinted courtesy of Cyril Pearl, *Dublin in Bloomtime*. New York: Viking Press, 1969.)

Molly's wearing the *Gentlewoman*'s corset and acceding to the claims of the advertisement would colonize her body by transforming her into a sexual and political commodity shaped by the ideology of the British-dominated magic system. The "correct" advertising discourse of the corset ad would reshape her body according to the rules of

Fig. 8.5. Contemporary advertisement for an American-made corset available from an English distributor. (Reprinted courtesy of Cyril Pearl, *Dublin in Bloomtime*. New York: Viking Press, 1969.)

English fashion, just as the speech of Menton, the Nameless One, and Boylan had earlier transformed her name into an exchangeable Dublin commodity. If we read English-Irish cultural politics typologically, we can further align the national and personal situations. As Ireland was brought into political union with England in 1800, Molly-as-Ireland would force her body into English clothing to satisfy the demands of a later form of imperialism. In 1904, Ireland is a British colony whose public mind is shaped by false, manufactured political images of itself. So, too, Molly falsely imagines herself having the "delightful figure line" of an upper-middle-class English woman of fashion.

We notice, however, a crucial mis-fit between the two kinds of discourse describing the corset as object of desire. Molly's voice self-consciously quotes some of the ad's text verbatim, and places it in the midst of her own differently-inflected monologue. In effect, Molly betrays the note of her characteristic voice by this quoted discourse about the corset. Her fantasy image of a transformed body is rendered through the ad's genteel, euphemistic style, which substitutes "lower back" for "bottom." But Molly has used the vernacular "bottom" earlier with no embarrassment, when she complains about the behavior of their former housemaid, Mary, in Ontario Terrace, "padding out her false bottom to exite him" (18.56–57). However, she rescues her body and her voice from this mistaken colonialist self-improvement project by her greater allegiance to a quintessential (Guinness-ential) Irish commodity. She says, leaving off the ad's discourse and resuming her own pattern of speech, "my belly is a bit too big Ill have to knock off the stout at dinner." But, given her liking for self-indulgence, her renouncing this particular Irish transformative commodity seems an unlikely prospect.

In her talk of corsets and their apparently wonderful powers, Molly comes closest to echoing the advertising language that surrounds Gerty MacDowell in "Nausicaa." Gerty is a true believer in advertising as the "magic system." She constantly expresses herself in the slogans of advertising, from the ad copy for eyebrowleine, to the mention of a favorite brand of hand cream, "queen of ointments," to the society-page prose that announces her fantasy marriage to Reggy Wylie (a marriage that can never take place, but figures large in her consciousness). As depicted by Joyce, Gerty becomes a type of the Irish consumer whose "womanly" goal, as defined by the ideology of consumerism, is frustrated: there will be no romantic marriage, no home to make beautiful.[4] Gerty, a Dubliner with aspirations to marry above her class, is among the women to whom the commodity culture addresses its most powerful messages. But Gerty never escapes the mentality or the social place of her assigned part in the colonial hierarchy. She is not empowered by the commodity system's promise of personal transformation, but remains one of its victims. An Irish-woman of the lower-middle class with a limited social function—a babysitter—she is a worker in the system of economic imperialism that British advertising has helped to produce. Thus she buys what is offered to her, including the image of Bloom as an exotic stranger. She cannot renounce the self-destructive colonial mentality, in which the colonized depend on the strong conquerors, and seek, perversely, to emulate them. Her dependence on Vera Verity's wisdom, and her belief in the rituals of the sentimental romance fiction of "The Princess Novelette" are signs confirming her colonial dependence.

Like Gerty on the strand, Molly in bed occupies a physically and socially marginal position in Dublin. However, Molly explicitly rejects the inculturated attitudes of female timidity and shame that Gerty has internalized. Molly participates in the advertising rituals of English commodity culture, but is not defined or contained by them, as Gerty clearly is. Instead Molly claims a symbolic relation to the natural world. She chooses a symbol which exists prior to and in opposition to the commodity culture of advertising when she identifies herself with a poetic image, "the flower of the mountain." Paradoxically, despite the conventionality of the floral image in the poetic tradition, the indi-vidual style and force of Molly's discourse break the pattern of passive cultural consumption. In the coda of "Penelope" Joyce's desire for ap-propriate narrative closure politicizes Molly's relationship to English commodity culture, but in a new way. With several rhetorical figures signaling Molly's mental disengagement from the world of commodi-ties and social goods, and the substitution of emotionally charged personal images, Joyce makes Molly "natural" and "Irish" once again.[5]

As she turns in bed trying to doze off, Molly's consciousness turns from absorption with commodities and their public symbolic value toward affirmation of the private symbolic value of "a flower of the mountain," Bloom's name for her when they were together on Howth head. This turn begins first with Molly's comment on flowers, as she notices the bedroom's wallpaper pattern: "what kind of flowers are those they invented like the stars the wallpaper in Lombard street was much nicer" (18.1545–46). Molly sees the wallpaper and is plunged into plans of ordering flowers from "Lambes there beside Findlaters," of Stephen as a potential visitor, and of "those fairy cakes in Liptons," of which she says "I love the smell of a rich big shop" (18.1548–54). At this point she is still entertaining sugar-coated commodity dreams, and it is worth noting in passing that "Liptons" refers to one of English merchant Thomas Lipton's tea shops in Dublin. But Molly's consciousness then turns from the fantasy world of the commodity and its mass-produced symbolic images. Her decolonization and corresponding reclamation of personal, poetic symbols begins when she declares her love of flowers and all nature: "I love flowers Id love to have the whole place swimming in roses God of heaven theres nothing like nature . . . rivers and lakes and flowers all sorts of shapes and smells and colours springing up even out of the ditches primroses and violets nature it is" (18.1557–63). Molly then remembers that flowers are a personally valuable symbol, invested with emotional significance on "the day I got him to propose to me." The process of refitting the poetic image over the marketplace image, of reclaiming the symbolic value of a "flower of the mountain" and letting fade "what kind of flowers . . . they invented" is nearly complete: "yes he said I was a flower of the mountain yes so we are flowers all a womans body yes that was one true thing he said in his life" (18.1576–77). In the coda of "Penelope," she repeats the phrase twice more, as she remembers "the rosegardens and the jessamine and geraniums and cactuses and Gibraltar as a girl where I was a Flower of the mountain." Finally, Molly remembers that September day in 1888 with Bloom on Howth, "and then I asked him with my eyes to ask again yes and then he asked me would I yes to say yes my mountain flower" (18.1602, 1605–6).

These passages are poetic, and their power derives from Joyce's exploitation of the rhetorical figures of poetic language—metaphor, meter, and repetition of images. Yet Molly's repeated affirmations in the coda of "Penelope" also indicate how Joyce employs her changing responses to commodities and their images. This dialectic of response is a poetic and a political process, beginning with her consumption of goods and discourses, working toward personal decolonization through her resistance to the invented images of commodities, finally achieving her reinstatement of the floral trope as personal symbol. Of course, the movement of her consciousness and response is always mediated through images, as Molly's thoughts turn from modern artifice to older artifice. From consumer products and mass-produced modern images, Molly's rhetorical turn is to woman-as-flower, the Petrarchan poetic tropes imitated and parodied by countless poets. We have seen that modern advertising is an economic and political construct, a social communication of goods and messages that shapes societies. So, too, the poet's floral trope is a social and aesthetic construct, a literary idea of the feminine, a symbol of Molly's personality and the great value of her experience.[6]

The flower remains a mediated image of Molly, not a universal metaphor for womanhood. It is true that in selecting a final image to represent Molly's life, an image that poets associated with women in elite culture and that subsequently became a popular cliché, Joyce risks trivializing her experience. Instead, I think her poetic association of her physical self with a flower is neither sentimentalism nor erotic mysticism, but a gesture with which Joyce reinforces Molly's imaginative force as a character in his novel. Molly's flower is a personal image retrieved from the stock poetic and popular images of women, and a political image with which she clearly rejects the commodification of woman's bodies promoted by the ideology of the *Gentlewoman* magazine. Molly therefore resists England's merchandizing and colonizing imperatives by reclaiming a symbol encoded with personal significance from the store of publically merchandised images.

With her rhetorical turn to the flower trope, Molly makes a significant political and aesthetic gesture. She asserts the value of the individually created image over the value of the mass-produced advertising image, which always denies the past and the future to feature the static and glamorized present. Thus, when Molly appropriates her floral image from the reified products of the cultural marketplace, she validates her personal history and its continuity with the present. By retrieving from memory and experience this important symbol of her history, she legitimizes her resistance to the spectacle of consumption and decolonizes her mind and body. As rhetorical closure and as "countersign" to the rest of *Ulysses*, then, Molly's last verbal turns in "Penelope" subvert the cultural and political dominance of the magic system. No longer a captive mind or an all-consuming colonial, Molly discards the fashionable vestments of the *Gentlewoman* and invests fresh meaning in a symbol of her past.

Notes

1. This illustration of the "beneficent" economic imperialism that characterized the mentality of turn-of-the-century English advertisers and manufacturers was published in 1902 in Thomas Dixon's *The Advertisers' Guardian*, (10).

2. In addition, I would claim that Leopold Bloom is part of the culture of resistance in Ireland. In his job as an advertising canvasser for the *Freeman*, Bloom forms part of the discourse of mass consumer culture in Ireland. As a politically informed individual, however, he acts in clandestine resistance to British rule, using the advertising he sells for commercial and political ends. The best example is the newspaper advertisement he proposes and designs for the wine merchant, Keyes. As Bloom envisions it, Keyes's ad has a promi-

nent subtext—a political endorsement of Home Rule—and Bloom explains this aspect of his design to Nanetti in "Aeolus."

3.   Don Gifford and Robert J. Seidman note that Joyce's realistic portrait of Irish urban life includes the significant fact that Dublin's population in 1904 is necessarily composed of consumers rather than producers. Yet these Irish consumers are far from affluent. The continuing disenfranchisement of the Irish middle-class by British economic policy meant, in Gifford and Seidman's words, that "outside of the church, law, medicine, civil service, and merchandising, there was precious little employment for members of the middle class, and the number of Bloom's contemporaries who are on their way down (and out) in the novel [is] not only testimony to Joyce's disaffection with middle-class Dublin, it is also a function of the hard realities that were the conditions of that Dublin world" (8).

4.   See Thomas Richards's chapter, "Those Lovely Seaside Girls," for an illuminating discussion of commodity advertising using images of "the seaside girl," and Gerty's place in this system.

5.   It would seem that Molly's Irishness is more metaphorical than literal, at least in terms of her family history. As Herring observes, Molly is a British colonial born in Gibraltar, of Irish, Spanish, and Jewish background. After a girlhood in which she belonged neither to the British garrison nor the Gibraltarian town, she came to Ireland and married Bloom at the age of eighteen. My point is that whatever her national status as Irishwoman or foreign-born British subject, Molly has always lived "beyond the pale" of English cultural norms, try as she might in 1904 to fit herself into the constraining styles of speech and dress advocated in the *Gentlewoman*. It is not simply that the "kid-fitting corset" advertised in this London woman's magazine will not fit Molly. Rather, the advertiser's display of such clothing is a symbolic communication of the social uniform and the proper attitudes required of the fashionable Englishwoman.

6.   See Margot Norris, "Joyce's Heliotrope," for a provocative study of flower tropes in Joyce.

Works Cited

Adorno, Theodor, "The Culture Industry Reconsidered." *New German Critique* 6 (1975): 12–19.

Barthes, Roland. *Sade/Fourier/Loyola*. Trans. Richard Miller. New York: Farrar, 1976.

Berger, John. *Ways of Seeing*. 1972. New York: Penguin, 1977.

Bowlby, Rachel. *Just Looking: Consumer Culture in Dreiser, Gissing, and Zola*. New York: Methuen, 1985.

Deane, Seamus. *Celtic Revivals: Essays in Modern Irish Literature 1880–1980*. New York: Faber, 1985.

Dixon, Thomas. *The Advertisers' Guardian*. London: Thomas Dixon, 1902.

Dyer, Gillian. *Advertising as Communication*. New York: Methuen, 1982.

Fanon, Frantz. *The Wretched of the Earth*. New York: Grove, 1966.

Fiske, John. *Understanding Popular Culture*. Boston: Unwin Hyman, 1989.

Gifford, Don, with Robert J. Seidman. "Introduction." *Ulysses Annotated: Notes for James Joyce's "Ulysses."* Berkeley: University of California Press, 1988.

Herring, Phillip F. "Toward An Historical Molly Bloom." *English Literary History* 45 (1978): 501–21.

Horkheimer, Max, and Theodor Adorno. *Dialectic of Enlightenment*. Trans. John Cumming. 1944. New York: Continuum, 1972.

Leiss, William, Stephen Kline, and Sut Jhally. *Social Communication in Advertising: Persons, Products, and Images of Well-Being*. New York: Methuen, 1986.

Lukács, Georg. "The Phenomenon of Reification." *History and Class Consciousness: Studies in Marxist Dialectics*. Trans. Rodney Livingstone. Cambridge: MIT Press, 1971. 83–110.

Norris, Margot. "Joyce's Heliotrope." *Coping with Joyce: Essays from the Copenhagen Symposium*. Ed. Morris Beja and Shari Benstock. Columbus: Ohio State University Press, 1989. 3–24.

Opie, Robert. *Rule Britannia: Trading on the British Image*. Harmondsworth: Penguin, 1985.

Richards, Thomas. *The Commodity Culture of Victorian England: Advertising and Spectacle, 1851–1914*. Stanford: Stanford University Press, 1990.

Said, Edward. "Yeats and Decolonization." *Field Day Pamphlet 15*. 1988.

Williams, Raymond. "Advertising: The Magic System." *Problems in Materialism and Culture*. London: New Left Books, 1980.

Williams, Raymond. *Keywords*. New York: Oxford University Press, 1983.

9

"Who's She When She's at Home?"
Molly Bloom and the Work of Consumption

Jennifer Wicke

Molly Bloom, in déshabillé, fingers shiny with butter from the morning toast, interrupts her breakfast in bed to determine the meaning of a word found in the thickets of *Ruby, Pride of the Ring,* marking it with her hairpin for the obliging Leopold to read. "Met him what? he asked. Here, she said. What does that mean?" "Metempyschosis? Yes. Who's he when he's at home? . . . Metempsychosis, he said, frowning. It's Greek: from the Greek. That means the transmigration of souls. O, rocks! she said. Tell us in plain words" (4.336–37, 339–43). This scene of instruction famously introduces a portentous term for the text, played out against its *mise-en-scene* of orange-keyed chamber pot, sibilant bedsprings, and rather squalid lingerie. Embedded, as it could be said to be, solidly within the domestic detritus of the everyday, metempsychosis, as a word, erupts out of acts of consumption—the desultory consuming of breakfast, the casual consumption of *Ruby,* left to lie unceremoniously underneath the bed. The multifarious affinities of metempsychosis with both the "mythologization" of the text, to follow Adorno's distinction, which differentiates the simple use of mythology as a theme from an embedded, linguistic, and textual mythologization process of the sort Joyce employs,[1] and with the issue of historicity, repetition and return, are crucial, and have been valuably discussed. However, the connection of "met him pike hoses"

174

with the activities of, and the consciousness entailed by, consumption is harder to discern. The transmigration of souls can beautifully analogize the nightmares of history, the wanderings and the eternal returns of material history as it is lived over time by disparate groups of people, and can offer a technique for the staging of shifts of identity from disparate ontological planes—Bloom as Moses as Christ as Ulysses as Parnell as Charlie Chaplin. But additionally, metempsychosis folds into the transformative labors of consumption—the logic of consumption, one could say, is metempsychotic.

As we attempt to grapple with consumption in theoretical, political, and aesthetic ways, the importance of consumption to Joyce's work has emerged as a powerful focus for new readings of his major texts.

The imbrication of *Dubliners* and *A Portrait, Ulysses,* and even *Finnegans Wake* in a material world awash in the detritus of consumer objects and the subjectivity of the everyday universe of consumption is now at least evident. Many questions follow from this recasting of our regard and the decision to take it as important that these texts are extravagantly interlaced with consumer minutiae—not the least of which is what critical paths we then choose to take through Joyce's texts. At this stage of discovery, however, the approach to consumption is still inevitably filtered through long-standing theories of consumer culture, the status of the commodity and commodity consciousness, or recent theoretical takes on those now pressing issues. Grateful as one is for the rereading of Joyce they are providing, it will be all the more useful to look at Joyce's texts not just as sites for the application of currently interesting rubrics like consumption, but as sources of privileged access to the problems of describing and defining consumption itself. In other words, very new things can be learned about the matrix of consumer society by reading Joyce, if these texts are seriously held to have the issue of consumption at their root. Here, I sketch the implications of this thesis by framing the topic of consumption as philosophically, aesthetically, and politically grand enough to warrant such attention, thereby guarding against any potential reductiveness in making this the scene of Joyce's textual labors. A crucial premise is that the culture of consumption *is* the culture of modernity, and that what we talk about when we talk about modernity is some form of consumptive relation. Joyce's *Ulysses* is the greater orbit of reference for my formulation of the work of consumption, within which Molly's situation traces its own concrete arc.

As critical fashions alter, and as other modes of inquiry arrive at a perhaps temporary exhaustion, increasing attention to the material concerns so evident in Joyce's work have emerged, sometimes under new historicist auspices, or in the form of Marxist or cultural materialist or even sheer empiricist analyses. This is definitely for the good, and it has served to shift the perception of *Ulysses*, for example, from a monument of aesthetic erudition to a dynamically social text. In line with these preoccupations, a new concentration on what could loosely be called the features of the marketplace, or modernity under the sign of capitalism, or of the forces of social exchange is also discerned. Attempts to locate the valences of advertising or the vagaries of the commodity form within Joyce are proliferating, and I also have contributed to this body of interpretation in emphasizing the centrality of advertisement to the aesthetic and social armature of *Ulysses*.

Many of the most sophisticated and valuable forays into the larger social resonances of the Joycean text have been predicated on theories of mass culture, of commodity fetishism, and of social reification in the historical processes of capitalism which have their own larger life in cultural debate. Among the contributors to this long and complex critical tradition are Georg Simmel, Max Weber, Thorstein Veblen, Walter Benjamin, Georg Lukacs, the Frankfurt School thinkers Theodor Adorno and Max Horkheimer, Jean Baudrillard, Pierre Bourdieu, Michel Foucault, and others, all essential in referring to the foundations of our present understanding of mass culture, consumption in general, and the commodity form. What can be claimed, in the shorthand contractions necessary here, is that whether issuing from the right or the left, the primary tenor of theories of consumption is distinctly negative. On the one, that is, the right, hand, consumption is a fallen if eminently necessary social process, which is mercifully refined out of existence in the rarefied circles of art and culture—*Ulysses*, for example, can be held up as an artifact impervious to the depradations of mass culture and rigorously defiant of consumption, having made itself unconsumable, the veritable proof of its artistic merit. The left hand of this argument doesn't require that texts attain a purity unsullied by signs of traffic with social relations, since the assumption is that texts arise from social contexts, or are social contexts themselves, but consumption arrives equally tainted in this arena, because it is the very marker of ideological control and the very symbol of capitalism's incursions into art and culture.

To elaborate this again through the lens of *Ulysses* is to recall the prescient and very intelligent considerations of Fredric Jameson, as he lauds *Ulysses* for its exhibition of the fragmented alienation of modern society and its critical refusal to be embedded in the Procrustean bed of consumption by the same token. Franco Moretti, in a similar if more hyperbolic vein, sees *Ulysses* as the embodiment of a principled refusal of mass culture and all the degraded commodities of capitalism; Bloom, in his reading, is the epitome of degraded consumer consciousness, and a species of cautionary tale for the reader's edification—do not do as Bloom does. The antipathy toward consumption at all levels, and the consequent celebration of what is difficult, avant-garde, or modernist as its counterpoint is a prevailing, I might even say the distinctive, feature of contemporary critical thinking in a variety of guises. Often this animus crystallizes in the valorizing of a more authentic, original, or folk culture now eradicated by consumption, or of a working-class culture thought to have more authenticity, or by extolling avant-garde practices precisely for their repudiation of consumptive strategies, in the quite stereotyped vision of what those strategies are thought to be. Even more ironically there is an attempt to recuperate aspects of mass culture as sites of resistance or struggle, with the hidden assumption that those participating in the consumption in the first place are entirely victimized by their contact with a hegemonic cultural industry enforcing its hierarchies in and through mass cultural schemes. That social hierarchies and exploitation are the order of the day is certainly my own starting premise, so my quarrel is not at all with the dimension of political critique visible in the legacy of critical theory. The problems arise when the social analysis proceeds from such a reductive view of consumption, which then obscures consumption's manifold possibilities, political and otherwise. Not the least of the results of this oversight, if perhaps less immediately relevant to many people, is the inability to locate the really majestic prescience of *Ulysses* in its understanding of consumption.

Far surpassing these examples in a supple approach to mass culture is the pioneering work done by Cheryl Herr, as one instance, where popular and mass forms of culture are traced through the ostensibly higher precincts of *Ulysses,* or the thoughtful contributions of Thomas Richards, Garry Leonard, Richard Simon, and others. Whatever the critical matrix, however, it has proven extremely difficult to avoid conceptualizing consumption under the auspices of the commodity, as a practice inherently partaking of the alienation or reification thought to haunt the commodity in its fetishized, indeed its only, form. Commodities are thrust upon one, they are the goods that speak, in Levi-Strauss's phrase, in this case, the goods that speak the subject (3–47). Human beings have been replaced by things, and human interrelations are shriveled to the phantom relation with objects so typifying modern social life. Following out this logic, it is distance from the commodity which is praiseworthy, or if such distance is not obtainable, then consumption is less a personal failing or an index of extreme alienation than symptomatic of any subjectivity in its fated, doomed encounter with the capitalist economy.

What I am proposing here is that consumption is a mode of work, that, in contrast to its reputation as the passive, effeminate, and mindless side of consciousness and modern social being, it is in fact a highly complex social and psychic labor, whose results are often contradictory or ambiguous, but never simply foregone conclusions. Work in this sense is not necessarily the physical labor involved in procuring the object of consumption—which, of course, can take form as a symbolic object (a book, a film, a poster, a museum exhibit) as readily as it may materialize as a can of Diet Pepsi on the supermarket shelf or a new lipstick from the department store cosmetics counter—nor only the labor sometimes required to physically transform the objects which enter our lives. Instead, this work may signify the time of possession, a particular context of presentation as a gift or as memorabilia, or the incorporation of a single object into a stylistic array which is used then to express the creator's place in relation to others similarly accoutered. The object is transformed by its intimate association with a particular individual or social group, or by the relationship between these, and such transformations are the work of consumption. This is not to say, of course, that all objects are or can be consumed in some transformative way; without question, there are networks of commodities deployed in powerfully oppressive ways, and the estrangements and refractions occasioned by that oppression are only too evident as the backdrop and even the substance of daily life. However, assigning an intrinsic negativity to the commodity, and an equally mordant and inescapable pathos to consumption, has highly reductive effects on how we gauge the social world and the possibilities inherent in it.[2]

To move back to textual terrain is to find *Ulysses* in some senses anticipating this quest for another means of qualifying the social relations of consumption, which are, in modern times, essentially what we call culture. Let me return to what I singled out as a common approach to *Ulysses'* greatness, or to its quintessential modernism, depending on the style of the critics involved: that while *Ulysses* may be engaged in a "dialectic with mass culture," either to its credit or to its loss it relentlessly reasserts its own imponderable difficulty, its avant-gardist or modernist critical edge, defying consumability. (I will set to one side momentarily Cheryl Herr's important alternative, that *Ulysses* be considered to have been written at least as much by its surrounding cultural practices as by a singular author.) Just as the stances

toward consumption I have delineated maintain that consumption or
its objects can invariably be traced back to the intentional authorship
of its producers, thereby ignoring consumption as a, or *the*, cultural
activity par excellence, so too these more local theories of the production of *Ulysses* insist, if not on an author succumbing to the Wim-
sattian fallacy, then at least to an omniscient producer able to outfox
the strategies of consumption. If we consider *Ulysses* to be engaged in
another kind of encounter with consumption, though, the boundary
lines are not so tidy. I am not implying that *Ulysses* is given over to
mass culture—that point, I hope, has already been broached. Rather,
I am taking *Ulysses* to be, at a high level of abstraction, an enactment
of the contradictions of consumption—as a work of consumption (an
artifact) on the work of, that is, the work entailed by, consumption.
Ulysses sets up a space, both a physical space (the book) and a temporal
space (the time involved in traversing the book), for the consideration
of this problem. The either/or insistence so embedded in the high art/
mass culture debates which swirl around *Ulysses* is alien to this text,
which parades itself as an exemplary work of consumption instead. I
will try to stage this perhaps outrageous claim more globally in con-
cluding, while now I retreat to more local spaces within *Ulysses* to
probe some of the implications, in particular to the realm of Molly
and "Penelope." To read Molly is to get a fix on what the work of
consumption, even including the work of the writing of *Ulysses*, may
entail.

It may seem counterintuitive to consider this book in any kind of
relation to the books we deem eminently consumable, examples of
which dot the text like candy—*Ruby, Pride of the Ring* will do as well
as any other. Its quasi-pornographic status would seem to put it at
farthest remove from the Joycean text, since we are convinced that
pornography completely bypasses intellection. In fact, *Sweets of Sin*,
the other delicacy shared in its reading by Leopold and Molly, as a title
is a nice synechdoche for the prevailing view of consumption, since
like candy its objects are presumed to go down easily and to vanish
into nothingness, while the appetite for more vacuous consumption
is ever whetted by the sinful temptations of those who produce the
objects. The book, though, is an incredibly rich text as consumed
by Bloom, who takes it up into his own psychosexual, class, and
national orbit and gets extraordinary mileage from rearrangements
of its fantasy components, not always for ecdysiastic purposes—the
book can hint to him of mortal thoughts or of philosophical specu-
lations concomitantly. *Ulysses*, too, however, consumes even its "soft
pornography" intertexts in this fashion—*Ruby, Pride of the Ring* is a

textual object within its panoply which is recontextualized, shifted and altered, made obsessive, used as a secret code, and so forth. That abundance, or perfusion, is excessive, is messy, and is also itself a synechdoche for the method of the book as a whole.

Joyce's statement that in *Ulysses* he wanted to render Dublin so materially that, if destroyed, it could be reconstituted from the book gives us additional access into the freeze-dried consumption process this text involves. I don't mean this pejoratively, as if in recapitulating Dublin as a whirling collection of objects in relation to one another he were deracinating the city—far from it. The quote overlooks the fact that the Dublin which might be destroyed would, anyway, be many years beyond 1904; the book never forgets the evanescence of the consumer world, and yet its perdurability as it becomes social relation, or material and intellectual culture.

To speak of consumption in Ireland is problematic because the Ireland of 1904 is a colony; in some measure its economic underdevelopment exists because Ireland is trapped in a backwater as a consumer market for British goods, without the independent means of production necessary to create its own goods for internal use. It is an ironic and well-known fact that the only really viable, indigenously manufactured product for internal consumption as well as for the export market at the time of *Ulysses* was Guinness Stout. Other than this liquidly circulating product, Ireland was systematically used—no other economic word will quite suffice—by England as the source of agricultural raw materials, including the cattle Mr. Deasy so blithely worries about, and perhaps primarily as a captive market for the injection of its own industrial goods, goods at every level from the necessities of life to the meta-consumptions of cultural forms.[3] This makes the consumption taking place within *Ulysses* consumption at a double remove. In other words, it is the consumption of commodities which are themselves already mediated by and through the colonial relation of British dominance over Ireland. The consumption operates in its own right, and then also as a consumption of the colonial status quo, of the unequal relations between Ireland and England which are crystallized in the distribution and consumption of commodities of all sorts.

Molly is in an even more mediated position as a consumer than the general run of characters in the text because her ties to Ireland are funneled through her youth spent in Gibraltar; as a resident of Dublin she is subjectively dispersed out over her past in another outpost and also mobilized by the presence on Irish soil of British artifacts and styles. Her doubleness doubles the equivocal position of the Irish consuming subject, while her gender contributes too to a straining at the seams of the consumptive norm, if such a thing can be said to exist. Molly is literally transmigratory, and if we have come to equate her very penumbra of being with Home, Molly as the plump period which marks the domestic spot, this is our own blindness to the migratory richness of her culture of consumption. Molly remains at home during much of 16 June 1904; during the peregrinations of the body of the text we merely see her white arm flung out from an upper window of the house in Eccles Street in the Wandering Rocks, as she tosses a coin to the old sailor, "for England, home and beauty," a slogan with considerable fantasmatic power for Molly Bloom. Her traveler's orbit, by domestic contrast, encompasses the home, but who she is when she's there is a mosaic of consuming travels, her placedness as a double refugee, her interior organization of the wanderings of the text.

The debates which have swirled around Molly Bloom as character, voice, or *ecriture* in the text have tended to constellate around the "Penelope" episode, and then to argue the case for Molly as a real woman, or a good woman, or a bad woman, or as not-woman, or as woman under erasure, with varying degrees of theoretical sophistication. "Penelope" can be valorized as expressing a female *jouissance* so acutely powerful it sweeps punctuation away in its wake, or be celebrated or anathematized as writing in drag, a linguistic imposture masquerading as the real, unsymbolizable thing, "woman."[4] I want to elide this debate by sidestepping it, in favor of tracing the metempsychotic consequences of Molly Bloom's consumption, a consumption which is assuredly gendered, but which has stakes beyond cataloguing the supposed sexual politics of *Ulysses* as a whole. My reading moves away from the argument that Joyce trivializes Molly by immersing her in consumer obsessions, but beyond this, claims that such immersion would not be trivial in any event. Molly as consumer subject is doing cognitive, analytic work. Moreover, the larger internationalist context of *Ulysses* as a whole is *recovered* from Molly's private consumer meditation—these are not divorced elements of the text. The reading of "Penelope" can't be closed down with gender concerns alone—or to do so forecloses on the historical, the national, the political in favor of a very narrow and privatized notion of sexual politics. Molly Bloom is a textual crucible of consumption, and I propose seriously that one can learn much from this about the conditions of modernity under consumption, and the consuming consciousness the modernist text refracts. To discuss this will require some slippage among designations for this "Molly Bloom." The emphasis falls on the textual, in other words, written construction of this discursive entity, but the sentimental and characterological elements of *Ulysses* are bracketed, I think, at some peril to the mass cultural frame of the text, so at times in my analysis "Molly Bloom" achieves character status too, although never as a flesh-and-blood simulacrum of "woman."

This doesn't amount to pointing out that Molly Bloom, as a character, is a consumer, or, more sexily, a consuming subject—features which make her no different from any other character in the text. Leopold Bloom is precisely such a consuming subject.[5] As a virtual litmus test of most politically progressive or materialist analysis, the condemnation of consumption follows naturally from a horror of the manipulative nature of the capitalism which depends on its consumptive matrix. There are other ways to conceive of this relation, however, if consumption can be accorded the status of a complex and intentional cultural mode. It is just such an oppositional version of consumption I suggest—an active, or a productive consumption, where the interest lies in the uses to which the consumptive strategy is put. Meaning is *use*, as Wittgenstein's phrase ever arrestingly warns us; in the absence of any social alternative to consuming, when we are talking about the circumstances of the modern world and the global economy, consumption cannot simply be equated with alienation or manipulation, and the curtain of analysis be pulled mercifully closed to hide its depradations. One can draw on the insight of Michel de Certeau, in his delineation of consumption as an active tactic of the weak, recasting the products shunted to them by their reformulation, and additionally on the emphasis Pierre Bourdieu places on the productive nature of social consumption, its constant making of meanings.[6] Further, in this analysis, consumption itself must be taken in an elaborated, expanded sense, since it more typically is conceived only as a shorthand for the act of buying mass-produced products; consumption refers not only to the regime of the commodity as literalized in shopping, or window shopping, or choosing to read *Ruby, Pride of the Ring*. Both material resources and semiotic and cultural forms are consumed—transport, clothing, food, the media, education, language and gesture, travel, thought, as John Fiske productively reminds us (7). Consumption is imbricated in every transaction, even, or especially, in the production of meaning which is language. Consumption should not be viewed with the transfixed, transfixing lens of the spectacular/specular, or with the dismay evinced at finding a slag· heap outside one's front door; above all, there is the final critical irony that *Ulysses* is a book which calmly expects to be consumed. Some of that tranquility needs to be recaptured in order to give appropriate consideration to the nature of consumption and what the book can tell us about it. The danger in these claims is that they have a Panglossian ring. They seem to suggest that we live in the best of all possible consumer worlds and that the best thing to do is lie back, consume, and enjoy it. For this reason, I should underscore the political framework of my own analysis by insisting that it is only by seriously exploring the extent to which all the operations of modern culture, including political critique, are performed under the sign of consumption, that clues about rearranging the disposition of consumption within culture will emerge.

Moreover, following the theorist of modernity perhaps most persuasive in interrogating the psychosocial aspects of consumption, Georg Simmel, I want to specify Molly Bloom's work of consumption as urban, national, even urbane, as well as domestic. Writing of the determinations of the metropolitan character in "The Metropolis and Mental Life," Simmel proposes that "it is the decisive nature of the metropolis that its inner life overflows by waves into a far-flung national or international area," and, correspondingly, that like the city "man does not end with the limits of his body or the area comprising his immediate activity. Rather is the range of the person constituted by the sum of effects emanating from him temporally and spatially" (419). Following out Molly Bloom's work of consumption requires mapping the range of her effects, tracing her emanations as they leave their commodified scent across a wide swath of metropolitan, national, and international geography, as well as textual space.

Just as we speak of the division of labor in the productive sphere, so we also should take seriously the idea of consumption as work, containing also its own versions of the divisions of labor. These divisions don't unpack neatly as the simple bifurcation of gender. Even so finely nuanced a commentary as Thomas Richard's chapter on "Nausicaa" in his *The Commodity Culture of Victorian England* collapses these divisions into two paths: "the female labor of consumption remains bracketed within male production and consumption as women become the go-betweens mediating men and their particular desires. The gendering of consumption works exclusively to masculine advantage, freezing women in postures prescribed by the watchful gaze of the male. Gerty does not stop Bloom dead in his tracks. The Medusan glance of 'Nausicaa' belongs not to her but to Bloom" (246–47). Here women's consumption is a matter of gilding the lily of male desire; that is not the sort of work I have in mind, for consumption or for Molly, who quite clearly is not stopped in her tracks by Leopold's gaze. Consumption so regarded offers nothing by way of active, tactical use of consumption by women, and thus cannot conceive of the productions of meaning immanent in even seemingly male-directed consumption.

The "Penelope" episode could be seen as a locus classicus for these varieties of work, for the divagations of consumption. The choice of the word "work," instead of its synonym, "labor," is important because the latter fits too neatly into the preexisting compartments of the labor theory of value, for instance, while "work" has a more sinuous semantic life—offering a word for labor, but more generally what Marx himself called the work of making the (individual's) world—his *homo faber*–definition—and just as insistently labeling a discrete piece of work, usually a work of art or creative labor. Certain interpretations of the "Penelope" episode have siphoned off the monological evidence of that labor, to regard it as expressive of Molly's quite individual characteristics, her supposed petty vanities and materialistic urgings, her resolute sluttish practicality; other readings submerge the materiality of consumption to arrive at an allegory of fertile, flowing, fructifying woman, the semiotic abundant. This analysis hopes to take the sheer productivity of the latter, and combine it with the cheese-paring accountancy of the former, to gauge the complexity of the consumptive moment in "Penelope."

the second pair of silkette stockings is laddered after one days wear I could have brought them back to Lewers this morning and kicked up a row and made that one change them only not to upset myself and run the risk of walking into him and ruining the whole thing and one of those kidfitting corsets Id want advertised cheap in the Gentlewoman with elastic gores on the hips he saved the one I have but thats no good what did they say they give a delightful figure line 11/6 obviating that unsightly broad appearance across the lower back to reduce flesh my belly is a bit too big Ill have to knock off the stout at dinner (18. 442–50)

The exfoliations of consumption as labor unfurl out of this little node of hosiery. The fact that the stockings have run requires some actual deliberative work—going to the store and fighting to exchange them; the purchasing of them in the first place was an orchestration of time and desire and money which, given the half-life of stockings, will have to be gone through time and again. These are surface acts of work, but they accompany of necessity the decision to buy the stockings at all, an invasion of Lewers for a commodity one can't be seen in public without. Molly's segue into the corset is another kind of interconnected work; rather than seeing this as the shallow rumination of a woman on the verge of losing her figure, the corset suggests itself as part of an interlaced commodity universe of extreme interest to a woman involved in the self-realizations of extramarital and marital sex. The actual words of the advertisement are memorized like a proof against spreading hips—a "delightful figure line" is only a trivial consideration when this act of sexual subjectivity is denied. Valerie Steele's recent work on fashion and eroticism in the late nineteenth century is able to show how mistaken is the assumption that corsets and other confining undergarments were part of the sexual oppression of women; the rage for reform of women's dress was in fact mounted by men who worried that women's reproductive abilities were threatened by sporting corsets; in that particular turn of the dialectical screw of fashion, the corset was clung to by sexually active women who had invested it as a talisman of nonreproductive sexual freedom. Molly is hardly so programmatic about this; nonetheless, her struggles with the lingerie demands of her perhaps burgeoning affair, and her problems with the toll exacted on carefully husbanded underwear by her husband's particular mode of sexual relief are highly specific to her constellation of consumptive labor. "I'll let him do it off on me behind provided he doesnt smear all my good drawers O I suppose that cant be helped" (18. 1527–29). For Blazes Boylan, "if its going to go on I want at least two other good chemises for one thing and but I dont know what kind of drawers he likes none at all I think" (18. 438–39). The "I want" should be taken in the sense of "I need," "I am wanting," the bare minimum for a complex adultery being several changes of bedroom attire. This last has nothing predatory or wanton about it, merely an acknowledgment that the conditions of sexual relations are entirely predicated on the world of style it is possible to carve out, producing the maximum erotic effects with the minimum of means, where eros itself arises out of the matrix of consumptive strategies. The flip side of these exigencies comes in a Gibraltar flashback, as Molly envisions herself in the athleticism of attending a bullfight "clothes we have to wear who invented them expecting you to walk up Killiney hill then for example at that picnic all staysed up you cant do a blessed thing in them in a crowd run or jump out of the way" (18. 627–29).

Taking mental inventory of her holdings, Molly can only count "the four paltry handkerchiefs about 6/ in all," and her weariness with these sentimental calculations prompts "sure you cant get on in this world without style all going in food and rent when I get it Ill lash it around I tell you in fine style" (18. 666–68). Style is Molly's end of things, her requisite contribution to the domestic economy, her labor, in short, and this is no mere gloss on shabby domestic proceedings. Where and how the Blooms live is a matter far beyond the reckoning out of expenses for food and shelter. Molly's consumptive efforts in this direction are part of the division of labor within consumption, because with their rocky downwardly mobile slide it is Molly's consumptive decisions which produce a viable habitus. Obviously, a habitus is not just a place to live; it is dwelling as a state of mind. Housework itself, for those above the level of destitution, becomes what Simmel was to call "ceremonial fetishism," since the "impersonal origin and easy replaceability" of "those numerous objects which swarm around us" emerges as "an interconnected closed world that has increasingly fewer points at which the subjective soul can interpose its will and feelings."[7] Molly's subjectivity as encoded in "Penelope" penetrates and invests and suffuses the objects of her household, the commodity swarm, however meager, with a ferocious amount of cathected consciousness. She is monumentally intimate with these items and with their place in an everchanging assemblage of unquantifiable style. Even shopping has no uniform status—Molly can move from "I hate those rich shops get on your nerves" to the peroration of "those fairy cakes in Liptons I love the smell of a big rich shop at $7\frac{1}{2}$d a lb or the other ones with the cherries in them and the pinky sugar" (18. 1554–58). This contradiction isn't about women's inconsistency, but reflects that shopping is both a terrifying labor of scrutiny and frustration, as well as the site of the dream of satisfaction. The effort involved in making, in constructing the petit bourgeois identity most commentators agree on as the proper pigeonhole for the Blooms is signaled in "Penelope" on every page.

Such efforts encompass the fashion consciousness so ambivalently assigned to Molly and to women in general. Molly is acutely attuned to the subtlest oscillations in fashion; she registers these changes like a template. The circumstances of her purchases are memorialized, the waxing and waning of her fashionable commodities exquisitely charted, and her narration of subjectivity uses fashion moments as the most highly charged and valorized nodal points. Do we have to contend here with a misogynist emphasis on women and their clothes? Or with women entrapped in a fashion system, paralyzed by the male gaze? It seems to me that neither scenario is satisfactory for reading this profusion of fashion, again because the labor of consumption is slighted and the richness of *Ulysses* thereby scanted. To borrow from Georg Simmel's study of fashion and consumption, fashion provides a surface which is partly expressive of social being, but which also in part protects individuals from having to expose their private world of taste to the public eye. In that oscillation between individuality and social definition the complexities of consumption are strongly at play.

Molly's mind is wafted back to Gibraltar on the fantasmatic wings of one of the best dresses she has ever possessed; her father's lady friend, Mrs. Stanhope, had sent it to her along with a letter detailing her own amorous adventures in Paris: "watching the sun all the time weltering down on you faded all that lovely frock fathers friend Mrs Stanhope sent me from the B Marche Paris." As she thinks of the letter, it intrudes like a wedge into the writing as "wd give anything to be back in Gib and hear you sing in old Madrid or Waiting Concone . . . he bought me one of those new some word I couldn't make out shawls amusing things but tear for the least thing still theyre lovely I think dont you will always think of the lovely teas we had together scrumptious currant scones and raspberry wafers I adore" (18. 616–21). The Paris frock is not only a gift from Paris, it comes from the Bon Marché, the first great department store in Paris and the model for the spectacular " 'people's palace,' an easily accessible center of luxury and display." [8] Molly receives both the garment and the evocative words as a direct hit from this center, as she persists on the fringes of the metropole, in Gibraltar, where the sun itself competes intensely against the glare of the spectacular commodity. Mrs. Stanhope's operative word, lovely, fans out to incorporate Molly into the nets of fashionability, even on the periphery—we believe that Molly can indeed imagine these cunningly delicate new shawls. While "Gib" seems to be well stocked with luxurious British tea things, the dress is really Molly's madeleine—fashion situates her, locates her, and also provides a terrain across which she can splay out her memories, as fragile as the shawls. From the mass-produced fashion of the Bon Marché, Molly draws out a highly particular, even recondite, engagement with social being. Her own nascent sexuality, her partial understanding of her father's circumstances, her placement in the zone of Gibraltar as a defender of British nationalism while being of mixed, eccentric parentage herself, her attempts to keep up with the international middle class through the weaponry of fashion—all these contradictions collocate in the dress.

Fashion is mysterious because of its cannibalizing of the new, its appearance of waste, its incriminating connection to conspicuous consumption. As Baudelaire says, "fashion is the essence of modernity, of the transient, the fleeting, the contingent" (403). The *flaneur* is valorized as the epitome of fashion, a fashion persona arranged as a work of art because of its thoroughgoing devotion to the ephemeral. No such distinction clings to the female fashion victim, who is presumed invaded by the fashion consciousness as a form of disease, or else, as in Thorstein Veblen's invaluable analysis, parasitic on the need of the husband to demonstrate wealth on the back of his wife. Leopold Bloom is incapable of these potlatch gestures, of course; as Molly says "Ive no clothes at all the brown costume and the skirt and jacket and the one at the cleaners 3 whats that for any woman cutting up this old hat and patching up the other the men wont look at you and women try to walk on you because they know youve no man" (18. 470–74). Fashion isn't an automatic system, so that Molly can simply take over an approved style as a slavish imitator. While fashion is a language of class, and its nuances map out the border territories of class overlap and conflict, Molly's interpolation of fashion should be understood as mental energy, a productive use of what she consumes. If the dandy analogy seems too excessively complimentary, there should be an equivalently lofty typology for the class self-construction entailed in the productive consumption of fashion. Walter Benjamin's phrase for fashion, in "Theses on the Philosophy of History," that it is "a tiger leaping out to devour the past," helps to explain the obsession in "Penelope" with fashion, which is also, at some level, attributable to Joyce (261, thesis XIV). This last aspect is often elided with the condescending amusement reserved for the underwear fetishist, but Joyce's immensely learned appreciation of fashion should in fact be celebrated as the mastery of an arcane language which materially situates the text in a tiger's leap of desire. One perhaps feels uneasy insisting on the importance of the minutiae of fashion within this monumental text, but such details parallel the mind-boggling finesse of the text, a replication on the cutting board of writing of the intricacy of fashion's tracings on the social board.

When Molly goes to plead with the implacable Mr. Cuffe to save Bloom's job, the moment is mediated through the fashion she employs as persuasion: "I felt rotten simply with the old rubbishy dress that I lost the leads out of the tails with no cut in it but theyre coming into fashion again I bought it simply to please him I knew it was no good by the finish" (18. 513–16). The dress had passed out of its instant, had lost any power to signify the distinctive differences needed to attract the merciful attention of Mr. Cuffe's social circle. Bloom has steered her wrong in this arena on many occasions—"every blessed hat I put on does that suit me yes take that thats alright the one like a wedding cake standing up miles off my head he said suited me or the dishcover one coming down on my backside" (18. 521–23).

In this light we need to consider those violet garters, the elastic suspenders of the text, spanning its length and engirdling its breadth. "I wonder is that antifat any good might overdo it thin ones are not so much the fashion now garters that much I have the violet pair I wore today" (18. 455–57). Like the nymph's speech in Circe: "I was hidden in cheap pink paper that smelled of rock oil. I was surrounded by the stale smut of clubmen, stories to disturb callow youths, ads for transparencies, trueup dice and bustpads, proprietary articles and why wear a truss with testimonial from ruptured gentleman. Useful hints to the married" (15. 3248–52). Molly's eros uncoils out of the antifat ads and the emblematic garters which subtend it. The violet garters also snap to a geographical pendant—they help to attach the materiality of Gibraltar to the thigh of Dublin, as it were, hoisting the multiple layers of history and colonial space aloft on consumer fasteners of erotica. The unquestionably pragmatic function of garters—they hold your stockings up—conjoins with their unquestionably fantasmatic role in a rather meager commodity sexuality (no one any longer has any other kind), to replicate the conjoining of the everyday with the transcendent in the book as a whole. As always, the avenue is through the commodity form as conceptualized by its users.

Molly has to confront a changing fashion which automatically excludes her, the fashion image of the girl on a bicycle, exemplified for her by the saucy exploits of her daughter Milly. "That old Bishop that spoke off the altar his long preach about womans higher functions about girls now riding the bicycle and wearing peak caps and the new woman bloomers God give him sense and me more money I suppose theyre called after him I never thought that would be my name Bloom" (18.837–41). Through the coincidental magic of mass culture the underwear fetishist Bloom seems to have provided the name for a woman's undergarment linked also to freedom, movement, and self-assertion; the "new woman" and the woman on the bicycle segue together in Molly's consciousness of her marginality to this feminine trend. As for Bloom, "hes mad on the subject of drawers always skeezing at those brazenfaced things on the bicycles with their skirts blowing up to their navels" (18.289–91). What is worth pointing out is that feminine self-determination itself is arising out of a consuming context, from within the nets of fashion and advertisement. Milly has already heeded the call; sent off to be a photo girl, she is freed from her precarious domestic situation by a free-fall into the photographic image. Molly's version of photographic immortalization involves either posing for erotic photographic postcards—"would I be like that bath of the nymph with my hair down yes only shes younger or Im a little like that dirty bitch in that Spanish photo he has" (18.562–64)—or, the apotheosis of her photographic image, her connection with Stephen Dedalus. She regrets having shown him her photo—"my photo is not good of me I ought to have got it taken in drapery that never looks out of fashion" (18.1302–4)—little realizing that Milly's photo girl photos are the ones now in fashion, but projects ahead to the publication of their two photos in the newspapers, after their affair has made her famous as his literary muse.

Molly herself is dispersed out over the mass cultural scene of Dublin, in the form of her participation in innumerable musicales, in her presence in shops, hotels, tea rooms and bazaars, in her newspaper reading and her glimpses of celebrity figures and her alluring erotic image. Her experiences of the sublime and her engagement with transcendence also derive from consumption—her attachment to the little statue Bloom brings home, "theres real beauty and poetry for you," "Id love to have the whole place swimming in roses" (18.1557–58).

The general movement of "Penelope" then is not so much the random exhalation and inhalation of female circularity, or the utterly formless and fluid stream of menstrualized consciousness named the feminine. Instead, my reading of the episode shows me an arc repeated again and again, a mental passage to Gibraltar or back from Gibraltar, mediated by the act of consumption. The largest example of the cognitive work of consumption is Gibraltar. Molly uses consumption to think through—to produce a situated analysis—of the relations of Gibraltar to Ireland, Gibraltar to England, England to Ireland. She is *metempsychosed* from one to another, on wings of consumer memory which displace, enter, and refract a cultural experience as profound as the meditations launched by Stephen in the "Nestor" episode or by Bloom in his colloquies with the Citizen.

Accordingly, Molly has been critically scanted on the political turf of the text. Gibraltar is not a utopian space beyond all commodity exchange in Molly's text, profuse with oranges and dark-eyed women, as it functions in Bloom's evocations of Molly's exotic otherness. Nonetheless, its opportunities for consumption are remarkably distinct from those of Dublin, involving catering to a British military presence superimposed on a Spanish and Arabic indigenous culture. Molly recalls Mrs. Rubio, her disobliging servant, "because she never could get over the Atlantic fleet coming in half the ships of the world and the Union Jack flying with her carabineros because 4 drunken English sailors took all the rock from them" (18.754–56). Gibraltar is flower and sun and the Moorish wall, donkeys and children and soldiers, a limbo land of consumption. "Penelope" moves in and out of the zone of Gibraltar by way of the exigencies of consumption in Dublin, its stringencies, its efforts, the attempt to get back to a Gibraltar with its plenitude of possibility. And yet, in Gibraltar, "people were always going away and we never," and "the days like years not a letter from a living soul except the odd few I posted to myself with bits of paper in them so bored sometimes I could fight with my nails listening to that old Arab with the one eye and his heass of an instrument" (18.668, 698–701).

Molly is in a lived relation with the modern world offered by no other figure in the text; an English colonial subject by her Irish nationality, she has also lived under Britain's colonial flag in the outpost of Gibraltar as a colonist, thanks to Major Tweedy, and is both of Gibraltar and not of it, forced to make and remake her "imagined community" of national identity (following Benedict Anderson) out of the scraps and bits of consumption which currently come her way.[9] The envelope of consumption within which she—and everyone else— lives is in her case elastically stretched to encompass a Gibraltar reachable now only through consumption or as consumption. "Id love to have a talk with an intelligent well educated person Id have to get a nice pair of red slippers like those Turks with the fez used to sell or yellow and a nice semitransparent morning gown that I badly want or a peachblossom dressing jacket like the one long ago in Walpoles" (18.1493–97).

If Molly's discourse seems centered in the home, then it is a home scored by traffic with an extended world, and in particular freighted with the ironic history of Gibraltar. "Penelope" alludes to this exoticism and its role in consumption by Molly's reading of The Moonstone—"that was the first I read of Wilkie Collins"—but also insists on the materiality of Molly's own historical past. She herself gives the dead Captain Gardner a ring, "as if it brought its bad luck with it like an opal or pearl", her own version of the moonstone. She imagines him wearing it as he dies of enteric fever in the Boer War—"those Boers killed him with their war and fever but they were well beaten all the same." The sexual delirium of Gibraltar for Molly also carries all the shock of empire, since Gibraltar is a way station for postings all over the globe. Through her sexual consumption Molly is witness to, and pays the price for, this centrifugal force. "there I was leaning over him with my white ricestraw hat to take the newness out of it the left side of my face the best my blouse open for his last day" (18.797–99). Even on Gibraltar social relations are consummated through the unspoken language of things: "I kept the handkerchief under my pillow for the smell of him there was no perfume to be got in that Gibraltar only that cheap peau dEspagne that faded and left a stink on you" (18.863–65).

When Bloom pronounces "metempsychosis" Molly smilingly answers with the exasperated epithet, "O rocks!" To put perhaps inordinate textual pressure on that phrase is to see the outline of the rock of Gibraltar in the distance. The transmigration of souls can entail, Bloom explains, changing "into an animal or a tree, for instance. What they called nymphs, for example." In and through consumption, in all its array, a transmigration of subjectivity is enacted into objects and back again. Such metempsychosis can be reifying, fragmenting, and objectifying, but it can *also* be enlarging, tactical, productive. To return to Simmel's darker view momentarily:

On the one hand, life is made infinitely easy for the personality in that stimulations, interests, uses of time, and consciousness are offered to it from all sides. They carry the person as if in a stream, and one hardly needs to swim for oneself. On the other hand, life is composed more and more of these impersonal contents and offerings which tend to displace the genuine personal colorations and incomparabilities . . . (the individual) has to exaggerate this personal element in order to remain audible even to himself. ("Metropolis," 422).

Molly Bloom's soliloquy, as it is known, doesn't so much speak the feminine as give a painstaking material recording of the work of consumption, a work which is as rhetorical and ardent and political as the rest of *Ulysses*. It is not a chaotic fragment, or a recapitulative coda, but a minutely tracked venture into the metempsychotic labors of Molly Bloom. Molly says "I hate a book with a Molly in it," apropos of her unhappy reading of Moll Flanders, whom she found "a whore always shoplifting anything she could cloth and stuff and yards of it" (18.657–59). This alone would prevent Molly from reading the book which she concludes. But the conclusion reenacts the arc of her labors, as her memory of her first kiss from Bloom pushes back past him to the trammeled world of Gibraltar. "I was thinking of so many things he didnt know of Mulvey and Mr Stanhope and Hester and father . . . and the Spanish girls laughing and the auctions in the morning and the Greeks and the jews and the Arabs and the devil knows who else from all the ends of Europe" (18.1582–89). Let me take this kiss as the epitome of consumption, an allegory of what it is mistakenly supposed to be. From Bloom's point of view, Molly's acceptance of the kiss is total, a promiscuous, erotic swoon, the very figure for the delirium of consumption, consumption's easy lay. But underneath lies what he doesn't and can never know—the skein of interwoven, thoroughly self-embroidered thoughts Molly produces which situate, deflect, and inflect her affirmative kiss, her historically sedimented kiss, the fabric of her kiss woven from the material of political life, Molly Bloom's work of consumption.

  Her work reveals, as does the writing of *Ulysses*, the manifold possibilities inherent in consumption, the consumption of language, of symbolic capital, the objectification of objects which then take up a place in a private universe. The ventriloquial or transvestite aspects of "Penelope" could be more carefully attributed to the parallels between

Joyce as writer and Molly Bloom as consumer—though the latter is not an author, her readjustments of her world of consumption are prompted by creativity, political resistance, and endless desire, as are Joyce's textual strategies in this book as the work of the consumption of Dublin. The inequalities and harrassments so evident in the consumptive universe of the market, and so specifically a feature of British colonialism in Ireland, are never eliminated by this text, but neither are the transformative and indeed positive features of the proliferating universe of material objects, whether these be books, ideas, violet garters, or *Sweets of Sin,* in the increasingly differentiated universe of modernity. It is the philosophical and political implications of the universe of consumption I think *Ulysses* takes up aesthetically, and the strong divide we are ready to make between consumable goods and rarefied literature is a distinction *Ulysses* does not want to make. As a later Joycean text will have it, "My consumers, are they not my producers?" In so saliently replicating the intricate mechanisms of consumption in its own construction and its own reading process, to say nothing of its material orbit, *Ulysses* prompts us to see the potential so rarely glimpsed or acknowledged in our attitudes toward consumption. Given that this is our cultural state, which *Ulysses* accepts with equanimity and realism, Joyce can teach us how we have been performing the work of consumption all our lives.

Notes

1.   Theodor Adorno famously contrasts "mythology" with "mythologization" to distinguish the latter, an inevitably mediating and self-aware aesthetic strategy, from the merely symbolic usage of the former (232).

2.   Recent richly suggestive works on consumption from disciplines other than literary criticism include Daniel Miller's *Material Culture and Mass Consumption,* Colin Campbell's *The Romantic Ethic and the Spirit of Modern Consumerism,* and Gerald McCracken's *Culture and Consumption.* Also see John Fiske's valuable contribution, *Understanding Popular Culture.*

3.   A wealth of historical analysis of these colonial contexts between Britain and Ireland now exists; in particular, the histories by R. F. Foster, *Modern Ireland,* and F. S. L. Lyons, *Ireland Since the Famine,* are noteworthy. The collection of essays edited by W. J. McCormack and Alistair Stead, *James Joyce and Modern Literature,* contains richly inflected historical essays on this context.

4.   I do not want to scant the complicated and valuable debate evoked here, but rather to point to other possibilities. Among the most suggestive works on Joyce and feminist questions are Julia Kristeva's "Joyce 'the Gracehoper' " (167–80); Cheryl Herr's " 'Penelope' as Period Piece" in this volume; Suzette

Henke and Elaine Unkeless, eds., *Women in Joyce;* and Bonnie Kime Scott's essays as well as her *James Joyce and Feminism*. Karen Lawrence gracefully delineates these issues in *The Cambridge Companion to James Joyce*.

5.   See my *Advertising Fictions: Literature, Advertisement, and Social Reading*, as well as Cheryl Herr's *Joyce's Anatomy of Culture*.

6.   Michel de Certeau's essay "Making Do: Uses and Tactics," in his *The Practice of Everyday Life*. For Bourdieu's contributions to these concepts, his book *Distinction: A Social Critique of the Judgment of Taste* is particularly relevant.

7.   These remarks occur in the final chapter of Simmel's majestic *The Philosophy of Money*. David Frisby's *Fragments of Modernity* is an excellent commentary on Simmel and other social theorists of modernity.

8.   Nicholas Xenos discusses the Bon Marché in his *Scarcity and Modernity*.

9.   Benedict Anderson's *Imagined Communities* has offered a vital understanding of nationality as a cultural and linguistic construction, refashioned and reproduced constantly by those who live its contours. The vital literature on nationalism now includes Eric Hobsbawm's *Nations and Nationalism Since 1780*, as well as numerous anthologies and readers.

Works Cited

Adorno, Theodor. *Aesthetic Theory*. New York: Routledge and Kegan Paul, 1984.

Anderson, Benedict. *Imagined Communities*. London: Verso, 1983.

Baudelaire, "The Painter of Modern Life." *Selected Writings on Art and Artists*. Trans. P. E. Charvet. Harmondsworth: Penguin, 1972.

Baudrillard, Jean. *For a Critique of the Political Economy of the Sign*. St. Louis: Telos Press, 1981.

Benjamin, Walter. "Theses on the Philosophy of History." *Illuminations*. Ed. Hannah Arendt. New York: Schocken, 1969. 260–65.

Bourdieu, Pierre. *Distinction: A Social Critique of the Judgment of Taste*. Cambridge: Harvard University Press, 1984.

Campbell, Colin. *The Romantic Ethic and the Spirit of Modern Consumerism*. Oxford: Basil Blackwell, 1987.

de Certeau, Michel. "Making Do: Uses and Tactics." *The Practice of Everyday Life*. Berkeley: University of California Press, 1984.

Fiske, John. *Understanding Popular Culture*. London: Unwin Hyman, 1989.

Foster, R. F. *Modern Ireland*. London: Allen Lane, 1988.

Frisby, David. *Fragments of Modernity*. Boston: MIT Press 1986.

Henke, Suzette, and Elaine Unkeless, eds. *Women in Joyce*. Urbana: University of Illinois Press, 1982.

Herr, Cheryl. *Joyce's Anatomy of Culture*. Urbana: University of Illinois Press, 1986.

Hobsbawm, Eric. *Nations and Nationalism Since 1780*. Cambridge: University of Cambridge Press, 1990.

Horkheimer, Max, and Theodor Adorno. *Dialectic of Enlightenment*. New York: Herder and Herder, 1972.

Jameson, Fredric. "Ulysses in History." *James Joyce and Modern Literature*. Ed. W. J. McCormack and Alistair Stead. London: Routledge, 1982. 126–41.

Kristeva, Julia. "Joyce 'the Gracehoper'." *James Joyce: The Augmented Ninth*. Ed. Bernard Benstock. Syracuse: Syracuse University Press, 1984. 147–52.

Lawrence, Karen. "Joyce and Feminism." *The Cambridge Companion to James Joyce*. Ed. Derek Attridge. Cambridge: Cambridge University Press, 1990. 237–58.

Leonard, Garry. "Women on the Market: Commodity Culture, 'Those Lovely Seaside Girls,' and 'Feminity' in *Ulysses*." *James Joyce Studies: An Annual, 1991*. Forthcoming.

Lévi-Strauss, Claude. *The Savage Mind*. Chicago: University of Chicago Press, 1966.

Lukács, Georg. *History and Class Consciousness*. London: Merlin, 1971.

Lyons, F. S. L. *Ireland Since the Famine*. London: Weidenfeld and Nicolson, 1971.

McCormack, W. J., and Alistair Stead, eds. *James Joyce and Modern Literature* London: Routledge, 1982.

McCracken, Gerald. *Culture and Consumption*. Bloomington: Indiana University Press, 1990.

Miller, Daniel. *Material Culture and Mass Consumption*. Oxford: Basil Blackwell, 1987.

Moretti, Franco. "The Long Goodbye." *Signs Taken for Wonders*. London: Verso, 1982.

Richards, Thomas Karr. *The Commodity Culture of Victorian England*. Stanford: Stanford University Press, 1990.

Scott, Bonnie Kime. *James Joyce and Feminism*. Brighton: Harvester, 1987.

Simmel, Georg. "The Metropolis and Mental Life." Reprinted in *The Sociology of Georg Simmel*. Tr. and ed. Kurt H. Wolff. New York: Free Press, 1950.

Simmel, Georg. *The Philosophy of Money*. Trans. Tom Bottomore and David Frisby. Boston: Routledge and Kegan Paul, 1978.

Steele, Valerie. *Fashion and Eroticism: Ideals of Feminine Beauty from the Victorian Through the Jazz Age*. New York: Oxford University Press, 1985.

Veblen, Thorstein. *The Theory of the Leisure Class*. New York: Viking, 1967.

Weber, Max. *Economy and Society*. Berkeley: University of California Press, 1978.

Wicke, Jennifer. *Advertising Fictions: Literature, Advertisement, and Social Reading*. New York: Columbia University Press, 1988.

Xenos, Nicholas. *Scarcity and Modernity*. Boston: MIT Press, 1989.

10

Molly Bloom's "Lifestyle"
The Performative as Normative

Garry Leonard

Consumption is not a passive mode of assimilation. . . . [It]
is an active mode of relations (not only to objects, but to the
collectivity and to the world), a systematic mode of activity
and a global response on which our whole cultural system is
founded . . .

(Jean Baudrillard)

sure you cant get on in this world without style all going in food
and rent when I get it Ill lash it around I tell you in fine style . . .

(Molly Bloom in *Ulysses*)

Money don't buy everything, it's true.
But what it don't buy, I can't use

(Barry Gordy)

Lifestyles of the Not Very Rich and the Not Yet Famous

"Life-style," according to the *Oxford English Dictionary*, was "a term
originally used by Alfred Adler (1870–1937) to denote a person's basic
character as established early in childhood which governs his re-
actions and behaviour." The idea that "lifestyle" (the word was hy-
phenated for a few decades, and appears now as one word) once
designated something as organic and precultural as "a person's basic
character" must strike us as odd given the word's current usage which
we might define as established patterns of consumption and social
exchange by individuals or groups. On the front page of the *New York
Times* on 30 March 1991, for example, we read: "If you look at the
records you find that on one of her trips Imelda [Marcos] was able to
spend $6,000 on the first day for chocolates. That is the kind of *lifestyle*

that used up the money" (emphasis added). Of course, Ms. Marcos's astonishing shoe collection is better known to the public than her prodigious sweet tooth, but her conspicuous pattern of excess consumption is consistently described and vilified as a "lifestyle." When this style of excessive consumption is directly compared to the poverty of the rural people in the Philippines—people who are understood to represent "real" life rather than a "lifestyle"—pejorative adjectives such as "obscene" are added. Such nomenclature is intended to reflect a general moral outrage that one individual should aggressively consume so many "luxury" items while her country people subsist on nothing more than their daily bread. To offer another example of the contemporary usage of the word "lifestyle," the popular American television show entitled "Lifestyles of the Rich and Famous" presents various "homes" as showcases of spectacular abundance. In this show, the "rich and famous" people are considerably less interesting to the viewer than their spectacular pattern of consumption (a "systematic mode of activity" to use Jean Baudrillard's term). Put another way, the people are no more and no less to the viewer than the signifying constellation of objects with which they surround themselves.

The point I want to make relative to the word "lifestyle" and Molly's complex ruminations in the final chapter of *Ulysses* is that although the word "lifestyle" is not available to her in 1904 (nor was it available to Joyce in 1922), her use of the word "style" to denote a *way of being* ("Ill lash it around") clearly forecasts the intricate integration of identity and commodity objects currently celebrated or denigrated as a "lifestyle."[1] Whereas a "style" may refer to the cut of a hat, or a mode of speaking and writing, "lifestyle" necessarily involves the transformation of commodities into a theatrical spectacle within which the consumer performs his or her "life" through the presentation of "style":

The consumer is not (just) an active appropriator of objects for sale. His or her entire identity, the constitution of the self as a social subject, a "citizen of consumer society," depends on the acquisition of appropriate objects: appropriate for the time (the seasons of fashion) and for the image which s/he is to project via the nuances of codes in dress and possessions—all the appurtenances of a "lifestyle" that can be recognized by other members of the society. (Bowlby 28)

The consumer's interior aspirations are signified approximately in a careful display intended for consumption by a mass audience. When Molly complains that "sure you cant get on in this world without style all going in food and rent when I get it Ill lash it around I tell you in fine style" (18.466–68), we can see in her juxtaposition of ideas, as

well as her awkward repetition of the word "style," that she is trying
to articulate an urge to be a modern consumer with a "lifestyle." Her
phrase "you cant get on in this world," for example, indicates that in
"this world"—that is to say, Molly's contemporary world—an individual whose money is "all going in food and rent" lacks what we
now call the "discretionary income" needed to support a "lifestyle"
that "authenticates" identity by soliciting the gaze of others. As Rachel
Bowlby points out, a "lifestyle," even though privately manufactured
by a consumer (what Jennifer Wicke, in this volume, calls "the work
of consumption"), still must be made visible to others or it cannot be
said to exist at all.

Ireland's colonial position relative to the British Empire makes the
adoption of a "lifestyle" particularly dramatic. Developing a "lifestyle"
is simply not possible for a citizen in any economy where one's income must "all go in food and rent"; and yet, with absentee British
landlords and economic restrictions on Irish Catholics, this was the
sort of economy Ireland had up until the early twentieth century. In
the *New York Times* (7 April 1991), an advertising executive had this
to say about the difficulty of introducing Western advertising into recently liberated Eastern Europe: "It would be a major mistake to try
lifestyle advertising, because their lifestyles are just beginning. . . .
They must develop their own style by drawing from their own heritage." Another executive stated "[a]t the moment, what our Western
clients are looking for is not advertising; it's understanding of their
markets." The goal of "understanding their markets" is to learn how
to commodify their "heritage" so that "life" can be recast into the marketable commodity of "lifestyle." I would suggest that the situation
of the West vis à vis Eastern Europe is not unlike that of nineteenth-
century England as it looked for a new market for commodities in
relatively rural Ireland.

Significantly, the so-called Celtic Twilight—championed by Yeats
and rejected by Joyce—resisted this commercial colonization by going
in search of the perfectly uncommodified peasant—one whose "own
style" would in no way reflect a British "lifestyle," and one whose
"heritage" would be incapable of being translated into a "market" by
England. But as the project by Haines demonstrates, even the clever
sayings of those Irish folk who have never heard of Plumtree's Potted
Meat is, if marketed correctly, a saleable commodity. The search for the
Irish peasant that Haines is conducting is the commercial equivalent
of Yeats's and Lady Gregory's more nationalistic project (and I sense
a deliberate juxtaposition of the two projects on Joyce's part). Where
Yeats would hold back the introduction of "commodity culture" into

Ireland, Joyce sees such a plan as impossible, self-delusional, and even selfish given that Yeats has no use for the sort of "trinkets" mass marketing and mass production make possible for the lower class. And yet, if Yeats has no patience with the vulgar trinkets of mass production, clearly they delight a character like Maria in Joyce's short story "Clay": "She took out her purse with the silver clasps and read again the words *A Present from Belfast*. She was very fond of that purse . . ." (*Dubliners* 100).

Baudrillard has defined consumption in the twentieth century not as the quantity of one's possessions, or the insatiable urge to gratify specific desires with specific commodities, but rather *the organization* of all these commodities—both inside the home and outside in the street— into a complex semiotic message that signifies the "life" we imagine we are living. One of Lacan's central premises is that desire is based on a permanent lack within the mythical construction of the subject's "self," and this lack requires the subject to move from word to word— from signifier to signifier—in the vain hope of finding an original signified to authenticate the (spurious) self-originating autonomy of his or her "identity." Although Baudrillard's theory of desire bears some resemblance to that of Lacan, he speaks of the "language" of *things* as well as words. For Baudrillard, the objects and desires strategically integrated by a consumer are signifiers that constitute a language of commodities that can be understood—by oneself in conjunction with others—as a "lifestyle." The language of things is publicized and made sacred by the ceremony of advertising, and this permits the "personalization" of commodities into the private prayer of an individual's immediate environment (an environment that, paradoxically, seeks to elicit a "global response" even while claiming to be "personal").

The "world" that results from this interpenetration of the global and the personal is a simulacrum within which the consumer experiences "life" as a "style" of consumption: "[I]n consumption objects become a vast paradigm designating another language through which something else speaks. . . . The flight from one signifier to another is no more than the surface reality of a desire, which is insatiable because it is founded on a lack. And this desire, which can never be satisfied, signifies itself locally in a succession of objects and needs" (Baudrillard 45). As long as this flight from one signifier to another is possible, then desire is a language that, like the best advertising, promises "complete satisfaction" in the near future (provided one continually "takes flight" to the "new" object). When Gallaher refers to Little Chandler's act of marrying as "putting your head in a sack," he is attacking Little Chandler's lifestyle, and belittling it in relation to his own apparently boundless ability to consume and be consumed: "Everything in Paris is gay. . . . They believe in enjoying life . . . they've a great feeling for the Irish there. When they heard I was from Ireland they were ready to eat me, man. . . . There's no woman like the Parisienne—*for style, for go*" (*Dubliners* 77, emphasis added). Both Molly and Gallaher link the word "style" to a verb phrase in an attempt to show the relationship of "style" to the dynamic, theatrical, and increasingly spectacular process of "life" and not merely to the static image of unstylish consumption where "all" goes "for food and rent." Gallaher struggles just as much as Molly does to describe something not adequately designated in the outmoded word "style."

For Gallaher, "style" somehow implies "go" just as Molly envisions a "style" as something that will allow her to "lash *it* around." What action does Gallaher wish to signify with "go"? To what action does Molly's pronoun "it" refer? Rather than the static image of style as the cut of a dress, this active, spectacular, and dramatic style—a style with "go" that can be "lashed around"—refers to the pre-scripted and carefully directed *life* style where "happiness" is performed daily for both a real and an imagined audience. When Little Chandler goes home, his final crisis of feeling "trapped" is brought on not by a particular thought or a particular person, but by the language of the objects that surround him. The furniture has a "pretty" style which he now finds "mean," perhaps because the word "go"—in Gallaher's dynamic sense of this term—is not in the vocabulary of his furniture's "language": "He found *something mean in the pretty furniture* which he had bought for his house on the hire system. . . . A dull resentment *against his life* awoke within him. Could he not escape from his little house? Was it too late for him to try to live bravely like Gallaher? . . . *There was the furniture still to be paid for*" (*Dubliners* 83, emphasis added). Little Chandler's resentment of his "life" is indistinguishable from his resentment of his furniture. He has bought a "lifestyle" on credit and now, spiritually bankrupt, he cannot abandon it because it, like the furniture, "is still to be paid for." The average Anglo-Irish domestic economy can purchase a basic "style" on an installment plan, but they are very far from the periodic pleasure of "lashing it around." Gallaher's insulting description of a married man as one who "puts his head in a sack" refers to a diminished capacity to see and be seen through the execution of a commodity-based performance of the "style" of one's "life."

Not unlike Molly, Little Gallaher attempts to alter the depressing

discourse of his "mean" lifestyle by making a "new" purchase: "How
he had suffered that day, waiting at the shop door until the shop was
empty, standing at his ease while the girl piled ladies' blouses before
him . . . striving to hide his blushes as he left the shop . . ." (*Dubliners*
82). This is a purchase not determined by the specific *style* of the blouse
(presumably, in his embarrassed haste, he simply plucks one from the
pile) but by his vague yearning for some variation in his life, a variation that perhaps might be inaugurated by a "new" erotic encounter
with his wife. Or, to restate my point using Gallaher's jargon, he made
his purchase *not* for style, but for *go*—not as a simple and single purchase, but as a concerted effort to buy an escape route to a "brave"
life: "Annie kissed him and said it was very pretty and stylish . . . she
was delighted with it, especially with the make of the sleeves . . ."
(*Dubliners* 83). His wife Annie, however, responds to the purchase
strictly by observing the particular cut of the blouse—"style" in the
more traditional and static sense—and also by professing horror that
he has paid too much for what is, after all, just a shirt. Her reaction
transforms Little Chandler's purchase from a magical attempt at tran-
scendance (not unlike what the boy of "Araby" also attempts relative
to Mangan's sister) to a pedestrian example of someone having failed
to barter properly for a "necessary" item. Annie further domesticates
any erotic component of the purchase by declaring the blouse, like
their furniture, is "pretty." Annie misses her cue, and Little Chandler's
purchase, with its vaguely articulated erotic component leads, both
literally and figuratively, to an anticlimax.

Through the Looking Glass: Dramatizing the Everyday

By the turn of the century, advertising had gone well beyond merely
announcing the price and availability of a product. Instead, both advertising copy and magazine articles operated together to formulate
what we might call "a philosophy of things." Countless ads suggested
that what one buys, where and when one buys it, the manner in which
one chooses to display it, and the imagined audience that is expected
to see it, all combine to produce a "stable" identity where a performative structure is tacitly (mis)construed as a normative personality.
In Lacanian parlance, the clothes we wear and the things we arrange
around us can function as our construction of the benevolent gaze of
the Other who can "see" that we are who we in fact can only imagine ourselves to be. In an "article" published in the July 1904 *Weldon's
Ladies' Journal,* the latest "fashion" is actually presented not merely as

a "style," but as a style of living, and the private act of shopping becomes an "off stage" endeavor that must be meticulously prosecuted
if one is to be a success when the curtain rises:

Fashions for July
What is Worn. THE halcyon days of an English summer encourage us to don
the prettiest raiment we possess. Our frothiest muslin frocks and smartest
of cool linen suits are none too bright and gay to grace the golden period
of the year. The prospect of holidays, and necessary outfits, are subject meet
for enthusiastic discussion at the present moment, and the pros and cons of
washing frocks, muslin robes, and lovely millinery usurp all our attention. . . .
Exquisite mercerised sateens and lawns, with all the appearance of the best
foulard silks, make up into inexpensive yet elegant little gowns.

As a first step in presenting the style of living, the advertisement
puts the scenery in place in a manner that also sets the consumer's
mood ("the halcyon days of an English summer"). From there, the
costumes appropriate to such a setting are detailed ("our frothiest
muslin frocks"); after this, the ad establishes the need to carefully syn-
chronize this display with the imagined audience. We can assume our
imagined audience has read the same ad we are reading, and that
they will applaud "style" or hiss at unauthorized deviations, just like
the well-primed audience of a melodrama. Phrases such as "necessary
outfits . . . enthusiastic discussion . . . pros and cons" constitute the
central paradox of fashion discourse: the ephemeral is imperative, at
least for now. The woman who buys in accordance with this multilay-
ered scenario consumes, as Baudrillard has phrased it, in "an active
mode of relations (not only to objects, but to the collectivity and to
the world.)" A "systematic mode of activity" is exercised in the pursuit of a hoped for "global response." This sense of others seeing us
as we wish to see ourselves may be likened to Lacan's theory of the
gaze "which circumscribes us, and which in the first instance makes
us beings who are looked at . . ." (75).[2]

Nineteenth-century theatre was also, as M. R. Booth suggests, obsessed with presenting on stage a spectacular display of materials,
fashions, and commodities for public consumption by the audience's
gaze: "The very existence of new materials, new stage machinery,
and new methods of lighting impelled them into a dramatic structure which in part existed to display the ingenuity of machinist, gas-
man, head carpenter, costume designer, and stage manager" (64). In
nineteenth-century popular theatre (especially pantomime and melodrama) a major consideration of a production became "how large
numbers of actors and quantities of expensive fabrics could best be

deployed" (Booth 64).[3] Indeed, a humorous contemporary poem describing "the Cave Scene" of the pantomime *Ali Baba and the Forty Thieves* suggested that the attitude of the audience for Victorian spectacular theatre was not simply that of a playgoer, but that of a shopper as well: "Whilst ladies, who with awe this sight regard, / Whisper, 'I'm sure it costs four pounds a yard'" (Booth 88–89). Like a clever lighting director or costume designer, the writer of the Weldon's article quoted above also offers tips to the would-be actress/consumer on how to design a wardrobe that looks expensive—but isn't: "*Exquisite mercerised sateens* and lawns, with all the appearance of the best foulard silks, make up into *inexpensive yet elegant* little gowns" (emphasis added). John Mercer was only one of several textile manufacturers who invented ways to treat ordinary cloth in a way that made it appear extraordinary; clothing submitted to the process he invented was referred to as "mercerised." As Molly's keen eye for detail suggests, part of the "fun," as well as the "drama," of developing and critiquing "lifestyles" is trying to see past someone's appearance directly to the theatrical process that has "enhanced" that appearance. At the same time, however, one must struggle to hide from one's own spectators the "mercerised" quality of one's own public performance. This is precisely what Gerty MacDowell does when she converts "shopsoiled" material into what appears as "a love of a hat" to all who observe her (or so she hopes).

There is little wonder that theatre audiences translated the appearance of costumes into estimates of what they were worth per yard; department stores at this time also benefited enormously from, and were completely transformed by, "the very existence" of "new materials, new stage machinery, and new methods of lighting." As Rachel Bowlby has said of the modern department store window that faces out into the street, "[g]lass and lighting . . . created a spectacular effect, a sense of theatrical excess coexisting with the simple availability of individual items for purchase. Commodities were put on show in an attractive guise, becoming unreal in that they were images set apart from everyday things, and real in that they were there to be bought and taken home to enhance the ordinary environment" (Bowlby 2). As Kimberly Devlin has noted in this volume, Molly "perceptively recognizes in the seemingly real the paradox of the genuinely fraudulent." And she does so, I would add, not out of some Hamlet-like "Nay, madam, I know not seems" disgust with the playacting of emotions, but rather as part of her constant effort to enhance the quotient of "genuine fraudulence" in her own performance. The idea of the home as a combination of "on stage" and "off stage," where Molly can either successfully perform or be caught between acts, is illustrated further by her aversion to answering the door for someone she is not expecting: "[Y]ou think its the vegetables then its somebody and you all undressed or the door of the filthy sloppy kitchen blows open the day old frosty face Boodwin called about the concert in Lombard street and I just after dinner all flushed and tossed with boiling old stew dont look at me professor I had to say Im a fright yet" (18.334–38).

The "scene" played with Boodwin is painfully awkward for Molly because it is unexpectedly real; she is "caught back stage" in two different ways: first, she is not prepared to step into the footlights of Boodwin's gaze ("don't look at me"); second, the house itself is not ready to have the curtain raised ("the door of the filthy sloppy kitchen blows open"), and finally these first two exposures are aggravated by the fact that Boodwin is there to discuss an even more carefully crafted dramatic and public performance: the concert in Lombard Street. As Leopold Bloom has noted to himself, there is a mirror in place by the door so that Molly can glance at her reflection before she opens it. It is also worth noting in this context that Molly's fondest memories (not to mention her most erotic—something I *will* mention later) all showcase her clear belief that for the duration of the recalled moment in which she appeared to the other person—in terms of her style, her strategy of consumption, and her posture—she exhibited herself exactly according to the theatrical *tableau* she had planned: "[T]here I was leaning over him with my white ricestraw hat to take the newness out of it the left side of my face the best my blouse open for his last day" (18.797–99). This memory is the fruit of the work of consumption. Molly experiences the "newness" of sex even as she is "taking the newness" out of her hat in a manner that keeps her best profile on display. The "everyday" is made dramatic by Molly's posture, her new hat, and the special style of her blouse (designed, like Gallaher's Parisienne women, "for go").[4]

Molly's feelings about being surprised at home also indicate that she stages and performs her lifestyle for an imagined audience that is of a particular social class: "You think its *the vegetables* and then its *somebody*." If someone from a different class were to observe her (the man who delivers vegetables, for example), she would not feel that she had been caught unaware because he is not part of the imagined audience for which she performs. Like the popular actresses of her time, Molly knows that an individual's persuasive presentation of a manner and an attitude—whether in the theatre or in the home—requires good costuming and appropriate set design. When Molly thinks about the possibility of taking Stephen as a lover, her first thought is that the "pre-publicity" photo Bloom has already shown him puts the specifics of her seduction scene into peril: "[S]howing him my photo its not good of me I ought to have got it taken in drapery that never looks out of fashion" (18.1302–4). Molly's momentary regret that she is not "in drapery" reflects the particular "plot" she has in mind with Stephen— a plot which involves her being cast as "the immortal woman" of his poetry. Such a woman, destined for immortality, should not be sporting this or that fashion; instead, her costume should call eternity to the audience's mind with an "immortal" style that seems impervious to the crude vagaries of time. By contrast, when Molly imagines the particulars of her wardrobe in reference to the gaze of Blazes Boylan, "drapery" and "classical" posing are the last things on her mind: "I wonder what kind of underwear he likes none at all I think." Certainly one could argue that Molly exhibits some phallocentrism in this passage, and that she appears to be more of a male fantasy than a woman, but I would suggest instead that Molly thinks of the men with whom she is involved (or with whom she might yet be involved) the way an actress thinks of her "leading man"; she is willing to cater to the needs of their performance, but only as a way to assure a more dramatic role for herself.

In this regard, Blazes Boylan has already proved a partial disappointment as a leading man for Molly because the second act of her imagined scenario with him calls for him to write her passionate love letters: "I wish somebody would write me a loveletter his wasnt much and *I told him he could write what he liked* yours ever Hugh Boylan" (18.734–35, emphasis added). Like Annie Chandler or Bartell D'Arcy, Boylan has missed his cue. Furthermore, Molly's deliberate prompting makes it clear that she is expecting an involved performance from Boylan that is not supposed to open and close on the same night. Significantly, she is not worried about the veracity of the letters, but only with their ability to make the everyday dramatic: "[T]rue or no it fills up your whole day and life always something to think about every moment and see it all round you like a new world" (18.737–39). Likewise, in the first act of her imagined tryst with Stephen Dedalus, she makes him faint with appreciation for the display of herself (a genuine form of applause which, unlike clapping, is not easily feigned). But in return, in the second act, he is to make her the sole subject of his poetry. Molly, in other words, dresses to please, but not without the expectation of producing pleasure for herself. Indeed, by casting herself as a performer in her own productions of pleasure, she performs not merely as an actress but as a director as well: "Ill read and study all I can find or learn a bit off by heart if I knew who he likes so he wont think me stupid . . . and I can teach him the other part Ill make him feel all over him till he half faints under me then hell write about me lover and mistress publicly too with our 2 photographs in all the papers when he becomes famous" (18.1361–67). The favorite technique employed by both Gabriel and Molly within the fantasy staging of their own erotic melodrama is the *tableau*—a "device of dramatury," Peter Brooks tells us where "we grasp melodrama's primordial concern to make its signs clear, unambiguous, and impressive" (48). As in the structure of melodrama, Molly envisions a mute *tableau* that reveals a "moment of truth" ("till he half faints under me") followed by the public and unambivalently triumphant achievement of all her long thwarted goals ("our 2 photographs in all the papers"). As Brooks has argued, melodrama is a genre where " 'life' has become wholly 'drama,' and . . . this offers the actor an unrivaled opportunity for *the uninhibited play with style* . . ." (48, emphasis added). Or, "lashing it around," as Molly would have it. Molly's urge to "play with style" leads her to wonder what style of underwear Boylan yearns to see and what style of poetry Stephen hopes to write. While she is willing to wear the one and recite the other, it is still *her* style she hopes to "lash around" in a production that features her own pleasure in a final *tableau* of spectacular excess.

"Oh! I'm Spending!": The Erotics of Shopping

As Jennifer Wicke has argued in this volume, "eros itself arises out of the matrix of consumptive strategies . . . shopping is both a terrifying labor of scrutiny and frustration, as well as the site of the dream of satisfaction. . . ." In theatrical terms, the "work of consumption" is also a "behind the scenes" endeavor that eventually, and hopefully invisibly, makes possible the public spectacle of a "lifestyle" performed before a live audience. When we are shopping, we imagine other people looking at what we are looking at, and from this vantage point try to imagine "what we will look like" when we are wearing it. In the passage from *Sweets of Sin* that catches Bloom's eye, the erotic triangle of "husband," "lover," and "the beautiful woman" is augmented by a different "site of the dream of satisfaction," the department store: "*—All the dollarbills her husband gave her were spent in the stores on wondrous gowns and costliest frillies*" (10.608–9). Here we need to recall that "spending" is Victorian slang for orgasm (Molly uses the term this way twice), and then we can see that "the beautiful woman" is causing her husband to "spend" dollarbills which she, through the act of shopping, converts into "costliest frillies," which in turn will cause her lover Raoul to "spend." Indeed, having been to the department store *en route* to meeting her lover, "the beautiful woman" is utterly confident that the silent *tableau* of her appearance—not unlike that of a mannequin in a department store window, or an actress doing a tried and true "star turn" on stage—will vanquish the "suspicious glare" with which Raoul initially greets her: *"—You are late, he spoke hoarsely, eyeing her with a suspicious glare. The beautiful woman threw off her sabletrimmed wrap, displaying her queenly shoulders and heaving embonpoint. An imperceptible smile played round her perfect lips as she turned to him calmly"* (10.614–17). If her smile is in fact "imperceptible" (as opposed to the more widely used cliché "*barely* perceptible"), then Raoul can't even see it, and this description of a woman "displaying" her fur coat, queenly shoulders, and "heaving embonpoint" should be read as a private expression of satisfaction and confidence that is emanating from a beautiful consumer who is well pleased *as a result of her own "spending."* Indeed, fresh from the Au Bon Marche department store, sporting her "imperceptible smile," she is the Mona Lisa of commodity culture.[5]

"Embonpoint" means excessive plumpness or stoutness, but it also carries the literal translation of "in good condition" which suggests that "the beautiful woman's" physical excess is also figured as a sort of perfectly maintained material abundance. One of the phrases that stays in Bloom's mind after his initial reading of the passage is "(*her heaving embonpoint!*)." This image of an abundant and spectacular excess deliciously threatening to overspill its confines ("heaving!") is also, as I have already suggested, a basic feature of set design in Victorian "spectacular theatre." It is, as well, a basic strategy of merchandise display in the newly illuminated department store windows. Once inside the store, shoppers faced bins filled to "overflowing" and products stacked in giant pyramids in an effort to overwhelm the shopper with the visual equivalent of luxury, pleasure, and satisfaction. Abundance, in other words, and excess as well, is an integral part of the seductive dynamic of spectacle, display, and "lifestyle." As Veblein's famous phrase, "conspicuous consumption" (coined in 1900) makes clear, a modern "lifestyle" is nothing if not visible, and the socially successful consumer must display a pattern of consumption as a visible "style." The idea of a "stout" woman's body as a metaphor for commodity excess and spectacular display is suggested by the description of how Raoul reacts to what "the beautiful woman" shows him: "*—Her mouth glued on his in a luscious voluptuous kiss while his hands felt for the opulent curves inside her déshabillé*" (10.611–12). "Luscious" has the connotation of "sweet to excess" and "voluptuous" implies "full of . . .

indulgence in luxury." Her "simple" kiss, then, overwhelms Raoul with the *sensual* equivalent of a "spectacle of excess." Furthermore, "opulent" denotes physical stoutness, but it is also used, especially in turn-of-the-century economic discussions, to characterize either a lavish display of merchandise or an abundance of "natural" (that is, undeveloped) resources.

In this context, Raoul's invasive and appropriating gesture ("his hands felt for the opulent curves") might additionally be read as a psychological echo of the foreign policy of an imperialist economy that is attracted to the "lusicous, voluptuous, opulent, and "untouched" resources of a land like India, Africa, or Ireland. Stephen Dedalus, in the "Proteus" episode, has already associated the idea of one mouth "glued" to another mouth as an image of vampirism, and so "the beautiful woman" has "her mouth glued on his" even as her natural resources are appropriated ("felt for"). She also poses—in the form of a seductively packaged object—as the sort of sensual and spectacular commodity that imperialism makes possible. My primary point, then, is that the scenario which stimulates Bloom at the turn of the century contains images of both commodity abundance and spectacular excess where the sensation of orgasm mirrors the act of consumption to the point where both foreplay and shopping lead to a climax of "spending."[6] Erotic experience for Molly and Leopold Bloom—in separate but equal ways—relates to a new form of market economy, a new style of merchandise display, and a new pattern of "individual" consumption. But this consumption is always collective in nature and always in search of a global response. "Lifestyle" permits the dramatization of the everday before the imagined audience of social "reality."

Bloom, of course, is not a wealthy imperialist and Ireland, in 1904, is still a colonized country. Accordingly, Bloom's erotic reverie is shattered by the intrusion of the indigent, therefore unerotic, Dublin shopkeeper:

The shopman's uncombed grey head came out and his unshaven reddened face, coughing. He raked his throat rudely, puked phlegm on the floor. . . . and bent, showing a rawskinned crown, scantily haired.
  Mr Bloom beheld it.
  Mastering his troubled breath, he said:
—I'll take this one.
  The shopman lifted eyes bleared with old rheum.
—*Sweets of Sin,* he said tapping on it. That's a good one. (10.633–41)

Aging and balding flesh, frank ill-health, disgusting secretion of body fluids—this shopman is as physical an anticlimax as "the beautiful woman" is a climax. The stimulating scenario of healthy, aggressive "masculine" imperialism and corresponding "feminine" display of opulence and submission is replaced by the unspectacular arrival of an old (perhaps dying) shopkeeper who makes a few shillings by selling pawed-over books from a street cart. The most crucial strategy of seductive display—a strategy employed equally by the spectacular theatre, the modern department store, and the "individual" consumer's attractive "lifestyle"—is to hide the unmediated reality that continues to exist behind the "displayed" illusion of "reality." When this unmediated reality comes to the fore in the form of the shopkeeper, Bloom is able to "master his troubled breath" all too easily.

In the "halcyon days" of British imperialism, it was Lily Langtry, with her famously opulent curves, who became the enviable standard for the "perfect" female form. Appropriately enough, it was widely understood that she was also the lover of Prince Edward—the reigning symbol of Empire—(a relationship Molly ruminates upon). In "Ivy Day in the Committee Room," King Edward is cast as a dubious character by Mr. Lyons, but Mr. Henchy quickly defends him as "an ordinary knockabout like you and me. He's fond of his glass of grog and he's a bit of a rake, perhaps, and he's a good sportsman. Damn it, can't we Irish play fair?" (*Dubliners* 132). The British Imperialist figure feeling for opulent curves is merely "a bit of a rake" while Parnell, the colonialist politician, is characterized by Mr. Lyons as "[not] a fit man to lead us." Clearly Henchy supports implicitly the idea that imperialism is never having to say you're sorry. Bloom's hesitant fascination with Raoul's aggressive and unapologetic consumption of "the beautiful woman" suggests the complex ambivalence that a colonialist like Bloom feels—both anger and awe—for the institutionalized indifference with which imperial leaders "spend" at his expense. The intersection of the Langtry/King Edward relationship with marketing is quite explicit in that Lily Langtry gave her name to a widely advertised corset that promised to give all women similarly "opulent" curves. Approaching this from a different angle, there is another article in the July 1904 *Weldon's Ladies' Journal* entitled "Beauty for Women" and subtitled "There is no Power like the Magnetism of Curves":

Beauty *rules the world.* . . . In every circle . . . there is *a woman who is ruler*— and there is also *a secret of her power.*

This question is of vital interest to every girl or woman in England. When a little silent struggle takes place between two or three women for supremacy in their set, or for the place of queen in the heart of some man, who wins? Always the woman of beautiful figure, of *attractive curves*—and who realises her power. . . . For those who lack the natural development of bust, a new and remarkable treatment has been devised. It is called "Diano." . . . This treatment will quickly develop the bust six inches, and any woman can use it at home . . . (xxiii, emphasis added)

Women of Empire who wish to "rule the world" with a "secret power," and who compete with other women for unrivaled "supremacy," must first develop their bust six inches more; that is to say, they must increase the attractiveness, from a "masculine"/imperialist point of view, of their "natural resources." Indeed, a contemporary translation of *"heaving embonpoint"* might be "well-endowed" which indicates that a woman's bust—those "opulent curves" that make "a woman a ruler"—is also viewed, in a patriarchal economy, as her permanent fund or source of income. The corset ad that Molly recalls, in addition to promising profitable curves, also promises to "obviate" ("eliminate disadvantages by effective measures") unprofitable ones.[7] This optimization of natural resources (the application of "Diano"), we are told, may be accomplished in a "personal" and "individual" act of consumption performed in the "privacy" of the home. But the collective nature of this act is apparent when we see, in a widely published advertisement, the "[opulent] curves" of a woman's breasts represented as the source of a secret and indomitable global power. "[H]e caressed them outside," Molly says when recalling the attention Mulvey paid to her breasts, "they love doing that its the roundness" (18.796–97). Thus, in keeping with the metaphor of a woman's body as a colonized country, the product "Diano" urges "the women of England" to "develop" their natural resources and capitalize on the result. The only way for women to capitalize on their resources is to pose successfully as a physical metaphor for the luxuriant and voloptuous excess of masculine imperialism; and, by doing so, seduce a man into "spending" some of his appropriated wealth back on to her. Or, as Molly Bloom states in her succinct summation of this same equation, "he's not the marrying type so someone should get it out of him" (18.411–12). Behind this act of seduction, as the *Sweets of Sin* excerpt suggests, there is a prior seduction to which the woman succumbs. "[T]he making of willing consumers readily fitted into the available ideological paradigm of a seduction of women by men, in which women would be addressed as yielding objects to the powerful male subject forming, and informing them of, their desires" (Bowlby 22). Raoul's suspicious accusation ("You're late") indicates his fear that he has been kept waiting while "the beautiful woman" satisfied herself elsewhere. Her "imperceptible smile" of "private and individual" pleasure (it is, in fact, social and collective) indicates to him that she must have been "spending" without him. His suspicions are well-founded—except that she has been seduced by the marketing techniques of a department store, and it is this—not another lover—that has caused her to "spend."

When Molly recalls a purchase *not made*, she describes this lost moment with the same nostalgic yearning that characterizes her recollections of Mulvey: "a peachblossom dressing jacket *like the one long ago* in Walpoles *only* ⅚ or ⅛⅙" (18.1496–97, emphasis added). One dimension of the "dear dead days beyond recall" is a nostalgia for a missed shopping opportunity. "I was thinking about a person *long ago*," Gretta tells Gabriel, in reference to Michael Furey (*Dubliners* 218, emphasis added). But "the one long ago" may also be a peachblossom dressing jacket! Accompanying Molly's regret is the vague recollection that, at the time, it seemed too much to spend ("⅚ or ⁸⁄₁₆"). The actual price has faded from memory, but the color of the dressing jacket—"peachblossom"—a term invented by the designer or the advertiser for marketing purposes, is nearly as vivid to her as the eyes of Michael Furey are to Gretta. The cycle of seduction in the bedroom and the department store finally comes full circle when we learn, in the closing moments of *Ulysses,* that the most powerfully seductive line Leopold Bloom has ever spoken to her—the one that prompts her to ask him with her eyes to ask again—is "you are a flower of the mountain *yes so we are flowers* all a womans body yes *that was one true thing he said in his life*" (18.1576–77, emphasis added). His observation that her body is a flower is as unforgettable and seductive to her as the *peachblossom* jacket. Both Leopold Bloom and the department store retailer seduce Molly because they formulate a slogan about her body that she considers to be a "true thing."

When Bloom happens upon this floral metaphor, a metaphor that is at the "normative" center of Molly's pleasure construction (which is to say she does not view it as a *role* performed solely for the benefit of a man's excitement), she pays him the sort of compliment that any manager of a department store would love to hear: "I saw he understood or felt what a woman is" (18.1578–79). At the turn of the century, it is the department stores, not men in general, who are most anxious to discover what makes a woman "spend." It is significant, therefore, that Molly's "normative" idea of pleasure echoes a marketer's "performative" advertising strategy: "Wear this *peachblossom* jacket because you're body is *a flower*." We can appreciate better the department store marketer as someone unusually motivated to discover "what a woman wants" (as opposed to what he wants her to do for him) by imagining what Corley would have come up with if asked to describe the color of the dressing jacket—"orange tart" is one possibility. Even

Freud's famous query, "What do women want?" sounds like the crucial question of a department store board meeting. Indeed, a saying
made famous by the founder of the Marshall Field's department store,
which later was used as the title of a book recounting the history of
the store, was *Give the Lady What She Wants*. Freud, of course, in line
with the grasping Raoul, thought a woman's body was not a flower
but "a dark continent"—which suggests to me that it is a good thing
he never went into retail sales—his suggestion for naming the color
of Molly's fondly recalled dressing jacket might have been "Savage
Sunset." Such an item, even with identical "styling," certainly would
have remained both on the shelf and out of Molly's mind.

Leopold Bloom, in keeping with his general sensitivity about marketing technique, rejects the novel *Fair Tyrants* in favor of *Sweets of
Sin*. The purchase is a highly erotic interlude for him, but this should
not blind us to the fact that he is a consumer making a "choice" in
the (sexual) marketplace: "No. She wouldn't like that much. Got her
it once. . . . *Sweets of Sin*. More in her line" (10.605). Granted this
purchase has a more demonstrable physical effect on Bloom than his
earlier purchase of lemon soap, but buying in a contemporary commodity culture, as the boy in "Araby" also demonstrates, frequently
has an erotic dimension. Nor is Bloom's production of pleasure "individual"; it is collective in that he imagines its effect on Molly even as
he experiences its effect on him. Bloom's phrase about the *Sweets of
Sin* ("more in her line") is really a marketing term normally used to
suggest the particular "line" of goods a merchant specializes in selling.

Bloom is correct that purchasing the book will not be an inducement for Molly to spend: "he brought me that twice I remember when
I came to page 50 the part about where she hangs him up out of a
hook with a cord flagellate sure theres nothing for a woman in that
all invention made up" (18.493–95). Molly objects to this scene as too
"stagy"—too obviously a performance. Like the excitement of watching a good play, eroticism depends on a suspension of disbelief. One
must at least pretend that the performative is normative. We see from
Molly's recollection that Bloom has tried to sell her on this idea not
once, but twice. Given that the female body/flower metaphor strikes
her as a "true thing," it is hardly surprising that she finds unstimu-
lating the role of whipping someone hanging from a hook ("there's
nothing for a woman in that"). The dressing jacket that so attracted
her, after all, was called "peachblossom" not "pink bottom." Indeed,
one of her central complaints about men (and Bloom in particular) is
that they excessively gaze at her buttocks where there is no possibility
for a woman to stimulate herself by doing a "star turn": "[A]ny man

thatd kiss a womans bottom Id throw my hat at him . . . where we havent 1 atom of any kind of expression in us all of us the same 2 lumps of lard" (18.1401–3). Molly wishes, like "the beautiful woman," to display herself in such a way that she can see from her lover's expression that her performance has that necessary erotic component of genuine fraudulence, the look that makes men spend: "I gave my eyes that look with my hair a bit loose from the tumbling and my tongue between my lips up to him the savage brute" (18.592–94). "Savage brute" is not so much what Boylan is; it is *the role* she has assigned to him as her "leading man" to facilitate his acting as a foil to heighten the brilliance of her own performance. Blazes's pleasure consists of an involuntary spasm, while Molly's is a sustained *tableau;* a "star turn" is what turns her on.

Satisfaction Guaranteed: Consumption and Pleasure Production

The act of sex in a commodity culture, like the act of consumption, is not motivated by "natural" and "individual" desire, but instead is a collective endeavor that *produces* pleasure as part of a collective enterprise:

> The truth about consumption is that it is a function of production and not a function of pleasure, and therefore, like material production, is not an individual function but one that is directly and totally collective. . . . Pleasure would define consumption for itself, as autonomous and final. But consumption is never thus. Although we experience pleasure for ourselves, when we consume we never do it on our own (the isolated consumer is the carefully maintained illusion of the ideological discourse on consumption). (Baurillard 46)

In a commodity culture, to wear is to be aware; to live is to have a visible and collectively affirmed "lifestyle." Likewise, what one buys to put in the room of a home also makes that room a stage. Dialogue between a husband and wife, against the backdrop of modern furnishings is a particularly popular advertising scenario at the turn of the century. In one advertisement, for example, the wife's purchase of inferior "ladder tapes" for window blinds is cited as "The Cause of Their First Quarrel." In the first drawing, the wrecked blinds serve as the background for the husband's denunciation of his wife's shoddy pattern of consumption: " 'Didn't I tell you to get Carr's Stamped Quality Ladder Tapes? Instead of which you get these wretched things, and'— (gives way to despair)". The drawing next to it is titled "Happy Reunion"; the binds are nicely shut behind them, and, as we are told by the ad copy printed beneath the second picture: "They Lived Happy Ever Afterwards." This two-act melodrama (the script even has stage directions) exclusively features the dramaturgical effect of the *tableau,* and thus converts the home into a stage. The "inferior" product serves as the "backdrop" against which the couple quarrels, and the advertised product provides the "improved" backdrop before which they enact their "Happy Reunion." The husband's ire has been aroused because he feels his wife has failed to observe the connection between a strategic pattern of consumption and the carefully maintained display of an enviable "lifestyle." The couple's quarrel is a "private" drama brought about by the husband's concern that their "normative" *performance,* produced for an imagined audience, will instantly reveal itself as contrived if their "props" are in disrepair; after all, nothing more quickly reminds a spectator that he is watching a performance than to have part of the scenery fall down. The resolution of domestic strife by the timely intervention of a product is so endemic to turn of the century advertising that one might well view the final tableau of "A Little Cloud" as the first panel of an advertisement for a product that fails to materialize.

In a different "two-act melodrama," one that also uses two contrasting "scenes" to advertise "Monkey Brand" soap, the first panel shows a husband shooting a pistol while he brandishes a decree of divorce before the tearstricken and horrified face of his wife. The man and woman are drawn with oversized heads to emphasize theatrical expression (recall Molly's despair that men prefer her expressionless "2 lumps of lard" to her face). The murder, mayhem, and marital discord of the first panel has resulted because supper was served late in a dirty pan. In the second panel, the "Monkey Brand" trademark presides over the two smiling and complacent heads: "Without strife/ Life's sublime; Married bliss,/Happiness," reads the copy beneath the drawing.[8] The connection made between soap, "life," and "happiness" illustrates the collective "pleasure production" in an age of spectacle and theatrical culture where only what can be dramatized is "real." As Rachel Bowlby puts it, " '[a]ll the world's a stage" takes its characteristic twentieth-century form in [the] novel of narcissistic consumer-actors, passively drifting up and down a line whose successive stages are marked by differences in the possession of wealth and commodities . . ." (65). In the production of pleasure, and in the construction of a "lifestyle," costume, scenery, expressive gesture, and dialogue are a collective illusion that structure's the individual consumer's reality. When Bloom gives a melodramatic recitation of his childhood to the court in "Circe," Joyce makes explicit the connection between advertising, patterns of consumption, "happiness," and the production of a "lifestyle" staged in the home:

[H]e wanted . . . to lead a homely life in the evening of his days, permeated by the affectionate surroundings of the heaving bosom of the family. An acclimatised Britisher, he had seen . . . through the windows of loveful households . . . scenes truly rural of happiness of the better land with Dockrell's wallpaper at one and ninepence a dozen. . . . [also] model young ladies playing on the pianoforte . . . what times the strains of the organtoned melodeon Brianniametalbound with four acting stops and twelvefold bellows, a sacrifice, greatest bargain ever . . . (15.907–22)

A piano is not only something to be played in Bloom's fantasy; it is also a prop in the presence of which we prepare to read aloud the ideal script of our lives. Bloom's idea of himself as an "acclimatised Britisher" also suggests that, at least to an extent, he has been successfully targeted by the British advertising firms attempt to create an expanded market in Ireland for British products (converting "heritage" and "tradition" into (British) "lifestyle." British advertising is as pervasive as the weather, thus "acclimatising" Irish consumers into "Britishers."

"Individuation, in the form of a modern self-image, is inseparable from appearance" (Bowlby 68). To not be able to afford "style"—to not have the means or the ability to "lash it around"—is to be invisible, and Molly is considerably ahead of her time in recognizing that how one looks is slowly becoming the dominant "reality" over one's invisible "reputation": "he [Bloom] says that little man he showed me without the neck is very intelligent the coming man Griffiths is he well he doesnt look it thats all I can say" (18.385–86). Molly's somewhat cryptic dismissal ("that's all I have to say") contains an implicit warning that if the public appearance of Griffith gives her so little to comment upon, then the idea of his approaching fame ("the coming man") seems quite doubtful. As Cheryl Herr has pointed out, Bloom's fanciful rise to the position of mayor in the "Circe" chapter is intensely—one might say exclusively—theatrical. Indeed, his rapid fall from power can be seen, in turn, as a failure to control *the spectacle* of his "greatness." Once the theatrical underpinning of his role as a "natural" leader is laid bare, his "audience" becomes especially vicious as a result of their "reality" having been suddenly exposed as illusion. The point of a "lifestyle," as well as a political campaign, or an advertising campaign, or a career as a "celebrity," is to make the performative appear normative. As Kimberly Devlin has pointed out in this volume, in reference to Molly's dismissal of Griffith, Molly re-

fuses "to be impressed by arbitrarily determined cultural differences."
Molly critiques the performances of others because she is, herself,
a performer bent on "self"-improvement; she is particularly critical
of *failed* or *shoddy* performances, rather than the idea of performance
itself.

But her most withering remarks are not for people who perform
poorly, but for people who would like to stop the show entirely: "[Mrs.
Riordan] greatest miser ever was . . . let us have a bit of fun first God
help the world if all the women were her sort down on bathingsuits
and lownecks of course nobody wanted her to wear them I suppose
she was pious because no man would look at her twice I hope Ill
never be like her a wonder she didnt want us to cover our faces"
(18.606–12). Mrs. Riordan has a private source of income, and so she
is "well-endowed" in a manner that does not require the accessories of
"bathingsuits and lownecks" to attract big-spenders. Her invisibility
("of course nobody wanted her to wear them") gives her a view of
"life" devoid of spectacle or drama ("pious") that is completely anti-
thetical to the idea of a consumer-constructed "lifestyle." One might
recall here the inscrutable Mrs. Mercer of "Araby" who, the narrator
tells us with frank puzzlement, "collected used stamps for some pious
purpose" (*Dubliners* 33). The very purpose of her existence baffles the
narrator who has already been electrified with desire following his
pledge to Mangan's sister that if he goes to the Araby Bazaar he will
"bring [her] something." The difference between a street market and
a department store is implicit in the form of the boy's pledge which
omits the idea of "buying" anything, and which does not make any
effort to conceive of what will be bought. Although Mrs. Riordan has
more than enough money for "food and rent," she saves it all up so as
to pay for masses conducted after she is dead. "[L]et us have a little
fun first," is Molly's rejection of this "pious" attitude in favor of publically performing in the (unacknowledged) carnival of competing and
staged "lifestyles" which produces the theatre without footlights that
dramatizes "the everyday."

"God knows hes a change in a way," Molly says of Blazes Boylan,
"not to be always and ever wearing the same old hat" (18.82–83). Here,
quite literally, Molly's physical desire is experienced as the equivalent
of moving from an "old hat" to a "new" one (the promise of even-
tual satisfaction stimulated by the flight from one signifier to another).
In this equation, eroticism may be generated by the acquisition of
a new lover or a new hat, and so shopping becomes an intercourse
with objects that is nearly as stimulating as intercourse with Boylan.
Indeed, in a later thought, shopping becomes a type of foreplay con-

ducted in "new" surroundings: "[I]t would be exciting going round with him shopping buying those things in a new city" (18.406–7). But here its interesting to note the distinction Molly makes between what she hopes will be "post-coital" shopping, and the "pre-coital" shopping that earlier she declined to do: "the second pair of silkette stockings is laddered after one days wear I could have brought them back to Lewers this morning and kicked up a row and made that one change them only not to upset myself and run the risk of walking into him and ruining the whole thing" (18.42–46). The difference in these two imagined shopping expeditions is that in one—the return trip to Lewers—Molly feels very much "off stage" vis-à-vis her later afternoon performance with Blazes Boylan. This sort of shopping is the equivalent of the "back stage" production so carefully screened from the play-going audience who are intended to view the "on-stage" scenes as being "natural" and "realistic."

It will not help Blazes Boylan to find her hosiery erotic if he is forced to recall having seen it, just hours before, crumpled in a bunch on a department store counter. "Appearance" and "display" are crucial to the "genuine fraudulence" of a modern self-image. In the same light, Raoul would not have been as impressed by the "queenly display" of "the beautiful woman" if he had bumped into her earlier when she was arguing over the price of her *déshabillé*. Leopold Bloom also recognizes the need to keep financial and hygiene matters "off stage" if a woman's erotic performance is to attain the necessary suspension of disbelief: "See her as she is spoil all" (12.855) And, like Molly, Gerty MacDowell carefully details the way she launders and irons her panties before she considers them fit to be seen. Little Chandler, for his part, is counting on Annie to somehow invest the recently purchased blouse with erotic allure, but instead she does just what Molly is anxious to avoid; she focuses on the monetary exchange that led to the purchase of the blouse, and demystifies it entirely: "when she heard the price she threw the blouse on the table and said it was a regular swindle to charge ten and elevenpence for that. At first she wanted to take it back . . ." (*Dubliners* 83). For his part, Blazes Boylan is always careful to present a predictable appearance that is as unified and consistent as any trademark; in fact, like a trademark (or a packaged commodity, or a theatrical performance), he is *all* appearance while betraying no visible sign of having manufactured his image: "lovely stuff in that blue suit he had on and stylish tie and socks with the skyblue silk thing on them hes certainly well off I know by the cut his clothes have" (18.420–22). The "skyblue silk thing" is a bit of embroidery around the ankle area of a sock called a "clock," and in the song "Those Lovely Seaside Girls" (which Millie Bloom associates with Blazes) it is the "girls" who wear such stockings and the men who notice them: "The boys observe the latest thing in socks,/They learn the time by looking at the clocks" (Gifford and Seidman 76). Perhaps our one-dimensional idea of Blazes Boylan as a voyeuristic and aggressive heterosexual man has blinded us to the fact that he also plays the part of a dandy—although he is a dandy without any of the requisite wit of a Beau Brummel or an Oscar Wilde. Blazes is most frequently characterized as a "rake" by readers, but I think his crude sensitivity to the advantages of "lifestyle" makes him *a new generation dandy*, one who understands, unlike Griffiths, that a rhetorical style is no longer as saleable a commodity as "personal" style.

Although "masculine" enough in his actions with Molly, the fact that Boylan wears the clocks by which Molly "tells the time"—a direct gender reversal of the situation in "Those Lovely Seaside Girls"—suggests that, relative to his "lifestyle," he operates within the supposedly "feminine" sphere of attracting the "masculine" gaze through an artfully constructed appearance. The song refers to the clocks as "the latest thing" which suggests that this item of clothing, with its deliberately rapid update of embroidery design, pioneered the sort of "instant fashion obsolescence" that is now common to such youthful fashion items as "designer jeans" or athletic shoes (where the brand names or "new" features publically indicate to any interested viewer whether the wearer possesses "the latest thing" or something that is "old hat"). The fact that boys "tell the time" by these "clocks" (and, as Molly demonstrates, girls do, too) indicates the extent to which an object (socks) becomes a sign ("clocks") in a commodity culture. This conversion exponentially increases the need to consume since the "use value" of a sock (something to keep one's feet warm) is replaced by the need the consumer feels to buy a "new" pair that features the latest "clock" well before the "old" sock has worn out. The conversion of objects into signs is what permits the construction of a "lifestyle" where the juxtaposition of objects designates a language through which desire speaks. The need to consume "the latest thing," a need Molly frequently expresses, is based on the hope of presenting to others a carefully staged image that operates as a visual correspondent to the individual myth of the self.

Blazes is the opposite of Griffiths. He is the *real* "coming man"—in that he makes a strong visual impression by displaying the flamboyant "lifestyle" that his salary permits ("lovely stuff . . . he's certainly well off"). But, as Molly can't help noting, his verbal skills consist of a dozen or so clichés that he fits to any occasion: "hes right enough in his way to pass the time as a joke sure you might as well be in bed with what with a lion God Im sure hed have something better to say for himself an old Lion would" (18.775–77). Blazes is not "a joke" in terms of the current connotations of this word—as someone pathetic and hopeless—but more in the sense of the "bit of fun" that she feels the ascetic Mrs Riordan would have outlawed if she could.[9] The idea of "fun," in the sense of something that provides enjoyment or sensation, is basic to the philosophy of a commodity culture where the pursuit of happiness has been refashioned not as a right, but as a *duty:* "Modern man *spends* less and less of life in production, and *more and more* in the continuous production and creation of personal needs and of personal well-being. He must constantly be ready to actualize all of his potential, all of his capacity for consumption. If he forgets, he will be gently and instantly reminded that he has no right not to be happy" (Baudrillard 48, emphasis added). "Double your pleasure, double your fun" begins a contemporary ad for chewing gum. What appears to be an invitation to increase our enjoyment of "life," is in fact a rather coercive reminder that we are required to have "fun" and that "having fun" involves the constant "trying" of "new" experiences and sensations that "double" our pleasure; "trying the new," of course, is the essence of a commodity culture where the consumer must be persuaded that "life" requires a "style" of "lashing around" all the products beyond "food and rent" that fulfill his or her duty to "have fun."

When Molly says of Blazes "hes a change in a way not to be always and ever wearing the same old hat," we can see that "trying" Blazes is an act of consumption even as it is an act of adultery. Indeed, Baudrillard talks about a *"fun morality* whose imperative is enjoyment and the complete exploitation of all the possibilities of being thrilled, experiencing pleasure, and being gratified" (Baudrillard 49). In this paradigm, Molly has a moral imperative to "try" Blazes if she is to obey the modern commandment: "Double Your Pleasure!" (*Ten* commandments are too confusing to market effectively, so we're down to one.) Bloom, too, states his (theoretical) readiness to "try" anything "new" with a sexual partner when he thinks of Gerty's limp as a possible "turn-on": "I wouldn't mind. Curiosity like a nun or a negress or a girl with glasses" (13.776–77). Likewise, Molly is not overly excited by the idea of having the prince of Wales as a lover because he is "old hat"; there is nothing "new" about him: "hes like the first man going the roads only for the name of a king." But a black man has enough of the requisite novelty for her to want to give it a try: "they're all made the one way only a black mans *Id like to try*" (18.483–

84, emphasis added). This is the worship of novelty, not the phallus. Any product that is "made the one way" for too long will stop selling (which is why, for example, automobiles are made a different way every year).

This operative word "try" is also what prompts Bloom's selection of the *Sweets of Sin*: "Yes. This. Here. *Try*" (10.610, emphasis added). One effect of commodity culture and "fun morality" is that "[a] *universal curiosity* has . . . been reawakened in the areas of cuisine, culture, science, religion, sexuality, etc. 'Try Jesus!' says an American slogan. *Everything* must be tried" (Baudrillard 48). In the contemporary definition of the word "try" as "experiencing something for the first time," one can only "try" something once; the citizen-consumer's duty to "experience pleasure" and "try things" requires the constant re-production of the everyday into the "new": "I wished I was one myself [a man]" Molly thinks, *"for a change just to try* with that thing they have swelling up on you so hard" (18.1381–82, emphasis added). It is not penis envy that prompts Molly's fantasy about being a man. She does not wish to *have* a penis, she wishes to *try* one; in fact, as far as any presumed worship of the phallus is concerned, it's rather deflating, from a patriarchal point of view, to think that Molly's impulse to have a penis—to "try" something new—is identical to the impulse that might prompt her to switch her brand of shampoo in order to "try" a "new" one in a differently shaped bottle.

This Time, You be the Imperialist and I'll be the Colonial Subject: The Fiscal and the Physical

The advent of a modern "lifestyle," with its paradoxical and insatiable requirement for the sensation of novelty as an everyday experience, also requires the increasingly detailed delineation and amplification of "pleasure." As Michel Foucault has stated in a different context, the purpose of various "polymorphous techniques of power" is "to reach the most tenuous and individual modes of behavior, the paths that give it access to the rare or scarcely perceivable forms of desire, how it penetrates and controls everyday pleasure" (Foucault 11). Another reason Molly would like "to try" being a man is that she is aware the female body has been thoroughly commodified as a "source" of pleasure; if she were to become a man, however, she could enjoy this commodification directly (rather than vicariously experiencing pleasure by watching the expression of a man who is looking at her): "I suppose its because they were so plump and tempting in my short petticoat he couldnt resist they excite myself sometimes its well for men all the amount of pleasure they get off a womans body" (18.78–80). The rise of "sexology" at the turn of the century, and its creation of such categories as "homosexual," "pervert," and "degenerate," as well as the corresponding insistence on "heterosexuality" as normative," helped to make "sexual preference" part of a "lifestyle"; indeed, one way to euphemistically express disapproval of someone else's sexual practices is to say "I don't approve of that lifestyle." Increasingly in a commodity culture, consumers visibly express how they consume products in order to make equally clear both how they wish to consume others and how they hope to be consumed by them in turn.[10]

The production of "everyday pleasure" requires the consumption of novelty, and the degree of "fun" we are able to reach through this "work of consumption" (to use Wicke's phrase) is mapped out—as all current advertisers are aware—by our "sexual preference" or "what turns us on" (which can also be understood as the "path" we most frequently choose to travel to reach our own "scarcely perceivable forms of desire"). Even within the "normative" practice of heterosexual intercourse there is still a nearly endless variety of "paths" (a variety that *Ulysses* maps, though not comprehensively). The fledgling science of sexology was a goldmine for the equally fledgling art of mass-marketers and advertisers because the detailed descriptions of the "polymorphous perversity" of the human being were easily converted to a "mapping out" of the polymorphous desire of the consumer. The scientific definition of "adolescence," for example, suggested an endless variety of products which are marketed as the appropriate fetish for all the permutations of "normal" and "perverse" sexuality (as Gerty is exquisitely aware). "Sexology expressed the same conviction about the domain of the consumer, starting with the assumption of the polymorphous desiring individual who eventually specializes in particular tastes. Through specialization, individuals starting out the same fulfill their individuality" (Birken 50). For the child growing to sexual maturity, or for the child developing his or her "own" lifestyle, the "healthy" goal in both cases is for the performative to be presented and perceived as the normative. Of course, "specialization," under the general rubric of "heterosexuality," is still "individually" expressed through strategic acts of consumption: "that black closed breeches he made me buy takes you half an hour to let them down wetting all myself always with some brandnew fad every other week" (18.251–53). The "use value" and "design" of the black closed breeches is dubious at best ("always wetting myself"), but Molly agrees to purchase breeches, and, despite the practical inconvenience, to wear them because she understands—albeit reluctantly—Bloom's modern duty in a commodity culture (experienced by the consumer as "need") to produce pleasure through the consumption of novelty.

But we need to notice that what is at issue for Molly is not Bloom's urge to "try" something new (an urge which she shares), but rather *the frequency* with which he wishes to do so. Because the production of "personal" pleasure requires other people's labor, issues of capitalization and exploitation arise. Interestingly, it is Wanda, the dominatrix in *Venus in Furs*, who delivers a manifesto of consumerism that reinterprets Hegel's "master/slave" paradigm in terms of who consumes pleasure, and whose labor makes this consumption possible. As with economic capitalism, the goal is to produce as much profit/pleasure as possible—to "spend" as long as possible—at someone else's expense:

Pleasure alone lends value to existence. . . . whoever wants to enjoy must take life gaily . . . he dare not hesitate *to enjoy at the expense of others.* . . . He must know how to make slaves of men who feel and would enjoy as he does, and use them for his service and pleasure without remorse. . . . He must always remember this, that if they had him in their power, as he has them they would act in exactly the same way, and he would have *to pay for their pleasure* with his sweat and blood and soul. (Sacher-Masoch 135–36, emphasis added)

The central dynamic of Wanda and Severin's relationship in *Venus in Furs* revolves around the complex playacting of a man and a woman who blur the line between who is laboring and who is "spending." First, Severin actively persuades Wanda to dominate him; but, after she grows to enjoy the role, the scenario reverses itself and soon he finds himself laboring for her pleasure. "I can't stop at make-believe, when once I begin" she tells him. "You know I hate all play-acting and comedy. You have wished it. Was it my idea or yours?" (70–71).

In still another reversal, Wanda abruptly forsakes her role as "Venus in Furs" and informs Severin about her "real" self: "didn't you know that everything was only make-believe and play-acting. . . . I have played my cruel role better than you expected, and now you will be satisfied with my being a good, little wife. . . . We will live like rational people—" (131). But "being a little wife" turns out to be the "real" performance, and what she disavowed as a *performative* mode ("my cruel role") emerges as her *normative* state of being. Under the guise of being a devoted "little wife," she persuades him to be tied up one more time ("I wonder if I can still do it"); then calls her new lover out from behind "the curtains of her four-poster bed" to administer Severin's most humiliating whipping yet. "You are indeed cruel," this lover says to Wanda. "Only inordinately fond of pleasure," she answers, a reply that supports my contention that the normative mode is often a performative mode that appears normative while allowing for a maximization of pleasure production in any given scenario of "reality." And yet, in the final reversal, it is Severin whose level of enjoyment deepens as a result of Wanda's "natural" cruelty: "The sensation of being whipped by a successful rival before the eyes of an adored woman cannot be described" (137). He then proceeds to recite everyone's role and position on stage to the accompaniment of his own mounting excitement, and finishes as the "star" at the center of his own ultimate (pleasure) "*tableau.*"

The theatrical production of pleasure in *Venus in Furs* suggests to me that, in the midst of feeling sorry for the cuckolded Bloom, we need to entertain the idea that Molly and Blazes's afternoon performance may be, in part, a matinee staged for Bloom's pleasure. Certainly it is Molly who suspects that, while directing her own satisfactory duet with Blazes, she also may be inadvertently performing for Bloom: "he has an idea about him and me hes not such a fool he said Im dining out and going to the Gaiety though Im not going to give him the satisfaction" (18.81–83). Later, when remembering how it is Bloom who insisted on sending Milly away to be a "photo girl," her suspicion that her affair with Blazes may be a play directed by Leopold Bloom becomes even more explicit: "on account of me and Boylan that's why he did it Im certain the way he plots and plans everything out" (18.1007–9). In "Circe," it is Molly who becomes a "photo girl" when Bloom asks permission from Blazes (who has invited him to "apply your eye to the keyhole . . . while I just go through her a few times") to "take a snapshot." Presumably, such a snapshot would find its way into his "secret" drawer along with the other staged photographs that he finds exciting. The earliest readings of *Ulysses*—which saw Molly as immoral and Bloom as a pathetically noble man who "bears up" under the strain of being made a cuckold—may still be obscuring the possibility that, relative to the affair of Molly and Blazes, Bloom is a man more sinning than sinned against. Just as we saw with Severin, production of a painful *tableau* may afford a "private" pleasure for the person who appears wronged according to "normative" standards. Pleasure production for a "masculine" colonial subject is not as straightforward as it is for Raoul and the German Emperor. As Bloom, the colonial subject, cannot hope to challenge power directly, he may design instead a scenario where an apparently abject posture conceals the pleasure of watching others unwittingly perform under his secret direction.

Certainly in the one encounter with a prostitute that Bloom recalls, he casts himself in the role of a director who hires an "actress" to recite a script he has prepared for her: "Girl in Meath street that night. All the dirty things I made her say" (18.867–68). Paradoxically, the "business" dimension of hiring a prostitute is also what makes it (potentially) erotic because the performance is paid for in advance, the actor or actress has been hired, and therefore the question of who is to labor for who's pleasure disappears as a hinderance to the enjoyment of the one who is "spending." In such an arrangement, who is spending fiscally and who is spending physically is contracted in advance. Bloom's "rehearsal" of the girl on Meath Street (who proves not ready yet for Bloom's "prime time") is a precursor to the contemporary phenomenon of "phone sex" where men and women offer to recite any script the client presents—but only after obtaining the client's credit card number.[11] Still, the exchange with the girl on Meath Street is unsatisfactory for Bloom because she is such an unconvincing performer: "All wrong of course. My arks she called it" (18.868–69). In contrast, when Bloom presents a script to Molly, and in the process gets a "free" performance from her, he reaches a climax; Molly, however, is resentful because this particular type of playacting leaves her unsatisfied, and thus feeling like an unpaid prostitute:

tell me who are you thinking of who is it tell me his name who tell me who the german Emperor is it yes imagine Im him think of him can you feel him *trying to make a whore out of me* what he never will he ought to give it up now at this age of his life simply ruination for any woman and *no satisfaction in it pretending to like it* till he comes and finish it off myself anyway (18.94–99, emphasis added).

As Don Gifford and Robert J. Seidman point out, the German emperor was William I who died in 1888—the year of Molly and Leopold's courtship—and his image dominated the newspapers at this time. Under his leadership, the new German empire rapidly became the chief economic and military power on the continent, rivaling England's empire.

Small wonder, then, that even sixteen years later Bloom is still excited by the erotic *tableau* of Raoul reaching for the beautiful woman's "opulent" curves. In calling Molly a "flower of the mountain," Bloom may have been thinking of her as unplowed countryside. In asking Molly to imagine it is the imperialistic German emperor who is exploring and appropriating her assets ("can you feel him"), Bloom is a sheep in wolf's clothing. Accordingly, Molly calls Blazes "Raoul" in the "Circe" chapter when she invites him to come see her step out of the bathtub: "Raoul darling, come and dry me. I'm in my pelt. Only my new hat and a carriage sponge" (15.3770–71). Molly's announcement

"I'm in my pelt" informs Blazes that she is naked. But it is also, as Gifford and Seidman note, an allusion to *Venus Im Pelz*. In a further echo of this novel, to "pelt" someone is to beat them unrelentingly. This refers us once more, of course, to the final *tableau* of Severin where his apparent complete humiliation is in fact his ultimate directorial triumph. In contrast to all this, Molly gets no satisfaction from her performance as a woman ravaged by a German emperor. She imagines instead that *she needs to hire someone herself*—spend in order to "spend"—if she expects someone to perform in a prearranged manner for her enjoyment: "unless I paid some nicelooking boy . . . I'd confuse him a little . . . *let him see my garters the new ones* and *make him turn red* looking at him seduce him" (18.84–87, emphasis added). Once again, just like "the beautiful woman," Molly links her ability to be a seductive display with her recollection of the purchase of new garters. Even when calling for Raoul/Blazes to see her in her "pelt," she announces at the same time that she is wearing a new hat.

Unlike Bloom and the girl on Meath Street, however, Molly does not enact her scenario. If she were ever to do so, she would run into a contradiction identical to Bloom's problem—how can someone who has already agreed to have sex in exchange for money still convince her that he is being seduced by the irresistable display of her body packaged in a new pair of garters? Even if the boy she hires is a good actor it is unlikely he will be able to blush on command—and yet Molly has included this as a specific stage direction! To use Devlin's term, what Molly wants from the boy is genuine fraudulence. She hopes to witness an apparently unrehearsed, involuntary, and physical expression of desire (confusion, blushing) from someone she has hired as a performer; he must convincingly present the performative as something that is normative. Buying a fantasy, and then seeking to ignore the relationship of the fiscal to the physical, is also basic to the experience of shopping in a modern department store: the prices are fixed to eliminate bartering, and customers are asked to pay, not at the point of purchase, but only as they leave the store (with contemporary credit cards, of course, one does not pay in the store at all). This is another reason that Molly considers the act of returning her "laddered" hosiery for money as potentially fatal to an erotic mood ("run the risk of walking into him and ruining the whole thing"), and yet also imagines it would be "exciting" to go shopping with Boylan in a "new city" where she could "spend" at his expense.

In the same way that a manufacturer who designs a product has a particular market or audience in mind, Molly Bloom, in designing her "lifestyle" (and in her desire to "improve" it), also has a particular market in mind; one might even go so far as to say that Blazes Boylan receives a "free sample" in return for his agreement to participate in a survey of her charms. In expressing rivalry with other women, Molly thinks of Boylan this way: "see if they [other women] can excite a swell with money that can pick and choose whoever he wants like Boylan to do it 4 or 5 times locked in each others arms" (18.993–95). With all due respect to Boylan, I think it is as unlikely that he "did it" five times as it is that Molly has had—as was once believed—twenty or more lovers. What is more interesting to note than Blaze's debatable stamina is that Molly keeps increasing the number of times Boylan has reached orgasm even as she recalls, with increasing alarm, that she is getting older and stouter. Different "lifestyles" require the credible presentation of different ages, and Molly, like Gerty, feels that her increasing age is forcing her out of the "lifestyle" she wishes to maintain. She understands, for example, that Mrs. Riordan's age is a factor in her ascetic world view: "I hope Ill never be like her" (18.17). Not surprisingly, then, each recollection of Boylan's increasingly numerous climaxes (her final quantification is "5 or 6 times") is accompanied by a mental note of what pose she struck to bring him to it: "I gave my eyes that look with my hair a bit loose from the tumbling and my tongue between my lips up to him the savage brute" (18.592–94). In terms of "spending" as Victorian slang for a sexual climax, we can see that Molly might also interpret Boylan's multiple orgasms as a sort of "shopping binge" which her display of herself has stimulated.

Indeed, Molly often catalogues and evaluates various features of her body—her hands, her feet, her breasts—in accordance with how capable they are of making men "spend" in the double sense of climaxing and buying her presents: "I saw his eyes on my feet going out through the turning door now how did that excite him because I was crossing them when we were in the other room . . . my hand is nice like that if I only had a ring with the stone for my month a nice aquamarine Ill stick him for one and a gold bracelet I dont like my foot so much still I made him spend once with my foot" (18.256–63). By "looking back," Molly has caught the gaze of an excited consumer and, like any good "manufacturer," she is eager to know what it was about her foot (which doesn't seem like much to her) that he found so exciting. Similarly, while thinking about getting a man to "spend" money for items that might dress up her hand, Molly's thoughts return once more to her apparently undervalued foot which—despite its unmarketable appearance to her—"made him spend once." If she could isolate what it is about her foot that is marketable, she could file this information away, or further refine it, just as she has evidently perfected "that look" which she "gives to her eyes" to make Boylan "spend." Significantly, the complaint about men that Molly voices most consistently is that there is no telling what will persuade men to spend ("they're all so different"). This, of course, is the perennial dilemma that the advertiser faces vis à vis the consumer.

Her contentment at having persuaded Boylan, as a wealthy consumer, to "spend" on her when he is free to "pick and choose" where he spends, is borne out by her silent refutation of what she takes to be Bloom's current perception of her as an unsaleable commodity: "I suppose he thinks Im finished out *and laid on the shelf* well Im not nor anything like it (18.1021–23, emphasis added). By understanding the implicit metaphor of marketing behind Molly's various strategies for getting men to "spend," we can see I think, that claiming she has the instincts of a "whore" misses the point. If she is a whore, then so is Blazes Boylan in his "sky blue" suit and "clocks." Indeed, so are all of us in the modern age who vie for attention through the spectacular "language" of lifestyle. To have a "lifestyle" at all is to try to determine, for the sake of advancement and profit, what is currently "selling" and what has been remaindered to "the shelf." "What's hot and what's not" is a staple article of contemporary magazines, whether it's *Vogue* for women or *GQ* for men. In the modern world of commodity culture, where all that is visible is for sale, and where everything has an exchange value relative to the visibility of something else, the person the public labels a "whore" is really no more than what Stephen calls a "bad merchant"—someone who "buys dear and sells cheap." It is these people who draw forth all the opprobrium that our culture can muster—not because they have "sold themselves"—but because they have failed to do so for profit. When selling leads to profit, as Molly seems well aware, it covers up a multitude of sins; "prostitution" becomes "good business."

But if Molly has been unfairly dismissed by some readers of *Ulysses* as a prostitute at heart rather than as a merchant who, like everyone else, buys cheap and sells dear, she makes a similar mistake when dismissing her famous namesake Moll Flanders: "I dont like books with a Molly in them like that one he brought me about the one from Flanders a whore always shoplifting anything she could cloth and stuff and yards of it" (18.656–59). And yet it is only after several marriages and a great deal of bad luck, more than two hundred pages into Defoe's novel, that Moll Flanders begins to shoplift. When Molly reflects that she could "do the indifferent" to reawaken Bloom's interest in her, she is echoing the same sort of "shop talk" that Moll Flanders consistently employs: "He pursued me close after this, and as I saw there was no need to fear losing him *I played the indifferent* part with him longer than prudence might otherwise have dictated to me" (Defoe 73, emphasis added). In looking back on her first sexual encounter with a man, Moll Flanders's primary regret is that she did not understand at that time that physical passion is just another occasion for commercial negotiation: "if he had known me and how easy the trifle he aimed at was to be had [her virginity], he would have troubled his head no farther, but have given me four or five guineas and have lain with me the next time he had come at me. On the other hand, if I had known his thoughts and how hard he supposed I would be to be gained, I might have made my own terms" (Defoe 27). Moll's ruminations on her "seduction" is not so much an admission of prostitution as a review of "Marketing 101": the exchange value of any "trifle," apart from its use value, may still be rendered cheaper or more expensive depending on supply and demand.

Quite a bit later in the book, Moll has become a skilled negotiator and is able to "make her own terms": "I played with this lover as an angler does with a trout: I found I had him fast on the hook, so I jested with his new proposal and put him off" (Defoe 125). So why does Moll end up shoplifting? Ah, there's the rub. For one thing, Defoe had to show her coming to no good because his reading public was not about to see her merely as a skillful negotiator. Of course, Defoe introduces so many absurdly coincidental hardships before he is able to reduce her to penury that her final downfall seems far from credible. Indeed, Moll Flanders can be read as Defoe's explicit inducement to women to learn to negotiate and barter if they expect to influence their destiny: "When a woman is . . . left desolate and void of counsel, she is just like a bag of money or a jewel dropped on the highway, which is a prey to the next comer" (Defoe 114). Moll's problem is one that Molly shares: "I had sufficient to live on, yet had no way of increasing it" (Defoe 115). Both Molly and Moll are fairly adept negotiators, but both have only their physical looks and acting abilities with which to barter. Molly is especially sensitive to the depreciation of her only capital—her body—because puberty is transforming Millie's body into the public attraction she once was: "[t]hey all look at her like me when I was her age of course any old rag looks well on you then . . . shes always making love to my things too the few old rags I have wanting to put her hair up at 15 my powder too only ruin her skin on her shes time enough for that all her life after of course shes restless knowing shes pretty with her lips so red a pity they wont stay that way" (18.1036–66). The "capital" of a woman's appearance within a patriarchal economy, in contrast to actual money, represents capital that inevitably depreciates over the course of time no matter how wisely it is invested ("shes pretty with her lips so red a pity they wont stay that way"). Significantly, the reason that Molly's and Millie's use of cosmetics intersect is that Millie wishes to look older and Molly to look younger. From their two ages—fifteen to thirty-three—we can see the outer limits of what we now call the "youth culture" (though one can see the nascent form of this "youth culture" in a popular advertising trope such as the "Seaside Girl").[12] The increasing mother-daughter tension between Molly and Millie needs to be understood in the context of a commodity culture where the "language of money and commodities has become an all-encompassing system—the very texture of everyday forms of ideology" (Bowlby 25). Millie's increasing marketability amplifies Molly's sense of her own devaluation.

Shopping as a Dress Rehearsal for "Life"

In the Sunday *New York Times* there is a section that appears under the headline "Lifestyle." In the issue for 5 February 1990, there was an article titled "Cards to Help the Tongue-Tied." The reporter writes of a stationery store in the financial district of Manhattan with a special alcove called "The Thoughtfulness Gallery." In this alcove the tongue-tied shopper will find the newest generation of Hallmark cards, published under the general rubric of "Just How I Feel" and "Between You and Me." The editorial manager of Hallmark explains that "[a] lot of today's consumers are feeling a need to share their thoughts but don't find the words." The new line of cards, she continues "express *the stuff* we *all* want to say" (emphasis added). What does it mean when a rhetorical message titled "Just How I Feel" and "Between You and Me" is marketed for mass consumption and thus understood to be "the stuff" we all speak (recall the headings of the turn-of-the-century ads: "The First Quarrel"; "Happily Ever After")? "It is what we call *universally specific*," continues the Hallmark editor. "It's where *everyone* thinks, 'This card was really written *for me*'" (emphasis added). The final frontier of commodity culture is consciousness where the mind, like one's livingroom, "talks stuff" and specific feelings are universal ("universal," that is, within the simulacrum—the supposedly Real World—of a given commodity culture).

A Hallmark competitor, Carlton Cards, has introduced a "complete" modern romance line of cards called "Couples." It is divided into four subcategories: "Falling in Love," "In Love," "Intimacies," and "Still in Love." Like Lacan's idea of the Real, the unrepresented fifth category of romantic love—"Get Lost"—hovers beyond these "universally specific" expressions, and yet also serves as the origin of the incomplete subjectivity that makes us misrecognize these four categories as complete. "Consumption [is] not a function of 'harmonious' individual satisfaction . . . but rather an infinite social activity. . . . Needs are strictly specified in advance in relation to finite objects" (Baudrillard 41). A customer with several cards in her hand told the *New York Times* reporter, "[t]hey capture what I feel and they save me time." Yes, and Molly, too, were she to find herself "just looking" in "The Thoughtfulness Gallery," might also discover that her thoughts had been "captured." She might send Bloom the one that begins "I Need to Feel Appreciated," and he could respond with the one titled "Please Give Me Another Chance"; tableaux of "true" love are given titles that "capture" what the performers are thinking. In contemporary commodity culture, we are what we buy, and the more we shop the more we are. We move from thing to thing—signifier to signifier—to "express the stuff we all want to say"—even though it is "the stuff" that is expressing us. Commodified desire is the consumer phenomenon known as "lifestyle" where we think we don't want what we have because we don't have what we think we want. Not surprisingly then, in "The Thoughtfulness Gallery," the card titled "I Need a Commitment" (the "latest" universal specific?) is sold out. But I'll conclude by citing my favorite title (as well this one as another): "This is the Real World." Yes.

Notes

1.   In her book *Dream Worlds: Mass Consumption in Late Nineteenth-Century France,* Rosalind H. Williams also uses the word "lifestyle" anachronistically to characterize the phenomenon in nineteenth-century France generally described—by contemporary writers—as "the democratization of luxury": "When in the late nineteenth century alternative models of consumption—alternative lifestyles, to use contemporary parlance—arose, they supplanted rather than replaced the aristocratic model" (21). Significantly, the image of Queen Victoria became a ubiquitous trademark of advertised goods. For a thorough discussion of the use of "aristocracy" to sell "democratic" goods, see Thomas Richards *The Commodity Culture of Victorian England.*

2.   Lacan makes it clear that the gaze is not manifested solely by our reaction to seeing someone who sees us; we react to objects, windows, or anything that triggers the urge to comprehend who we are by imagining what we look like to the Other: "The gaze is not located just at the level of the eyes. The eyes may very well not appear, they may be masked. The gaze is not necessarily the face of our fellow being, it could just as easily be the window

behind which we assume he is lying in wait for us. It is an x, the object when faced with which the subject becomes object" (220).

3. I am indebted to Cheryl Herr's book *Joyce's Anatomy of Culture* for pointing out the relationship between Joyce's depiction of gender/sexuality and the popular theatre of his time.

4. Henri Lefebvre, as Jules David Law notes, designated 16 June 1904 as the "momentous eruption of everyday life into literature" (2). Law examines this concept further and asks: "The history and the culture of everyday life: are these parodic oxymorons, or modernist ideologies par excellence? And if it is possible to write the history and the culture of everyday life, is Joyce's work an authentic—or even, perhaps, a unique—contribution to that project?" (197). Law goes on to suggest that the quotidian, or the "everyday," is the realm of the unintentional: "Freudian everyday life is defined precisely as that realm of experience in which our actions and expressions are so habitual and un-thought-out at the conscious level that their disruption by unconscious intentions is all the more likely to be noticed" (202). But the effect of pursuing a "lifestyle" is that the unintentional (the Freudian everyday) is what commodity culture converts into the intention to consume (the commodification of the everyday). In a current commercial for a candy called "Skittles," a group of visibly bored people are shown (in a museum listening to a lecture), their thoughts wandering, until the action of popping a skittle into one's mouth causes a flood of noise and color to escalate the moment into one of spectacle and sensation. The quotidian is equated with boredom and sensory deprivation, and countless products with a varying degree of sophistication (candy, hand-held video games, walkman radios) puncture and punctuate the "unintentional" world with intentions to buy, sell, and "have fun."

5. The representation of "the beautiful woman" in *The Sweets of Sin* can also be seen as a complex example of Irigaray's theory that the woman acts as an economic conduit through which men communicate to other men the "spending" of eroticism as well as the "spending" of consumerism. Ellen Carol Jones, in an unpublished manuscript delivered at the Joyce Symposium in Monte Carlo, applied Irigaray's theory to the exchange of the sailor's postcard and Molly's photograph in "Eumaeus." Linda H. Williams points out that the moment in contemporary pornographic films where the male actor climaxes is called "the money shot." At this same moment, the female actor is portrayed, illogically enough, as achieving equally orgasmic pleasure just by looking: " 'The Money Shot' could thus finally be viewed as that moment when the male 'homosexual' economy falters, almost reverts to an absolute and unitary standard of value" (117). For a discussion of the patriarchal economy in "Eveline," see my essay " 'Wondering Where All the Dust Comes From': *Jouissance* and 'Reality' in Joyce's 'Eveline.' " For a discussion of women as commodities in the music hall song "Those Lovely Seaside Girls" (which also discusses and utilizes Irigaray's theory of a closed "homosexual" economy), see my essay "Women on the Market: Commodity Culture, 'Those Lovely Seaside Girls,' and 'Femininity' in Joyce's *Ulysses*."

6. Another scenario he recalls as exciting is the pornographic "muto-

scope" titled "a dream of wellfilled hose"—also a staged image where a commodity (hosiery) allows a woman to become a spectacle of abundance ("wellfilled"). This, in turn, produces erotic pleasure and results, in the "Nausicaa" chapter, in the "spending" of Bloom's "wellfilled hose."

7.   The advertising strategy illustrated by the "Diano" ad has changed very little over the years. As I discuss in my essay " 'The Woman is Perfected': Sylvia Plath and *Mademoiselle*," brassiere and girdle ads America in the fifties made such comments as "[a] body is not a figure. A body is what you're given, a figure is what you make of it," and "make your torso more so." Just a few months ago, an ad in the *New York Times* urged women to upgrade their wardrobe by wearing tight-fitting skirts with the statement "[i]mprove your bottom line."

8.   Looking back from the perspective of the age of television, we can see the "Monkey Brand Melodrama" as a precursor to a much more complex, but essentially similar phenomenon known as the daytime "Soap Opera." The continual melodrama of the show is punctuated by the commercials which, in direct contrast to the endlessly unfolding story of the soap opera, present a mini-crisis that is resolved, in thirty seconds, by the *tableau* of the product. The Wisk commercial, to offer just one example, shows a woman at a business party with her husband. Such matters as raises and career advancement for her husband are clearly in the air, when a disembodied God-like voice declares "Ring Around the Collar" and the camera moves in for a *tableau* of the woman's guilt-stricken face. The Wisk is purchased and used by her— as opposed to advising the man, next time, to wash his grubby neck before getting dressed—and when the party resumes (the equivalent of the "second panel" in the ladder tape and soap ad), the woman listens contentedly as her husband garners the praise of others. What is at issue in the ad is not just one dirty shirt, or one party, or one missed opportunity, but the ability to sustain a "lifestyle" that allows one to "Live Happily Ever After."

9.   A recent pop-psychology term, retrospectively appropriate for Mrs. Riordan, is "pleasure anorexic"; the term was coined to describe people who reacted to the conspicuous consumption of the eighties by cutting back their use of commodities and "luxury" items. The term further implies that the subject derives a sense of identity by denying himself or herself "popular" or "stylish" objects. Finally, the term insists that only consumption of the "new" produces enjoyment ("doubles" one's "fun"), and therefore the refusal to consume is also a willful self-denial of pleasure. But "pleasure anorexics," in their attempt to do away with "lifestyle," still must define themselves in direct relation to the very phenomenon they wish to banish. Mrs. Riordan, for example, may "perversely" enjoy restricting her degree of mass consumption, but when Parnell is denounced by the priesthood, her complex and enduring rage is acted out for Stephen's benefit in a manner he has never forgotten: "Dante had ripped the green velvet back off the brush that was for Parnell one day with her scissors and had told him that Parnell was a bad man" (*Portrait* 16). Indeed, if Simon Dedalus is to be credited, Mrs. Riordan's self-imposed aus-

terity is thoroughly implicated in the wealth of imperialism and commodity culture: "But he had heard his father say that she was a spoiled nun and that she had come out of the convent in the Alleghanies when her brother had got the money from the savages for the trinkets and the chainies" (*Portrait*, 35). Gifford and Seidman report: "According to Ellmann, Mrs. Riordan's real-life counterpart 'had been on the verge of becoming a nun in America when her brother, who had made a fortune out of trading with African natives, died and left her 30,000 pounds" (145). Mrs. Riordan's very vocal refusal to "lash it around" is motivated, at least in part, because the commodity culture she disparages made her wealthy in the first place.

10.   In her book *Idylls of the Marketplace: Oscar Wilde and the Victorian Public*, Reginia Gagnier makes the point that men who shared homosexual desire in the nineteenth century referred to themselves not as "gay," or "homosexual" but as "modern." The desire of men for men was publically communicated through fashion and patterns of consumption in a collectively understood blend of "sexual preference" and "consumer selection." This blend shows the conjunction of physical desire and lifestyle: " 'life-style'—the neologism has come to represent precisely the convergence of such phenomena—of identifiable costume and predictable presents (cigarette cases, sleevelinks, etc.), holidays . . . and ostentatious dining out at all hours . . ." (Gagnier 140). Even more to the point, perhaps, a new brand of condom, just released on the marketplace, is called "Life Styles." Here we can see a product—a condom—being marketed as something "polymorphously perverse" in order to attract a range of consumers with different sexual preferences: heterosexual men, homosexual men, women with heterosexual lovers, unmarried couples, married couples, adulterous couples, threesomes . . . A glance at the "personal ads" in the *Village Voice* indicates that my list is quite brief and inconclusive. Indeed, these personals suggest that the handful of "sexual deviations" described by Masoch, Ellis Krafft-Ebbing, and even Joyce are increasingly blurred as meaningful categories. The adult consumer is becoming as polymorphously perverse as Freud's infant. Marketers now see sexuality as performative ("Life Styles") rather than "normative" (that is, patriarchal and heterosexual, as implied by a brandname like "Trojans").

11.   In a skit I saw on the television show "Saturday Night Live," the performative dimension of phone sex was wonderfully highlighted by showing the hired woman as a housewife scurrying around the kitchen getting supper ready for her family while she "talks sexy" to the man who cannot see her. "I'm so hot I can't stand it," she tells her breathless caller while bending over to check on the meat loaf in the oven.

12.   In his discussion of the "Nausicaa" episode of *Ulysses*, Thomas Richards discusses the relationship between the definition of "adolescence" and turn-of-the-century advertising (205–48).

Works Cited

Baudrillard, Jean. *Selected Writings*. Ed. Mark Poster. Stanford: Stanford University Press, 1988.

Birken, Lawrence. *Consuming Desire: Sexual Science and the Emergence of a Culture of Abundance, 1871–1914*. New York: Cornell University Press, 1988.

Booth, M. R. *Victorian Spectacular Theatre: 1850–1910*. Boston: Routledge and Kegan Paul, 1981.

Bowlby, Rachel. *Just Looking: Consumer Culture in Dreiser, Gissing and Zola*. New York: Methuen, 1985.

Brooks, Peter. *The Melodramatic Imagination: Balzac, Henry James, Melodrama and the Mode of Excess*. New Haven: Yale University Press, 1976.

Defoe, Daniel. *The Fortunes and Misfortunes of the Famous Moll Flanders*. New York: New American Library, 1964.

Foucault, Michel. *The History of Sexuality. Vol. I: An Introduction*. New York: Vintage Books, 1980.

Gagnier, Regina. *Idylls of the Marketplace: Oscar Wilde and the Victorian Public*. Stanford: Stanford University Press, 1986.

Gifford, Don, with Robert Seidman. *Ulysses Annotated: Notes for James Joyce's Ulysses*. Berkeley: University of California Press, 1988.

Herr, Cheryl. *Joyce's Anatomy of Culture*. Urbana: University of Illinois Press, 1986.

Joyce, James. *Dubliners*. Ed. Robert Scholes, in consultation with Richard Ellmann. New York: Viking Press, 1967.

Joyce, James. *A Portrait of the Artist as a Young Man: Text, Criticism, and Notes*. Ed. Chester G. Anderson. New York: Viking Press, 1968.

Lacan, Jacques. *The Four Fundamental Concepts of Psycho-Analysis*. New York: W. W. Norton & Co., 1981.

Law, Jules David. "Simulation, Pluralism, and the Politics of Everyday Life." *Coping with Joyce: Essays from the Copenhagen Symposium*. Ed. Morris Beja and Shari Benstock Columbus: Ohio State University Press, 1989. 195–205.

Leonard, Garry. "Women on the Market: Commodity Culture, 'Those Lovely Seaside Girls,' and 'Femininity' in Joyce's *Ulysses*." *James Joyce Studies: An Annual, 1991*.

Leonard, Garry. " 'The Woman is Perfected': Sylvia Plath and *Mademoiselle*." *College Literature*. 19.2 (1992): 60–82.

Leonard, Garry. " 'Wondering Where All the Dust Comes From': *Jouissance* and 'Reality' in Joyce's 'Eveline'." *James Joyce Quarterly: Special Issue on Joyce and Lacan* 28.3 (1991): 23–42.

Richards, Thomas. *The Commodity Culture of Victorian England: Advertising and Spectacle 1851–1914*. Stanford: Stanford University Press, 1990.

Sacher-Masoch, Leopold Von. *Venus in Furs*. New York: Sylvan Press, 1947.

Williams, Linda H. "Fetishism and Hard Core: Marx, Freud and the 'Money Shot'." *Hard Core: Power, Pleasure and the "Frenzy of the Visible"* Los Angeles: University of California Press, 1989.

Williams, Rosalind H. *Dream Worlds: Mass Consumption in Late Nineteenth-Century France*. Los Angeles: University of California Press, 1982.

PART 5

MOLLY AS BODY AND EMBODIED

11

"Taken in Drapery"
Dressing the Narrative in the *Odyssey* and "Penelope"

Margaret Mills Harper

The voice with which Joyce unveiled the last of the main characters of *Ulysses* makes an extraordinary number of references to various states of dress and partial undress—and, as if by extension, to a variety of items made from fabric. In attending to some of the material covering the body of this character, my interests coincide with those of several contributors to this volume. But I do not consider clothing in primarily cultural or historical terms, as a sign of consumption or costume. Instead, I look at fabric in the *Odyssey*, that well-worn text with which to dress interpretations of *Ulysses*. I discuss the Homeric story and the "Penelope" episode using terms borrowed from mythic criticism and structuralism, methods more or less discarded by my generation of critics, uneasy as we have been with atemporality and universality in methodologies.[1] Mythic and formal structural pattern- ing were part of Joyce's cultural milieu, however, and are invoked in the "Penelope" episode, although these patterns prove upon second glance to be in a state of serious disrepair, not unlike much of the wardrobe of Mrs. Bloom. The dirty or ripped clothes covering Molly also uncover holes, or at least areas that have been worn awfully thin, in the meanings the episode suggests by means of myth and form. Several layers of suggestive holes in the fabric of expectations intrigue me, for "Penelope" ultimately displays neither seamless art nor naked epiphany but a text stretched out of ordinary shape in order to cover inadequacies in a form it suggests for itself, thus revealing the outline of the elements that trouble its proposed structures.

This gesture, of offering a principle or conclusion and simultaneously retreating from or undercutting it, is common to Joyce's writing generally. As Seamus Deane remarks of the political and social rhetoric of *Ulysses,*

Rather than consign his fiction to any single structure or set of structures, [Joyce] investigated the activity of structuration itself as it was revealed through the exploration of language, discovering always that there is something excessive in language, something which is of its nature beyond the reach of any structuring principle that can be articulated and yet is within reach of a structuring activity. For language is itself that structuring activity. (106)

One such "something excessive" in "Penelope" is the idea of gender, necessary to the ordering principles of the episode and of its place in the novel but also preposterous in that contemporary issues had metamorphosed gender from a regulating principle, fundamental to novelistic plot and subject-positioning, to a questionable, uncontrollable quality. The episode registers and finds a form to contain the effects of a broad cultural shift in whose unpredictable movement Joyce wrote. "Penelope" draws attention to the significant relationship between construction of gender and literary structuration by tampering with the resolution of *Ulysses,* using and abusing gender and genre, and in the process disclosing dissonances in the powerfully resonant cultural and literary institutions that plots, and particularly conclusions to plots, support and are supported by.[2]

I might begin with any number of passages from "Penelope" to discuss clothing or other items made from fabric, such as sheets, bandages, pillows, mosquito nets, thread, carpet, or rags. These references may be, and to varying degrees have been, used in several kinds of studies. First, Molly's clothes and underclothes may function as examples in a number of differing interpretations of her character. Her preoccupation with dress may be taken to indicate deficient intellectual capacity, excessive sexuality, narcissism, bourgeois values, interest in appearance as a semi-professional performer, or enactment of an engendered role which requires the veiling of unencoded desires.[3] In "Penelope" such references give information about the personality and social position of this character, as well as her position as subject or object.

Second, and more typical of the analyses in this volume, Molly's clothing may be regarded as proof of cultural, historical, or political practices; in other words, dressing in the episode is understood to function as the dressing of it. Kimberly Devlin's consideration of masquerade in the "Penelope" episode and Jennifer Wicke's presentation of consumption as work and metempsychosis, with Molly "a textual crucible of consumption," are readings that begin with this kind of observation.

A third variety of critical study leads me closer to the use to which I finally put clothing and fabric in "Penelope." The text/texture/textile metaphor has been a common trope of poststructuralist and feminist criticism, although these approaches have tended to appropriate the metaphor to somewhat different ends. If Molly Bloom is granted mythic status, considered as emblematic of the text in which she is embedded, she joins other symbols like Arachne and Ariadne, figures favored by J. Hillis Miller as metaphors for the creative and destructive forces at work in narrative. According to Miller, Ariadne signifies "both the labyrinth and a means of safely retracing the labyrinth," and Arachne signifies both artist and monster, spinning narrative webs that are beautiful and dangerous ("Ariadne," 156; see also J. Hillis Miller, "Ariachne's Broken Woof" and Nancy K. Miller, "Arachnologies"). If read as "female," Molly can illustrate the spatializing which Julia Kristeva elaborates as the sociohistorical intuition of "women's time." A measurement whose problematic nature Kristeva stresses, women's time "essentially retains *repetition* and *eternity* from among the multiple modalities of time known through the history of civilizations." Female subjectivity might seem to spatialize time by adhering to "cycles, gestation, the eternal recurrence of a biological rhythm" and, "perhaps as a consequence," to "a monumental temporality, without cleavage or escape, . . . all-encompassing and infinite like imaginary space" (191). Ariadne and Arachne being female, it was predictable that they be appropriated by feminist critics (the discussion of Emily Dickinson as spider by Sandra Gilbert and Susan Gubar is one example of such a practice). Such readings soon became commonplace, as Elaine Showalter complained in 1986, although Showalter follows her assertion that the metaphor has become clichéd by using it to analyze American women's fiction and criticism:

> The repertoire of the Victorian lady who could knit, net, knot, and tat, has become that of the feminist critic, in whose theoretical writing metaphors of text and textile, thread and theme, weaver and web, abound. The Spinster who spins stories, Ariadne and her labyrinthine thread, Penelope who weaves and unweaves her theoretical tapestry in the halls of Ithaca or New Haven, are the feminist culture heroines of the critical age. (224)

Applying this metaphor to *Ulysses* shows "Penelope" evoking the traditionally feminine textile arts and unraveling the "action" of the novel, to the extent that "action" in *Ulysses* occurs on a diagetic level. Layered, woven, or labyrinthine rather than linear in presentation, "Penelope" also alters the relation of interior and exterior action so that memory and present consciousness coexist in closer relation to each other than they do in other episodes of the novel, except perhaps "Circe," where enlivening of memory operates to different purposes.[4] The episode also valorizes space, the bulk of bed or body, as a mechanism for making sense and thus assuming power. "Penelope" thus seems to attempt a redefinition of time and space, two vital qualities of narrative. It succeeds at this attempt, if only partially.

The ubiquitous association of Molly Bloom with textile consumption and production is reminiscent of weaving, the art of the Odyssean Penelope. Indeed, a textile metaphor may be as apt as the liquid one which is usually associated with the "Penelope" episode: Molly is covered as often as she flows, and her discourse can be regarded as "woven"—or perhaps "entangled"—as easily as "fluid."[5] Fabric in both *Ulysses* and the *Odyssey* stands in metonymic relation to the idea of power over and through time, of which women's arts such as weaving and spinning have been powerful literary and cultural emblems. In writing an "indispensable countersign to Bloom's passport to eternity" (*Letters* 1:160), Joyce clearly designed Molly's discourse to halt whatever teleological expectations might remain after the other episodes of the book, to set a seal on *Ulysses* by providing not so much the end of its story as the end of story itself. Although Joyce indicated movement when he wrote to Frank Budgen that "Penelope" "turns like the huge earth ball slowly surely and evenly round and round spinning" (*Letters* 1:170), the movement is repetitive and circular, not linear. It has "no beginning, middle or end," as Joyce emphasized to Harriet Weaver (*Letters* 1:172), and in fact it partakes more of stasis than kinesis, a state anticipated at the end of the "Ithaca" episode where the Blooms are defined as lying "[a]t rest relatively to themselves and to each other. In motion being each and both carried westward, forward and rereward respectively, by the proper perpetual motion of the earth through everchanging tracks of neverchanging space" (17.2307–10). From the perspective of the female center about which the males of the novel have swirled, questing looks like circumambulation or perhaps orbiting, inscribing a circle or sphere rather than a linear progression.

Molly's "spheres" include not only the round emblems with which she is associated by her husband, herself, and others ("anterior and posterior female hemispheres" [17.2232], "such a mixture of plum and apple" [18.1535], "earth ball" and the like) but also the domestic sphere. Repetitive action and slow change characterize the routine world of the space culturally designated as domestic: preparation of meals, maintenance of clothing, caring for children and the aged. Daily, monthly (menstrual as well as lunar), yearly, and generational time is measured in cyclical patterns. In the slow way of life at the hub of the wheel, time slows to a virtual standstill. Paradoxically, however, in this space the passage of time is also revealed in its aspects that Kristeva calls "monumental": birth, growth from infancy into adulthood, marriage, aging, and death all take place in it.

There is little to distract people whose existence is circumscribed by domestic walls, unlike life in the space defined as "outside," where less rigidly defined areas of activity and segments of time are of greater significance. In the enclosed, nocturnal, last episode of *Ulysses*, domestic time replaces the action-driven time of the street and the workplace. This replacement accomplishes the paradox outlined above: time seems to stop and its unstoppability is also revealed. For the first time in the novel the couple in the bed are old, with more of their lives behind than before them. History, Stephen Dedalus's nightmare, is a product of the "outside" world. It is finally less disturbing, and arguably less real, than the end of its hegemony in the wide-awake sphere of domesticity, which is never included in historical memory but dominates the lives of most humans—Stephen's mother, the central figure of his most potent nightmare, most definitely included.

Like Yeats's dancers and gyres or Eliot's figure of the ten stairs, Molly's time, according to this scheme, seems to be motion in fixity.[6] It is perhaps reminiscent of a spinning wheel, a woman's machine which does not transport anything but which makes thread, emblematic in Greek mythology for human destiny. One does not travel away from the past as one moves into the future, as Oedipus made the mistake of thinking; rather, past and future are spun together in an ineluctable, predetermined pattern.

The *Odyssey*, we recall, neatly emphasizes feminine power over time in the episodes which feature the hero's wife. The shroud which Penelope weaves and unravels as a ploy to hold her suitors at bay (first described, Homer, 2.87–110) symbolizes her attempt to control the speed of the story of the epic. In fact, although her ruse of weaving the shroud by day and unraveling it by night is eventually unsuccessful, the actions over which she presides in the *Odyssey* do make the Ithaka narrative pace itself to the time it takes for Odysseus to wind his way home.[7] It is Penelope who decides to tell the suitors that the time is right for her to marry one of them since Telemakhos's beard has begun to grow (18.260–73), and it is she who decides upon and orders the shooting contest that precipitates the final slaughter

(19.570–80; 21.73–79). Significantly, the mnemonic tags and repeated phrases associated with her often indicate delay or prevention of a single course of action: she is "prudent," taking her time before she acts. She "neither refuses the hateful wedding nor can she make an end of it," and "she gives them all hope, and she promises each man,/ sending out messages. But her mind wants other things."[8]

Like Penelope's sections of the *Odyssey*, Molly's episode acts like a web to catch and halt time in *Ulysses*. The book ends in a domestic place presided over by a woman in an episode studded with references to textile production and consumption. We might note that the various textile arts, like many of the arts practiced traditionally by women, are not temporal but spatial in orientation. Women in traditional cultures often create designs or pictures, working with textiles or food to make items for private or public consumption. While women also tell stories or make music, activities which exist in time, these entertainment arts are frequently the province of men, whose spheres of activity are less restricted to home and family.[9]

Molly Bloom is, of course, a singer and probably a fair storyteller, but we do not read of her engaging in these activities nearly as often as she refers to fabric in one context or other. In fact, she seems to be more interested in what she has on at concerts than in what is on the programme. Her first chain of reminiscences—within the first thirty-five lines of the episode—pull up Mrs. Riordan, a woman of many flaws in Molly's eyes, one of the worst of which was her disapproval of "bathingsuits and lownecks of course nobody wanted her to wear them I suppose she was pious because no man would look at her twice I hope Ill never be like her a wonder she didnt want us to cover our faces" (18.10–12). A few lines later, Molly's memory of Mrs. Riordan's dog centers on his interest in her petticoats; she recalls an outdoor party by picturing the dress she wore; then her attention is diverted by noticing a damp spot on the bedsheet.

The sheets, which were changed earlier in the day in preparation for her afternoon visitor, are in danger of being soiled later in the episode as well, when Molly's menses arrive. Immediately before she makes the discovery of this inconvenience, the thought of a dirty rag left behind by a forgetful cleaning woman dusts off images of another dog, then Simon Dedalus, Stephen, and Bloom in close proximity, surrounded by four articles of dress ranging from head to toe and areas in between. Reminded of the "rotten old smelly dishcloth that got lost behind the dresser," Molly recalls:

I knew there was something and opened the area window to let out the smell bringing in his friends to entertain them like the night he walked home with a dog if you please that might have been mad especially Simon Dedalus son his father such a criticiser with his glasses up with his tall hat on him at the cricket match and a great big hole in his sock one thing laughing at the other and his son that got all those prizes for whatever he won them in the intermediate imagine climbing over the railings if anybody saw him that knew us I wonder he didnt tear a big hole in his grand funeral trousers as if the one nature gave wasnt enough for anybody hawking him down into the dirty old kitchen now is he right in his head I ask pity it wasnt washing day my old pair of drawers might have been hanging up too on the line on exhibition for all hed ever care (18.1084–96)

It was doubtless the clean sheets, and the clean underclothing as well, that brought on her period, she gripes. Irony next becomes annoyance at the monthly timing which will interfere with her next meeting with Boylan. She then generalizes and extends her personal and temporary affliction: "damn it damn it and they always want to see a stain on the bed to know youre a virgin for them . . . O Jamesy let me up out of this pooh sweets of sin whoever suggested that business for women what between clothes and cooking and children" (18.1125–30).

Her railing is a bit exaggerated on this subject. Of her triad of female duties, "clothes and cooking and children," we remember, Molly is actively engaged in only one in *Ulysses*. The one meal we have witnessed her eating was prepared for her, and mothering Milly is not daily physical work. Molly's connection with the "work" of clothing is also ambiguous, for Molly's participation in the garment industry is far removed from the historical "business for women" that cloth and clothing production have been.[10] She usually has a servant to do the washing, ironing, and mending, and her wardrobe comes from stores. There is little indication elsewhere in "Penelope" that the task of keeping herself decently groomed is so demanding that the "sweets of sin" are too great an extra burden to bear, if this is what she means by the labor of clothing. Still, in this passage she is displayed as weary and frustrated—perhaps enough so to warrant her famous complaint to "Jamesy" to "let me up out of this."[11]

Reading "Penelope" as a novel-stopper, a web of associations that catches narrative time in its mesh, has its limitations, however. To begin with, it is problematic, to say the least, to assert the end of narrative in "Penelope" when the novel as a whole wrestles conventional narrativity almost out of recognition. Colin MacCabe's study of Joyce's "concern with the material effects of language and . . . the possibilities of transformation" (2), Karen Lawrence's odyssey of style, Patrick McGee's examination of style as ideology, and Richard Pearce's attention to "the voice of the body-text" (60) are a few of the many readings of *Ulysses* which assert that the drama or desire of the book is rendered most palpably outside the action of the plot. Indeed, "Penelope" exhibits, confusion over pronouns aside, more detail about the matter of the plot, in plainer prose, than several of the other episodes.

In addition, the evocation of Molly's discomfort with the fabric with which she is surrounded, even as she finds it irresistible, points to two further difficulties. First, the undoing of diegetical time is illusory: repetition and cycles do not negate time's passage.[12] The Blooms who will breakfast on 17 June 1904 are older than the couple whose tea, toast, and kidney were consumed the morning before, and they have probably aged less during the diegesis than the reader who has come from the beginning to end of the novel. Nor does the "Penelope" episode eliminate time stylistically: the syntax and discourse of the episode suggest the temporality of ordinary speech.

Second, and as a direct result of this time-ridden quality of "Penelope," the totalizing effect of narrative as conceived structurally or spatially is itself undone when Bloom's consciousness yields to Molly's, when, in other words, the hero or male authorial presence is presumably replaced as subject by the object who has stood for the satisfaction of desire throughout the book. When Joyce has Molly speak, those words disorient the projection of space within the fictional world as boundary or obstacle, an act which also dislodges reading eyes from positioning themselves vis-à-vis textual space in trained deference to narrative convention: progress against stasis, moving lines of text to back cover. In *Ulysses* Bloom has moved; so have Stephen, the progression of episodes, authorial or arranging voices, the urgency of philosophical, psychological, social, or other issues, and readers' eyes and minds. But these varying kinds of motion have required a space that is itself motionless, a ground against which their relative motion might be reckoned. The unmaking of that space, in a seeming paradox, dismantles the dechronologizing structures formed by the motion of the other actors in the text, whether they are characters, ideas, styles, or readers. The movement of time is measured and perceived only as a timeless structure, as writers from Augustine to Barthes have recognized.[13]

This disturbance of narrative synchrony probably ratifies Joyce's intentions, as Patrick McGee has noted, commenting on Joyce's assertion to Frank Budgen that the "last word" given to Penelope "is the indispensable countersign to Bloom's passport to eternity" (*Selected Letters* 289). According to McGee,

The word of this other is central because the first signature lacks authenticity without the second to endorse and recognize it; the central character lacks centrality without the chief attraction, without a figure to posit him as radically other in relation to another center. Without the supplementary sign, the name of Leopold Bloom functions as a mere mask or disguise, a mouthpiece for the author. (171)

McGee's attention to Molly as sign and his plays on the word *center* indicate the repositioning that occurs in "Penelope." When Molly's word becomes "central," a shift in perspective skews the dimensions of the narrativized space that required her body to be the center of attention so that Bloom (and the readers of the novel) could move through its action and its pages. Molly's countersign stops Bloom, defining him as if her episode were a document sending him out of time "to eternity," placing him not as "central" in the sense that the hero of a story is central but as "center" in a non-narrative orientation.

It is worthwhile noting, too, that the unremitting attention to clothing suggests a staging of the feminine. A "female narrative," to use Joyce's term, that attains its identity by mimicry would seem to subvert its gender. Surely female impersonation, of the kind stressed by Kimberly Devlin or by Cheryl Herr's view of "Penelope" as a "clou" or "star turn," both in this volume, is a less than perfect vehicle for readings that depend upon the notion of "woman" for their cogency. Thus, it would seem, generalized theories of mythic and female time in *Ulysses* are invalid, undercut by the style of the novel and deconstructed by inadequacies of their own logic.

Not exactly—or, rather, not entirely. The strongly value-driven opinions that were expressed about "Penelope," especially in the first several decades of criticism (and about "Nausicaa," for similar reasons), whether approving or disapproving, point not only to critics' culturally fashioned aesthetic and moral expectations—Molly Bloom reading her readers—but also to the partial satisfaction and partial denial that "Penelope" offers to such expectations. "Penelope" is both a daring display and an unsettling exposé of gender construction, similar in this regard to the other sections of *Ulysses* in which female characters are featured prominently as speakers. And just as false trappings exposed by other episodes may be located in the genres into which they are mockingly cast, "Nausicaa" and "Circe" reproducing popular romantic fiction and pantomime, for example, so in "Penelope" considerations of genre show the locations of contradictions in the powerful cultural institutions invoked by the ends of narratives.[14] The difference between other episodes and "Penelope" in this regard is that in "Penelope" the genre at issue is not that represented in its style as clearly as in the generic structure in which it participates, the coda, the ending after the ending of a fiction.

Ulysses is hardly the first text to express irresolution in the material of its resolution. Homeric epics also participate in this activity, although some common misreadings of them hide their internal ambivalences. Attention to Homeric parallels in *Ulysses* can modify such misreadings, however, exchanging them for others which may be no less creative but have the virtues of drawing attention to fabrication, their own and artifice in general, in addition to resembling "nature" in the sense of structures already existing in the minds of their consumers. As McGee notices, *Ulysses* continually encourages attention to Homer: it "seems to invite its reader to seek in the structural connections to Homeric narrative ready-made answers to the questions set up by Stephen's search for paternal authority and by Bloom's attempt to recover his lost sexual relations with his wife." But these Homeric red herrings do not provide "the structural closure" which McGee claims "can be achieved only by repressing the other formal properties of the book" (193). Indeed, readings of the *Odyssey* that offer such closure repress formal aspects of both Homer and *Ulysses*.

In a number of ways, Joyce's "strong misreadings" of the *Odyssey*, to use Harold Bloom's terminology, do not display the assumptions about ancient texts that have been made by some of his critics. Joyce's novel does not merely use and discard Homeric form; it also makes available a Homeric form other than might be expected by readers searching for parallels. In other words, in leading us back to the epic Joyce can influence Homer just as Homer can influence Joyce, if we keep in mind that Joyce's Homer is not necessarily the poet who has reflected, reinforced, or defined cultural values for varying readers over the centuries.[15]

Thus, for example, we know that Joyce's favorite interpretations of the *Odyssey* included Victor Bérard's iconoclastic *Les Phéniciens et l'Odyssée*.[16] It is a long jump from Bérard's Phoenician Odysseus to Joyce's Jewish Bloom, and the trajectory of that jump provides a useful course to follow in reading Joyce. The determining text for such a reading is not that of Homer, whoever and wherever that may be, nor of Bérard, nor of Joyce, but a signifying field consisting of possible engagements that may occur between a particular reader and the *Odyssey*. Closure is not a necessary result of such an event.

Another of Joyce's sources for interpretation of the *Odyssey*, which has been mentioned with less frequency or seriousness than Bérard, was Samuel Butler's *The Authoress of the Odyssey*, a relatively well-known book whose conclusions, despite sales figures, were no more universally accepted in Joyce's day than in ours.[17] Noticing the preponderance of females and domesticity in the *Odyssey*, the fact that "it is sweetness rather than strength that fascinates us" (106) in the epic, and numerous other suggestive details such as "a kind of art for art's sake love of a small lie, and a determination to have things both ways whenever it suits her purpose" (119), Butler proves to his own satisfaction, at least, that the author of the epic was a woman— an unmarried woman, from Trapani, on the west coast of Sicily, and most probably the basis for the autobiographical character Nausikaa.

The aspect of Butler's theory most relevant here is his perception that quite a few of the gaps in the logic of the epic's narrative are clustered around the character of Penelope. According to Butler, the authoress's "determination to have things both ways" includes most prominently taking on "the impossible task of making Penelope at the same time plausible and virtuous" (123). Penelope simultaneously encourages and rebuffs the suitors and remains the paradigm of fidelity despite persistent rumors to the contrary.[18] Surely there must be some explanation for this unlikely state of affairs: "In all Penelope's devotion to her husband there is an ever present sense that the lady doth protest too much" (126).

Butler's critical vision was heavily colored by his intimacy with nineteenth-century British novels, including many anonymous novels written by women, which, he asserts, provide good practice in discerning a woman's authorial hand. Nonetheless, he is not alone in noticing the fault lines in logic and emotion that accompany Penelope. In a recent discussion, John J. Winkler remarks that "in a sense, [Butler's] reading is only the most extreme form of the typical modern reaction to the *Odyssey*, which has regularly seen its female characters as strangely important, albeit in a puzzling and even contradictory way" (132). In my own, and perhaps Joyce's, "typical modern reaction," Penelope functions as the locus of several contradictions with regard to the relations of gender and time in the *Odyssey*.

It would seem as though Odysseus, moving through twenty years' time and a Mediterranean world of space in his journey home, masters both dimensions. Penelope exists in the repetitive and slow world of kingless Ithaka while the narrative of the epic, pacing itself to Odysseus' adventures, draws attention to the speed of his story. Homeric narrative is characterized by the lack of movement in time outside the primary diegesis; thus the Ithaka story is rendered timeless whenever Odysseus is the focus of attention. Paradoxically, however, in providing the stopping point for her husband's wanderings, interrupting his movement through space, Penelope's role makes palpable the changes rendered by time to the characters of the epic. In the stasis of a domestic world, where a bed is rooted to the earth and two decades of absence cannot prevent recognition, Odysseus and she grow old and Telemakhos grows up. Once Odysseus is home there are no more goddesses or young girls vying for his love, no more young bachelors competing for Penelope's hand as if she were their own age, no more question about the status of Telemakhos as boy or man.[19] When the female sphere influences the events of the epic, the paradox of "women's time" is evident: the rhythm of the quest, which has a timeless quality caused by the infinite renewability of its episodes, is balanced by the rhythm of daily life, whose slow pace displays the inexorable transformations it causes. It is worth noting that the story of the reconciliation of Odysseus and Penelope ends with the couple in bed telling each other their respective stories, an action which admits a plurality of modes of time in that the stories are temporally incompatible. In addition, the Ithaka story is temporally implausible: the four years' ruse of the shroud and Penelope's instant decision to marry just when Odysseus returns are two examples of illogical pacing. Nevertheless, the epic itself ends with a strange exertion of divine power over the next chapter of the revenge plot, the retaliation of the suitors' families. Only Zeus can control the inexorable narrative, apparently.

As we have seen, the "Penelope" episode of *Ulysses*, like the Ithaka narratives in the *Odyssey*, is a pressure point for issues concerning the dimensionality of time and the gendering of narrative: whether time is cyclical or linear (or, indeed, just what time it is) and whether the voice of the language can be defined as feminine in any locatable way have been provoking questions. Both of these issues surface in the passage mentioned earlier and can be explored by asking again the rhetorical question, "sweets of sin whoever suggested that business for women." As we know, *Sweets of Sin* refers not only to Molly's afternoon assignation with Boylan but also is the title of the novel her husband bought for her earlier in the day. And interestingly, the passages from it which Bloom read and which convinced him that the book was "in her line" are also laced with mentions of clothing:
"—*All the dollarbills her husband gave her were spent in the stores on wondrous gowns and costliest frillies. For him! For Raoul! . . . —Her mouth glued on his in a luscious voluptuous kiss while his hands felt for the opulent curves inside her déshabillé. . . . —You are late, he spoke hoarsely. . . . The beautiful woman threw off her sabletrimmed wrap, displaying her queenly shoulders and heaving embonpoint*" (10.608–16). In complaining about the business of "sweets of sin," Molly perhaps protests fabrication in two texts. One *Sweets of Sin* is the book she now owns, which is already written but as yet unread by her, although she presumably

knows a great deal about it from having read similar novels. The other is the *mythos* created from sexual activities such as she engaged in that afternoon, activities which are already known but as yet unwritten, in the sense that "Jamesy" will compose his novel well after 1904. Note, too, that the passages from the already-written romance novel that have been visible to us were chosen by Bloom.

It is arguable, then, that at least four answers are implied in Molly's rhetorical question "sweets of sin whoever suggested that business for women." In one, generalized sense, patriarchy at large has suspected women of being temperamentally faithless. Second, perhaps, is the author of the novel *Sweets of Sin*, who certainly suggested "that business for women," even if he or she were not the first to have done so. Third, of course, is Molly's husband, who has been fantasizing about and perhaps passively encouraging her to cuckold him. Indeed, he inserts her into the text of *Sweets of Sin* in "Eumaeus," confusing wife's body with both book and photograph while admiring "the slightly soiled photo creased by opulent curves, none the worse for wear however, . . . gauging her symmetry of heaving *embonpoint* (16.1464–68). And fourth is Joyce, who more than any other agent created the story of Molly's adultery.

Molly's discourse is an extended protest of the tales made up by all of these bearers of assumptions about women. Her protest operates by denying not the facts, however, but their use to generate a certain kind of story. Her defense against the unnamed interlocutor to whom her language responds, of whom Jacques Derrida perhaps speaks when he poses "the Father or . . . the Lord" whose signature Joyce countersigns, leaving "the last word to the woman who in her turn will have said 'we' and 'yes'" ("Two Words," 158), depends upon a state of mind that has little to do with what may or may not have happened, or when—the stuff of narrative. Instead, her language gathers together characters, scenes, and states of consciousness that a chronological narrative would separate, and she justifies her actions by means of compilations of data. Her argument rests upon simultaneity, not sequence. For instance, the arrangement and rhetoric suggest that Bloom's acquiescence on the Hill of Howth triumphs over Boylan's sexual prowess in her mind, a logical seedcake offered up that posits faithfulness to be a result of attitude, not action: all her men are present in her mind, piled up in a jumble of associations, and the one to whom she is loyal is the one she mentally places above the others (hence the memory of the hill), not the earliest, latest, or next lover.[20]

Molly's spatialized discourse, like Penelope's woven and unraveled

shroud, is an attempt at power over time that is discovered and undone. Her construction of meaning, like a linear narrative, ends in
death. Her own more-or-less "woven" shroud appears juxtaposed
with her husband's tacit urging as if both exist in the same temporal
mode. The "woolen thing" she knitted for her infant son Rudy inter-
twines with "him trying to make a whore of me what he never will
he ought to give it up now at this age of his life simply ruination for
any woman and no satisfaction in it" (18.92, 95–97). The same jacket
reenters her musings, along with another mention of dogs (signs of
recognition, as they are in the *Odyssey*[21]) at the end of a tightly as-
sembled cluster of emblematic moments of consciousness: the recent
memory of Stephen's visit, the older memory of mourning for Rudy,
the fantasies of becoming Stephen's lover and of mothering him, and
the awareness of the present state of affairs between Poldy and herself
(18.1300–1455). Significantly, this montage of essentially static areas
of awareness begins with the photograph Bloom showed Stephen,
which Molly regrets not having had "taken in drapery" (18.1303). The
voice that we identify as Molly Bloom tries to dismantle the story of
her adultery by revealing its fabrication as an action dependent upon
time instead of an absolute state.

"Penelope" also attempts to uncover the incomplete relationships
between the main characters which have served as catalysts for such
action as there has been in *Ulysses*: the causes for Stephen and Bloom
wandering around town; the reasons why Molly has taken a lover.
Through the perspective of the final episode, the "whys" which have
driven the narrative are converted into a long "because," dependent
upon the clause begun in the first line ("Yes because he never did
a thing like that before" [18.1]). The propulsion implicit in a question, the linguistic structure which underlies narrative, has become
the stasis implicit in statement—or, more specifically, the actionless
form of an explanatory clause. The search is over; all is now laid out,
explained. More specifically, the *becauses* extend through the first two
of the eight "sentences" into which the monologue is organized, as
Diana E. Henderson (519) has noticed, then dwindle in number, replaced by *ands*: "I was thinking of so many things he didnt know
of Mulvey and Mr Stanhope and Hester and father and old captain
Groves and the sailors playing all birds fly and I say stoop and washing up dishes they called it on the pier and the sentry . . . and the
Spanish girls laughing in their shawls and their tall combs and the
auctions in the morning" (18.1582–87).[22] By the last two "sentences"
the causal mode itself seems to have been undermined. The voice
no longer speaks in terms of the drive of cause to effect, agency to

action, but in the less urgent but automatic unfolding implied by parataxis. Language is always temporal, but the piling up of phrases with the seams joined by the connective least associated with temporality seems to minimize this unskirtable fact.

But narrative temporality cannot be easily banished. It reappears through the interstices left by the very parataxis that hides it, in the gaps between the grammatical and the intellectual or emotional connectives of the discourse. A similar phenomenon occurs in biblical narrative, in which a typically repetitive and additive structure in effect makes the very act of reading into an encounter with ineffable and timeless divinity. One of the most obvious strategies of biblical rhetoric is to join elements of a story which are related in complex ways with the deceptively simple connective *ve* (and), so that, for instance, after Adam and Eve have eaten the forbidden fruit, "[t]hey heard the sound of the Lord God moving about the garden at the breezy time of day; and the man and his wife hid from the Lord God among the trees of the garden" (Genesis 3:8)—their reasons left to the reader's imagination, to be partially explained by the direct speech in the next verse. But this phenomenon in biblical narrative points not only, or even primarily, to the omniscience and timelessness of God or the narrator, but to the lack of these qualities on the part of the reader of divine signs and stories: the biblical text demands exegesis and teaches humility. The partial suppression of information has the rather jarring effect of forcing readers to interpret in order to make sense of the action and at the same time of denying absolute value to any particular interpretative act. We are given events but not motivation, sequence but not cause, truth but not whole truth. Ultimately such a technique highlights the disparity between the imperfect knowledge of readers and the perfect vision possessed by God. As Meir Sternberg has argued, "the world and the meaning are always hypothetical, subject to change from one stage of the reading *process* to another, and irreducible to any simple formula" (47).

Sternberg is surely correct in adducing that biblical structures gain a measure of their force from the power they assume over the subjectivity of their readers. Similarly, the discourse of "Penelope" as it nears the end of the book asserts absolute power on its own behalf and denies that power to its readers. If I want a story, I must become an exegete, or psychoanalyst, and make one, reconnecting passages with my own narrative sense and creating the "real" narrative from the almost mystical reminiscences, comments, and explanations Molly's voice offers. Indeed, as the voice builds through parataxis and rising lyricality to its conclusion of flowers and *yeses*, it increasingly denies contradiction and encourages interpretation, in the sense that it does not explain why the ending clauses seem to propose orgasmic, narcotic, happy-ever-afterness. Divine authority and, indirectly, creative power are invoked: "as for them saying theres no God I wouldnt give a snap of my two fingers for all their learning why dont they go and create something I often asked him" (18.1563–65). Once, as if perhaps surprised by its power, the voice checks for corroboration of its dominion over time: "16 years ago my God" (18.1575).[23]

Time, like narrative, can be figured as a product of a reader's desire in mythic or mythic-derived texts, and, as in biblical narrative, this observation both asserts timeless divinity and reveals the time-ridden relationship between a reader and the text. Augustine takes this position when the rhetoric of his meditations on time in Book 11 of the *Confessions* swerves from the question of the position of God and time to an analysis of what happens when someone recites a psalm: time is implicated in the expectations and memories of a reader, not in the inexplicable nature of the deity. Thus too Derrida, despite his claim that "[t]he concept of time, in all its aspects, belongs to metaphysics, and it names the domination of presence," opens the structural into the temporal by building into his concepts of trace and *différance* the form of desire ("Ousia and Gramme" 63). Trace implies an imaginary if impossible relation to something it might be trace *of*, and *différance* similarly implies even though it denies a presence always deferred. Thus Gayatri Spivak writes of "postponement" to define Derrida's "law of difference" (lvii). Analyzing the implications of deconstruction for a philosophy of time, David Wood likewise mentions that this imaginary temporal quality would mean that "[s]ignification, and hence language, would then essentially involve an imaginary or virtual temporality" (330).

The discourse of "Penelope" strips away the story of *Ulysses*, then, partially by language that is stereotypically "female" and at first glance technically flamboyant in comparison to other episodes, and partially by a seeming retreat from diegetical time into timeless revery. But the unremitting "femaleness," like that of Samuel Butler's Penelope, may itself "protest too much" to allow genuine comfort to readers who have placed a heavy burden of meaning on it. The protest is generated by language which draws attention to its own illogic and fabrication and, by extension, to those of a presumed reader.[24] The sources of the fallacies and falsity of Molly's discourse lie ultimately in the needs of a consumer of her voice. In confronting what I might perceive as the inadequacy of her definition of fidelity, for example, I may find myself wondering if my ideas are grounded in a truer reality. If I am unconvinced by the imagistic final passage, I might be led to wonder why I might have been persuaded by rhetoric elsewhere in the novel that opposes the rhetoric of the ending. Molly Bloom shows that my reading is desirous, a voyeuristic peep at an object clothed in expectations or traditions that are in poor repair or at the very least in need of cleaning. Similarly, an examination of time in "Penelope" reveals that temporal dimensionality is also relative, both in itself and with regard to space, in an Einsteinian manner: how quickly time passes, where objects or people might be situated in it, what its implied relationship is to the language of the episode, and whether it moves forward from past to present to future are all debatable issues. As in the *Odyssey*, considerations of gender are implicated in these questions, and desire is the force which sets them in motion.

In rendering problematic the relationships between gender and narrative in "Penelope" and simultaneously offering the "monologue (female)" as absolute and essential in its patterning of experience, Joyce's novel reveals a structural flaw, or gap, in the idea of a story. Hélène Cixous's Medusa laughs at this flaw: it might also be described as the answer Oedipus cannot give to the Sphinx, the site of the unwritten and unfigurable, without which patriarchal structure cannot exist. Teresa de Lauretis describes this site as the point at which desire drives narrative, rereading the work of Vladimir Propp and later morphologists to show that "the work of narrative . . . is a mapping of differences, and specifically, first and foremost, of sexual difference into each text" (121).

More specifically, Propp argues that "plots do not 'reflect' a given social order, but rather emerge out of the conflict, the contradictions, of different social orders as they succeed or replace one another" (113). Elaborating on this concept, Jurij Lotman defines two separate cultural mechanisms out of which narratives were formed, one which generated myths and another which recorded incidents or anomalies.[25] According to Lotman, there are likewise two kinds of characters: "It is not difficult to notice that characters can be divided into those who are mobile, who enjoy freedom with regard to plot-space, who can change their place in the structure of the artistic world and cross the frontier, the basic topological feature of this space, and those who are immobile, who represent, in fact, a function of this space" (167). Unfortunately, of course, this freedom extends only to the *man* who is capable, in the homology which the first mechanism contributes to plots, of exerting his will and acting. The character who cannot so move and act falls into the second of the two categories. This mythological quality of texts is most closely figured by lyric poetry with its positioning of

"I" and "he/she/you," and may be reduced to an open-ended chain: "entry into closed space—emergence from it" (Lotman 167).

Just who "I" and "you" are allowed to be is revealed by Lotman's next observation, that "inasmuch as closed space can be interpreted as 'a cave,' 'the grave,' 'a house,' 'woman' (and correspondingly, be allotted the features of darkness, warmth, dampness) . . . , entry into it is interpreted on various levels as 'death,' 'conception,' 'return home' and so on; moreover all these acts are thought of as mutually identical" (168). De Lauretis takes this argument a step further, noticing that "if the work of the mythical structuration is to establish distinctions, the primary distinction on which all others depend is not, say, life and death, but rather sexual difference" (119). All other oppositions may be reduced to the figure of a man moving vis-à-vis closed space. He establishes differences; "she (it) is an element of plot-space, a topos, a resistance, matrix and matter" (119). Furthermore, in the sense that the mythic mechanism operates through narrative, performing its regulating function by positioning integrated characters as subject or object, narrative assumes the position of the mythic subject and creates difference, specifically, sexual difference, throughout its work. The desire at work in narrativity, then, the propulsion or tension that incites it, is force against a resisting topos that is typologically female. A corresponding female desire must be denied, since actionless plot-space may react with one of few options: consent, seduction, or coercion. Thus de Lauretis corroborates Laura Mulvey's assertion that narrativity is inherently sadistic, since, according to Mulvey, "[s]adism demands a story, depends on making something happen, forcing a change in another person, a battle of will and strength, victory/defeat, all occurring in a linear time with a beginning and an end" (14).

For the purposes of my reading of "Penelope," there is twofold value in rereading these structuralist arguments with attention to the gender distinctions necessary to their formulation. First, if a bipolar concept of gender is inextricable from the propulsion of narrative, then ending *Ulysses* with a remarkably unstable conclusion by a flamboyantly female voice appears sensible and just. "Penelope" is an outlandishly overstated exposé of the dirty linen of narrative, an appropriate finish to an excessively self-conscious and self-parodying novel. Second, it is important to bear in mind the heavy reliance of these theories upon the idea of cultural origin. Social tension causes these elaborate aesthetic patterns to arise, and the continuance of the cultural phenomena that underlie them is required for them to endure. That the structures are extremely durable and powerful indicates the persistence of gender definition and the tensions inherent in rigid oppositionalism and hierarchy. Narratives "work" only when they can be written, read, or acted in by subjects who are embedded in historical and material reality—indeed, who are created, at least in part, by the very narratives they engage in. Conversely, points at which narratives in texts become disturbed may indicate interruptions in historical and experiential patterns of behavior.

All this is to say that "Penelope" makes difficult the job of narrative to construct readers, authors, and texts, placing them in one of the two positions open to them, "male-hero-human, on the side of the subject; and female-obstacle-boundary-space, on the other" (de Lauretis 121). The "yes"-saying, disagreeable, assertive, stereotypical, hidden, scantily-clad Molly Bloom, and the lack of closure in an episode redolent with mythic structures, point to an imperfectly defined gender division underlying genre and subject. In Molly's discourse none of the subjects implied by it—Joyce, "I," Molly, I—may rest. Figurations of time, space, and identity in the text, and desires that put these structures into effect, are in poor repair. Their worn state engages the world that surrounded Joyce as he wrote his epic, and the environment in which many readers still find themselves, if contentious and continuous reaction to the episode indicates the liveliness of textual and extra-textual issues. When Joyce took advantage of the *Odyssey* to write his own epic, his world was undergoing shifts in gender definition that express themselves in narrative and subject-positions, in *Ulysses* as in other Modernist texts.[26]

For me, then, the deteriorating garments and undergarments which provide enjoyment and irritation for Mr. and Mrs. Bloom are a display, a striptease which reveals some of the distributions of power implicit in plot and language even as it participates in this economy. Like the readers of biblical texts, as a reader of *Ulysses* I have not stopped positioning myself as an interpreter, but I recognize that in this activity I am myself an image of (and to) the maker of the textual system. Or, to formulate this concept in the Lacanian terms Laura Mulvey applies to narrative film, the scopophilia implicit in my gaze has not ceased but it has itself become visible. I am still watching, but I am looking from holes into holes.

Like Bloom's favorite photograph, the pose in which Joyce took Molly Bloom has both stopped time and shown its inexorable passing. It has elevated her to the state of a goddess and demonstrated the inadequacy inherent in formulations of divinity. It has rounded off *Ulysses* and refused to participate in the novel that precedes it. However, as I listen to the voice of "Penelope" the holes or stains in the novelistic fabric are encouraging, as, for different reasons, the old picture of Molly is pleasing to Bloom. "[T]he slight soiling" of the photo, he believes, "was only an added charm like the case of linen slightly soiled, good as new, much better in fact with the starch out" (16.1468–70). His recorded remarks earlier in "Eumaeus" did not tell Stephen the whole truth of his attitude toward the "female form" of the "antique statues" in the "Kildare street museum" or, by contrast, "women here": "An exception here and there. Handsome yes, pretty in a way you find but what I'm talking about is the female form. Besides they have so little taste in dress, most of them, which greatly enhances a woman's natural beauty, no matter what you say. Rumpled stockings, it may be, possibly is, a foible of mine but still it's a thing I simply hate to see" (16.890–98). Like his creator, who was also partial to representations of ancient women, Bloom was something of a connoisseur of such apparel. Or perhaps Bloom was telling more truth than he knew, if what "greatly enhances a woman's natural beauty" is women's having "so little taste in dress" and what he "hate[s] to see" is that "foible of mine." The language of the last episode of the book offers both options, a voice clad in enhancements and foibles, taste in dress and things we might hate to see. It hides the desires that write it as it reveals the look of them, making representations from biology and exposing their artificiality in one gesture: "theyre supposed to represent beauty placed up there like those statues in the museum one of them pretending to hide it with her hand are they so beautiful of course compared with what a man looks like" (18.540–42). In "Penelope" the gendered nature of narrative and the artificiality of gender are put on show, in a performance that reveals actors and spectators alike.

Notes

1.   "Mythic" approaches to Joyce, in which religious or anthropological values are placed upon characters, scenes, objects, or styles, have a long history in Joyce criticism. Structuralism, too, had its moment in American Joyce studies: probably the most important such analyses of Joyce were written by Robert Scholes (see especially his essay "*Ulysses:* A Structuralist Perspective," reprinted in *Structuralism in Literature* 180–90).

2.   Many critics have commented on the relationship between patriarchy, in particular, and conclusions to novelistic plots. For an extended treatment of this relationship see Rachel Blau DuPlessis.

3.   See Bonnie Kime Scott 156–83; Suzette A. Henke, *James Joyce and the Politics of Desire* 248n; and Kathleen McCormick, in this volume, for overviews of critical attitudes toward Molly Bloom.

4.   Interestingly, Joyce did describe "Circe" using a woven metaphor in a

letter to Harriet Weaver: "Her [Circe's] web is so vast and of such intricate zoological design that I suppose it must be hard to follow in such a typescript. A few threads have fallen out to say nothing of the rent made in it" (*Letters*, I:164). The "rent," as Ellmann (507–8) and McGee (115–16) note, refers to the burning of part of the manuscript by the scandalized husband of a typist.

5.   Derek Attridge examines the logic supporting the fluid metaphors usually associated with "Penelope."

6.   See, for examples, Yeats's "Among School Children" and "The Double Vision of Michael Robartes" for dancers who image forth a state in which "Mind moved yet seemed to stop / As 'twere a spinning-top" (*Poems* 172). See also *A Vision*, which illustrates in great detail Yeats's preoccupation with the dynamic quality of changeless abstraction. Eliot's "figure of the ten stairs" is in "Burnt Norton" (l. 160); it alludes to St. John of the Cross, *Dark Night of the Soul*, book 2, chap. 18.

7.   Actually, one might argue that Penelope's trick does accomplish her ends in that it postpones the moment in which she will have to give in to the suitors' demands until Athene, the primary divine manipulator of events in the *Odyssey*, takes over the task of making the story when in book I she convinces Zeus to allow Odysseus' return at last.

8.   περίφρων, "prudent," is of course the most common adjective linked with Penelope's name in the poem: see, for example, lines 1.329, 4.787, 4.808, 4.830, 5.216, 11.446, 15.41, 19.103, 19.559, 23.10, and 24.404. The other two phrases are ἡ δ' οὔτ' ἀρνεῖται στυγερὸν γάμον οὔτε τελευτὴν / ποιῆσαι δύναται (1.249–50, 16.126–7); πάντας μέν ῥ' ἔλπει καὶ ὑπίσχεται ἀνδρὶ ἑκάστῳ, / ἀγγελίας προϊεῖσα νόος δέ οἱ ἄλλα μενοινᾷ (2.91–2, 13.380–81). Translations mine.

9.   Elaine Showalter makes a similar point in examining spatial techniques used by American women writers in relation to quilting, a craft practiced by women in most classes and regions, and throughout most of American history. Quoting Lucy Lippard, Showalter discusses scenic composition as appropriate for "those whose time comes in small squares" (Lippard 32), a phrase which neatly spatializes time.

10.   There was a business in clothing rental some time before the time of the novel, about which Simon Dedalus comes up with a catchy phrase in "Sirens" ("Mrs Marion Bloom has left off clothes of all descriptions" [11. 496–97]). For two discussions of the gradual displacement of women in premodern Europe from industries which had been theirs, such as weaving, dying, knitting, tailoring, and mending, see Merry Wiesner and Judith C. Brown.

11.   Of course, she may be pleading with herself to get off the increasingly wet sheet—up out of textile/fabric, not text/fabrication. Or pleading with Joyce, the maker of the plot, to allow her to do the same, annoyed at being displayed during the "business for women" of menstruation. Or perhaps Joyce is pleading with himself. James McMichael devotes an essay to this passage.

12.   See, in this regard, John Paul Riquelme's discussion of time in *Ulysses* as a spiral (218–22).

13.   See Augustine's *Confessions*, book 11 (esp. chaps. 26–30). See also Ricoeur, who uses the *Confessions* and Aristotle's *Poetics* as the central texts for his meditations on time and narrative. "Dechronologizing" is Roland Barthes' term; he notes that "all contemporary researchers . . . could subscribe to Lévi-Strauss's proposition that 'the order of chronological succession is absorbed in an atemporal matrix structure.' Analysis today tends to 'dechronologize' the narrative continuum and to 'relogicize' it," in other words, "[to give] a structural description of the chronological illusion" (98–99).

14.   For generic analyses of "Nausicaa" and "Circe," see Henke, "Gerty MacDowell," and Herr. See also Devlin and Norris for discussions on related topics such as the implications of exhibitionism and the rewriting and undercutting of myth in "Nausicaa."

15.   I am indebted to Fritz Senn for suggesting to me the idea of Joyce's influence on Homer. Richard Brown notices that Joyce was interested in readings of Homer that stress marital concerns (25). See Joseph A. Kestner for an illustrated tour of Victorian Odyssean iconography (most of which depicts scantily dressed female characters).

16.   Among other scholars who have discussed Joyce's interest in Bérard are Groden and Seidel.

17.   Richard Ellmann includes this book in his list of the contents of Joyce's Trieste library, although it is no longer in the collection. It is marked with the stamp that Joyce first used in Zurich and left behind in Trieste in 1920, however, and thus was presumably owned by him during this period (*The Consciousness of Joyce*, 103). See Kenner's examination of this and other sources for Odyssean inspiration (41–50). Winkler (129) notes that, according to H. F. Jones's preface to the second edition of Butler's *Authoress of the Odyssey*, George Bernard Shaw was among the book's few enthusiastic readers. Butler mentions Shaw's approval but does not identify him (*Authoress*, 208–9).

18.   Fritz Senn makes the suggestion, using homophones from the Greek text, that Penelope's faithfulness may be ambiguous in the *Odyssey* as well (Senn 82–83). It certainly is in other renderings of the Odysseus story, and the many comparisons of Penelope with Helen or Klytemnestra in the epic also encourage such readings. Note especially Agamemnon's words in 11.433–34 and 24.200–1.

19.   Odysseus' father Laertes also appears as a man of great age in the final books of the epic. See also Mihoko Suzuki's useful study of Helen of Troy for an analysis of Penelope's desirability and ageless quality.

20.   Recalling Derrida's invocation of Joyce's signature to "forgive God," laughter overcoming the "resentment *a priori*" that charcterizes the "God of Babel" who prevents and orders translation of His name ("Two Words" 158), we should perhaps note that Molly's argument for return to a previous state replaces forgiveness, the concept within Christian thinking which allows one to undo the results of one's actions. Anger, memory, and pleasure are agents which Molly uses to replace μετάνοια, literally "change of mind" or repentance, which is the necessary first step toward forgiveness in theological terms. She is far from sorry about how she spent her afternoon but asserts the

recovery of an earlier state of being nonetheless, as perhaps does the rhetoric of the novel in general. In this action we may also, perhaps, see linearity problematized: repentance, linear in that it is linked to salvation history (although itself as disjunctive as Kierkegaard's leap), is undone not by its opposite, which contains it as necessary other, but by the aporia that provokes such states as laughter, anger, memory, and desire.

21. Her husband also remembers these dogs, whose coupling precipitated the lovemaking in which Rudy was conceived (6.77–81). Interestingly, this act, which resonates throughout the novel and participates in no one frame of action, was accomplished when Molly "had that cream gown on with the rip she never stitched," Leopold remembers—more rumpled clothing (6.80). In the *Odyssey*, of course, Odysseus' dog Argos is not fooled by the twenty years' change in his master's appearance but does not live through the recognition (17.291–327), any more than Rudolph Bloom's "infirm dog" Athos survived his master's death (17.1890).

22. According to Derek Attridge, the Rosenbach manuscript shows that there were at first periods at the end of each of the "sentences," removed later (549).

23. See Frances Restuccia for an examination of the psychological and theological inversions through which Joyce attributed divine power to Molly Bloom.

24. The ironizing of the totalizing and countersigning femaleness of "Penelope" is thus similar to other motions toward all-inclusivity in the novel. For example, the idea that art is "a totalization of particular and universal" suffers the same fate. Terry Eagleton points to "the enormous irony with which the novel manages this remorseless totalization, which gestures to its own flagrant arbitrariness in its very poker-faced exhaustiveness." In general, Eagleton remarks, "[i]f *Ulysses* 'resolves' contradictions, . . . the sweated Flaubertian labor with which this is accomplished points to the effective impossibility of the whole project" (34–35).

25. Lotman asserts, following Lévi-Strauss, that a forward trajectory, the motion of a story from beginning to end, is illusory in mythic texts. To a modern reader coming into secondary contact with myths, a narrative which can be fit into a linear, propulsive pattern may be read or heard, because later cultures produce readers trained to recognize plots: the mythic mechanism is translated through the now-dominant narrative system. In fact, however, the actions in individual myths are part of a repetitive, cyclical system: "the text is thought of as a mechanism which constantly repeats itself, synchronized with the cyclical processes of nature: the seasons of the year, the hours of the day, the astral calendar" (161). Mythical texts are essentially topological in organization, drawing together and unifying remote spheres of objects and actions (so that, for instance, winter and death are different names for the same thing); featuring actors which are not discrete identities but isomorphic or homomorphic phenomena; and "constructed on the principle of an integrated structural whole, a sentence" (173). Their function, according to Lotman, was to classify and regulate, to reduce the unruly elements of the world.

26.   It is worth asking what the ending of the *Odyssey* might indicate about the Achaean culture from the age of the pre-Homeric cycles upon which the *Odyssey* was based through the eighth or seventh century B.C.E., since similarities to sensitive elements of structure in the *Odyssey* suggest that shifts of equal importance may have been occurring during those periods. Yet ancient history tends to register most clearly the attitudes of historians, and my reading of Homer, like Joyce's, doubtless speaks of my own age as much as it reflects Homeric or pre-Homeric culture.

Works Cited

Attridge, Derek. "Molly's Flow: The Writing of 'Penelope' and the Question of Women's Language." *Modern Fiction Studies* 35 (1989): 543–65.

Augustine. *St. Augustine's Confessions.* Trans. William Watts. Loeb Classical Library. London: Heinemann; New York: Putnam, 1925.

Barthes, Roland. "Introduction to the Structural Analysis of Narratives." *Image-Music-Text.* Trans. Stephen Heath. London: Fontana; New York: Hill and Wang, 1977. 79–124.

Bérard, Victor. *Les Phéniciens et l'Odyssée.* 2 vols. Paris, 1902–3.

Bloom, Harold. *The Anxiety of Influence: A Theory of Poetry.* New York: Oxford University Press, 1973.

The Book of J. Trans. David Rosenberg. Interpreted by Harold Bloom. New York: Grove Weidenfeld, 1990.

Brown, Judith C. "A Woman's Place Was in the Home: Women's Work in Renaissance Tuscany." *Rewriting the Renaissance: The Discourses of Sexual Difference in Early Modern Europe.* Ed. Margaret W. Ferguson, Maureen Quilligan, and Nancy J. Vickers. Chicago: University of Chicago Press, 1986. 206–24.

Brown, Richard. *James Joyce and Sexuality.* Cambridge: Cambridge University Press, 1985.

Butler, Samuel. *The Authoress of the Odyssey, where and when she wrote, who she was, the use she made of the Iliad, & how the poem grew under her hands.* London, 1897. Rpt. with new introduction by David Greene. Chicago: University of Chicago Press, 1967.

Cixous, Hélène. "The Laugh of the Medusa." Trans. Keith Cohen and Paula Cohen. *New French Feminisms: An Anthology.* Ed. Elaine Marks and Isabelle de Courtivron. Amherst: University of Massachusetts Press, 1980. 245–64.

Deane, Seamus. "Joyce and Nationalism." *Celtic Revivals: Essays in Modern Irish Literature 1880–1980.* Winston-Salem, N.C.: Wake Forest University Press, 1985. 92–107.

de Lauretis, Teresa. "Desire in Narrative." *Alice Doesn't: Feminism, Semiotics, Cinema.* Bloomington: Indiana University Press, 1984. 103–57.

Derrida, Jacques. *Of Grammatology.* Trans. Gayatri Chakravorty Spivak. Baltimore: Johns Hopkins University Press, 1976.

Derrida, Jacques. "Ousia and Gramme." *Margins of Philosophy.* Trans. Alan Bass. Chicago: University of Chicago Press, 1982. 29–67.

Derrida, Jacques. "Two Words for Joyce." *Post-Structuralist Joyce: Essays from the French.* Ed. Derek Attridge and Daniel Ferrer. Cambridge: Cambridge University Press, 1984. 145–59.

Devlin, Kimberly. "The Female Eye: Joyce's Voyeuristic Narcissists." *New Alliances in Joyce Studies: "When it's aped to foul a Delfian."* Ed. Bonnie Kime Scott. Newark: University of Delaware Press, 1988. 135–43.

DuPlessis, Rachel Blau. *Writing beyond the Ending: Narrative Strategies of Twentieth-Century Women Writers.* Bloomington: Indiana University Press, 1985.

Eagleton, Terry. "Nationalism: Irony and Commitment." *Nationalism, Colonialism, and Literature.* Introduction by Seamus Deane. Field Day; Minneapolis: University of Minnesota Press, 1990. 23–39.

Eliot, T. S. *The Complete Poems and Plays, 1909–1950.* San Diego: Harcourt, 1952.

Ellmann, Richard. *The Consciousness of Joyce.* New York: Oxford University Press, 1977.

Ellmann, Richard. *James Joyce.* New York: Oxford University Press, 1982.

Gilbert, Sandra M., and Gubar, Susan. *Madwoman in the Attic: The Woman Writer and The Nineteenth-Century Literary Imagination.* New Haven: Yale University Press, 1979.

Groden, Michael. *"Ulysses" in Progress.* Princeton: Princeton University Press, 1977.

Henderson, Diana E. "Joyce's Modernist Woman: Whose Last Word?" *Modern Fiction Studies* 35 (1989): 517–28.

Henke, Suzette A. "Gerty MacDowell: Joyce's Sentimental Heroine." *Women in Joyce.* Ed. Suzette Henke and Elaine Unkeless. Carbondale: Southern Illinois University Press, 1982. 132–49.

Henke, Suzette A. *James Joyce and the Politics of Desire.* New York and London: Routledge, 1990.

Herr, Cheryl. *Joyce's Anatomy of Culture.* Urbana: University of Illinois Press, 1986.

Homer, *Odysseae.* Ed. Thomas W. Allen. Scriptorum Classicorum Bibliotheca Oxoniensis. Vols. 3–4. London: Oxford University Press, 1917.

Joyce, James. *Letters of James Joyce.* Vol. 1, ed. Stuart Gilbert, New York: Viking Press, 1957; reissued with corrections, 1966.

Kenner, Hugh. *The Pound Era.* Berkeley: University of California Press, 1971.

Kestner, Joseph A. "Before *Ulysses:* Victorian Iconography of the Odysseus Myth." *James Joyce Quarterly* 28 (1991): 565–94.

Kristeva, Julia. "Women's Time." *The Kristeva Reader.* Ed. Toril Moi. New York: Columbia University Press, 1986. 187–213.

Lawrence, Karen. *The Odyssey of Style in "Ulysses."* Princeton: Princeton University Press, 1981.

Lippard, Lucy. "Up, Down and Across: A New Frame for New Quilts." *The Artist and the Quilt.* Ed. Charlotte Robinson. New York: Knopf, 1983. 32–43.

Lotman, Jurij M. "The Origin of Plot in the Light of Typology." Trans. Julian Graffy. *Poetics Today* 1 (1979): 161–84.

MacCabe, Colin. *James Joyce and the Revolution of the Word*. London: Macmillan, 1978.

McGee, Patrick. *Paperspace: Style as Ideology in Joyce's "Ulysses."* Lincoln: University of Nebraska Press, 1988.

McMichael, James. "Real, Schlemiel." *Critical Enquiry* 7 (1985): 474–85.

Miller, J. Hillis. "Ariachne's Broken Woof." *Georgia Review* 31 (1977): 36–48.

Miller, J. Hillis. "Ariadne's Thread: Repetition and the Narrative Line." *Interpretation of Narrative*. Ed. Mario J. Valdes and Owen J. Miller. Toronto: University of Toronto Press, 1976. 148–66.

Miller, Nancy K. "Arachnologies: The Woman, The Text, and the Critic." *The Poetics of Gender*. Ed. Nancy K. Miller. New York: Columbia University Press, 1986. 270–95.

Mulvey, Laura. "Visual Pleasure and Narrative Cinema." *Screen* 16:3 (1975): 3–18.

Norris, Margot. "Modernism, Myth, and Desire in 'Nausicaa.'" *James Joyce Quarterly* 26 (1988): 37–50.

Pearce, Richard. *The Politics of Narration: James Joyce, William Faulkner, and Virginia Woolf*. New Brunswick and London: Rutgers University Press, 1991.

Restuccia, Frances L. *Joyce and the Law of the Father*. New Haven: Yale University Press, 1989.

Ricoeur, Paul. *Time and Narrative*. 3 vols. Trans. Kathleen McLaughlin and David Pellauer. Chicago: University of Chicago Press, 1984.

Riquelme, John Paul. *Teller and Tale in Joyce's Fiction*. Baltimore: Johns Hopkins University Press, 1983.

St. John of the Cross. *Dark Night of the Soul*. Trans. E. Allison Peers. New York: Doubleday, 1959.

Scholes, Robert. "*Ulysses:* A Structuralist Perspective." *James Joyce Quarterly* 10 (1972): 161–71.

Scholes, Robert. *Structuralism in Literature: An Introduction*. New Haven and London: Yale University Press, 1974.

Scott, Bonnie Kime. *Joyce and Feminism*. Bloomington: Indiana University Press, 1984.

Seidel, Michael. *Epic Geography: James Joyce's "Ulysses."* Princeton: Princeton University Press, 1976.

Senn, Fritz. "Remodeling Homer." *Light Rays: James Joyce and Modernism*. Ed. Heyward Ehrlich. New York: New Horizon Press Publishers, 1984. 70–92.

Showalter, Elaine. "Piecing and Writing." *The Poetics of Gender*. Ed. Nancy K. Miller. New York: Columbia University Press, 1986. 222–47.

Spivak, Gayatri Chakravorty. "Translator's Preface." *Of Grammatology*. By Jacques Derrida. Baltimore and London: Johns Hopkins, 1976.

Sternberg, Meir. *The Poetics of Biblical Narrative: Ideological Literature and the Drama of Reading*. Bloomington: Indiana University Press, 1985.

Suzuki, Mihoko. *Metamorphoses of Helen: Authority, Difference, and the Epic*. Ithaca: Cornell University Press, 1989.

Wiesner, Merry E. "Spinsters and Seamstresses: Women in Cloth and Clothing Production." *Rewriting the Renaissance: The Discourses of Sexual Difference in Early Modern Europe.* Ed. Margaret W. Ferguson, Maureen Quilligan, and Nancy J. Vickers. Chicago: University of Chicago Press, 1986. 191–205.

Winkler, John J. *The Constraints of Desire: The Anthropology of Sex and Gender in Ancient Greece.* New York: Routledge, 1990.

Wood, David. *The Deconstruction of Time.* Atlantic Highlands, N.J.: Humanities Press International, 1989.

Yeats, William Butler. *The Poems.* Ed. Richard J. Finneran. New York: Macmillan, 1983.

Yeats, William Butler. *A Vision.* London: Macmillan, 1937.

12

The Female Body, Technology, and Memory in "Penelope"

Ewa Ziarek

My reading of the female body in "Penelope" starts in fact with the last, unanswered, question of "Ithaca": "Where?" Providing a transition of sorts to Molly's monologue, this suspended question problematizes the discursive location of the female body. Indeed, where is she when she is at home—seemingly in the most familiar and intimate space? Where is the meaning of the female body, and by extension, of sexual difference to be found? In what discursive space? An inquiry into the discursive position of the female body in the context of modernity involves rethinking not only the public and private distinction but also the problem of a specific rhetoric through which this distinction is expressed. My reading of "Penelope" focuses on the contrast between the private space, intertwined with the pronounced rhetoric of organicism, and the public space, associated with the equally compelling, though much less frequently discussed, rhetoric of mechanical reproduction. Consider, for instance, the sharp difference between Molly's fantasy of extramarital sex on the train and her *memory* of Bloom's proposal:

O I love jaunting in a train or a car with lovely soft cushions I wonder will he take a 1st class for me he might want to do it in the train by tipping the guard . . . 1 or 2 tunnels perhaps then you have to look out of the window all the nicer than coming back suppose I never came back what would they say eloped with him (18.366–75)

O that awful deepdown torrent O and the sea the sea crimson sometimes like fire and the glorious sunsets and the figtrees in the Alameda gardens . . . and the rosegardens and the jessamine and geraniums and cactuses and Gibraltar as a girl where I was a Flower of the mountain . . . and how he kissed me under the Moorish wall and I thought well as well him as another and then I asked him with my eyes to ask again yes and then he asked me would I yes to say yes my mountain flower (18.1597–1606)

The contrast between these two passages implies that the dynamics of female desire can be articulated in two very different discourses. Obviously synchronized with the movement of the machine in the first passage, female desire circulates in the public and cultural space, which, at the turn of the century, undergoes increasing technologization. Assimilated to the organic torrents of the sea and the blossoming of flowers in the second quotation, female desire retreats to the private and natural space. Producing a strange bifurcation of female desire, these oppositions between technology and organicism, between the public and the private, suggest not only a certain nostalgia for "natural" sexual identity but also a promise that the organic female body might be a site of resistance to the mechanization of public life.

Such nostalgia is implied in the way these two kinds of desire are valorized: if the passion incited by the onward movement of the machine is associated with Molly's infidelity, the passion in harmony with nature stands for her faithfulness and marital union. In contrast to deception, duplicity, and pretense associated with the sex on the train ("then you have to look out of the window all the nicer"), the celebrated erotic union among the rhododendrons conveys the authenticity of experience, preserved and recuperated by erotic memory: "the day we were lying among the rhododendrons on the Howth . . . it was leapyear like now yes 16 years ago" (18.1572–75). Thus, by retreating to the natural and private space, the union of eroticism and memory promises the possibility of an authentic subjective experience—experience which seems to be increasingly endangered in the technologized public sphere.

By contrasting the rhetoric of organicism with mechanical reproduction on the one hand, and the public and the private spheres on the other, female desire in "Penelope" performs two very different functions. When assimilated to the inner work of memory, the movement of female desire recuperates the authenticity of experience, subjective identity, and the temporal continuity of life, dissipating in this way the modern anxiety about the effects of technology. Yet, on the other hand, when associated with technological and public means of transport, such a desire intensifies the deceitful play of appearances, discontinuity of experience, and the possibility of a radical break from the past. It is not by accident that the fantasy of sex on the train, intertwined with speculation about elopement, takes Molly to a point almost beyond return: "suppose I never came back." The recuperation of experience by female erotic memory is no doubt nourishing, even if excessively so; however, the motif of the breast milk, or sharing of the famous seedcake, is ironically juxtaposed with the nervous spilling of the soup on the platform, with antifat ads, or most drastically, with the motif of poison administered by an unfaithful wife. In contrast to the rhetoric of life, the unfaithful female desire displays the threatening effects of technology in terms of nonsatisfaction, privation, and finally, death.

What the rhetoric of organicism consistently implies is a singular and private form of enunciation, based on the unity of voice, experience, and erotic memory. This subjective identity in turn suggests that the truth of female sexuality is to be found in the natural body.[1] Because the rhetoric of organicism consolidates desire with memory on the one hand, and sexuality with nature on the other, such a desire bears the mark of "fidelity." Consider, for instance, that Molly does not even have to articulate her desire to Bloom—it is enough that she "asks" with her eyes. What this scene suggests is that the authentic female passion communicates immediately, without the slightest detour of voice, without any mediation of the artifice of language. Consequently, only memory could preserve the immediacy and authenticity of such a wordless experience. I would like to suggest that this profound complicity between a singular form of private enunciation and a "naturalized" sexual identity constitutes the paradigm of Molly's fidelity in the text. In contrast, the convergence of mechanical reproduction and female sexuality intensifies the effects of infidelity and inauthenticity. Taken as a rhetorical figure, "infidelity" indicates not only a breakdown of the epistemological unity of memory, experience, and voice, not only the dissolution of sexual identity, but also the disturbance of the distinction between the public and the private. The trope of infidelity questions, therefore, both the role of the subject as the origin of signification *and* the role of the body as the location of sexual truth. From this perspective, I would like to raise once again the performative aspect of Molly's monologue, discussed in different ways by Cheryl Herr and Kimberly Devlin in this volume, and to examine it from the discursive rather than the subjective angle.

That is, what interests me here is the question of performance exceeding the function of the subject, that is, performance as an effect of the overlapping discourses in a textual "machinery."

In order to elucidate further why Molly's infidelity is linked both with a dissolution of sexual identity and with a mode of enunciation under the conditions of mechanical reproduction, I would like to refer to Walter Benjamin's two famous essays "The Work of Art in the Age of Mechanical Reproduction" and "On Some Motifs in Baudelaire." As one of the first theorists of modernity, Benjamin not only emphasizes the theme of technology in modern literature but also underscores the impact of mechanical reproduction on the structure of the work of art and on subjective experience. By exploring some of the familiar tropes of modernity, (which Joyce also deploys and elaborates in *Ulysses*[2]), like the crowds of the passersby, gambling, new means of public transportation, newspaper headlines, printing techniques, advertizing, telephone communication, and photography, Benjamin calls our attention to the technologization of the public sphere and to the subsequent fragmentation of subjective experience. No longer a neutral tool of domination over nature, modern technology transforms both social relations in the public sphere and subjective experience in the private sphere.[3] In his "Civilization and Its Discontents," Freud speaks in a similar way about the effects of the technologization of the body: "man has, as it were, become a kind of prosthetic God" (38–39). Freud suggests that the supposedly neutral technological tools function in fact as prosthetic devices, reshaping and destabilizing the contours and the significance of the body.

As Benjamin argues, modernity represents first of all an epistemological shift from the familiar philosophical model of experience rooted in memory to the technological conditions of mechanical reproduction (most evident in film or photography).[4] The consequences of this shift can be seen in the destruction of the uniqueness of the text, the autonomy of the subject, and the self-evidence of the real. By supplanting memory (which preserves individual experience) or tradition (which preserves collective experience), mechanical reproduction shatters the authority of the original, and consequently, destroys the authenticity of the work of art—or, what Benjamin calls, its *aura*. In contrast to memory's faithful recreation of the past, mechanical reproduction obliterates the authenticity of experience not only because it substitutes mechanically produced copies for the original, but also because its technological apparatus penetrates into the very structure of reality, fragments it, and then reassembles it under its own technological laws. In this context, the anxiety linked to the modes of mechanical reproduction, in particular to photography, indicates a certain crisis of the real.

Similarly, the conditions of mechanical reproduction penetrate into the structure of subjective experience, causing the fragmentation of the subject. This change is evident in the erosion of memory by shock, which Benjamin describes as a breakdown of the protective shield of consciousness under the pressure of the mechanisms of the urban life. If memory allows the subject to recover both the individual and the collective past, shock merely discloses an interruption of the mental life which assigns "to an incident a precise point in time in consciousness at the cost of the integrity of its contents" (163). Such fragmentation of the subject makes him or her even more dependent on the resources of mechanical reproduction to preserve the past. Consequently, shock destroys the autonomy of the subject and connects it to a larger social mechanism: pedestrians in the crowd, workers at the assembly line, and even crowds in the amusement parks "act as if they had adapted themselves to the machines and could express themselves only automatically" (176). "They live their lives as automatons and resemble Bergson's fictitious characters who *have completely liquidated their memories*" (178, emphasis added). Thus, the figure of shock blurs the boundaries between private and public, inner and outer, natural and technological, subjective and collective. As a mode of enunciation, the figure of shock indicates that the decentered subject is included in the larger, external mechanisms of signification, whose operations it can no longer control or contain.

The emblems of this disintegration of the public sphere and subjective experience abound in the iconography of modernism—the modern metropolis, the shock effect, and finally and above all, the image of the urban crowd replacing rational critical public. What is characteristic about the urban crowd, according to Benjamin, is the erasure of intersubjectivity. If the crowd appears uncanny, inanimate, and inhuman, it is because the mutual interdependence of its members is achieved by an efficient regulation of the social apparatus and not by the communicative consensus of the subjects themselves. What Benjamin emphasizes in his account of modernity is a different subject position in the modern public: no longer a rational agent acting in a community of debate, the modern subject is placed alongside the machine and subjected to its regulatory power. In a similar way, Jürgen Habermas argues that the effects of the disintegration of the public sphere can be seen in the decreased importance of the two major social roles—the worker and the citizen: the role of the worker is taken over by the consumer, that of the citizen by the client of the state bureaucracies.

Benjamin's account of the modern subject alongside the machine is still motivated by a nostalgia for the authentic structure of inner experience based on memory. Such nostalgia is conspicuously absent in postmodern views of textuality, which regard the text itself as a discursive machinery. Take, for instance, Derrida's discussion of "the gramophone effect" in *Ulysses*. Although Derrida's metaphor of the text as a gramophone develops Benjamin's insight that mechanical reproduction penetrates into the structure, production, and reception of the work of art, it provides a more positive view of these changes.[5] No longer preoccupied solely with the intentionality or memory of the subject, Derrida's interpretation of *Ulysses* focuses instead on the performative effect of the text itself. Such performance never assumes a singular form of enunciation—that is, textual production does not refer back to its point of origin in the subject—but is irreducibly linked to external signifying mechanisms, to other discourses, to other re-corded voices. Derrida describes this polyphonic form of enunciation as a "gramophone effect." A certain telephonic *techné* not only de-stroys the intimacy of voice, but also mediates between the self and the other. In this context, Derrida juxtaposes a singular mode of enun-ciation of Molly's final "yes" with the figure of Bloom speaking at the telephone. Displacing the rhetoric of organicism, such "gramophonic enunciation" exposes the subject addressing itself to the adventures of repetition, difference, and technological networks of communication (27–71).

By interpreting "Penelope" in the context of Benjamin's or Derrida's approaches to modernity, we are confronted first of all with the ques-tion of the significance of the female body in the age of mechanical reproduction. As the example of *Ulysses* makes clear, the discourse of modernity defines femininity in contradictory ways: on the one hand, femininity promises an illusory escape from the technologization of the public space, but on the other hand, it dramatizes the effects of mechanical reproduction at the very core of inner subjective experi-ence.[6] As Mary Ann Doane, for instance, argues, the anxiety about mechanical reproduction is often displaced onto the female body and reinterpreted within a more familiar framework of castration threat ("Technophilia" 163–75). Although this is not the place for a detailed discussion, I would like to suggest briefly why this displacement from mechanical reproduction to female sexuality is possible in the first place. The interrelation between mechanical reproduction and female sexuality once again returns us to the psychoanalytic construction of femininity as masquerade, discussed at great length by Kimberly Devlin in this volume. What Benjamin's discussion of mechanical reproduction and the psychoanalytic account of female sexuality have in common, therefore, is the erasure of authenticity and the authority of the real. In psychoanalytic theory, in particular in its Lacanian version, the woman masquerading as the phallus both confirms the power of the paternal signifier and reduces it to the order of appearances (Lacan 290). As Judith Butler argues, we can interpret female masquerade either as a loss of authentic femininity or as a disclosure that all forms of being, including male and female subjects, belong to the order of appearances (43–57). The complicity between mechanical reproduction and female masquerade, therefore, threatens to invalidate the fundamental notions of authenticity, originality, and identity. Instead of securing the hierarchy of the original and the copy, mechanical reproduction and female masquerade postulate that origin is only a performative effect of discursive operations.

At the same time, however, femininity, defined in opposition to mechanical reproduction, seems to provide an imaginary means of escape from the increasing technologization of the public life. Because of the materiality of the body and its possible link to natural reproduction, and because of the historical exclusion of women from the public sphere, female sexuality seems to limit the negative effects of technology and to promise the epistemic security of origins. As Stephen claims in "Scylla and Charybdis," paternity may be "a legal fiction" but the maternal body remains the only true thing in life, immune to the impact of technology. We could say that femininity replenishes the *aura*, that is, authenticity and uniqueness, destroyed by mechanical reproduction.[7] By positing femininity between natural and mechanical reproduction, "Penelope" simultaneously secures the stability of origins and subverts any claims to authentic experience.

Interpreting "Penelope" in the double context of female sexuality and mechanical reproduction, rather than female sexuality alone, we are in a better position to understand why Molly is both faithful and unfaithful, and why the episode as a whole is both conventional and subversive. Whether interpreted as affirmative, subversive, or regressive,[8] the episode has often been taken as a retreat from the technological conditions of urban life. Because of the sexist ideology linking femininity with nature, and because of the historical exclusion of women from the public life, Joyce imagines a retreat from the threat of mechanical reproduction only through the mediation of female eroticism. As an alternative site of male self-elaboration, the female body could appease the modernist nostalgia for a more authentic way of being and for the structure of experience rooted in memory. It is not surprising, therefore, that critics who, like Karen Lawrence, appreciate the adventures of textuality in *Ulysses*,[9] are clearly disappointed with this function of femininity: "The 'Penelope' chapter seems to me to be regressive, to present something denied by the rest of the book (the authority of consciousness). If Molly's monologue contains the truth or resolution, hasn't the book implicitly suggested that we cannot trust messages or any version of the truth?" (*Odyssey* 206). With such a reversal, the finale of *Ulysses* seems to stress the affirmation of life rather than technology, the origin rather than reproduction of meaning, memory rather than the heterogenous operations of discourse.[10] Yet, as Lawrence argues, this simplification of textuality offers something in return—the episode provides a sense of emotional relief after the ordeal of reading more "depersonalized" episodes: "After the stark abstractions and cold 'precision' of 'Ithaca,' the breakdown of grammatical and syntactic categories into lush, emotional rhythms provides *a release of tension* in the narrative, soothing to the beleaguered reader" (205).

According to Lawrence's interpretation, Molly's monologue dissipates the anxieties connected with "the cold impersonality" of the mechanically reproducible discourse and secures a retreat to a more personal, more "emotional" language, based on the authority of experience and memory. I would like to suggest that this reading of "Penelope," prepared in advance by the composition of previous episodes, is in fact an extension of male desires, expressed so straightforwardly by Bloom earlier in the text: "Be near her ample bedwarmed flesh. Yes, yes" (4.238–39). Not to mention that the calming effect of Molly's "large soft bubs, sloping within her nightdress like a shegoat's udder" (4.304–5) rescues Bloom from the bleak moments of despair and emptiness. Secluded in the privacy of home or situated in proximity to nature, Molly's "bedwarmed" body alone can replenish the humanity of the modern Odysseus—an advertizing agent—after his exhausting peregrinations through the modern urban landscape. Not surprisingly, Molly's memory of Bloom's proposal mirrors faithfully his fantasy of her body: "I put my arms around him yes and drew him down to me so he could feel my breasts all perfume yes and his heart was going like mad and yes I said yes I will Yes" (18.1606–9). By reflecting Bloom's desires so closely, Molly's final words seem to restore his personality, as if to compensate for a dissolution of his identity in "Ithaca." In all of these examples, the performative effect of femininity in *Ulysses* bridges the gap between memory, affectivity, and the economy of mechanical reproduction. In all of them Molly becomes a textual device that nostalgically recovers memory ("its just like yesterday to me"), emotional rhythms ("yes because I felt lovely") underlying language, and the authority of inner subjective experience.

However, the episode promises us the pleasure of recovery only when we accept this male fantasy of the female body—that is, only when we already "understood or felt what a woman is": "we are flowers all a womans body" (18.1576–79). As Annette Shandler Levitt suggests (and I think Joseph Heininger's argument in this volume about Molly's decolonization follows in a somewhat similar direction), the pleasure of the text depends on accepting the proffered flower as an emblem of diffuse female sexuality which partakes both in the abundance of the natural world and the richness of female language (507-17). Such pleasure, I argue, springs from the notion of Molly's language as preserving an immediate link to bodily experiences and female memory. Rich and alive, such language would be free not only from cultural mediation, but also from any sense of arbitrariness, discontinuity, or artificiality:

I love flowers Id love to have the whole place swimming in roses God of heaven theres nothing like nature the wild mountains then the sea and the waves rushing then the beautiful country with the fields of oats and wheat and all kinds of things . . . that would do your heart to see rivers and lakes and flowers all sorts of shapes and smells and colors springing up even out of the ditches (18.1557–63).

This passage shows us why Molly's flowers are so exciting: by grounding female language and body in the rhetoric of organicism, the text suggests that it is possible to integrate language, memory, and the natural body into one flow and to protect it from the impact of technology. In this natural landscape the human body seems to be immune from technologization: it would be difficult to imagine in this passage a human heart as an "old rusty pump" (6.675). Unlike Molly's empty letters, the rhetoric of organicism consistently implies a singular form of enunciation, based on the unity of language, experience, and erotic memory. As I have suggested, this singular form of enunciation, in complicity with the natural truth of sexual difference, constitutes the paradigm of Molly's fidelity. And the only additional form of pleasure that such fidelity would allow for is female narcissism: a spectacle of a woman addressing herself, caressing herself, gathering herself in the rich flow of her memories and her pleasures.

In this context, it is not surprising that the critics' defense of Molly's fidelity is often intertwined with the admiration for her memory, which, according to Hayman, preserves both "the texture of an experience" and the unity of time as "one continuous erotic present" (127). It is as if Molly's memory itself constituted a sufficient "proof" of her fidelity. Molly's memory is seen as faithful to the structure of experience in so far as it is posited as unreflective and involuntary, preserving and itself preserved by the immediacy of sensations. This unity of memory and experience—the paradigm of epistemological fidelity in the episode—precludes any external ordering, either by technology, culture, discourse, or even by intellect. Seemingly unmediated sense impressions, smells, perfumes, sounds, and sights in the episode— "the smell of the sea excited me of course"—provide a sense of continuity between the past, present, and future without any "omissions." In the economy of unmediated memory nothing seems to be lost, especially not the authenticity and intensity of erotic experience.

And yet "omissions" trouble Molly, and not only gaps in her memories, but paradoxically, even "omissions" in the closed circle of her auto-affection.[11] And even though "emissions" of memory function for Molly as an extension of masturbation,[12] always bringing her into a close intimacy with herself, she is perturbed by a sense of emptiness she would like to "fill up." In spite of her vivid recollections, Molly is not satisfied with memories and sex alone and wishes for more clothes, gifts, love letters, and even for sensational publicity in newspapers, which would finally "fill up your whole day and life." This void that even memories cannot fill up is, not surprisingly, represented as a castrated female body. Despite all the joy that Molly can find in the admiration of her body, and despite all the pragmatic value of her natural charms, Molly complains: "I never in all my life felt anyone had one the size of that *to make you feel full up* . . . whats the idea making us like that *with a big hole in the middle of us*" (18.149–51, emphasis added). Like the empty letters that Molly posts to herself, the erotic memory closes the circle of narcissism only by covering over the "omission," the void, represented by female sexuality.

Although Molly's "bedwarmed flesh" and her "large soft bubs" might dissipate anxieties concerning technology and mechanical reproduction (it is as if sexual pleasure were the last vestige of authenticity in the urban landscape[13]), the female body proves to be a disorderly figure in its own way. The early history of the reception of "Penelope," analyzed by Kathleen McCormick in this volume, seems only to confirm the anxiety associated with female sexuality. It shows that Joyce's construction of femininity has been anything but soothing to his critics. In her discussion of the excesses, extremes, and exaggerations in the critical reponses to Molly, McCormick demonstrates that the episode has tended precisely to beleaguer and shock, rather than to sooth Joyce's readers. By provoking a simultaneous reaction of "titillation and fear," Molly's explicit display of female sexuality parallels closely the effects of mechanical reproduction and shows that the Benjaminian notion of shock could be transferred to the sphere of sexuality. It was not until the impact of feminist and post-structuralist critics, like Cixous, Kristeva, Boheemen-Saaf, Henke, Scott, or McGee, that female sexuality in *Ulysses* could be linked to the subversive effects of writing, since both disturb rather than consolidate the mastery of male authorship.[14] However, by locating the unsettling or subversive effects of "Penelope" in female sexuality and language, these interpretations risk avoiding the social context of technology and mechanical reproduction altogether. We may wonder in fact whether the effects of mechanical reproduction, in particular its fragmentation of subjective identity, are not once again displaced onto the female body and reinterpreted through the tropes of subversive sexuality.

The strategy of displacement from technology to sexuality is particularly evident in the mythical approaches to "Penelope." Although Margaret Mills Harper's suggestive essay in this volume rescues "mythical method" for feminist analysis, I would argue that mythical interpretations of Molly have been so productive in Joyce criticism because they dissipate both the shock of technology *and* the fear of female sexuality. In a famous misreading of *Ulysses* ("*Ulysses*, Order, and Myth," 1923), T.S. Eliot postulates myth as an aesthetic ordering principle, capable of bracketing "the anarchy and chaos" of contemporary history (177). By placing the work of art outside the chaos of history, and by securing its "timeless organic unity," these mythical interpretations of *Ulysses* separate modern aesthetics from the impact of technology and mechanical reproduction. In fact, to use Benjamin's term again, the function of mythical interpretations is to restore the decayed *aura* of the work of art. However, as Kristeva reminds us in "Women's Time," such transformation of historical time into timeless myth, or the "organic spatial form," is invariably carried on along the traditional gender lines. The implicit connection between the nostalgia for myth and nature, or more precisely, for the myth of nature, presupposes the gendering of linear historical time as paternal (time as project, departure, arrival, as well as technological progress) and cyclical natural time as maternal (time of gestation and biological rhythms). Therefore, the escape from history to myth not only restores the *aura* of the work of art, but sooner or later evokes a "belief in the omnipotence of an archaic, full, total englobing mother with no frustration, no separation, with no break-producing symbolism (with no castration, in other words)" (205). Kristeva's critique of the myth of the archaic mother can be fruitfully extended to the "timeless, archaic Gea-Tellus" interpretation of Molly Bloom. The function of the Gea-Tellus myth is to replace mechanical reproduction with maternal reproduction. By translating the anxiety of technology as yet another symptom of castration anxiety, the myth of the archaic mother eventually provides the means for appeasing both.

Bearing in mind this function of myth, let us turn to a more witty discourse—to jokes. Jokes might reveal to us the historical and discursive function of femininity that the myth of the archaic mother tries to cover over.[15] In place of the Gea-Tellus myth, let us then consider the riddle of female sexuality in the light of the following joke from the "Aeolus" episode:

What opera is like a railwayline?
—Opera? Mr O'Madden Burke's sphinx face reriddled.
Lenehan announced gladly:
—*The Rose of Castile.* See the wheeze? Rows of cast steel. Gee! (7.588–91)

Restaging the Oedipal drama (the sphinx, the riddle) within the technological space, the joke parodies the rhetoric of organicism associated with sexual difference. Its performative effect collapses the boundaries between the binary oppositions on which the logic of the myth of the archaic mother depends: between art (opera) and technology (railway), nature (rose) and culture, body and the machine and, as we shall see, between the circulation of female desire and the technological means of traffic. As a result of this performative force of the joke, which is explicitly about performance itself, an exotic discourse of music, romantic love, and organicism appears as an effect of the impersonal operation of technology.

Yet, this overt anxiety about the technologization of both art (opera) and the female body is expressed once again in terms of female infidelity. Taking a hint from Freud, we might suspect that this linguistic punning articulates both hostility and attraction to an unfaithful woman. After all, "The Rose of Castile" refers not only to the title of the opera but also to the name of its main heroine—a beautiful but false woman (Elvira, Rose of Castile)—who chooses "rank and empire" over her lover, in other words, social power over authentic erotic experience. In order to deflate the exotic charms of unstable female sexuality, the joke compares this "unnatural" and unfaithful circulation of female desire to a different sort of traffic—to technological means of transport. As the punning of the joke implies, the interplay between technology and treacherous female sexuality not only reduces authenticity to the order of appearances but also destabilizes the binary oppositions, such as nature and culture, art and technology, the male and the female.

If I pay more attention to jokes than to myths, it is because jokes both articulate *and* perform different aspects of infidelity in *Ulysses* associated with the motifs of femininity, language, and mechanical reproduction. It is not by accident that this particular joke is embedded in the chapter of *Ulysses* that explicitly experiments with new forms of mechanical reproduction and the circulation of discourse, like printing techniques and newspapers headlines. Advertizing various forms of writing and rhetoric divorced from the authority of experience and memory,[16] "Aeolus" as a whole dramatizes both anonymity and contingency of signifying effects. At the same time, however, it consistently returns to another, somewhat less joyful, mode of circulation and betrayal, that is, adultery: "—Onehandled adulterer, he said smiling grimly. That tickles me, I must say" (7.1072–73).

By condensing the effects of language, mechanical reproduction, and female sexuality, the "Rose of Castile" joke articulates in fact some of the main concerns of "Penelope": it brings to our attention the fact that Molly's explicit preoccupation with flowers, nature, and sexuality cannot be separated from the pervasive technologization of the body and the public sphere. It is as if the coda of *Ulysses* replays the joke in reverse and converts the textual web of "rows of cast steel" into a seductive and exotic "Rose of Castile," or as Molly is fond of calling herself—"a flower of the mountain." A strange flower of rhetoric unfolding at the intersection of sexuality and technology, Molly seems to offer us "excitement like a rose." But "Penelope" returns to the rhetoric of organicism and to the immediacy of experience preserved by memory only to disrupt it by quite a different tonality—by the train whistle, which provides instrumental music for Molly's nocturnal concert. Although we do not know its point of departure or destination, we can take this distant train as a synecdoche for the pervasive effects of mechanical reproduction displayed not only in the previous episodes of *Ulysses* but in "Penelope" itself. Ranging from the circulation of photos (all kinds of photos, including "smutty" ones), ads, newspapers, and mass-produced clothes to the circulation of new sex objects—girls on bicycles—the examples of mechanical reproduction in Molly's monologue are in fact as numerous as the figures of flowers. The repetition of the mechanical noise in Molly's monologue has a double function: on the one hand, it points to a technologization of the female body and subjective experience, but, on the other hand, it demystifies the rhetoric of organicism and shows that such rhetoric— like the flowers on the wallpaper Molly so fondly remembers—is itself an effect of mechanical reproduction.

Even though "Penelope" capitalizes so much on the function of female erotic memory, the episode equally forcefully suggests its extension and replacement through photography, which for Benjamin constitutes the paradigm of mechanical reproduction *par excellence*. As a mechanical extension of memory, photography "fills up" the "omissions" in human recollections. However, if memory makes the original experience alive again, photography seems to freeze the moment and to replace the original through its representation. As Benjamin shows in "The Work of Art in the Age of Mechanical Reproduction," photography precisely undermines our notions of the original experience, immediacy, and authenticity. Similarly, whenever photography replaces erotic memory in "Penelope," it "denaturalizes" desire itself, connecting it with pornography, prostitution, and commodity. We remember, for instance, Bloom's suggestion that Molly should pose for nude pictures in the time of economic hardship, a suggestion which triggers Molly's imitations of other photographic representations of women. Even though Molly burns semi-pornographic Photo Bits, her memory, as Kimberly Devlin shows, is sustained and mediated by photographic images and stock representations of femininity in popular culture: "would I be like that bath of the nymph with my hair down yes only shes younger or Im a little like that dirty bitch in that Spanish photo" (18.562–64). In this context it is significant that Milly, coming to terms with her adolescent sexuality, no longer relies on the maternal resources of erotic memory but studies photography.

If photography mediates the flow of Molly's memories, the noise of the train interferes with the seductive power of her voice. The train's whistle merges most often with the sentimental songs from Molly's repertoire, as if to disrupt the natural unity of voice and memory, of hearing and seeing: "that was Gardner yes I can see his face clean shaven Frseeeeeeeeeeeeeeeeeeeeefrong that train again weeping tone once in the dear deaead days beyondre call close my eyes breath my lips forward kiss sad look eyes open piano ere oer the world the mists began I hate that istsbeg comes loves sweet soooooooooong Ill let that out full when I get in front of the footlights again" (18.873–78). The distant noise of the engine not only provides a strange accompaniment to the popular sentimental songs from Molly's repertoire, but is explicitly compared to them: at one point, the noise of the engine appears "like the end of Loves old sweeetsonnnng." As its last stanza suggests ("Footsteps may falter, weary grow the way,/Still we can hear it, at the close of the day;/So till the end, when life's dim shadows fall,/Love will be found the sweetest song of all" [17]), "the sweetest song of all" expresses simultaneously a nostalgia for the past and the pathos of memory and voice, which can withstand the passage of time. Such unity of voice, memory, and love restores the shadows to life, the past

to the presence of consciousness. With a touch of perversity, however, Joyce interrupts this seductive unity of voice, song, and memory
with the noise of the machine. The intrusion of a purely mechanical
noise into the melody of the song reminds me of Joyce's description
of his authorship in a letter to Miss Weaver: "I am really one of the
greatest engineers, if not the greatest, in the world besides being a
musicmaker, philosophist and heaps of other things. All the engines
I know are wrong. Simplicity. I am making an engine with only one
wheel (*Letters* 1:251).[18] Although this description refers to the composition of *Finnegans Wake*, even in the most organic chapter of *Ulysses*,
Joyce the musicmaker joins hands with the great engineer over the
"bedwarmed" female body.

But what would this conjunction of music and engineering mean
in "Penelope"? In one sense Molly's entire monologue is like "loves
sweet song"—an expression of faith that the unity of memory, art,
and voice can revive "dear deaead days beyondre call," withstand
the passage of time, and bring the past erotic experience back to the
subject. As the words of the song suggest, forgetting and omissions
are deadly. Yet, maybe because Molly experiences some trouble performing to the full capacity of her voice and her memory, because
"letting that out full" is increasingly more difficult for her, this vocal
deficiency reveals an other, and equally compelling, aspect of this episode: the mediation of textual technique even within the most intimate
recesses of body and voice. By supplanting the function of memory
and voice, textual machinery interrupts the immediacy of experience
and reinserts a sense of distance, artificiality and exteriority. And here
again, what is revealing is the contrast between Molly the singer, who
desires to recover the fullness of voice, with Molly the letter writer,
who either dispatches the empty letters or else reproduces clichés with
spelling mistakes: "your sad bereavement sympathy I always make
that mistake and nephew with 2 double yous" (18.729–31). Unlike recollections which always come from oneself to oneself, the mechanical
noise—just as the mute graphics of the text—implies a movement
from an unknown origin to an obscure destination. As a synecdoche
for mechanical reproduction (but a synecdoche that fails to command
the entirety of its effects), the train signals a possibility of nonrecu-
peration: the circle of memory is broken by the onward movement of
the engine, the "weeping tone" of the lyrical song by the purely mechanical whistle, the performance of the singer by the performance of
the machine.

In contrast to the end of the episode, Molly's figuration of desire,
her "heat" of passion, and even her admiration for male and female

bodies quite consistently fuse the rhetoric of organicism and technology. At the great finale of Molly's performance, voice, memory,
and the rhetoric of organicism are intertwined not only to secure the
singular form of enunciation but also to restore the "natural" gender
difference and, it must be added, their "natural" hierarchy as well.
The closure of the episode reveals a profound complicity between the
affirmation of voice and the affirmation of the "natural" sexual difference. Ironically, it is the technologization of the body that reveals the
fluidity of sexual difference and disarticulates its natural order:

> the savage brute Thursday Friday one Saturday two Sunday three O Lord I
> cant wait till Monday
>   frseeeeeeeefronnnng train somewhere whistling *the strength those engines*
> *have in them like big giants* and the water rolling all over and out of them all
> sides like the end of Loves old sweeeetsonnnng the poor men that have to
> be out all the night from their wives and families in those roasting engines
> (18.594–600, emphasis added)

Molly's recollection and impatient anticipation of intercourse with
Boylan turns into the paradoxical image of men trapped inside "those
roasting" machines and separated from their wives. Molly not only
reminds us of the role technology has played in the male conquering
of nature but also stresses the effects of the machine on "the poor
men." Given this image of the male romance with technology turned
sour, we would expect at this point some vision of the organic body
as a source of resistance to male domination. However, this is not the
case—the passage neither deplores technological power as domination nor mystifies nature as a source of resistance. On the contrary,
it is by acknowledging technologization of the body and desire that
Molly feels empowered to rewrite the story of sexual difference. By
implicitly rejecting the notion that the truth of female sexuality re-
sides in nature or in the privacy of experience, Molly produces an
androgynous fantasy, in which machine occupies both masculine and
feminine positions. Clearly supplanting natural reproduction, Molly's
phantasmatic machine becomes on the one hand a sort of technological womb, trapping men in its interior. I would like to suggest that this
image of entrapment parodies the male myth of "Gea-Tellus" receiving
"the childman weary" into her womb. But on the other hand, the machine also assumes the attributes of phallic power ("the strength those
engines have") similar to the potency of "the savage brute." It even
reproduces the intensity of male and female desire—"all fire" that
Molly feels inside her is articulated in this passage as an unbearable
heat inside the engine. Furthermore, Molly's description of the engine

deploys the tropes reserved for the Gibraltar rock ("like big giants") and for the oceanic torrents ("the water rolling all over"), which so frequently function as a metaphor for the "flow" of her erotic memories. Needless to say, Molly's fantasy is conspicuous for its refusal (or "failure") to reproduce the binary gender roles faithfully. Usurping the rhetoric of organicism, Molly's androgynous machine disarticulates the binary gender opposition and demonstrates that the nature of sexual difference is in fact constructed by discursive operations.

Because of these consistent intersections with mechanical reproduction, feminine sexuality in "Penelope" participates in two contradictory economies of signification. On the one hand, the female body facilitates a retreat from the technologized public space into a singular form of enunciation and the privacy of subjective experience. As I have been arguing, this authority of subjectivity in the production of meaning is emphasized by the rhetoric of organicism, which restores not only the unity of voice, experience, and memory, but also the "natural" gender hierarchy. These qualities of Molly's monologue qualify it as a *faithful* site of male self-elaboration. On the other hand, the technologization of the female body reveals it as a site of diverse cultural inscriptions, which cannot be unified into a singular form of enunciation. Moreover, the female body no longer reproduces those inscriptions faithfully. Whereas the faithfulness of "Penelope" is orchestrated as a recuperative movement of erotic memory, her infidelity indicates a breakdown of the singular form of enunciation and, even more importantly, a re-vision of gender differences.

My reading of "Penelope" has concentrated on the points of interruptions of the female voice, indeed, on the moments when technology seems to intrude upon the work of female memory. These moments of discord (rather than Molly's inner contradictions) disclose how the pressure of technology redefines the function of femininity and the epistemological and social stakes attached to it. The overlapping discourses of sexuality, memory, and mechanical reproduction in the coda of *Ulysses* disclose two performative effects of femininity. On the one hand, Joyce's display of female sexuality, no matter how audacious or subversive for his times, betrays a certain nostalgia for a more traditional paradigm of experience based on memory and for a more "natural" sense of gender difference. It is as if Joyce could imagine the female sexual body as the last remnant of authenticity in the increasingly technologized social space. On the other hand, however, the trope of female infidelity not only divulges a complicity between female masquerade and mechanical reproduction but also indicates that this unity of language, memory, and natural sexual identity has been irreparably broken. Consequently, in the last act of the textual performance, Molly's body functions as an alternative stage where paradigmatic shifts of modernity could be once again reenacted but their "shocking" effects immediately dissipated.[19]

Notes

1.   No doubt, this interpretation has been invited by Joyce's frequently quoted description of the episode: "It begins and ends with the female word *Yes*. It turns like the huge earthball slowly surely and evenly round and round spinning. Its four cardinal points being the female breasts, arse, womb and . . . cunt expressed by the words *because, bottom* (in all senses, bottom button, bottom of the glass, bottom of the sea, bottom of his heart) *woman, yes*. Though probably more obscene than any preceding episode it seems to me to be perfectly sane full amoral fertilisable untrustworthy engaging shrewd limited prudent indifferent *Weib*" [*Letters* 1:170]. For a discussion of this description from a feminist point of view, see for instance, Bonnie Kime Scott (119).

2.   This deliberate inclusion of the elements of urban experience in *Ulysses* has been very well documented in Joyce criticism, which often pays tribute to Joyce's ambition to render the cultural phenomenon of a modern metropolis: "If I can get to the heart of Dublin I can get to the heart of all the cities in the world" (Ellmann, 505). For a discussion of the city in *Ulysses* see among others, Frederick Jameson (173–88), Hugh Kenner (4–6), and Christopher Butler (269–70). For a general discussion of modernity and technology, see Astradur Eysteinsson (18–22).

3.   For a discussion of the impact of technology on the social relations in modernity, see for instance, Herbert Marcuse (138–63) and Jürgen Habermas.

4.   Walter Benjamin articulates this paradigm of modernity primarily in his two essays: "On Some Motifs in Baudelaire" (155–200) and "The Work of Art in the Age of Mechanical Reproduction" (217–51).

5.   For another discussion of the text as a machinery, see Gilles Deleuze and Félix Guattari (81–88).

6.   For postmodern approaches to this question see, for instance, Donna Haraway, "A Manifesto for Cyborgs: Science, Technology, and Social Feminism in the 1980" and a series of responses to this paper in Elizabeth Weed's *Coming to Terms*. See also Theresa de Laurentis's *Technologies of Gender*.

7.   For a discussion of femininity in the context of Benjamin's concept of aura, see for instance, Mary Ann Doane's *The Desire to Desire* (29–33).

8.   According to Jameson, for instance, "Penelope" collapses into "vitalist ideology" (188).

9.   In a similar manner, Derek Attridge castigates critics, especially feminist critics, for overemphasizing stylistic complexity of the episode and turning it into an example of subversive *écriture féminine* (543–64).

10.   See also in this context Jean-Michel Rabaté, who sees "Penelope" as "an unexpected return to oral discourse" (*James Joyce*, 105). A more positive

evaluation of textuality in "Penelope" as staging of otherness can be found in Patrick McGee (170–72).

11. Derrida explains the term of auto-affection as the basic trope of the mastery of the subject: "The lure of the I, of consciousness as hearing-oneself-speak would consist in . . . transforming hetero-affection into auto-affection" (*Margins of Philosophy*, 297).

12. For a critique of the representation of Molly as a conventional narcissistic woman, see Elaine Unkeless (150–68).

13. As Mary Ann Doane eloquently points out in her response to Foucault, "the unified and coherent bourgeois subject, threatened increasingly by a fragmentation imposed from without, finds its heaven in a sexualized, orgasmic body" ("Commentary" 70–71).

14. See for instance, Hélène Cixous (15–30), Julia Kristeva (*Powers of Horror* 22–23), Christine Van Boheemen-Saaf (29–36), Suzette A. Henke (126–63), Bonnie Kime Scott (107–27), Patrick McGee (37–68, 150–81), and Ewa Ziarek (51–60). For a good discussion of feminist readings of Joyce, see Karen Lawrence ("Joyce and feminism" 241).

15. As Freud suggests, the pleasure of the joke depends on evading the restraints of logic and cultural censorship. The first source of pleasure is purely linguistic—we delight in throwing off the constraints of rational discourse and enjoy the linguistic play characteristic of the primary process. The second source of pleasure comes from a release of the unconscious hostile or sexual thought, that is, a release from inhibitions and moral censorship (117–39).

16. For an excellent discussion of this episode, see Karen Lawrence (*The Odyssey of Style* 63–67).

17. The text of the song is reproduced in Don Gifford and Robert J. Seidman (56–57).

18. For a discussion of Joyce's "triple profession" and interpretation of the text as a machine in the context of *Finnegans Wake,* see Jean-Michel Rabaté ("Lapsus ex machina" 80).

19. Some ideas that went into the preparation of this essay were initially suggested by Nancy Amstrong's lectures "The Work of Art in the Age of Sexual Reproduction" and "High Culture, Savage Art, and the Uses of Pornography" delivered at the University of Notre Dame on 9 and 11 April 1981 and the informal exchange after the lectures. Also, I would like to express my gratitude to my colleagues, Theresa Krier and Richard Pearce, whose attentive reading and generous comments strengthened my argument.

Works Cited

Attridge, Derek. "Molly's Flow: The Writing of 'Penelope' and the Question of Women's Language." *Modern Fiction Studies* 35 (1989): 543–65.

Benjamin, Walter. *Illuminations.* Ed. Hannah Arendt. Trans. Harry Zohn. New York: Schocken, 1969.

Boheemen-Saaf, Christine Van. "Deconstruction after Joyce." *New Alliances in*

Joyce Studies. Ed. Bonnie Kime Scott. Newark: University of Delaware Press, 1988. 29–36.

Butler, Christopher. "Joyce, Modernism, Post-modernism." *The Cambridge Companion to James Joyce.* Ed. Derek Attridge. New York: Cambridge University Press, 1990. 259–288.

Butler, Judith. *Gender Trouble: Feminism and the Subversion of Identity.* New York: Routledge, 1990.

Cixous, Hélène. "Joyce: the (r)use of writing." *Post-structuralist Joyce: Essays from French.* Ed. Derek Attridge and Daniel Ferrer. Cambridge: Cambridge University Press, 1984. 15–30.

Deleuze, Gilles, and Félix Guattari. *Kafka: Toward a Minor Literature.* Trans. Dana Polan. Minneapolis: University of Minnesota Press, 1986.

Derrida, Jacques. *Margins of Philosophy.* Trans. Alan Bass. Chicago: University of Chicago Press, 1982.

Derrida, Jacques. "Ulysses Gramophone: Hear say yes in Joyce." *The Augmented Ninth: Proceedings of the Ninth International James Joyce Symposium, Frankfurt, 1984.* Ed. Bernard Benstock. Syracuse: Syracuse University Press, 1988. 27-75.

Doane, Mary Ann. "Commentary: Pos-Utopian Difference." Weed, *Coming to Terms* 70–78.

Doane, Mary Ann. *The Desire to Desire: The Woman's Film in the 1940s.* Bloomington: Indiana University Press, 1987.

Doane, Mary Ann. "Technophilia: Technology, Representation, and the Feminine." *Body/Politics: Women and the Discourses of Science.* Ed. Mary Jacobus, Evelyn Fox Keller, and Sally Shuttleworth. New York: Routledge, 1990. 163–75.

Eliot, T. S. *Selected Prose of T. S. Eliot.* Ed. Frank Kermode. New York: Harcourt Brace Jovanovich, 1975.

Ellmann, Richard. *James Joyce.* New York: Oxford University Press, 1982.

Eysteinsson, Astradur. *The Concept of Modernism.* Ithaca: Cornell University Press, 1990.

Freud, Sigmund. *Civilization and Its Discontents.* Trans. James Strachey. New York: Norton, 1961.

Freud, Sigmund. *Jokes and Their Relation to the Unconscious.* Trans. James Strachey. London: Routledge and Kegan Paul, 1966.

Gifford, Don, and Robert J. Seidman. *Notes for Joyce: An Annotation of James Joyce's "Ulysses".* New York: Dutton, 1974.

Habermas, Jürgen. *The Structural Transformation of the Public Sphere: An Inquiry into a Category of Bourgeois Society.* Trans. Thomas Burger. Cambridge: MIT Press, 1989.

Hayman, David. "The Empirical Molly." *Approaches to "Ulysses": Ten Essays.* Ed. Thomas F. Staley and Bernard Benstock Pittsburg: University of Pittsburg Press, 1970. 103–35.

Henke, Suzette A. *James Joyce and the Politics of Desire.* New York: Routledge, 1990.

Jameson, Frederick. "*Ulysses* in History" *James Joyce*. Ed. Harold Bloom. New York: Chelsea, 1986. 173–88.

Kenner, Hugh. "Notes toward an Anatomy of 'Modernism.'" *A Starchamber Quiry: A James Joyce Centennial Volume, 1882–1982*. Ed. E. L. Epstein. London: Methuen, 1982. 3–42.

Kristeva, Julia. *Powers of Horror: An Essay on Abjection*. Trans. Leon S. Roudiez. New York: Columbia University Press, 1982.

Kristeva, Julia. "Women's Time." Trans. Alice Jardine and Harry Blake. *The Kristeva Reader*. Ed. Toril Moi. New York: Columbia University Press, 1986. 188–213.

Lacan, Jacques. *Écrits: A Selection*. Trans. Alan Sheridan. New York: Norton, 1977.

Lauretis, Theresa de. *Technologies of Gender: Essays on Theory, Film and Fiction*. Bloomington: Indiana University Press, 1987.

Lawrence, Karen. "Joyce and feminism." *The Cambridge Companion to James Joyce*. Ed. Derek Attridge, Cambridge: Cambridge University Press, 1990. 237–58.

Lawrence, Karen. *The Odyssey of Style in "Ulysses."* Princeton: Princeton University Press, 1981.

Levitt, Annette Shandler. "The Pattern Out of the Wallpaper: Luce Irigaray and Molly Bloom." *Modern Fiction Studies* 35 (1989): 507–16.

Marcuse, Herbert. "Some Social Implications of Modern Technology." *The Essential Frankfurt Reader*. Ed. Andrew Arato and Eike Gerhardt. New York: Urizen Books, 1978. 138–62.

McGee, Patrick. *Paperspace: Style as Ideology in Joyce's "Ulysses."* Lincoln: University of Nebraska Press, 1989.

Rabaté, Jean-Michel. *James Joyce, Authorized Reader*. Trans. Jean-Michel Rabaté. Baltimore: Johns Hopkins University Press, 1991.

Rabaté, Jean-Michel. "Lapsus ex machina." *Post-structuralist Joyce: Essays from the French*. Ed. Derek Attridge and Daniel Ferrer, Cambridge: Cambridge University Press, 1990. 79–102.

Scott, Bonnie Kime. *James Joyce*. Atlantic Highlands: Humanities Press International, 1987.

Unkeless, Elaine. "The Conventional Molly Bloom." *Women in Joyce*. Ed. Suzette Henke and Elaine Unkeless. Chicago: University of Illinois Press, 1982. 150–68.

Weed, Elizabeth, ed. *Coming to Terms: Feminism, Theory, Politics*. New York: Routledge, 1989.

Ziarek, Ewa. "'Circe': Joyce's *Argumentum ad Feminam*." *James Joyce Quarterly* 30 (1992): 51–68.

Index

Index